Content and Copywriting

Content and Copywriting

The Complete Toolkit for Strategic Marketing

Second Edition

Margo Berman

WILEY Blackwell

Registered Offices
John Wiley & Sons, Inc., 111 River Street, Hoboken, NJ 07030, USA
John Wiley & Sons Ltd, The Atrium, Southern Gate, Chichester, West Sussex, PO19 8SQ, UK

For details of our global editorial offices, customer services, and more information about Wiley products visit
us at www.wiley.com.

Wiley also publishes its books in a variety of electronic formats and by print-on-demand. Some content that
appears in standard print versions of this book may not be available in other formats.

Library of Congress Cataloging-in-Publication Data
Names: Berman, Margo, 1947– author. | John Wiley & Sons, publisher.
Title: Content and copywriting : the complete toolkit for strategic
    marketing / Margo Berman.
Description: Second edition. | Hoboken, NJ : Wiley-Blackwell, 2024. |
    Includes index.
Identifiers: LCCN 2023042918 (print) | LCCN 2023042919 (ebook) | ISBN
    9781119866503 (paperback) | ISBN 9781119866510 (adobe pdf) | ISBN
    9781119866527 (epub)
Subjects: LCSH: Advertising copy–Handbooks, manuals, etc. |
    Marketing–Handbooks, manuals, etc.
Classification: LCC HF5825 .B467 2024 (print) | LCC HF5825 (ebook) | DDC
    659.13/2–dc23/eng/20231107
LC record available at https://lccn.loc.gov/2023042918
LC ebook record available at https://lccn.loc.gov/2023042919

Cover Design: Wiley
Cover Image: © aelitta/Getty Images

Set in 11.5/13.5 STIXTwoText by Straive, Pondicherry, India
Printed and bound by CPI Group (UK) Ltd, Croydon, CR0 4YY

C9781119866503_260724

*I would like to dedicate this book to
my parents, who gave me the discipline
and creative freedom to
solve complex problems.*

Brief Contents

Contents

CHAPTER FOUR
The Experiential Word: Immersive, MR (Mixed Reality), and Interactive Engagement

CHAPTER NINE

CHAPTER TEN

CHAPTER ELEVEN

Preface

I t doesn't matter whether you're a student, novice, or seasoned professional, this book will hone your content and copywriting skills. It is divided into three parts: (1) Content Writing: Content Versus Copywriting; (2) Copywriting for Three Platforms: Video, Audio, Print, plus, Cross-platform Campaigns; and (3) Resources, including useful terminology. The work begins with social media content, templates, and experiential campaigns, followed by Part II with strategy and technique. The subsequent chapters focus on writing for specific traditional media: from print and broadcast to out-of-home, ambient, and multiplatform. Content and copywriting examples offer a gamut of industry standard formats, which are useful reference points when writing. You'll quickly see how digital content differs from traditional advertising writing. Television and video storyboards and scripts will serve as examples for client presentations.

You'll discover why first thinking from the channel and platform helps writers create more consumer engagement. Starting with the end result in mind helps you consider the purpose and audience before actually starting to write. For video content, it will also direct which talent to cast, what type of visuals to choose, and what sound effects or music cuts to include. These conscious choices force you to write for a specific voice for a professionally produced result. Other discussions will help you avoid other writing errors, like inaccurate content or broadcast script length, legal issues created by the absence of talent releases, and screen safety problems in video post-production. Special callout boxes will make major principles easy to remember and simple to apply.

You may already realize that it's not enough for you to know how to develop catchy social media content or create exciting slogans to write strong copy. You must also know how to create gripping messages on every channel, platform, and device. Writers today must be as comfortable creating YouTube videos as they are developing immersive experiences. Besides having an understanding of current trends, you should also challenge yourself to invent new forms of engagement. Try to avoid creative stagnation and innovative inertia. With all your mental muscle, push your imagination past the status quo. Influence new modes of expression. In order to achieve this, you must have a solid writing foundation. You need to understand audience segmentation, message creation, creative brief application, and content-length restrictions, as well as layout design options.

Then, you need to build on that knowledge and cement it with strategic thinking, analytical insights, audience-relevant messages, and sound writing techniques.

This book will give you an entire toolkit of tips to write in all size spaces, all marketing ecosystems, all formats, and all touchpoints. Whether you're creating messages for mobile devices, packaging, or "ginormous" billboards, interactive or any other media, you'll be able to apply the principles set forth in this volume and succeed in writing compelling copy.

Great marketing writing isn't just clever. It's convincing. It's persuasive. It's interruptive. It's intrusive. Most of all, it's unforgettable.

The videos, podcasts, posts, or campaigns that prompt shares, reposts, and follows, or promote "street cred" (brand credibility), or "talk value" (are talked about over office water coolers or virtual meetings) also generate live events, comments, and other free press that propels the brand into mainstream consciousness.

How do you begin to create these kinds of messages? You start by understanding that every assignment has a purpose and a goal. An audience that it's targeting. An array of touchpoints where it encounters that consumer. And a specific strategy to deliver that message.

To help you get started, chapters are devoted to content, templates, strategies, and specific writing. I would recommend you begin with the first six chapters, so you have a solid foundation of the basics: creating content, understanding your audience, and presenting solutions to common pain points (Chapter 1); applying analytics to channel selection (Chapter 2); using templates (Chapter 3); comprehending immersive campaigns (Chapter 4); developing a strategically targeted creative brief (Chapter 5); and, adopting a successful strategy (Chapter 6). After that, you can read any chapter in any order for preparing traditional media (from Chapters 7 through 14). That's because the book is modular. Therefore, each chapter stands on its own.

So, if you'd like to read about writing for social media, you could read that chapter. Or, if you're interested in immersive and experiential campaigns, you could go to that chapter. Or, if you're curious about cross-platform campaigns, you start with the last chapter. People learn best when they satisfy their curiosity. With that said, you can begin wherever you want. Then, go to whatever section interests you most. Here's the order of each medium that's explored.

- Chapter 7: TV and Video
- Chapter 8: Radio
- Chapter 9: Copywriting Tips
- Chapter 10: Headline and Slogan Techniques
- Chapter 11: Print Messaging
- Chapter 12: Ambient and Moving

- Chapter 13: Abridged: Small-space Writing
- Chapter 14: Cross-platform Campaigns

I also recommend familiarizing yourself with the content set in callout boxes. They're designed so you can find what you're looking for. If you want to review the checklists, you can see them listed in the table of contents or the index. If you want to read tips for writing, simply look those up. Or, if you want to check out the info boxes, rules, tips from the pros, and so on, go right ahead. You can also scan the book and read the callout quotes. They're little bites of wisdom that are easily digestible.

To best absorb the information in each chapter, allow yourself the necessary time to do the following:

1. Read the copy in all the examples.

2. See how it relates to the image.

3. Look carefully at typography for a hierarchy of message. (See what's emphasized by the size, position, and style of the type.)

4. Review the terminology list.

5. Examine examples and templates.

6. Complete, or at least, check out the exercises.

7. Become an active observer. Notice new media everywhere.

8. Practice your analytical skills every day, whenever you see advertising messages.

9. Be a gracious recipient of criticism. You'll grow faster.

10. Read more. Be receptive to all kinds of writing. In all channels, platforms, and formats, from plays to promotions.

What I have intended to set forth is a "Writer's Depot" where you can browse all the tools on the virtual shelf and select the ones you need to add to your creative tool shed. Take what you want, review what you'd like, and cart off as many as you can. That way, you'll be prepared for any upcoming project.

If you're committed to your own creative growth, you'll become a stronger writer, even if you jump around from channel to channel or medium to medium. You'll soon discover, after reading this complete guide, you'll be prepared to create compelling copy in any marketing ecosystem. Mostly, because you'll be equipped with a handy, all-in-one toolkit.

Acknowledgments

This edition would not have been completed without generous help of many people who gave their time and attention throughout the creative process. I am excited to thank each of them individually to show my gratitude. I can hear their reply, "Oh, that's not necessary." But, I assure you, it is. If by any chance, I unintentionally omitted anyone, please accept my deepest apology.

The first person I would like to thank is my husband, Jack. I've been hidden away for extended periods to write. So much so, he's always surprised to see me. Next, I would like to applaud Jennifer and Paul Minnich, co-creative directors of M2Design, for supporting my resolute determination to complete this. They wholeheartedly joined my celebratory moments when I received another approved image or quote. Third, I wish to recognize Monica Hudson, who eagerly assisted in acquiring new campaign examples. Fourth, I must celebrate my sister, Sue, who fills my life with fun and giggles. Fifth, I would like to honor my niece, Ronni Alexander, who is an irreplaceable, unwavering life compass.

Next, I must thank some people at Wiley-Blackwell. First, Nicole Allen, commissioning editor, Wiley-Blackwell Humanities Editorial, who not only enthusiastically supported my vision but also allowed me to modify the manuscript into what it has become. Second, I wish to acknowledge Laura Matthews, assistant managing editor, Authored Books, who aided in reviewing the images. Third, I would like to thank Rosie Hayden, managing editor, who oversaw the project from its inception. Fourth, I want to express my heartfelt gratitude to Liz Wingett, executive managing editor, who diligently oversaw the final edits and brought the book to publication, as well as the team of proofreaders, especially Roger Bullen, for his invaluable copy editing expertise. In addition, I would also wish to recognize Simon Eckley, assistant director, Intellectual Property Licensing & Post-Production Operations, for his careful assistance in permissions confirmation. Also, a grateful thanks goes to Ed Robinson, editorial assistant, who helped coordinate the cover design and marketing content.

I want to thank all of the creative talents and advertising executives (in alphabetical order), who helped me complete this second edition. They quickly responded to my complex requests of image acquisition with correct specification, text content edits, and caption and credit approvals.

Independent creative talents

Sheena Brady, commercial director/creative director, for eagerly providing wonderfully informative remarks.

Curt Mueller, freelance creative director/writer, for offering invaluable writing tips and background information on Red Brick Beer and other campaigns.

Sara Rose, executive creative director, for her prompt reply to all my questions and for her illuminating comments.

Agencies and companies

At Augusta Free Press: Chris Graham, global editor, for graciously granting permission to freely quote from one of his articles on digital trends.

At Convince&Convert: Michelle Saunders, director of content marketing, for kindly allowing me to use excerpts from several articles including those by Nathan Ellering and Anna Hrach.

At Craig Miller Creative: Craig Miller, creative director/copywriter, for sharing his writing tips and campaign-development insights.

At DeVito/Verdi: Ellis Verdi for his generous approval of many outstanding agency campaigns; Nick Ryan, marketing director, for the careful overseeing of image specifications and caption approvals.

At Digital Surgeons: Peter Sena II, founder and chief technology officer, for his astute comments about the digital development of creative work for Lovesac StealthTech and Naboso Sensory Sticks.

At Drayton Bird Associates: Drayton Bird, founder, writer, marketer, for generously sharing his noteworthy articles, blogs, and insights.

At Planet Propaganda: Teddy Brown, group creative director, for his indispensable insight into Taco Bell campaigns.

At Rain the Growth: Benazhir Maratuech, associate director of content strategy, for her quick response to provide clarification about content- and web-development strategy.

At The Escape Pod: Vinny Warren, founder and creative director, for his commentary on strategic planning; images, scripts, and writing tips; and innovative campaign examples, such as Feckin Irish Whiskey and Wheat Thins.

At Tom & Eric 911: Tom Amico, creative director/writer, for his detailed explanation of the strategic planning and creative thinking behind Natürlich, Siggi's yogurt, and Upcycle campaigns.

At Top Tog Media: Melonie Dodaro, CEO, for granting permission to freely quote from her blog that detailed interesting topics.

At WordStream: Kristen McCormick, senior managing editor (USA Today Network), for her generous permission to liberally quote from her articles and those of Megan Marrs and Céillie Clarke-Keane.

At Young & Laramore: Tom Denari, president, for his consent to include exciting agency work; Carolyn Hadlock, principal and executive creative director, for providing images, interviews, and comments about the creative process; Charlie Hopper, principal, for sharing the strategic thinking behind various campaigns; Brad Bobenmoyer, vice president of marketing, for overseeing the quote, image and permission process; and Kinsey Whitt, associate account manager, for her tireless work of ushering through to completion the complex task of image curation, resizing, and caption approvals.

At Zimmerman Advertising: Juan Valente, creative director, for his content and website writing tips.

I would also like to thank the following people for their encouragement and generosity. At Florida International University: Brian Schriner, Dean, College of Communication, Architecture + The Arts, for his unwavering commitment to my research; Lillian Kopenhaver, founder and executive director of the Lillian Lodge Kopenhaver Center for the Advancement of Women in Communication, for her enthusiastic, continuous encouragement; Aileen Izquierdo, department chair of the FIU School of Communication and founding director of Lee Caplin School of Journalism & Media, for her support and professional-leave approval to finish this work; and Brian Friedman, in IT services, for his invaluable assistance in digital image refinement.

In addition, I would also like to thank my colleagues, university students, and seminar audiences who inspire me and drive my inquisitive nature to seek out new avenues of research.

Finally, I want to express my gratitude to all those who had faith in this project right from its inception, when it was merely a concept in my mind.

Introduction

There are several significant changes to this work. First, the book is restructured into three sections for quick access to relevant topics. Each part will start with an explanation of that section, as follows:

Part One – Content Writing: Content Versus Copywriting

Part Two – Copywriting for Three Platforms: (1) Video, (2) Audio, (3) Print, plus Cross-platform Campaigns

Part Three – Resources

Suggested Reading
Index

Other changes to help navigate through the 2nd edition include:

1. New content in the first four chapters, plus some content from Chapters 10 through 12 (1st edition)

2. A hundred new images of innovative social media, interactive, experiential, TV, out-of-home, transit, print, and radio campaigns

3. Dozens of new TV and radio storyboards and scripts

4. New charts, infographics, content-writing templates, and campaign examples

5. New social media, video, and other handy templates (Chapter 3)

6. A new resource section (Part Three), which will help readers gain access to a curated list of skill-building references

7. Some new in-chapter terminology lists, checklists, and other reference lists, as well as new exercises, callout quotes, writing tips, and end-of-the-book terminology

Below are the section-by-section and chapter-by-chapter summaries for easy reference.

Part One – Content Writing: Content Versus Copywriting

The first part discusses writing techniques with some exciting forms of engagement, such as interactive and experiential content.

Chapter 1 – The Shareable Word: Content Creation Process

This chapter discusses how to develop the topics for content writing. It includes a "Seven-step Content Writing Process" detailed below. This is similar to the Creative Brief in Chapter 1 in the first edition. These kinds of comparisons will help guide writers in the idea- and campaign-development process. (Chapter 2 will begin with step four.)

1. Why are you sharing or advertising? Purpose/goal

To help writers focus their ideas, they should write down in one sentence the reason for this message. What is it supposed to do: inform, entertain, educate, inspire, generate shares, solve a problem, etc.? Once the purpose of the content is clear, the writing can begin.

2. What are you saying? Content/message (Copy development)

We next ask writers to consider what they want the reader to know and ask them to think about what attracts them to continue reading? We review ways to present the message, such as quick checklists, quick peeks, in-depth explanations, etc. We point out the importance of tailoring content because consumers look for information on specific topics.

3. To whom are you speaking? Segments/audience

We look into which audience they want to reach. We also examine how these consumers process information and where they consume content. We study the three buying states: (1) awareness, (2) consideration, and (3) decision. We also examine the five targets in the buying process: (1) Initiator, (2) Influencer, (3) Decider, (4) Buyer, and (5) User. Plus, we cover other audience-targeting techniques, including segmentation, to maximize the content impact.

Chapter 2 – The Digital Storytelling Word: Audience Engagement

This chapter continues the "Seven-step Content Writing Process," starting with step four below:

4. Which tools are you using? Audience analytics/research

This is a discussion of content formats and frameworks. How and where is it going to be presented? Is it written, as in a social media post, an email, a blog, or a mini post? Is it in audio format for a podcast or Clubhouse discussion? Is it a recorded video for TikTok, YouTube, or an Amazon review? Is it a live streaming video for Facebook Live, Instagram Live, or gamers on Twitch? Is it a visual depiction in a pictographic, an illustration, or an infographic? Is it a shoppable post for social commerce? Techniques and templates will clarify the format options.

5. Where are you reaching them? Channel content/platform strategies

This section will show how to apply analytics to create multichannel communication, segment targeting, personalization, and more. The immediate application of consumer insights strengthens content, as well as the readers' comprehension and retention. Discussed are specific ways to integrate consumer data into usable content on myriad platforms.

6. *How are you presenting the content? Format/vehicles*

This covers an analysis of social and interactive and formats, plus how they guide writing development. By understanding how the communication will be delivered, writers can more accurately design effective marketing campaigns for Facebook, LinkedIn, X (previously Twitter), Instagram, Pinterest, YouTube, AR/VR/MR, AI-powered content, and more.

7. *When are you scheduling the content? Scheduling/media plan and social media options*

Here we discuss how to tailor the release times to best reach the audience. As usual, we review the first steps in content creation: (1) purpose and (2) audience. Again, we examine the initial audience questions: Who's reading or watching it? Where are they seeing it? When are they consuming content? How will the product help them? Then, we move on to detail the importance of a release schedule and calendar to keep track of the campaign's post or release dates.

Chapter 3 – The Template Word: Visual Engagement for Cross-platform Use

This section shows different templates that can be modified for use in different channels and platforms. Included are layout examples, script formats, social media video formats, and TV storyboards. This chapter shows how to apply templates as shortcuts in the content-development process. Included are channel content length, layout formats, image selection, and types of social media posts and/or ads.

Chapter 4 – The Experiential Word: Immersive, MR (Mixed Reality), and Interactive Engagement

Here we explore the user experience and interfacing in immersive and experiential environments. We emphasize how consumers became influencers with persuasive opinions on social media platforms. Also, we examine the commercialization of social media sites that allowed consumers to shop directly from links on influencer, marketing, and brand posts. We then look at how marketers, in response to these changes, designed content around followers' and customers' preferences. We highlight how marketers personalized audience-driven interactions in live events, digital environments, and immersive experiences.

Part Two – Copywriting for Three Platforms: 1) Video, 2) Audio, 3) Print, plus Cross-platform Campaigns

The second part discusses traditional copywriting techniques with some new applications, such as interactive TV spots.

Chapter 5 – The Persuasive Word: Strategy ABCs: Audience, Benefits, and Creative Briefs

In this chapter, we examine how the creative brief directs the campaign. We cover both the shorter and longer briefs, as well as audience types by demographics, psychographics, geographics, VALS (values and lifestyles), age/interest groups, and more. The focus is on the connection between what marketers want the audience to know about the brand, how the brand will help them, and why they should buy it. It also explains where the audience will discover or collide with the message (*touchpoints*) and which *tactics* or media vehicles would work best. Also discussed are *tone of voice*, *point of view*, types of research methods, and differences between primary and secondary audiences, as well as consumer insights.

Chapter 6 – The Strategic Word: Strategy Categories

Here we explain the six basic strategy categories broken down into: (1) *Consumer-focused*, (2) *Product-focused*, (3) *Savings as the Star*, (4) *Emotional Approach*, (5) *Storytelling*, and (6) *Audience Engagement*. Fifty types of content-writing strategies fall into the six main, above-mentioned categories. We review Maslow's Hierarchy of Needs, Jib Fowles' Advertising's 15 Basic Appeals, types of brand positioning, and more.

Chapter 7 – The Animated Word: TV, Interactive Spots, and Video Scripts

In this section, we study the basic writing rules for TV and the various formats, including scripts and storyboards. We explain how: (1) "The Five Rs" drive results and (2) *universal truths* apply to TV.

In addition, we identify different types of commercials, including the talking head, continuing characters, reason why, and more. First-hand TV writing tips are shared by several successful copywriters. These include Tom Amico, who created the copy for the Aflac Duck, and Vinny Warren, best known for the Budweiser "Whassup!" campaign.

Finally, the list of commonly used industry terms will strengthen copywriters' pre- and post-production communication skills.

Chapter 8 – The Spoken Word: Radio Script Writing and Formats

Here, we explore the main radio script formats. A common one, often used at radio stations, is double-spaced, all caps, and breaks each line at the end of a phrase. We cover a few other radio "rules," including: (1) leaving two seconds for sound effects and music cuts; (2) using ellipses to "billboard" (emphasize) a word or phrase; (3) considering production while writing, such as the talent, delivery, sound effects, and music; and (4) writing for the ear. Also discussed are casting, booking, and directing talent; creating scripts for specific celebrities; and targeting different radio *dayparts* (times the spots air on radio). Again, industry-used terms are included in a terminology list.

Chapter 9 – The Chosen Word: Copywriting Techniques

This section analyzes the correct use of the vernacular and when to digress from the grammatical rules to deliver a more natural writing style. The list of writing tips is an invaluable guide to reach that goal.

The useful writing techniques assist in concept development, execution, and production across all platforms. These include *tone of voice* (how you speak to the audience), *point of view* (who's speaking), *ABA* (referring back to the headline in the closing line), *weave* (connecting one main idea from the headline throughout the copy), and more, to design a strong message.

Chapter 10 – The Sticky Word: Headline and Slogan Techniques

Here the focus is on the 16 specific techniques to develop sticky headlines and impossible-to-forget slogans. We also explain the differences between eyebrows, headlines, subheads, body copy, call-to-action wording, closing lines, and taglines. We evaluate the types of headlines to guide in idea generation. These include: the celebrity endorsement, the metaphor, the story, and many more.

More emphasis is placed on writing from the consumers' perspective by applying consumer insights into how they shop, where they shop, what's important to them. Writers discover more invaluable copy tips from master copywriters.

Chapter 11 – The Written Word: Print Ads, Posters, Brochures, and More

We show how exciting print can be with the inclusion of scent, sound, 3D, holograms, pop-ups, QR codes, and so on. Readers are reminded to appeal to the needs and desires of their audience. As with content writing, copywriting should address the target's pain points and show how to relieve them with specific products. This chapter (1) reviews writing techniques and strategies, (2) explains basic copy format, (3) discusses categories of effective messages, and (4) introduces new terminology, such as: *mandatories* and *eyebrows*. Here readers learn to connect audience analysis, consumer benefits, appropriate *tone of voice*, message relevance, concept design, and idea presentation and delivery.

The presentation of powerful print ad examples will illustrate successful campaigns. A writing checklist and copy tips enhance strong copywriting skills.

Chapter 12 – The Ambient and Moving Word: Out-of-home and Transit

In this chapter, we point out unexpected *touchpoints*, such as manhole covers, retail store sliding glass doors, and pedestrian crosswalks. We also showcase traditional media with surprising copy that elevates a transit sign or billboard into a direct-to-consumer, almost intimate message. Visual examples demonstrate the clever, humorous, and irreverent copy with campaigns for Legal Sea Foods, Feckin Irish Whiskey, Pet Supplies Plus, and 7-Eleven.

We also examine the use of technology in signage to create interactive, targeted messages, such as the ASICS campaign for New York City marathoners, their friends, and families.

Chapter 13 – The Abridged Word: Small-space Writing: Direct Mail, Package Copy, Coupons, Freebies, etc.

We explore the challenges of small-space writing, including out-of-home, packaging, in-store signage, and sales letters, as well as detail the differences between direct mail and direct response. We refer back to the 50 types of strategies discussed in Chapter 6.

Further discussion covers reaching audiences through email marketing, mobile coupons, product-related apps, games, catalogs, and interactive ads. Examples and writing tips reinforce the techniques discussed.

Chapter 14 – The Cross-platform Word: Integrated Campaigns: Traditional, Social Media, and Interactive

This summative chapter shows how concepts can work across all channels, platforms, and formats, supported by strategic thinking, idea execution, audience segmentation, and targeted distribution.

We study how new technology builds consumer relationships and increases brand loyalty. Included are exciting visual examples of campaigns for Hotel Tango alcohol, Natürlich yogurt, Trane heating and cooling systems, Upcycle waste recycling, and Mount Sinai Medical Center. Successful campaigns, regardless of the platform, are remembered because their messages are unique, informative, interactive, and entertaining. A big idea will shine across platforms through consumer-engaging campaigns.

Part Three – Resources

This section is devoted to handy references from resource lists and terminology to suggested reading and the index.

- **A Short, Handy List of Resource Links**
- **Terminology**
- **Suggested Reading**
- **Index**

In conclusion, this work is designed to facilitate the learning process for new writers in all communication styles and guide them from idea generation to content and copywriting development. We encourage readers to carefully review all examples, writing tips, terminology lists, and to embrace the exercises. The goal is to make learning as exciting as writing!

About the Companion Website

This book is accompanied by a companion website:

www.wiley.com/go/contentandcopywriting

The website includes Powerpoints, an Instructor's Guide, and a Test Bank

Content Writing: Content Versus Copywriting

1 The Shareable Word: Content Creation Process

"The same writer works across all the platforms for an account, whether it's a TV spot or a tweet."

Carolyn Hadlock, Principal and Executive Creative Director, Young & Laramore[1]

A quick look into the history of communication will reveal the inner drive to share with others and express oneself. This is evident in early forms of communication from cave drawings and oral tradition, such as town criers. Sharing information then moved into the printed or written word, which

Content and Copywriting: The Complete Toolkit for Strategic Marketing,
Second Edition. Margo Berman.
© 2024 Margo Berman. Published 2024 by John Wiley & Sons Ltd.
Companion website: www.wiley.com/go/contentandcopywriting

ultimately led to digital and visual delivery. Postable, shareable social media posts merged into shoppable systems. Consumer experience and interaction drove content development.

With the significant change in advertising strategy, messaging has transitioned from a brand monologue that spoke to the customer into an interactive, customer-focused relationship. The biggest transformation is that advertising, integrated communication, and public relations have migrated from segregated silos into interrelated, multichannel marketing. It is no longer a "push" to sell to the customer, but rather a "pull" from the customer to learn more about the brand.

Even the language has changed. What was previously called "opt-in advertising" is now "pull marketing." "Advertising sales" is now also called "inbound marketing." "Free-info-sales bait" is now "conversion-designed content." A "multiplatform campaign" is now "cross-platform integration and content recycling." Advertising is no longer linear, but a series of multipronged digital interactions and consumer *touchpoints*. This social media marketing cycle is designed to convert followers into buyers.

With the shift from copywriting and public relations writing to content writing, writers in all communications fields must learn new ways to reach their audiences. Messaging has shifted from brand-centric selling to information-to-consumer storytelling. Marketers in all positions often must know both kinds of delivery: content writing and copywriting. Many also use traditional public relations techniques.

Marketers also need to understand new platforms, templates, and terminology. What was once under the domain of ad agency media planners is now in the hands of many writers, who often handle scheduling and calendaring. What was once just social media has morphed into cross-integrated delivery that includes shareable and shoppable content.

Today, more than ever, communicators need to master myriad formats and storytelling templates. This work will include lists that compare the differences between content writers and copywriters to clarify several questions:

- Who writes which assignments?
- What are the writing and format templates?
- How to apply content development processes?
- What do the new terms mean?

With technology evolving daily, communicators must keep pace. Tutorials delivered by social media and technology giants, such as Google and

Facebook, now train students and professionals for careers in the field. This is why accessing these tutorials will sharpen your content-composition skills. Remember to learn first. Write second.

As in all marketing, strategic thinking will support effective consumer engagement.

Basically, this work will help writers write, right now.

Seeing how this section works

In this first part, you'll see how content writing is different from copywriting. You'll learn to strategically compare the similarities and differences between message development, audience targeting, creative processes, and terminology usage.

When you can see how to write social media content and advertising copy, you will be a more versatile professional.

To write content, begin with a seven-step process similar to the 14-question creative brief in Chapter 5. Here's a quick look at the creative brief, so you don't have to move out of this chapter:

1. *Why* are you advertising?

2. *Whom* are you targeting?

3. *Who* are the competitors?

4. *What* do consumers currently think about the brand?

5. *What* do you want them to think?

6. *Why* should they buy this product?

7. *What's* the big message?

8. *What's* the brand's *positioning*?

9. *What's* the brand's *USP*?

10. *What's* the brand's *personality*?

11. *What's* the tone of voice?

12. *Who's* speaking?

13. *What* tactics will you use?

14. *How* can the campaign create buzz (press coverage/earned media)?

In Chapter 1, we'll cover the first three steps of the Seven-step Content Writing Process. Chapter 2 begins with step four and explains each subsequent step through number seven in detail.

Pay attention to idea-generating steps in different channels. These kinds of comparisons will help guide you in the idea- and campaign-development process. The core questions for content messaging are the same, namely:

1. *Why are you sharing content or advertising?* Purpose/goal
   Content writing begins with the same question as in the creative brief (to be discussed in Chapter 5): What is the point of this communication?
   If you don't know what you're trying to say, you don't have a definite destination. Where are you headed? Why are you going there? What do you want to accomplish?

2. *What are you saying?* Content/message (Copy development)
   After you answer why you need to develop content, next you need to consider what you want the reader to know.
   When you're consuming content, what compels you to read on? Do you like a quick checklist, a sneak peek, or a detailed explanation? Realize that people digest and search for content differently regarding specific information.

3. *To whom are you speaking?* Segments/audience
   In order to reach your audience, you need to first know how to reach a segmented and custom-curated audience. You also need to understand how they process and where they consume content.

Now, let's take a closer look at each of these first three steps, one by one.

Determining the reason for the message

Q1. *Why are you sharing or advertising?* Purpose/goal

If you had to write down one sentence about why you need to get the message out, what would be the reason? Is it to teach? Inspire? Motivate? Share? Help? Why does the brand need to communicate and interact with its audience? What's the ultimate goal or result you're trying to achieve?

You could start by creating a *sales funnel*. But, which type? There are so many from which to choose, from marketing to sales. However, there are several types of those as well. For example:[2]

1. *Opt-in lead-generating* – Create content with perceived value that merits the release of contact information, including email, mailing address, and/or phone number.

2. *Free-item-plus-shipping* – Offer a physical product for free with only the shipping costs billed to the consumer.

3. *Pays-for-itself* – Present a paid-for offer that covers the cost of publicizing it, ensuring immediate profitability.

4. *Subscription (membership)* – Create valuable content that others want to receive on a regular basis.

5. *Tutorial (webinar)* – Deliver digestible instruction on narrow-focused topics.

6. *New product introduction* – Launch just-developed products and illustrate their problem-solving features.

7. *Consultation (coaching)* – Highlight expertise and experience to get hired.

8. *Expensive product sales* – Present high-end items with a deep discount to reflect value and savings.

If you decide to use a five-part sales funnel that (1) drives traffic, (2) offers free content, (3) distributes the content, (4) converts respondents on a website landing page, and (5) establishes new leads, you could break the five key parts into a more detailed, content-specific list, such as:

1. *Introduce the brand* – Announce a new product or service.

2. *Educate with information and tips* – Explain how the brand is different from its competitors and how it can help consumers.

3. *Present a bait click* – Entice readers with a valuable *lead magnet* (free offer) to gain their contact information.

4. *Show a value* – Describe why the product is worth consideration and purchase.

5. *Build a list* – Collect a preliminary, consumer-contact list, cull it down to a targeted audience, and establish a relationship.

6. *Create a community* – Develop a group of followers interested in your content to grow your network.

7. *Drive traffic to a website* – Create relevant, clickable content to guide readers to your URL.

8. *Guide a purchasing decision* – Virtually take the viewers' hand and shepherd them through a step-by-step buying cycle, as mentioned in the above paragraph.

9. *Convert visitors, followers, and subscribers into buyers* – Stay in touch with people replying to multiple offers to convert interested followers into consumers.

10. *Offer multiple buying methods* – Make it easy to purchase by providing different ways to purchase, for example: Amazon Pay, Apple Pay, Google Pay, PayPal, monthly credit card installments, etc.

11. *Manage customer relationships* – Maintain and boost brand loyalty among consumers with ongoing content and offers.

12. *Repurpose content for other channels and platforms* – Reuse created content in various formats, channels, and platforms to extend exposure and increase output.

If you want to increase shares and reposts, you might start by researching common questions on Quora. You could write about areas not covered. Then, your purpose might be to build a content list such as:

1. *Pique curiosity with a unique topic* – If it hasn't been discussed, yet needs attention, cover it.

2. *Solve a common problem* – Examine the most frequently posted issue that many people are trying to solve – and answer it.

3. *Show a proven solution* – Illustrate the answer and show successful examples.

4. *Change an opinion* – Create a paradigm shift by explaining substantial reasons to do so.

5. *Inspire action* – Explain the next steps with multiple ways to subscribe, opt-in, register, purchase, etc.

6. *Ignite audience engagement* – Invite readers to share their thoughts, pose or answer questions, and/or even challenge the information.

7. *Lure and interact with an influencer's followers* – Appeal to what interests them and offer exciting and relevant content to ignite engagement.

You could choose to use fewer or more steps in your sales funnel, such as these six: (1) awareness, (2) interest, (3) consideration, (4) intention, (5) decision, and (6) purchase. Whatever your buying process or sales funnel categories (Figures 1.1, 1.2, and 1.3), developing a content list will keep you focused on your overall goal of reaching out to a new or existing audience.

Most importantly, as with all messaging, it needs to be relevant and authentic. Therefore, narrowly focused content speaks to a targeted audience. A general topic talks to a wider audience. Before writing anything, you must answer these and other questions: What is the purpose of this communication? What do I want people to do?

1. Subscribe to a series of articles?

2. Follow a blog?

3. Register for a course, webinar, or event?

4. Get a special offer?

5. Order a tutorial, e-book, or guide?

6. Sign up for a trial offer?

Asking yourself why you're creating content will focus your attention. Starting with a clever idea might be the completely wrong direction for someone who wants to learn how to create a webinar.

If you begin by considering what your audience needs to solve a problem or resolve an issue, your overall purpose is to show how your product/service can offer the solution.

Looking at different sales funnels

Although marketing has morphed, don't overlook that a decades-old sales funnel, A-I-D-A, is still being used: Attention, Interest, Desire, and Action. It can be relabeled for social media in many ways. Often, it's seen from the consumers' perspective as: Awareness, Interest, Decision (or Discovery), and Action. In addition, you could also see it as Awareness, Interaction, Decision, and Advocacy. Or, you could see your role as a content writer as someone who will affect consumer behavior in the following ways: Activate, Influence, Deliberate, and Adopt.

Other sales funnels used some of the earlier labels and added other ones, such as these six: (1) Awareness, (2) Discovery, (3) Evaluation, (4) Engagement, (5) Sales, and (6) Loyalty. You can also add this one: (7) Advocacy: This is an easy way to understand the funnel from the consumer's perspective (Figure 1.1):

7-Part Social Media/Sales Funnel

Awareness: What is it?

Discovery: How will it help me?

Evaluation: Do I need it?

Engagement: I'll play along.

Sales: I want it.

Loyalty: I love it.

Advocacy: I'll brag about it.

Awareness

Discovery

Evaluation

Engagement

Sales

Loyalty

Advocacy

FIGURE 1.1 This "7-Part Social Media/Sales Funnel" chart was created by Juan Bermeo. Image courtesy of Juan Bermeo.

Awareness – What is it?

Discovery – How will it help me?

Evaluation – Do I need it?

Engagement – I'll play along.

Sales – I want it.

Loyalty – I love it.

Advocacy – I'll brag about it.

Sales funnels have even been simplified to three key areas: (1) Leads, (2) Prospects, and (3) Customers. Another way to look at a three-part funnel (Figure 1.2) is (1) Get Found, (2) Get Conversions, and (3) Get SEO (Search Engine Optimization) Analytics. These break down into (1) ToFu (top of funnel), (2) MoFu (middle of funnel), and (3) BoFu (bottom of funnel). Pay attention to the bottom of the funnel because it includes loyalty and analysis.

With so many types of sales funnels, it's easy to get confused here. Just sit down and think through the steps you need to guide your audience from learning about your brand to embracing it.

The seven steps can be viewed as a map that outlines customers' journeys from what they know (Awareness) to what they want to promote (Advocacy).

Now, let's consider why content is so important? It's because it drives customer relationships, loyalty, and sales. So, now you need to think carefully about what the most relevant message would be.

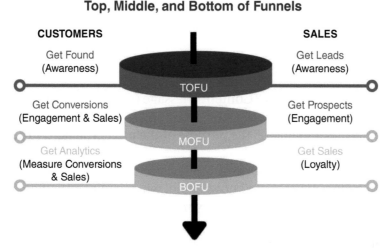

FIGURE 1.2 This "Top, Middle, and Bottom of Funnels" chart was created by Juan Bermeo. Image courtesy of Juan Bermeo.

Hooking the audience

If you want someone to order something, you need to create a *bait piece* of free content. This, once simply called a "free offer," is designed to hook the reader into providing contact information, such as an email, to receive the item. Remember, when you provide content that people value, they'll be willing to opt in (sign up for more material).

The point is, to just list the purpose as "writing digital content" won't work because it isn't specific enough. That's like ordering eggs at a restaurant. How do you want them prepared: scrambled, fried, over easy, in an omelet? Are they for dine in or take out? Before you begin to write any content, you must know exactly where it will be consumed. Marketers and clients might ask for digital content. You, as the creative talent, must learn exactly what that means to them. For some, it's social media. For others, it's a landing page. For several, it might mean email marketing. For a number of them, it might be growing webinar attendance, podcast followers, content subscriptions, tutorial registrations, or marketing-consultation contracts. You need to know where you're headed before writing one word of content.

To begin, review the statistics in different channels to determine which ones support your purpose before deciding which one to use. As you can imagine, the stats change quickly. So, whatever you're reading may be from a few months or years ago. Keep reviewing them and make your own comparisons.

One of the easiest ways to entice your audience is to ask what you provide that they need. How can you enrich their lives, assist in their personal growth, or improve their professional skills? Then, find a way to package your assistance in clear, concise, and informative content.

Learning how to craft the message

> Q2. *What are you saying?* Content/message (Copy development)

Just as you need to understand the purpose of the piece, you need to determine the actual content.

Imagine that you're sitting next to a few consumers. Just speak out loud and say what you want them to know. Often, when you picture them as three-dimensional people, not statistics, they magically come to life. What do they need to hear? What do you want to say?

Your content can be crafted by the easiest communiqué: the spoken voice. Even if it's in a digital delivery system, it should sound natural and authentic. Casual and relaxed. Unless, of course, it's focused on serious topics.

Here you need to consider how to develop content specifically designed to: (1) generate digital and mobile consumer engagement, (2) be organized into *content grouping*, (3) mimic the *brand voice*, (4) promote shares, and (5) create more ways to populate interactivity.

Next, you need to decide among different topic categories. Take a look at the six *strategy categories*, discussed later in Chapter 6, which include: (1) *Consumer-focused*, (2) *Product-focused*, (3) *Savings as the Star*, (4) *Emotional Approach*, (5) *Storytelling*, and (6) *Audience Engagement*. Now, instead of using those core categories for copywriting, you would use the topics below or many others for content writing. The list goes on with whatever you wish to discuss. If you need more suggestions, there are many sources, including the Convince&Convert website (www.convinceandconvert.com), where you would search under marketing/content ideas by Anna Hrach and Nathan Ellering.[3] Here's a handy reference list:

1. *Spotlight on people* – Feature members of the team, a successful entrepreneur, a recognized expert in the field.

2. *Core info* – Provide basic information for the novice. Build the content with the beginner in mind. Imagine it's the first time you heard about this topic. What would you need to understand first?

3. *Beyond the basics* – Focus on the more technical aspects after people know all the basics. Think about intermediate- or advanced-level professionals. They want to move forward and not spend time on areas they already understand.

4. *Learn-how tutorial* – Show the reader how to do something in an easy-to-understand, step-by-step sequence. Make sure it's clear and concise.

5. *Handy list* – Curate a must-have list that you would find helpful and personally use as a reference.

6. *New product intro* – Explain in detail how this product is different from earlier models. Or, if it's the first of its kind on the market, describe why it's needed. Be sure to showcase the exact features that deliver specific consumer benefits or solutions.

7. *Product comparison* – Compare it to others in the market to help buyers navigate the choices and select yours.

8. *Trend-focused* – Highlight what's happening in the industry at this moment. What has changed? What has improved? What do readers need to know to stay current?

9. *New technology* – What new software can help them grow their business, improve their professional skills, and/or shortcut some of the content development and editing time? Which search engines (Google), social media networks (Instagram), blogs (QuickSprout), CRM (customer relationship management) platforms (HubSpot), video-sharing channels (YouTube), design platforms (Canva), podcasts (Buzzsprout), etc., offer tutorials on this new technology? Show them where to find what they want to learn.

10. *Behind-the-scenes* – Give readers a peek inside the product/company/technology, etc. Present something that would satisfy their curiosity.

11. *Opinion pieces* – Share your personal views and detail how you reached your opinion. People like to follow the thinking behind the evaluations.

12. *Success stories* – Spotlight how others managed to reach their goals when facing similar challenges. What exactly did they do to overcome obstacles, learn new processes, and adopt new technology?

13. *Quizzes* – Illustrate new information in a fun and engaging way.

14. *Answers to common questions* – Provide a go-to resource of what many people are searching to learn with easy-to-find answers.

For example, if the product is complicated, you may want to break it down into digestible bites of content. If it's a lighthearted family-entertainment activity, you might choose a behind-the-scenes look at how a movie was shot or how a Disney character got ready to greet fans.

You want to grow your audience and build communities around the content you're creating. You can do this in many formats, such as live videos or podcasts (edited) or streaming content (as-it-happens without editing). Do you want people to be able to engage with you while you're presenting content, as in a webinar with questions and answers? Or do you want people to comment after viewing it, as with many YouTube videos? Do you want to invite your followers to create their own TikTok video challenge? Do you want to interact with them at in-person events? Do you want to enlighten them on membership or subscription perks? Each of these questions will help you think through the purpose of your post, tutorial, webinar, podcast, live interaction, etc.

Always remember that you want to frequently update and improve your content to enrich audience engagement, deepen the connection, and enhance the experience. To assist in boosting the frequency of your post, blog, etc., you may want to look into *AI-powered copy*. This is content that is written by artificial intelligence. It's auto-generated content created by computer tools. Many marketers are turning to these time-saving, content generators for everything from blogs and social media posts to websites and articles. In addition to the well-known ChatGPT, here are five *AI content-generation tools* compiled by digital marketer Alex Tucker[4]: (1) Jarvis, (2) Frase, (3) ClosersCopy, (4) Simplified, and (5) Anyword. He also listed Invideo for video content assistance in animation and editing, as well as Grammarly, the often-used grammar-checker software program. Others, including Karl at DreamGrow,[5] listed and reviewed sources for various formats, such as long documents, screenplays, grammar, SEO, and advertising. He and others listed the following SEO writing tools: (1) Surfer and (2) Topic – as well as Woven (now part of Slack), the catch-all, content calendar, and ProWritingAid, in addition to Grammarly, for grammar corrections. Many content writers recommend the Hemingway app for content and ad copy.

Continue to always look for new tools and keep an eye on the influence of current and emerging social media, gaming, streaming, and other platforms. You're probably familiar with the ones listed by HubSpot[6]: (1) Twitch, (2) Discord, (3) TikTok, (4) Clubhouse, (5) X Spaces (formerly Twitter Spaces), (6) Caffeine, (7) Instagram, and (8) Reels. In six months or less, there could be new communication instruments, as well as new devices. What works on one platform may or may not carry over to the next. Whatever does transfer, tweak the content, so you can repurpose it. Also keep in mind that, as mentioned in the preceding text, some marketers turn to auto-generated (AI) content.

Targeting the consumer group

Q3. *To whom are you speaking?* Segments/audience

To influence your audience, you also want to reach them wherever they are in the three buying states: (1) awareness, (2) consideration, and (3) decision.

Compare these three with the *five particular shoppers in the buying process*: (1) Initiator, (2) Influencer, (3) Decider, (4) Buyer, and (5) User.

After determining your audience(s), you will focus on audience-targeting techniques, such as segmented marketing.

It's important to integrate behavioral marketing because it examines many aspects of consumer engagement. This includes, but is not limited to, which sites and how often they visit, what offers they respond to, what content they follow, when they purchase, and *click-through rates* (to measure the effectiveness of ads, offers, content-embedded links, and more). Brand marketers who use behavioral-based statistics can increase engagement, subscriptions, loyalty, and sales.

HubSpot[7] shows how technology drives marketing automation and answers the question, "What is behavioral marketing?" This includes gathering data in the following areas of consumer insight: (1) *geolocation*, specifically, where the audience is physically located; (2) *visitor frequency*, namely if this is a first-time or prior guest; (3) *needs and goals*, including what motivates them and why they're searching; (4) *purchase statistics*, showing which consumers bought and may do so again; (5) *visitor interaction*, answering how they perceive and engage with the brand; and (6) *calendar-related buys*, mainly whether visitors make buying decisions on holidays or randomly throughout the year.

It's imperative to learn about the audience's patterns of behavior to customize content and scheduling. When do they look at content? What do they intend to learn? How soon are they going to make a purchase? How often have they searched or returned for the answer?

Now, let's look more closely at exploring market segments. You can't tell followers anything if you don't know where to reach them or what they want to learn. What's interesting is the similarity between targeting traditional audiences in advertising compared to social media communities in content marketing. There are three areas on which to focus. Two out of the three are the same: demographics and geographics. The only difference is behavioral habits for content writing and psychographics or values and lifestyles (*VALS*) for ad copy.

1. Demographics

2. Geographics

3. Behavioral habits (content writing) vs. Psychographics (copywriting)

VALS is discussed in detail in Chapter 5 and refer to audiences who fall into four key categories. Here is a quick overview: (1) Need-driven (Survivors/ Sustainers), (2) Outer-directed (Belongers/Emulators/Achievers), (3) Inner-directed (I-Am-Me's/ Experientials/Societally Conscious), and (4) Integrateds. Those in the fourth group have achieved ultimate financial and professional success, and even global recognition. (Please see the chart in Useful Info 5.3 in Chapter 5.)

Although content writers must learn how consumers behave (*behavioral habits*), copywriters often focus on how they live (*psychographics*). What is their lifestyle, and what are their personal preferences? Later, in Chapter 5, we will discuss demographics and geographics as they appear in the creative brief charts (Templates 5.1 and 5.2). Although you may know these words, here are handy reminders. *Demographics* describe the audience's age, education, gender, household income, occupation (e.g., mid-management), etc. This helps you qualify your leads. *Geographics* details where they live, from rural and suburban to urban settings (see Useful Info 1.1). Now, geographics has morphed into detailed *geolocation* analysis to more specifically pinpoint consumers' whereabouts – not just where they live and work, but also where they go during the day – via GPS and WiFi connections.

Here's a quick visual comparison of labels used by content writers and copywriters for three-part audience segments (Useful Info 1.1).

USEFUL INFO 1.1 Three-part audience segmentation

CONTENT WRITERS	COPYWRITERS
1. Demographics	1. Demographics
2. *Behavioral habits*	2. *Psychographics*
3. Geographics	3. Geographics

However, today, writers use both behavioral habits and psychographics, turning the three categories into four (see Useful Info 1.2) – sometimes even adding a fifth: *firmographics* – to study a targeted firm's data.

USEFUL INFO 1.2 Four-part audience segmentation

CONTENT WRITERS	COPYWRITERS
Demographics	Demographics
Behavioral habits	*Psychographics*
Psychographics	Behavioral habits
Geographics	Geographics

The similarities continue with targeting audiences. For social media segmentation, there are eight main areas:

1. *Know your consumers* – Know where they consume content, what's important to them, what's stopping them (objections), and what they need to fix or correct.

2. *Apply built-in social media controls* – As you may know, Facebook enables business accounts to reach their audience via demographics, common interests, and location (geographics). LinkedIn offers industry and company filters.

3. *Build content communities* – Engage with or build common-interest groups, such as those on Facebook and LinkedIn, and those centered around your content.

4. *Curate targeted-lead lists* – As mentioned earlier, list creation is key to any successful content marketing campaign. Some social networks help their audiences connect with their friends, followers, family members, and like-minded people or enthusiastic event participants.

5. *Schedule posts at different times (day parts)* – Grow your segments by targeting worldwide audiences who will be viewing at myriad hours around the clock.

6. *Use various touchpoints (channels and platforms)* – Parlay one group of followers into a legion of many by exploiting the power of each platform. You can expand or pinpoint your market by reaching them on their preferred channel or platform. For example, for teens, pick TikTok. For interested adults, use Instagram. Or use YouTube channels for specific, audience-centric topics.

7. *Simplify your procedures* – Reduce your workload by creating or using content, infographics, and design templates that are available from seemingly endless sources, including tutorials, blogs, podcasts, and videos, such as those from HubSpot, Hootsuite, Canva, Brandwatch (formerly Falcon), and more. There are many sources for learning about and automating content, as well as scheduling. Some, such as Brandwatch, offer a one-stop source for *social media management*, including designing social posts and ads; *managing customer relationships, scheduling*, and *content calendars*; developing customized audiences; and more.

8. *Assess your campaign strategies* – Check what's working and what isn't by testing the effectiveness of your content and distribution. Then,

you can create more relevant and targeted messaging and tactics by using social media testing, which can be found on HubSpot and elsewhere.[8]

In addition to strategies, there are also eight benefits that will help you learn about your consumers, decide what's missing in the marketplace, and determine how to market your product's solution:

1. *Develop more powerful content* – Speak their language and respond to their needs.

2. *Select the most successful tactics* – Evaluate different platforms and determine where to reach them.

3. *Create highly focused, targeted messages* – Write relevant, authentic content that will make them respond.

4. *Generate leads and convert them into buyers* – First entice, then qualify consumers.

5. *Show what makes your brand unique* – Exemplify what separates your product from your competitors, so they know why they should choose it.

6. *Strengthen consumer insight* – Evaluate and analyze your audiences, so you can see their point of view.

7. *Recognize niche opportunities* – Determine which narrowly focused markets suit your brand.

8. *Keep your eye on the market* – Examine the trends and needs of consumers to fine-tune your offers.[9]

Understanding the consumer journey: Sales funnel to audience loyalty

The goal is to move the audience through from the sales funnel to audience *advocacy*. Simply put, you're guiding the experience from learning to *loyalty*. Just making one sale isn't the objective. You want to create long-term fans. After they've opted in for content, you want to establish an ongoing relationship or focus on a *CRM* or *Customer Relationship Management* plan. Sending multiple, free, content-rich offers solidifies consumers' connection to the brand.

These people will be your vocal and virtual supporters who share and comment on your content and/or positively review your products, postings, podcasts, videos, tutorials, and so on. Once they buy in, you want them to get others to do so. In essence, they will become your advocates, who speak honestly and favorably on your behalf.

To get a clearer idea of this journey, here's what it looks like in a more condensed version. The decades-old adage *A-I-D-A* (Attention, Interest, Desire, and Action), as we mentioned earlier, looks similar, but can also be different. You will decide which formula works best or create a new one. For example:

A – *Attention* can be changed to *Awareness* (product introduction)

I – *Interest* can be turned into *Interaction* or *Intention* (engagement or likelihood to buy)

D – *Desire* can be categorized as *Decision* (actual purchase)

A – *Action* can be converted into *Advocacy* (product promoter)

If you then divide the top two into getting the consumer and second two into keeping the consumer: A-I and D-A. This would work well in a social media campaign:

1. *Get them* or *Acquire leads* before purchase: (A-I) Awareness and Interaction happens before a purchase.

2. *Keep them* or *Convert leads*: (D-A) Decision and Advocacy occurs after a purchase.

Ultimately, you're looking to reach them as they're deciding to buy and after they have purchased. Picture an actual individual to whom you're speaking. See them in your mind as an actual person or *persona*, not just as data based on their demographics and geographics. Focus on their psychographics. How they live their lives and what matters to them. Be sure that you follow the 6 Ps from the customers' point of view and focus on these points:

1. *Pique interest* (bring awareness) – Clearly inform consumers about the brand or service to spark their attention.

2. *Pain point* (problem) – What are they trying to learn or solve? What are the common issues many people are struggling to fix? Is it knowledge? Time management? Social media techniques? Marketing objectives?

3. *Prescription* (remedy) – Show how your brand/product is the cure for the problem. Explain what makes it better and detail the features that deliver the solution.

4. *Promise* (benefit) – Highlight what consumers gain when they move forward. Be sure the promise is one that the brand can keep. Negative reviews from unhappy shoppers will crush repeat and possibly new business.

5. *Payment* (buying options) – Make it easy for shoppers to buy. Offer several different payment methods. Their preferences should be readily available. For example, if they prefer mobile payment (like Apple Pay and Google Pay), credit card, PayPal, ACH (Automated Clearing House connects bank and billing accounts), or bitcoin, they should be able to pay the way they want.

6. *Product promoters* (brand fan) – Convert contented customers into your marketing team by encouraging them to share their opinions. Ask them to write reviews, post comments, or refer others. Add incentives for them to do it by offering free items, credit toward other products, points, etc. Create a loyalty program if you don't have one. Everyone likes to feel appreciated.

Always keep in mind the various reasons why consumers search for a solution. Then, consider these questions when preparing content. Where are they looking for this information? Whom are they listening to when deciding? What messages are influencing their choices? What do they need to hear to make the next step? If they follow macro (major) influencers or microbloggers, reach out to them where they are.

Consider the steps that move people from "What should I buy?" and "I'm ready to purchase" to "I love what I bought" and "I can't wait to tell others." These four phases include other stops along the route. The overall social media cycle could also be broken into a two-part, seven-stage customer-buying process:

- *Part one* (before the purchase): (1) Awareness, (2) Interest, and (3) Consideration

- *Part two* (after the purchase): (4) Conversion, (5) Use, (6) Opinion, and (7) Share

The point is that you can create a cycle customized to your customer, product, and marketing goals, or you can adopt existing sales funnels and marketing cycles. Another way to look at the *customer journey* is as a *three-part, eight-step process*, as in Figure 1.3. Review several funnels or charts to find the one that works for your campaign.

- *Part one "Customer Prospects"* (before the purchase) = *Getting relevant audience's attention*: (1) Audience Insight, (2) Awareness, and (3) Discovery

- *Part two "Customer Acquisition"* (during the purchasing process) = *Converting them into buyers*: (4) Evaluation and (5) Engagement

8-Step Customer Journey

ATTENTION: CUSTOMER PROSPECTS

  1 *Audience Insight:* How do I fix it? What do they need to solve? **KNOW THEM.**
  2 *Awareness:* What is it (the solution)? What they know. **SHOW THEM.**
  3 *Discovery:* How will it help me? Where to learn more. **TEACH THEM.**

CONVERSION: CUSTOMER ACQUISITION

  4 *Evaluation:* Do I need it? How they decide. **CONVINCE THEM.**
  5 *Engagement:* I'll play along. How they interact. **INVOLVE THEM.**

REPEAT PURCHASE: CUSTOMER RETENTION

  6 *Sales:* I want it. What and where they buy. **PERSUADE THEM.**
  7 *Loyalty:* I love it. What they cherish. **APPRECIATE THEM.**
  8 *Advocacy:* I'll brag about it. How they share. **ENCOURAGE THEM.**

FIGURE 1.3 This "8-Step Customer Journey" chart was created by Margo Berman. Image courtesy of Margo Berman.

- *Part three "Retaining Customers"* (after the sale) = *Developing repeat purchases*: (6) Sales, (7) Loyalty, and (8) Advocacy

Learning about tracking tools

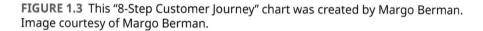

Although, as a content writer, you might not be involved in tracking research, you would still want to be familiar with the tools being used. These help obtain as-it-happens consumer data.[10] By now, you've probably heard of *Google Analytics*, a web analytics service provided by Google that helps you understand visitors' engagement and buying stages. Google actually has an entire toolkit of data-gathering instruments, including: (1) Google Trends and (2) Google Forms. So, whether you need to develop content based on what's happening in the marketplace (Trends); or create a response form to gauge your audience's pain, desire, or chosen action (Forms), you can quickly do that using these instruments.

There are also these and other such tools available:

1. *YouTube Analytics* to see how well your video is performing, as well as what are the popular tutorials/product demos that you also might want to create.

2. *Facebook Audience Insights* to gain demographic and psychographic data to more precisely target your consumer. Here, you could discover Facebook Groups, with members who might want to learn about your brand.

3. *Brightpearl CRM* for e-retailers who want to study and follow consumer behavior after they make a purchase.

You can organize the information into eight main areas on which to focus, including:

1. *Ad response* – Which ones worked and from where (website, app, social media post, YouTube video, etc.)?

2. *Brand interest* – Which products or brand categories interested the audience?

3. *App adoptions* – Which ones did consumers have and use most frequently?

4. *Cell phone providers* – Which carriers did they use?

5. *Topic interest* – What did they want to know?

6. *Demographics* – What were their ages, gender, personal income, education, household income, etc.?

7. *Mobile device* – What were they using: tablet or cell phone, and which model type and operating system (iOS, Android, etc.)?

8. *Geolocation (geographics)* – Where were users located via their GPS or WiFi?[11]

Making connections when writing

Often, the question is asked, "What's the difference between content writing and copywriting?" The core difference is that content starts by dispensing information, and ad copy begins with a pitch. It's interesting to note that both address a consumer issue that's resolved with a benefit-driven message.

Content writers offer nibbles of teachable information or "bait" before they purchase. They want users to know about something, then click on a link and gain access to the content. They feed, then lead the audience, and finally convert consumers into advocates. They initiate the relationship. Copywriters persuade and motivate the audience into buying right away. They want their ideas to stick and drive a purchasing decision. They plant the desire-to-have-it-now seed, show them why they must have it, and plead with them to buy now. Ultimately, they create shopping sirens, alerting the audience to something they might not have thought they needed. They instigate the need to buy.

An easy-to-remember comparison chart to use when creating content or copy is found in Useful Info 1.3. We learn rhyme when we learn to read because it's so easy to recall. Notice the deliberate use of rhyme listed in this chart. Of course, there are many other rhymes that could work in each column, such as "share" and "dare." This list could get you thinking about creating your own handy comparisons. Although content developers often train, both types of writers also edutain, as listed first in the "Common techniques writing chart" (Useful Info 1.4).

i USEFUL INFO 1.3 Writing purpose comparison chart

CONTENT WRITERS	COPYWRITERS
Tell	Sell
Bait	Manipulate
Click	Stick (ideas)
Feed	Seed
Know	Show
Lead	Plead
Teach	Preach
Initiate	Instigate
Convert	Alert

i USEFUL INFO 1.4 Common techniques writing chart

CONTENT WRITERS	COPYWRITERS
Explain (features)	Edutain (information)
Articulate (details)	Necessitate (action)
Alleviate (pain)	Validate (purchase)
Curate (audience)	Populate (buzz)
Animate (brand promise)	Relate (to audience)
Guide (decision)	Provide (pay options)
Demonstrate (solutions)	Perpetuate (purchases)

Applying social media content writing templates

Notice when you find excellent content that you can modify and use. In addition to automated content, these examples will simplify your writing process. As you run into them, save them and refer to them later as a resource file. Here's one more list (Useful Info 1.5) that you might find invaluable. The article, titled "The Proven Mechanics of Successful Social Media Writing,"[12] was written by Convince&Convert author Nathan Ellering, who was mentioned earlier.

Examine how this template list offers topics and content to attract interest. Don't just read the list. Analyze it. Consider each title one by one and see if any can work for you. Here's one way to begin. Think about what common problem your audience faces and how your product/service can help solve it.

Right now, with the mountains of available information in tutorials, webinars, podcasts, and blogs, it's difficult to sort through all of it and find the most relevant content. If you can condense it down to a review of curated resources for your readers, that could be very helpful. You could focus on the one skill that

USEFUL INFO 1.5 Content writing templates for all social media by Nathan Ellering[13]

1   How you feel when you (*do something desirable*).

2   Are you (*doing something*) like you should be?

3   Here's why you need a (*commonly held belief*).

4   Want to (*get something desirable*)?

5   [#] reasons your (*something a majority of your audience typically has*) sucks (*and how to make it the best*).

6   Nothing is (*commonly held belief*).

7   The secret to (*something desirable*) lies in (*unexpected advice*).

8   (*Influencer*) said, (*quote*). Here's how to do it.

9   What if you could (*get something desirable*) while (*getting something desirable*)?

10 Let's be honest. No one has enough time to (*do something desirable*). Smart (*audience*) do this.

11 Want to (*experience something desirable*)? Here is the (*way to get it*).

12 Turns out (*something desirable*) is actually (*something humorous*).

13 There's bound to be a (*something desirable*) for you.

14 Have you noticed anything different about (*something audience community does*)?

your content could teach. Or, suggest one problem-solving software that easily handles CRM data. Or, even recommend one design tool that could generate useful templates for multiple channels or platforms.

Let's go through just a few of these topic suggestions, one by one.

- **How you feel when you (*do something desirable*).**
  What's the one positive experience that directly relates to your offerings? If you're a content marketer, perhaps the "something desirable" is developing an effective content calendar. Focus your writing on free-content calendar templates as lead magnets or other content that also helps them.

- **Here's why you need a (*commonly held belief*).**
  Most marketers want to create a list of interested, ready-to-buy consumers. As mentioned earlier, in a sales funnel, they are referred to as "BoFu" (bottom of funnel). You could offer tips that explain how to narrow down opt-in consumers and/or how this list will increase sales. Relevant tips are handy and often saved, then shared.

- **Want to (*get something desirable*)?**
  It's difficult to get out as much content as you may want. Therefore, explaining how to repurpose blogs, articles, posts, etc., would keep your audience interested. Evaluating various AI-based software for auto-generation of content would help guide writers through the selection process. This is useful if they wanted to explore writing helpers.

- **[#] reasons your (*something a majority of your audience typically has*) sucks (*and how to make it the best*).**
  Using vernacular language, such as "suck," makes your content more casual and familiar. Your writing sounds the way members of your audience speak. It shows you understand their point of view. You feel their pain. Now, decide the number of suggestions you want to share. Don't pad the list. Offer only the most important ones. Writers sometimes think that more is better. It is if each one on the list is great.

- **The secret to (*something desirable*) lies in (*unexpected advice*).**
  What's something you wish you knew when you were facing an often-searched-for challenge? Did you run into an easy fix from a surprising source? Use that as your secret.

- **Let's be honest. No one has enough time to (*do something desirable*). Smart (*audience*) do this.**
  What's your biggest time waster? How did you alleviate it? Share what you discovered because it will help others who will then turn to you for future time-management advice.

- ▪ **Want to (*experience something desirable*)? Here is the (*way to get it*).**
Think about something most of your audience would like to enjoy. Perhaps, you could turn a dreaded task into a rewarding achievement. Let's say they need to constantly find content topics. What if you suggested a digital scavenger hunt, where they would look for and save great ideas in one place? You could include a list of linked clues to start. Remind them to bookmark or create a file with the ones they like. Then, they could either open the bookmarks or resource file and, in minutes, have lots of exciting ideas from which to choose. Instead of hating to hunt for topics, now they can review many applicable options.

- ▪ **Have you noticed anything different about (*something audience community does*)?**
This doesn't just have to refer to an audience community. It could refer to top-ranked bloggers. What are the techniques, templates, tutorials, software, etc., that they use? After checking these out, share them with your group. Perhaps, members haven't discovered their suggested resources. You could copy that link and, in effect, become an information scout. Be sure to cite your source(s).

This should give you some insight into how to use these content titles. Later, in Chapter 2, we'll also examine other social media writing templates, specifically those for Facebook, Instagram, X (formerly Twitter), and LinkedIn. Right now, this provides a jump start on formulaic content creation. Now when you create an effective lead, you can modify and repurpose it. Pay attention to what's working when you write. You may have found the most powerful topics for your audience. You just need to know which ones they are.

Writing with a purpose

With all the easy-to-find references, you won't have any problem discovering best practices. Just search for the key words "content writing" or "content marketing" and you'll run into miles of ideas. There are many lists of words and phrases that are chosen to tap into and spark an emotional response. Some articles break them into specific categories to help writers find the most relevant ones for that reaction, for example, reduce risk, build trust, etc. Here's a handy list of categories by Kristen McCormick, senior managing editor at WordStream:

1. Reduce risk

2. Reduce uncertainty

3. Build trust

4. Invite purchasing

5. Create urgency

6. Spark curiosity

7. Connect with your audience

8. Communicate value

9. Convey authority

10. Infer growth or benefit

Next, we'll examine these categories with a few successful words and phrases as examples (Tips and Rules 1.6), referenced in Ms. McCormick's article, "120 of the Best Words and Phrases for Marketing with Emotion,"[14] which you can try.

TIPS AND RULES 1.6
Best words and phrases for marketing with emotion

1	Reduce risk	Guaranteed or your money back
		a No obligation
		b No purchase necessary
		c Try it first
2	Reduce uncertainty	First month/time period free
		a See for yourself
		b No hidden fees
		c The [business name] guarantee
		d Risk-free guarantee
3	Build trust	Check out our testimonials page
		a See our reviews
		h See our resource library
		c Check out our FAQ section
4	Invite purchasing	What do you have to lose?
		a Give us a shot!
		b Take advantage of this special offer
		c A bargain you can't beat
		d See the results you want/Real results
5	Create urgency	For a limited time only
		a Save your spot
		b Sale ends [Saturday]
		c Download now
		d Call today

6	*Spark curiosity*	What if. . .?
		a Learn how to. . .
		b Discover
		c Find out
		d See why
7	*Connect with your audience*	Finally. . .
		a At last. . .
		b Are you tired of. . .
		c We get it. . .
		d We've got you/We've got your back. . .
		e It's about time. . .
8	*Communicate value*	Top/top-notch
		a Premium
		b Custom-built
		c Only
		d One-of-a-kind
9	*Convey authority*	Ultimate
		a Expert-approved
		b Cutting-edge
		c Leading
		d Specialized
10	*Infer growth or benefit*	Boost
		a Improve
		b Achieve
		c Learn
		d Grow

Of course, there are more categories and hundreds of tested expressions. Just do a quick search for powerful marketing words and phrases.

Content today needs to bring the readers into a state of readiness. As they're considering what to order, subscribe to, opt in for, and so on, they're making conscious choices. They're also going through a decision process. That's why the words you use need to escort the consumer from preview to purchase and from consideration to consumption. If you'd like to look at it another way, you could consider this list of categories as an additional reference: (1) Instill brand confidence. (2) Remove buying hesitation. (3) Turn shoppers into buyers. (4) Promise a solution. (5) Show quality. (6) Ignite a buy-now mentality. (7) Build customer rapport. (8) Create exclusivity. (9) Deliver a benefit.

(10) Inspire belief and loyalty. (11) Generate excitement. (12) Offer a hard-to-turn-down incentive or reward.

The point is that your customers are evaluating their options. They're choosing from an endless list of products or services. They're also reading reviews and listening to others' opinions. If it works for someone they follow or trust, they believe it could also work for them. That's why reviews are so important. Consumers trust each other when they might not trust marketing messages. Make sure that whatever you offer will flourish, not fold under honest reviews.

Whatever you can do to inspire trust and confidence, do it. That's why using the right words is so important and effective.

Using trends for content writing

In addition to new language, you need to pay attention to communication trends. What's happening now? What do you need to do to stay relevant? What's the hot topic at the moment? Here are seven trends to watch (Useful Info 1.7), listed by blogger Céillie Clark-Keane in her WordStream article.[15] Realize that all trends will change and you need to be watching out for what's new.

USEFUL INFO 1.7 7 trends to watch by Céillie Clark-Keane

1   Building content communities

2   Going live with video and webinars

3   Improving content experience

4   Focusing on products and services

5   Testing AI-powered copy

6   Doubling down on SEO

7   Repurposing content across channels

Let's take a closer look at each of these trends and see how they can help you create more engaging content.

- *Building content communities* – Think of this as a goal to grow communities of content teams. More and more teams are looking for resources to collaborate online. They need to find easy work-think-and-share spaces. This is why groups on various platforms, such as Facebook, X (formerly Twitter), LinkedIn, Slack, Microsoft Teams, Google Chat, Pumble, and Discord (not just for gaming),[16] have become easy gathering spots. Finding a way to build your own communities will make you a content source.

■ *Going live with video and webinars* – Look to design streaming videos, podcasts, and webinar tutorials because live videos continue to gain in popularity. Webinar audiences want to engage with the speaker and appreciate the opportunity to ask questions and offer comments. This is particularly appreciated in how-to-do-this tutorials.

■ *Improving content experience* – Enhance customer experience with relevant content because consumers want to quickly search and find what they need. They don't like being bombarded with superfluous content, annoying pitches, or other distractions. This is why marketers who pay attention to the overall user experience and create engaging, interactive content will provide topic-focused answers in videos, podcasts, blogs, etc. Some bloggers with a large following, such as Pat Flynn and Steve J. Larsen, do just that. You might want to check out their YouTube videos and notice their enticing prompts that get viewers to take the next step and respond.

■ *Focusing on products and services* – You want to highlight benefit-related product features. As marketing budgets become more streamlined, companies are looking to focus on targeting the BoFu, ready-to-buy groups in the sales funnel. Products need to immediately instill a why-buy mentality for consumers to take the next step and choose them.

■ *Testing AI-powered copy* – Why not explore AI content solutions? You might find they're a time-saver. You'll find product comparisons in blogs like Alex Tucker's,[17] as mentioned earlier, with these and other recommendations: (1) Jarvis for short blogs, websites, and posts; (2) Frase for help writing paragraphs; and (3) Simplified for idea organization. Mike Kaput,[18] Chief Content Officer at Marketing AI Institute, discusses the following: (1) Automated Insights, which offers spreadsheet software that creates written content from data-derived formats; (2) HyperWrite, which even constructs full paragraphs of completely new content; and other sources for marketing strategies, content topic research, performance analytics, and more. Other content writers have favored Contentyze for AI-written copy. To help with background information, writers also turn to the popular, already discussed AI chatbot, Chat-GPT. It provides answers to commonly asked questions and explanations of simple to complex topics. It's also designed to recognize text, write content, be conversational, and be easy to use. However, as with all AI copy, users must check all facts for unintended errors.

- *Doubling down on SEO* – Marketers evaluate SEO results to stand out among the major name brands. Two ways they do this are: (1) by developing specific SEO strategies, and (2) by designing uniquely targeted and lengthy (long-tail) keywords. They are watching what strategies their competitors are implementing, which content they're creating, and what keywords they're using. They are success observers. They see what their rivals are doing. Then, outdo them.

- *Repurposing content across channels* – Once you've written effective, inviting content, why discard it? Instead, find another home for it on another channel or platform. Ask yourself, could it be reused as a blog, podcast, or video? Could it be edited down for a social media post or lengthened for a webinar or live event? With all the pressure to produce content every day, find ways to streamline your process by repurposing well-written, targeted content.

Studying content marketing resources

Stay current on some of the best content to improve your writing. Useful Info 1.8 will guide you to the most relevant information. Kristi Hines, a Content Marketing Specialist, included 39 sources in her review of the *best content marketing blogs*.[19] Use the edited list in Useful Info 1.8, reduced from 39 to 14, as a quick reference.

USEFUL INFO 1.8 14 top content marketing blogs

1   *Content Marketing Institute* – Presents how-to advice guides in content development and creates new marketing and educational benchmarks delivered in print, online, and through live sessions

2   *Contentful* – Provides blogging tutorials on e-commerce replatforming, strategic content design, and digital creation

3   *Convince&Convert* – Explains how to use digital marketing and social media strategy to enhance content and engagement

4   *Copyblogger* – Shares content writing and copywriting tips for entrepreneurs

5   *CopyPress* – Keeps readers informed on what's happening in the industry, technology, the market, and content marketing

6   *Curata* – Teaches how to develop and execute content market strategies and how they relate to performance metrics with content-curation software

7   *Grow and Convert* (Newest content marketing articles) – Curates some of the latest marketing-based articles

8   *Heidi Cohen* (Actionable Marketing Guide blog) – Explains in plain language the complexities of an ever-changing marketing environment and the barrage of new subjects and terminology

9   *HubSpot* – Shows how to develop effective strategies to engage targeted consumers and convert them into buyers

10 *Influence & Co.* – Offers content marketing to help companies strategize, develop, distribute, and analyze content to strengthen branding and increase leads and sales

11 *Marketo* – Provides automated and targeted marketing software to increase lead generation, track behavior, and measure audience engagement

12 *MarketingProfs* – Produces educational materials in webinars, articles, live and hybrid events, and other tutorials, to build marketers' skills

13 *Semrush* – Evaluates online rankings, keyword performance, consumer response to content and analytics, and offers other SEO tools to optimize campaign effectiveness

14 *WordStream* – Presents rich insights into content marketing through detailed articles that outline trends, share tips, provide templates, and showcase strategies to build traffic, generate leads, and maximize digital marketing performance

Also, keep an eye out for new social media, streaming, and other platforms. This short list will probably be old in minutes:[20] (1) Triller, (2) Vimeo, (3) Valence, (4) Untappd, (5) Elpha, (6) Yubo, (7) Peanut, and (8) Caffeine. You can find hundreds more in a quick search. For a quick look at how quickly social media continues to grow, imagine billions of new users in a handful of years, with 56.8% of the world population on board in July 2021, boasting a 13.1% increase from the previous year.[21]

Talking about terminology

Terminology has also changed. As a professional, you want to keep up with the current language. Here is a tiny example of the different wording used by writers of content and copy (Useful Info 1.9). Of course, there are many more, plus new ones emerging as digital content morphs.

Become a permanent student and avid reader. Follow blogs on content marketing and digital writing. Each time you come across words or abbreviations that you don't know, look them up. (See the "Terminology" section under Resources in Part Three.) Add them to your writing arsenal. Learn the latest catch phrases and connect what you already know to what you're learning. Are there similarities? Is this phrase another way to express

USEFUL INFO 1.9 Terminology comparison chart

CONTENT WRITERS	COPYWRITERS
Analytics	Audience research
Cross-channel marketing	Spin out
Community	Online audience
Content	Copy
Conversion	Sale
Co-produce	Cross-promote
Curate	Assimilate
Format	Layout
Listening	Focus groups, surveys
Marketing funnel	Purchasing process
Purpose	Goal
Repost	Quote
Repurpose	Repackage
Share	Word-of-mouth
Social media integration	Cross-platform campaign
Title	Headline

something already familiar? By making these links, you'll become better versed and eventually fluent in what may at first seem like learning a new language.

Comparing channels and platforms

These words are sometimes confusing because they can have different meanings in different contexts. A quick way to understand channels is to see them as personal audience communication methods or portals that speak directly to a specific group. It helps to assign channels three basic functions. They let marketers: (1) create and post, (2) share or distribute, and (3) analyze. Analysis can include content effectiveness, as well as audience engagement, topic trends, and more. Let's use a YouTube video as an example. Marketers can create a video, upload it, distribute it, and collect analytics about it on their YouTube channels. All their videos are housed on the YouTube video platform. Likewise, content that they create for social media channels, such as Instagram, Facebook, LinkedIn, etc., is stored on social media platforms.

The platforms provide a content hub for greater distribution and analysis of one or multiple sources.

You already know about many kinds of platforms, including: (1) video platforms, (2) social media platforms, (3) search engine platforms, (4) content marketing platforms (e.g., customer retention), (5) email platforms, (6) e-commerce platforms (for shopping), and (7) influencer platforms. Sometimes, they are grouped into online and offline platforms. They can also be labeled as digital or mobile platforms, content or marketing platforms, and so on. Notice how often you come across the word "platform" and its many references. For example, you are probably already familiar with cross-platform apps that work on both major mobile operating systems: Android and iOS.

Basically, platforms offer tools with myriad functions, which can help to: (1) increase name recognition; (2) build brand fans, engagement, and referrals; (3) grow common-interest audiences; (4) generate reviews and endorsements; (5) demonstrate product use; (6) guide consumer journey; (7) improve search engine rankings; (8) offer analysis for consumer insight; (9) aid in CRM; (10) provide educational hubs; and more. One way to help understand platforms is to see how they work as tools to connect companies to consumers. Here are just a few examples for clarification (Useful Info 1.10). Of course, many others could be added.

In later chapters, we will see that advertisers use the word "platform" to refer to multimedia or cross-platform campaigns. For example, messages can be created for TV, radio, and social media, as well as out-of-home, immersive, and interactive platforms.

USEFUL INFO 1.10 Platforms provide services to help marketers. . .

1 *Design and create templates* – Canva

2 *Distribute content* – Amazon, YouTube, etc.

3 *Manage relationships* – HubSpot Marketing (CRM)

4 *Sell product*s – Shopify (e-commerce), pay-per-click (to initiate purchases), etc.

5 *Educate audiences* – Convince&Convert, LinkedIn, etc.

6 *Schedule content* – Hootsuite (calendaring)

7 *Analyze audience and campaign results* – Facebook, Google, Amazon, Sprout Social, etc.

8 *Optimize search results* – Google SEO

9 *Integrate campaigns* – Cross-platform marketing

Content writing checklist

It's always helpful to have a to-do list before you begin writing. Of course, you can create your own reference guide depending on your purpose and audience. Or, you can refer to the checklists given here. As always, start with why you're writing, what you're saying, and to whom you're speaking. Are you looking to write about the consumer journey? Are you looking for topics to discuss? Are you trying to write a comprehensive explanation or a marketing overview?

Let's review: (1) "The 6 Ps of the consumer journey checklist" (Checklist 1.11), as mentioned earlier, before we move to "The 7 Ps for content development" (Tips and Rules 1.12); and (2) "The 18 Rs for content writing checklist" (Checklist 1.13). As you compare Checklist 1.11 and Tips and Rules 1.12 side-by-side, you'll see how "consumer journey" and "content development" are different from each other. The consumer journey checklist addresses who consumers are, what they get, how they buy it, and how they can share it. On the other hand, the content development checklist outlines what marketers can do to get the message out. Now, closely review the above-mentioned content writing checklist (Checklist 1.13). Notice how it offers reminders of key initiatives to grow and retain the audience through timely and informative content.

CHECKLIST 1.11 The 6 Ps of the consumer journey checklist

Use the 6 Ps from the customer's point of view to focus on the following:

1   *Pique interest* – (bring awareness) What do they need to know about the brand/service?

2   *Pain point* – (problem) What's torturing them?

3   *Prescription* – (remedy) What do you offer?

4   *Promise* (benefit) – What do they get?

5   *Payment* (buying options) – How can they pay for it?

6   *Product promoters* (brand fan) – How can consumers promote it?

TIPS AND RULES 1.12
The 7 Ps for content development

You can also use these seven Ps for social media marketing as a handy list:

1   *Plan* – Determine your strategy, audience, and message. Know what you want to say, to whom you're speaking, and where you'll share the content.

2   *Prepare* – Evaluate commonly posted pain points and develop content to speak to those issues.

3   *Pinpoint the Persona* – (specific person) Who are these people? Picture an actual individual to whom you're speaking. See them in your mind three-dimensionally, not just as statistics based on their demographics and geographics. Focus on their psychographics. How they live their lives and what matters to them.

4   *Produce* – Create relevant, actionable content that prompts a response.

5   *Persuade* – Explain how this information/service/product will solve the prevailing problem.

6   *Publish* – Post and repurpose the content on multiple platforms and across channels.

7   *Promote* – Loyalty and advocacy from fan base.

Now, we'll look at the longer list for many content writing projects. You could refer to it as "The 18 Rs" to remember as you develop content. As you can see, this is a general list. You can easily expand or shorten it, as needed.

CHECKLIST 1.13 The 18 Rs for content
writing checklist

1   *Research* the most effective communication strategies and decide the purpose, content, audience, and channels/platforms.

2   *Recognize* the audience as individual people and write a brief persona description.

3   *Reach* them where they absorb/share content.

4   *Restate* widespread challenges/problems.

5   *Represent* their core values, so they connect to the brand.

6   *Reveal* the remedy for pain to resolve the problem.

7   *Relate to* and realize the audience's challenges.

8   *Recap* benefits as reasons to buy.

9   *Repeat* and reconsider content to generate leads.

10 *Reduce* risk with free trials:

    a Remove buying fears with guarantees.

11 *Repurpose* content and repost across channels.

12 *Retain* customers with a robust CRM program.

13 *Recruit* advocates and reap the benefits of positive reviews.

14 *Revive* former consumers, renew their interest, and redirect them into buying.

15 *Respond* to followers:

    a Refer them to useful resources.

    b Reward them and reciprocate with free content and special offers.

16 *Report* new trends and recommend new innovations.

17 *Review* analytics (record reactions, engagements, and visits), reevaluate campaigns, and revise as needed.

18 *Refer* to relevant resources regularly and release fresh content.

In the next chapters, we'll present content and format templates for each channel. We'll also examine analytics and learn how they relate to content design. We'll explore the content length for different social media channels and suggest some templates as applicable learning tools.

Content writing exercises

Exercise 1: What current trend could you use as a content topic?

Part 1   Pick a health-related product that just announced a new or improved formula.

Part 2   Write a list of topics that discuss how the new treatment can offer results.

Part 3   Answer these questions:

- Which trend would help consumers who use that product to solve a problem, such as acne?

- How can you get other users to share their success stories?

Exercise 2: What content could you repurpose for a blogger you follow?

Part 1   Choose one of your favorite bloggers.

Part 2   Select a particularly helpful article.

Part 3   Answer these questions:

- How could you reuse the content?
- Where else could you post it?
- How could you get followers to engage with the material?
- For example, could you ask for audience suggestions?

Exercise 3: Search online for a common problem and find a product that promises to solve it.

Part 1   Design a marketing direction.

Part 2   Write content using the following four of the 7 Ps for content development listed in Tips and Rules 1.12:

1. First, *plan* your strategy, audience, and message.
2. Then, *prepare* content for consumers' pain points.
3. Next, *produce* response-driven content.
4. Last, *persuade* consumers that this product will resolve the problem.

Part 3   Remember to find and include fact-based statistics, product reviews, and customer testimonials. If you don't find any, write some to support the product claims.

Notes

1. Carolyn Hadlock, personal communication, March 16, 2022.
2. https://www.funnelkarma.com/types-of-sales-funnel/ (accessed December 26, 2021).
3. https://www.convinceandconvert.com/content-marketing/content-ideas/ (accessed December 20, 2021)
4. https://alextucker.ca/ai-content-creation/ (accessed December 27, 2021).

5. https://www.dreamgrow.com/content-writing-tools/ (accessed December 20, 2021).

6. https://blog.HubSpot.com/marketing/new-social-media?utm_campaign= Newsletter%25202021&utm_medium=email&utm_content=177731513&utm_source=hs_email (accessed December 27, 2021).

7. https://blog.HubSpot.com/marketing/what-is-behavioral-marketing (accessed January 3, 2022).

8. https://blog.HubSpot.com/marketing/segment-social-media-audience (accessed January. 3, 2022).

9. https://www.theverge.com/2022/4/28/23047026/amazon-alexa-voice-data-targeted-ads-research-report (accessed February 26, 2024).

10. Keith A. Quesenberry, *Social Media Strategy: Marketing Advertising, and Public Relations in the Consumer Revolution*, 3rd ed. (Lanham, MD: Rowman & Littlefield, 2021), 114.

11. https://www.verfacto.com/blog/data-driven-marketing/tracking-consumer-behavior-online/ (accessed February 26, 2024).

12. https://www.convinceandconvert.com/social-media-strategy/successful-social-media-writing/ (accessed December 16, 2021).

13. https://www.convinceandconvert.com/social-media-strategy/successful-social-media-writing/ (accessed December 16, 2021).

14. https://www.wordstream.com/blog/ws/2021/01/13/best-words-and-phrases-for-marketing (accessed January 22, 2022).

15. https://www.wordstream.com/blog/ws/2020/11/23/content-marketing-trends (accessed May 21, 2021).

16. https://solutionsuggest.com/slack-alternatives/ (accessed January 21, 2022).

17. https://alextucker.ca/ai-content-creation/ (accessed December 27, 2021).

18. https://www.marketingaiinstitute.com/blog/ai-tools-for-content-strategy (access January 21, 2022).

19. https://kristihines.com/content-marketing-blogs/ (accessed January 20, 2022).

20. https://influencermarketinghub.com/social-media-sites/ (accessed January 12, 2022).

21. https://influencermarketinghub.com/social-media-marketing-benchmark-report/ (accessed January 12, 2022).

2

The Digital Storytelling Word
Audience Engagement

.

"By determining your audience, writing short and descriptive paragraphs and utilizing SEO keywords, you can attract more customers and create trackable results."

Sabina Escalada, Senior Product Manager, Target[1]

Content and Copywriting: The Complete Toolkit for Strategic Marketing,
Second Edition. Margo Berman.
© 2024 Margo Berman. Published 2024 by John Wiley & Sons Ltd.
Companion website: www.wiley.com/go/contentandcopywriting

T his chapter continues the Seven-step Content Writing Process, starting with step four. Remember that the first three steps were: (1) *Why* are you sharing content or advertising? (2) *What* are you saying? and (3) *To whom* are you speaking?

Now, we'll look at the last four steps: (4) *Which* analytical tools can you apply to writing? (5) *Where* are you publishing the content (channels/platforms)? (6) *How* are you presenting the content? and (7) *When* are you scheduling the content? Notice how similar this Seven-step Content Writing Process is to the 14 questions in a creative brief, covered later in Chapter 5.

Here's a handy creative brief question list as a reference: (1) *Why* are you advertising? (2) *Whom* are you targeting? (3) *Who* are the competitors? (4) *What* do consumers currently think about the brand? (5) *What* do you want them to think? (6) *Why* should they buy this product? (7) *What's* the big message? (8) *What's* the brand's positioning? (9) *What's* the brand's USP? (10) *What's* the brand's personality? (11) *What's* the tone of voice? (12) *Who's* speaking? (13) *What* tactics will you use? (14) *How* can the campaign create buzz (press coverage/earned media)?

Whatever the campaign strategy, content writers and ad copywriters have to answer the who, what, where, when, and how before they create a relevant, result-driven message. All writing starts at the end goal and moves backward. It begins with where the message is heading, to whom it's directed, how it's written, and finally, where and when it appears.

Campaign analysis and consumer-insight research has always been part of the marketing equation. Today, it's even more precisely integrated into the campaign tactics and messaging. It directs which types of communication vehicles (channels and platforms) speak best to the target and what consumer insights can be used to fine-tune the content. Let's look at how the analytics tools work for writing content.

Understanding how to apply analytics

Q4. *Which tools are you using?* Audience analytics/research

How are you going to apply audience insights to content development? How does what you learn guide what you write? What's the connection between data and content?

It's important to see how you can use *social media analytics* to guide marketing strategies and content writing. Here's a short list to guide your thinking when developing content. As always, pay attention to new trends. Notice if influencers and brand marketers are integrating them.

- *Conversation analysis* – Learn what people are saying and where they're learning it.

- *Consumer opinion* – Discover how they feel about brands, products, and services.

- *Audience-response measurement* – Determine how they're reacting to posts, comments, and other social media communication, such as reviews, podcasts, videos, etc.

- *Product-feature importance* – Find out what brand traits consumers value.

- *Competition chatter* – Reveal what competitors are talking about.

- *Evaluate affiliates and channels* – Uncover in what ways partners and social media channels could influence performance success.

Ultimately, applying this information steers marketers in the design of campaign strategies. For example, if they learn about a negative product review or post, they can address the product problem or specific complaint. They could also apply the insights to revise the content to better fit the audience. Review Useful Info 2.1 for easy-to-apply explanations of how to use analytics to drive content.

 USEFUL INFO 2.1 How analytics drive content

1 *Audience segmentation* – Ascertain the details of your audience, as mentioned in Chapter 1, by demographics, psychographics and geographics. Who are the influencers you wish to inspire to create and to share content with targeted, topic communities?

2 *Behavior analysis* – Comprehend consumers' opinions and conduct. Do they support the brand, critique it, or promote it as advocates?

3 *Attitude evaluation* – Focus on what people feel and how they're expressing those sentiments in their comments, posts, podcasts, blogs, etc. If you're picking up a great deal of negative chatter, you would want to address those issues. With social media listening, you can follow audience opinions.

4 *Customer experience* – Apply the shift from brand-focused to consumer-driven experiences to improve engagement and brand loyalty.

5   *Share of voice* – Examine how often and to what depth consumers are talking about companies and their products and services. You can learn the common concerns and opinions in these conversations.

6   *Content customization* – Modify communication to speak directly to the consumer community. What do they care about? What problems can your brand solve? How can you showcase the benefits?

7   *Platform-specific* – Confirm where your consumers absorb content. Then, repurpose the content to best fit those platforms.

8   *Topic relevance* – Write about what they care about. Give them quality content in digestible and informative pieces.

9   *Operational performance* – Use analytics to determine product popularity to adjust overall production in response to need.

10 *Clustering study* – Reveal connections between keywords or commonly used phrases to see if you can create a topic around a perceived interest. If people are talking about peanut butter and holiday-related recipes, you might publish a cooking video or podcast.

11 *Product enhancement* – Analyze an accumulation of posts and Amazon product reviews, which can deliver a clearer picture of customer pain points, shifting needs, and desired features. Trends can be identified and used to shape the modifications of existing products or guide new product development. You could then publicize these product updates.

12 *Competitor evaluation* – Examine the competition's activity. What products are they introducing? Which channels are they using? What new technologies are they integrating? Taking a marketing pulse might shed light on new markets, platforms, trends, or opportunities. Can you create content around these insights?

13 *Budget control* – Determine how well the budget is working. Are there areas to reassign marketing costs to strengthen the communication? Where else could you distribute content?

14 *Visual depiction* – Design charts, graphs, and infographics to share social media data with the audience in an easy-to-grasp manner.

15 *Quality content* – Identify what resonates with your audience and apply these findings to future content.

16 *KPI analysis* – Detect and monitor the key performance indicators (KPIs), such as audience likes, shares, reactions, engagement, impressions (number of times a visitor saw the content), and views (number of times consumers take action after reading the message). These are the topics, channels, and platforms to watch closely because they resonate most with the widest audience.

17 *Common interests and trends* – Focus on the topics *du jour*. What's getting everyone's attention? Use this info to develop timely content.

In addition, there are other ways to apply consumer data and analytics. You could use social media analytics to evaluate content subjects, keywords, and long-tail keyword phrases to see which ones are favored. Then, you could carefully incorporate those words or phrases into meaningful content. You could use social media listening to assess what's being said on reviews, comments, and posts. This could lead to product and/or content improvement. It could also help you detect answers to specific questions to help you develop pinpointed content. You could more precisely target audiences and personalize content for segments interested in those topics or trends.

Director of social media at VML, Benazhir Maratuech offered insights about how analytics can drive content writing:

> Social analytics is the needle that moves content and strategy. This is where we learn about our audiences, our competitors, performance, etc. Understanding our audience and how they react to content is key to optimizing current content or creating new one [content]. Everything in social moves at lightning speed, so being on top of performance, including social listening, is key for any brand to remain current and top of mind.
>
> From social data, you can learn about the tone, slang, and most importantly, sentiment! And this information should fuel your writing to create data-driven content.[2]

The fact is that analytics can also help determine what and where to publish; who's reading, engaging with, and sharing your content; what's getting the most reach; which topics are receiving the most visits and views. Use analytics to find answers to specific campaign results you want to learn.

Deciding where to publish

Q5. *Where are you reaching them?* Channel content/platform strategies

After receiving insights from social media analytics and listening, you have a better idea of where your audience is most often engaged. Consider if they're listeners, viewers, readers, and/or creators. Do they like to tune into podcasts? Do they prefer YouTube or live streaming videos? Do they like to follow influencers? Do they enjoy creating TikTok or YouTube videos?

What are their interests? What matters to them? What information are they seeking? What problems are they discussing? Once you know this, you can personalize your content on multiple channels for specific, segmented targets.

The immediate application of knowledge strengthens the readers' comprehension and retention. Discussed below are specific ways to integrate consumer data into usable content on myriad platforms.

Once you choose the channels, you need to know the correct ways to craft the content. What are the formats? What are the length restrictions? What are the visual requirements? What are the best practices for maximum impact?

Choosing how to write content

Q6. *How are you presenting the content?* Format/vehicles

Your choice of content vehicles will guide your writing process. By understanding how the communication will be delivered, you can more accurately design effective marketing campaigns for Facebook, LinkedIn, X (formerly Twitter), Instagram, Pinterest, YouTube, AR/VR/MR, AI-powered content, and more.

Next, you need to consider which format or framework to use for the content. How is it going to be presented? Is it for:

1. A *written* format, as in a social media post, an email, a blog, or a mini post on X?

2. An *audio* format for a podcast or Clubhouse discussion?

3. A *recorded* or *skippable video* for TikTok or YouTube?

4. A *live streaming video* for Facebook Live, or Instagram Live, or for gamers on Twitch?

5. A *visual depiction* in a pictographic, an illustration, or an infographic?

6. A *shoppable post* for social commerce?

7. An *immersive experience*?

8. Something else?

Each is a unique communication vehicle. Each uses different content-development and visual-design techniques. Some have templates. Others have specific requirements, such as getting the message up in the first five seconds for YouTube videos. Each should be designed to be best optimized for that specific social network. For example, simple visual changes, such as the Facebook profile picture that went from square to circular, could be important if you have any text within or around the image. You might have to edit it down or change the direction of the text. Or realizing that the Facebook "Our Story" section was removed, you would need to upload your company or personal information under the "About" section. Likes changed to followers, as well as various types of new calls-to-action emerged. These changes would affect how you write content.

In addition, Facebook offers a template menu to create the following with just a click: (1) posts, (2) stories, (3) video chats, (4) new pages, (5) new groups, (6) events, (7) marketplace listings, or (8) fundraisers. For business pages, you'll find these options: (1) live streams, (2) an event, (3) an offer, and (4) a job listing. You can also repurpose your Instagram stories directly to your Facebook pages.

It's imperative to stay up-to-date with design and content modifications for all social media channels and advertising platforms. Creating appropriate visuals will make engagement much easier for your social followers and brand fans.

As you review them, think about which senses you're targeting: sight, sound, hearing, touch, or even smell. Although some of the senses might be more applicable in traditional advertising, such as scent strips in magazine ads, perhaps, there will be a virtual scent "strip" or taste "spray" built into VR/AR headsets of the future.

Also, before writing, consider the types of content marketing. What are you creating? Is it any of these six or something else? Is it for these reasons or others? Know your goals up front, so you can tailor your content.

1. Social media posts to boost followers or sales?

2. Infographics as reference tools?

3. Blog articles to increase engagement?

4. Podcasts to share insights, educate, or entertain?

5. Videos as product descriptions or tutorials?

6. Paid ads for awareness or sales?

According to Carolyn Hadlock, principal and executive creative director at Young & Laramore, regardless of the channel or platform, strong writers still have to be able to distill the brand message into one singular point. Here's a quick way to find out how well a writer can encapsulate the core content:

> While writers have gotten more versed in long form content, many writers coming out of schools today are unable to write a headline or distill the idea.[3]

Scheduling the content and calendaring

Q7. *When are you scheduling the content?* Scheduling/media plan and social media options

This, of course, will be tailored to your audience and channel. We will go into detail later in the chapter, starting with this section: "Learning the best times to post." It appears after we examine the writing styles of many social media and video channels, including Facebook, Instagram, and YouTube.

As with all content and advertising, you start with your purpose and audience. Why are you creating this message? Who's reading or watching it? Where are they seeing it? When are they consuming content? Then, create a schedule that fits the brand's purpose and the audience's need to learn about it. Remember to ask: How will it help them?

Scheduling and calendaring, and when to post will appear in this upcoming section: "Learning the best times to post." Scheduling is when you plan when to post. Calendaring is the outline you create after you've decided when you'll release the content.

Analyzing storytelling formats, channels, and platforms

For now, carefully examine the format options. Ask what content "container" works best? Which one best speaks to your audience? Are they readers, watchers, listeners, sharers, experiencers, or creators? What's the best way to awaken their curiosity and engage their senses?

Here are some useful social media templates and tips (Templates 2.2, Templates 2.3, Templates 2.4, Templates 2.5) by Nathan Ellering for Convince&Convert that you can use as references.

 TEMPLATES 2.2 Facebook content writing templates

How can (*your audience*) do (*action*) better with (*your product/service*)?

(*Insert problem*)? We've got your solution.

Do (*insert task*) better.

(*Insert problem*) sucks. (*Insert your product/service*) doesn't.

What's your favorite (*insert product*) feature?

How can (*insert product*) make (*insert task*) easier?

What's your top (*insert task*) tip?

(*Insert achievement*) in just (*insert length of time*)?

The best (*insert technique*) for (*insert task*) isn't what you think.

Your (*insert task*) could be this easy, too. (*Include photo of completed task*).[4]

TEMPLATES 2.3 X content writing templates

That feeling when (*insert action*). #(*insert hashtag*)

How we increased our (*insert metric*) by (*insert percentage*) with (*insert something unexpected*).

Time's running out! Sign up for (*insert event*) by (*insert date*). #(*insert hashtag*)

Here's how we (*insert achievement*) (and you can too). #(*insert hashtag*).

Here's what (*insert credible source*) uses to (*insert task*) by (*insert percentage*).

Great news! You can now (*insert action*) with (*insert product*).

Could using (*insert product*) to (*insert task*) improve (*insert metric*)?

(*Insert percentage*) of (*insert audience*) use (*insert product*) to (*insert task*) more (*insert benefit*). Be one of them.

Still doing (*insert task*) the old way?

No more (*insert problem*). Say hello to (*insert product/service featured*).[5]

TEMPLATES 2.4 LinkedIn content writing templates

What makes (*insert your company*) the best (*insert company type*) in the (*insert industry*)?

How did (*insert your company*) achieve (*insert achievement*) with (*insert something unexpected*).

Be the best at (*insert task*) with this (*insert content type*) from (*insert source*).

The best (*insert audience*) need the best (*insert product/service*).

We had a problem with (*insert problem*). So, we solved it with (*insert product/ service*). Could this work for you, too?

(*Insert audience*) often struggle with (*insert task*). Here's how (*insert product/ service*) turns (*insert task*) from failure to success.

The old way: Doing (*insert task*) by (*insert action*). The new way? (*insert product/service*).[6]

TEMPLATES 2.5 Instagram content writing templates

That Friday feeling. (*insert photo*) # (*insert hashtag*)

Shout out to (*insert photo*) for this awesome pic! (*insert photo*)

Love (*insert product/hobby/trend/etc.*)? Then you'll love this. (*insert photo*) (*insert customer testimonial*) (*insert customer photo*)

Later. (*insert problem*) (*insert photo*)

Wish you were here? (*insert photo of location*)

Here's one way to get the job done. (*insert photo*)

We spotted (*insert your product*) in the wild! (*insert photo*)

If you worked here, this could be you. (*insert office photo*)

What's going on at (*insert your company*) today? (*insert office photo*)[7]

Nathan Ellering in his article, "The Proven Mechanics of Successful Social Media Writing," suggested the following as optimal post lengths and content:

1. *Facebook* – 111 characters with no hashtags and one emoji: best results with links, 2nd best with images, and 3rd with text.

2. *X (formerly Twitter)* – 103 characters (including links for best engagement), two hashtags, and one emoji: best engagement with images, 2nd best with text only, 3rd with links.

3. *Instagram* – 241 characters, best posts have 11 hashtags (2nd best have five, 3rd place has ten hashtags) and three emojis: best results with images, 2nd best with videos.

4. *Pinterest* – 215 characters: best results with images.

5. *LinkedIn* – 149 characters, with no hashtags or emojis: best results with links, 2nd best with text, and 3rd with images.[8]

According to director of social media at VML, Benazhir Maratuech, when writing for social media consider the following:

> *Attention span on social is short and varies from platform to platform and from audience to audience. For example, having an older generation consuming content on Facebook or Pinterest, for example, (Gen X and Older Millennials) writing – captions and scripts – needs to be informative and always have a clear CTA [Call To Action]. People tend to visit Facebook for brand updates and promos.*[9]

In Advice from the Pros 2.6, social media strategist Maratuech offers three more valuable content writing tips.

 ADVICE FROM THE PROS 2.6 Three content writing tips from Benazhir Maratuech

1 *Instagram* continues to be highly visual, so long captions lose their intent quickly, and because the platform still does not allow for clickable links in captions,* this is not likely a conversion platform but more an awareness and engagement one. Instagram is where you build communities so writing for this platform should be fluid, simple, and personable. Writing successful copy online is all about filtering out the noise and tuning into the channel.

2 *X* (formerly Twitter) used to be considered the go-to for news and updates, but today its role is more fluid and fun! Writing here has the

true potential to go viral – a few simple words have the power to take a brand from anonymity to the spotlight in a positive or negative way. So, back to understanding data – know your audience before typing.

3   *Side Tip:* writing is not only for words. Think about emojis! These small visuals can also convey an idea, fun and powerful – and social media is the right place to include them.[10]

*You can add a link in bio.
(Comments courtesy of Benazhir Maratuech, director of social media at VML.)

In addition to writing content, you should also be familiar with required format specifications or "specs" for the various channels, including: (1) character count or content length, (2) image size, (3) image format, (4) video length, (5) adjustments for mobile posts, and more. However, requirements change over time. So, remember to check and update them, as needed.

Other established content writers and copywriters offered insights into different types of writing. Juan Valente, creative director at Zimmerman Advertising, explained how he judiciously used social media analytics to write content, as follows:

> *Social media analytics should be used carefully and only as a guide. It's good for spotting trends and patterns which you can incorporate in social posts, so that you're a part of the conversation.*
>
> *Spending too much time on research will only slow you down. Social media moves quickly, and when something goes viral, you have a very small window to jump on board.*
>
> *If you wait too long, you'll miss the boat, and nothing looks worse jumping on after the trend has moved on.[11]*

In answer to the question: Why do some clients use skippable ads? Juan stated:

> *Using skippable ads is a monetary strategy. You only pay YouTube if your video is watched from start to finish. You don't pay YouTube if it's skipped.*
>
> *So the strategy is getting the main message into the first 5 seconds, so a viewer gets the main selling point. . .and the marketer does not have to pay for it.[12]*

He also shared these writing tips (Advice from the Pros 2.7) for social media and YouTube.

ADVICE FROM THE PROS 2.7 Seven content writing tips from Juan Valente

1 I've written a lot of posts and carousels for Facebook and Instagram. What I've discovered is that you need to take advantage of every space you can use. For example, a carousel has 3 main parts: the post, the headline, and sometimes the copy on the picture/image. Use all these parts to create variety in the story or message. Use the post to write the main story line, then add variety in the headlines by expanding the story, and use the copy on the image to create even more variety. This way, if the reader is interested, they'll be enticed by all the different messages you've created.

2 With Facebook, I would use the same approach as Instagram.

3 For YouTube, all I can say is find the main message you have to say, and say it in the first 5 seconds. Especially if you're creating a skippable YouTube ad. Be creative if you can, but not overly clever. Five seconds goes by fast, and you need to hit the punch line quickly.

4 There is a big difference in writing skippable versus TV spots. It comes down to the storytelling. In a traditional :30 (30-second) TV spot, you have the time to tell the story you want to share. There's a beginning, middle, and end. There's time for the concept to develop before you establish why your product is worth buying or using. Now, when it comes to skippable spots, your storytelling becomes drastically altered. You need to lead with the ending. In the first 5 seconds you need to explain why your product is worth buying or using. Essentially, you have to start with the end, then you can explain the rest of the story after the intro. To summarize, :30 TV spot = storytelling, skippable spot = *storyselling* (you need to sell in 5 seconds).

5 Instagram is similar to creating a billboard. Use a strong image to create interest and keep the copy short to compliment the image. Use post copy and links to give consumers the opportunity to learn more about the product or service. If you're creating a carousel, expand your message. Use images to expand the story, and when possible have the headlines play off each other, in other words, have the carousel frame continue the message from the previous frame.

6 TikTok is all about following the trends. Focus on entertaining and not selling. This is a great platform to help humanize your brand.

7 For X, keep the copy/message short and sweet. You have a 280-character limit, but you don't need to use them all. Learn to be frugal with your words.[13]

(Comments courtesy of Juan Valente, creative director at Zimmerman Advertising.)

When asked about writing for websites, Valente said:

I think of websites as just digital brochures. Break the copy up in to small chunks so they can be easily digested.[14]

Let's look at writing for different platforms, one by one. Each one requires a little different approach to make the content easily digestible for your audience. Take note of the similarities and differences as you continue to read through them. Also, keep in mind the following list (Tips and Rules 2.8) of general content creation tips when you start drafting content.

TIPS AND RULES 2.8
General content creation tips

1 *Write quality content* – Just writing a lot with the hopes of getting higher search engine rankings doesn't work. It's about useful, informative content, not just length.

2 *Picture your followers/customers/fans* – If you have different audiences, write content specifically for them. What do they want to know? Why would they read and share your content?

3 *Write enticing headlines* – Focus on writing headlines that explain the benefits, differences, and usefulness, as well as a sense of urgency. It's not just why someone should read it, but why they should want more of it.

4 *Make it timeless* – Some information, such as the basics of sound writing, stands up against trend-of-the-moment content. Both are valuable. Just remember to look for topics with longer shelf life.

5 *Keep it relevant* – With technology changing by the second, old content makes your company appear stale and dated.

6 *Create regularly* – Think of your best friends. They don't come and go. They stay in touch all the time. The same is true for your content. Remember to not be a fair-weather, but a year-round friend.

7 *Watch your competition* – You might mine some excellent ideas from competitors. It could be a theme, a how-to, or a bulleted list that sparks a new approach. Read and follow as much as you can.

8 *Ask for their opinion* – Engage with your content community. They may have tips that could benefit everyone. Ask them questions. Invite their feedback. Generate a comfortable environment where they feel safe to share.

9 *Track results* – Is what you're doing working? Keep an eye on this through analytics to follow your results and adjust your writing.

Writing content for Facebook

According to WordStream, there are ten areas to consider before you start drafting content. These include:

1. Post content that interests your customers.

2. Post a variety of content.

3. End every post with a question.

4. Don't post too frequently.

5. Allow fans to write on your wall.

6. Don't share X (formerly Twitter) posts on your Facebook page.

7. Use contests, but use them in moderation.

8. Get creative with the contests.

9. Try selecting a monthly topic.

10. Be interesting.[15]

Let's analyze each of them.

1. *Post content that interests your customers* – If you don't write about what interests them, they'll tune out. Your goal is to establish a rapport and an ongoing conversation with them, so they feel a connection and even a relationship with you and your brand. Notice the companies you follow. What makes you enjoy their content? Is it entertaining, fun, or informative? Pay attention to what attracts you. Then, see your content from your readers' point of view before you start posting.

2. *Post a variety of content* – Don't just stick to one format. That's boring. Offer a smorgasbord of content, which will keep them up-to-date on the latest news and events, in myriad formats, such as:

   a. *Blog posts*

   b. *Photos*

   c. *Press releases*

   d. *Videos*

3. *End every post with a question* – Why? To draw in your visitors and get them involved. Ask them their opinion. Ask them for advice. Ask them to clarify something people are struggling to learn.

4. *Don't post too frequently* – People unfriend others because they get sick of reading frivolous, self-absorbed posts. If there's nothing to benefit them, they get turned off.

5. *Allow fans to write on your wall* – Be sure to check that you haven't disabled this feature. How can people engage with you if you lock the "door" and don't let them in?

6. *Don't share X (formerly Twitter) posts on your Facebook page* – It's fine if you want to share the same content on both platforms. Just remember to rewrite it and remove the #&@s, etc. for Facebook. Those symbols are not appropriate on every channel and may be construed differently, or even as an unintended, rude comment.

7. *Use contests, but use them in moderation* – Just as seasonal flavors are appreciated when they're absent, contests should be offered occasionally, to be best enjoyed. Peppermint coffee isn't as exciting if it were always available.

8. *Get creative with the contests* – Contests should be imaginative and enticing, not predictable and dull. Think about contests that ask you to guess the number of jelly beans in a jar or the number of tennis balls in a car. The fun part is guessing because you can't actually count them. What can you create that would spark curiosity and participation?

9. *Try selecting a monthly topic* – It might be helpful to center your posts around one central theme that others can embrace and look forward to reading each month. They might start wondering what's coming up next and regularly look out for it.

10. *Be interesting* – Exactly! Fans don't want to be bored after reading your content. Next time, they could choose to skip your posts because they might think they'll read the same old "stuff." It's easier to lose fans than it is to keep them. So, challenge yourself to find ways to create imaginative and thought-provoking posts.

Writing content for LinkedIn

If the question for LinkedIn is what to post, here are some topic suggestions. Remember, professionals are looking for company information, networking opportunities, and possible job listings. Companies want to showcase exciting news, share product updates, recruit candidates, promote engagement, and more. The key with all content is to write to your target with a specific purpose. Here are just a few topic ideas inspired by Robin Ryan's post on *Forbes* that still work today:

Professionals can:

- Showcase newly earned certificates to make them more marketable.
- Highlight their latest creative work or professional project.
- Show new photos that highlight their personality and events they attended. Tag others who attended.

- Share others' posts or applaud their achievements. Be sure to credit all repost sources.

- Announce a new job position or just-received promotion. Their friends would like to hear about this and congratulate them.

- Ask for recommendations, for example for improving skills or applying for positions.

- Identify influencers who have helped them grow professionally.

Companies can:

- Post an informative video or short tutorial.

- Include relevant, interesting, and unexpected stats to generate interest.

- Announce job posts and a few requirements.

- Welcome new hires.

- Showcase new technology advances that take the work out of work.

- Introduce new management systems.

- Identify emerging trends and ask others to share what they've discovered.

- Ask a thought-provoking question to spark engagement.

- Promote registration for online learning, on-site training, or virtual/ live conferences.

- Share insightful research. Everyone loves staying informed.

- Repurpose content-rich articles that offer useful advice, skill-building information, and instantly applicable tips.

- Comment on influencers' posts.[10]

To boost your status as an expert, consider some other key tips by Melonie Dodaro, CEO of Top Dog Social Media. She referred to "pillar posts." These are the core topics that are of particular interest to your readers. (1) Wrap your content around what they wish to learn, whether you're creating visuals, such as infographics, videos, or blog articles. (2) Prepare 10 go-to content pieces, based on the most commonly discussed topics. These will help strengthen your brand traction and improve your SEO rankings, whether it's for your personal profile or a company page. (3) As with other types of social media, engage your audience by asking them to participate. What's their opinion? What else can they add to the topic? What other tips might they suggest? (4) Remember to suggest some kind of action after reading. (5) Post regularly, so your audience will know when to expect to see new content.

She listed the following seven types of posts to spark conversations and interaction.

1. *Thought leadership* – Offer provocative and/or educational content that proves your authority in that area.

2. *Curated content* – Share what others, especially influencers, are posting, especially if the topics are trending or in-the-news.

3. *Promotional content* – Drive visitors to your website, podcast, tutorial videos, and wherever you post. Use this to repurpose and highlight your material.

4. *Engagement* – Ask followers to respond with their own ideas and suggestions.

5. *Opinion* – Give them a forum to state what they really think. Ask how they feel about that issue or subject. Encourage them to express themselves.

6. *Celebration* – Spotlight an accomplishment, award, certificate, new product, and any other achievement worthy of attention.

7. *Current events* – Join the most talked-about topics. Add some interesting ideas to the discussion of what's happening right now.[17]

One other point, when writing to a general audience, is to keep the reading level to eighth graders, ages 13 to 14. That's based on the Flesch–Kincaid readability score of 70–80, so that 80% of Americans can quickly comprehend your message. Of course, if you're addressing professionals with college degrees, you could up your reading score to over 90. You can read more about this score, but here's a quick look. It's based on 1 to 100.

There are two scores: (1) Flesch Reading Ease and (2) Flesch–Kincaid Grade Level. Both measure sentence and word length. Shorter sentences and lower-syllabic words are grasped more quickly. However, for the reading-ease score, the higher the number, the easier the content is to read. For the grade-level score, the higher the number, the more difficult the material, and 100 would target a university-level audience.[18]

Writing content for X (formerly Twitter)

For X, with its limited 280-word content count, increased from the original 140-word limit, this article, "Good Copy, Bad Copy: Tips for Writing Effective Tweets," by Brian Peters for X Business,[19] can guide you. Many would work well in other social media posts. So, keep them handy.

1. *Sound urgent*
   Consumers don't have the time to figure out whether or not the post should be read. That's why you want to make readers feel that they should do something right now. Be clear what you want them to do: Make a purchase, click for more information, download from a link, and so on. Emphasize that they could miss out if they don't respond.

2. *Make offers based on psychology*
   Research has shown that under-$100 products receive a greater response with a percent off rather than a dollar discount. Buyers think that 25% off sounds like a better deal than "save $25" (on a $100 item). So, use that information, which has been shown to work best during the buying-decision process to maximize conversions.

3. *Add a button for your website*
   Website buttons enhance X's posts by making them more engaging with images, video clips, and animations that increase web traffic. X's research shows that visuals increase interactions by 43%. So, why not use them? But, first get your website card installed. (These are small, flexible designs with company information, icons, clickable call-to-action buttons, and linkable images to drive website traffic.)

4. *Keep hashtags down to two*
   Here's a case where less is more. Just two hashtags are all you need. Test out a few and pick the two that get the most reactions. Remember to create one brand-driven hashtag to increase name awareness and use one that's trending to draw a larger audience.

5. *Avoid all caps in your posts*
   Use of upper and lower case sounds more natural. As you know, reading all caps gives you a feeling that someone's shouting. Take on a relaxed, personal tone, as if you're speaking with your audience.[20]

Remember, to be personable and entertaining. You could add a touch of humor, share some interesting posts, offer a novel approach to a trending topic, and intrigue others to share your ideas. Be sure to hold your followers' attention and interest.

> *Tweet. Learning to be relevant and humorous and interesting (and retweetable!) in 280 characters is a great exercise. Besides, it's a fun way to meet strangers without having to make eye contact or think about how you're dressed.* Charlie Hopper, Principal, Young & Laramore[21]

Writing content for Instagram

To use Instagram as a marketing tool, whether it's for your business or yourself as the industry expert, here are some useful tips. The first five are by content specialist, Nadira Also, from her article: "The Best 5 Instagram Marketing Tips For 2022." Whether or not you're a business, you want to look professional. Therefore, you want to do the following:

1. *Create a business account* – You won't be able to create sales using a personal account. The business account offers these and other professional Instagram features: insights, ads, e-commerce links, messaging inboxes for communication, contact info, and call-to-action buttons.

2. *Keep it short* – Instagram is visual. Use great ones [visuals] that tell the story. Then, just add captions.

3. *Set specific objectives* – Know what you're trying to accomplish when you use Instagram to not only reach content communities, but also to market to them. For example, you could be trying to do any or all of these:

   ■ Create a digital footprint for yourself or your company.

   ■ Establish name recognition.

   ■ Grow new prospects (leads).

   ■ Become recognized as the expert in that area.

   ■ Convert readers into buyers.

4. *Boost your company and personal profile* – See it as an introduction. It might be the first time you or your brand speak to your followers. You only have 150 characters, to say " hi, " establish trust, and welcome them. Don't waste this opportunity. Seize it. Be friendly, warm, and personable. Put them at ease as you tell them about you. Be sure you remember to include your (1) name, (2) username, (3) web address, (4) a few details about your company or service, and of course, (5) contact information, so they know how to reach you.

5. *Develop a specific design and tone of voice* – Your look and sound should be distinctive and recognizable, so it strengthens brand awareness. The posts should have the same brand voice and be consistent in the choice of colors, type, and visual effects. People should become familiar with what you say, as well as how you express your brand verbally and visually. Consider how your brand speaks and looks.[22]

6. *Use videos* – They get more attention and shares.

7. *Be choosy with hashtags* – Just because you can use dozens, actually 30, doesn't mean you should. Instead, use them sparingly. Select only those that speak to your:

   - Audience's interest
   - Core content (niche topic)

8. *Make it fun* – How can you entertain them while showcasing your abilities?

9. *Have a solid call to action* – What do you want them to do? Always remember to tell them how to take the next step. If you don't tell them, they don't know.

These are just a few ideas. As you develop your strategy, revise the checklist to suit your goals.

Taking a look at Instagram video formats

Although new features are often introduced, here are four types of formats to consider before you start writing. These formats are presented by Alexa Nizam in her article, "Video for Instagram: How to Choose Between a Post, a Story, a Reel, and IGTV" on www.LemonLight.com.

1. *Posts* – These one-minute videos, which can look formal and polished, stay on your profile permanently for ongoing access. Use this for your current fans and for these types of videos: (1) promos, (2) consumer testimonials, company staff features, and new product introductions.

2. *Stories* – These short videos, with 15-second runtimes, can be created as interrelated episodes to allow you to provide more details. They have a tiny, 24-hour lifespan, which can be prolonged if you save them as Story Highlights. Then, they remain on your profile indefinitely. Use this format: (1) to chunk down longer videos into smaller clips and (2) if you're looking to invite interaction through fun polls, then with their short expiration date, any message with urgency, or an "act-now" intent would work. For more personality, you can add filters and doodles.

3. *Reels* – Similar to TikTok, these are 60-second clips that can be created individually or linked together. They can have superimposed text, music, captions, and various special visual effects. Use these to attract new fans and make them exciting and entertaining, as well as tutorials.

4. *IGTV* – (Instagram TV) is like YouTube, which allows for longer content. Mobile devices can hold 15-minute clips and computers can allow 60-minute clips. Use these to showcase how products work, as instructional content and for step-by-step teaching tools.[23]

Just looking at the Instagram options makes you realize how important the format is to your content. Do you have a lot to share? Does it need to be available for a day or more? Does it need to have music and visual effects? Answering these questions first will help as you're developing your video content.

Writing content for YouTube

As with most content, you'll find that most of the same key steps apply. For YouTube, you would add the last one, number ten (#10), and design your own channel around your brand and followers. This allows you to create a unique outlet with an identifiable content that's relevant to the brand's core content and key consumers' interests. Here's an overview of the most common YouTube campaign components and standard practices.

1. *Start with a purpose*: What are you trying to achieve?

2. *Identify your target*: Who's interested in this content?

3. *Decide your distribution*: Which communication channels and media platforms should you use? Ask: Where do viewers search for information and share content?

4. *Write your core content*: Why would it matter to these targeted viewers? How can it improve SEO (search engine optimization) and raise the search rankings?

5. *Share your research*: What's new that others would like to know? Can you partner with another YouTuber and create more useful videos?

6. *Design a production plan*: For efficiency and when sensible, shoot several videos at the same time. What's the look, feel, and sound of your brand? Consider visuals and music that resonate with your consumers.

7. *Create a schedule*: How often will you create content? Plan ahead and "bank" extra videos to stay on schedule.

8. *Include a call to action*: Build an audience by asking viewers to like the video and subscribe to your channel.

9. *Track content performance*: Which channels resulted in the most clicks? What topics received the most views? Which videos were saved and/ or shared?

10. *Develop your own channel around your brand*: Establish what you have to offer. Create quality content: Keep it fresh and relevant to encourage future views.

Think about what your audience wants to see. So, if your followers enjoy learning, you'd choose channels where consumers are searching for information. Let's say you're creating a how-to-write-a-business-blog tutorial. You could consider the following because people would be looking to learn this or are asking for an answer.

- *Quora* – Check to see if your content is coming up with many questions.
- *Reddit* – Examine the forums to see if your topic is a fit.
- *Facebook Groups* – See if this is a common topic of interest.
- *LinkedIn Groups* – Follow the posts to discover if your content would help others.

Be careful that you align your content with appropriate venues. You wouldn't expect to see a wedding planner seeding content on LinkedIn. But, you wouldn't be surprised to see references to a how-to-pick-a-wedding-planner video on Instagram, Facebook, or Pinterest. Propose your content to a hyper-narrow market. Think niche.

Here a few places to garner topic ideas for your next videos.

1. *Quora.com* – People ask questions on this site and others answer them. Here's where you can easily get ideas about what people are searching to learn. Then, create a video and post the answers.

2. *Ubersuggest* – With this site, you can discover popular titles, frequently used keywords and favorite topics. Just enter your content idea and find out how many times it has been searched each month, how easily it increases rankings, what are the most common keywords, the cost per click, and what websites show high rankings and shares.

3. *TubeBuddy* – Here you can get an estimated ranking for your topic idea.

4. *Google Trends* – Quickly find out what's trending at the moment. You might find a good topic here when you see what's gaining or losing traction.

5. *Hashtags* – Notice what people are chatting about on the different social media channels, from Instagram to Facebook. If a topic crops up often, you may want to consider creating video content around a current theme.

6. *YouTube comments* – Read through viewers' comments and see if there's a nugget of a topic idea. Look for commonly asked, but still unanswered questions. Be the one to provide the answer in an on-point video.

7. *Piggyback off the news* – As with other platforms, tune into breaking news and borrow or hijack the subject matter. You already know that people are hearing about it at this moment. You can ask for others' ideas and/or state your thoughts to stimulate engagement.

8. *Suggested search* – Look at Google and YouTube to see if your topic is being commonly discussed. Just type it in for a quick answer.[24]

When are you targeting them? Just knowing what to post and whom to target isn't enough. You need to consider when you should distribute content. Successful marketers today examine all the social media options, create media calendars, carefully schedule the content, and then track engagement. If a channel isn't working it might be the right channel, but the wrong time or day to post.

It's crucial to develop a social media, as well as a cross-platform calendar. This way, you'll have all of your scheduling in an organized system. There are many free calendar templates that are easy to find with a quick search, including those by Keith Quesenberry, Influencer Marketing Hub, HubSpot, Hootsuite, Canva, Sprout Social, Semrush, ContentStudio, and others. There are also many blogs and tutorials that teach you how to design your own calendar. Don't skip over this. The short amount of time it will take for you to download or create a calendar will pay for itself by boosting your productivity.

Learning the best times to post

We mentioned earlier in this chapter that we would return to question #7: When should you schedule the content? As you know, social media changes by the second. Be sure you regularly check which times are recommended, channel-by-channel, and review your purpose and audiences. Many marketers feel frustrated because there are many sources with differing statistics. However, one of the most useful and comprehensive social-media-performance comparisons is the research done by Professor Imed Bouchrika, chief data scientist and head of content at www.Research.com. In this article, "The Best Times to Post on Social Media: 2022 Studies & Statistics," he reviews 27 reports by some of the most frequently referenced sources, including the recommended times and days for easy access. This all-in-one, detailed list includes findings from:

1. Sprout Social

2. American Marketing Association

3. CoSchedule

4. TrackMaven

5. HuffPost

6. Neil Patel

7. Jon Loomer

8. Harvard Business Review

9. Later

10. Buffer

11. Hootsuite

12. FreeCodeCamp

13. Oberlo

14. The Balance

15. Raka Creative

16. Unmetric (now part of Brandwatch)

17. HubSpot

18. Post Planner

19. Falcon.io (now part of Brandwatch)

20. SurePayroll

21. TruConversion

22. Boot Camp Digital

23. QuickSprout

24. The Drum

25. Search Engine Journal

26. Mariah Althoff

27. Impulse Creative[25]

Be sure to follow his research because it will help guide your social marketing content decisions. His company also presents scholarly conferences for academicians to share their most current and important research.

For a quick reference, you'll find some of the best-times-to-post lists by various sources below.

1. **Best times to post on X (formerly Twitter)** According to Mariia Kovalenko, content strategist and editor at Digital Marketer's World, the optimal days and times as listed in "Best Time to Post on Twitter to Boost Engagement (2022 Guide)" are most mornings from 9 to noon:

   ■ Monday: 9 a.m. to 1 p.m.

   ■ Tuesday: 8 a.m. to 2 p.m.

   ■ Wednesday: 8 a.m. to 5 p.m.

   ■ Thursday: 9 a.m. to 1 p.m.

   ■ Friday: 9 a.m. to 1 p.m.

   ■ Saturday: 9 a.m. to 11 a.m.

   ■ Sunday: 9 a.m. to 1 p.m.[26]

2. **Best times to post on TikTok:**

   a. Kovalenko also suggested when to post on TikTok in "Best Time & Day to Post on TikTok & Tips for More Views in 2022." (Bold type shows highest engagement levels.)

      ■ Monday: 6 a.m., 10 a.m., 10 p.m.

      ■ Tuesday: 2 a.m., 4 a.m., **9 a.m.**

      ■ Wednesday: 7 a.m., 8 a.m., 11 p.m.

      ■ Thursday: 9 a.m., **12 p.m.,** 7 p.m.

      ■ Friday: **5 a.m.,** 1 p.m., 3 p.m.

      ■ Saturday: 11 a.m., 7 p.m., 8 p.m.

      ■ Sunday: 7 a.m., 8 a.m., 4 p.m.[27]

   b. Another study conducted by Hootsuite and discussed by Stacey McLachlan compared TikTok against Instagram Reels and learned that TikTok videos prevailed at these day times:

- Tuesday: 7 a.m.
- Thursday: 10 a.m.
- Friday: 5 a.m.[28]

In her article "The Best Times to Post on Social Media in 2022," Mary Keu-telian, SEO specialist at Sprout Social, offered the following best times for global engagement in Facebook, Instagram, X, TikTok, and LinkedIn, as well as optimal times for nine industries. She also included the list below for best times to post for maximum press coverage. These stats, shown in Eastern Standard Time, are regularly updated. Refer to this list to engage with a global audience.

1. *What are the best times to post on Facebook?*
   - Best times: Monday through Friday 3 a.m., Tuesdays 10 a.m. and noon
   - Best days: Tuesday through Friday
   - Worst day: Saturday

2. *What are the best times to post on Instagram?*
   - Best times: Monday 11 a.m., Tuesday and Wednesday 10 a.m. –1 p.m., Thursday and Friday 10 a.m. and 11 a.m.
   - Best days: Tuesday and Wednesday
   - Worst day: Sunday

3. *What are the best times to post on X (formerly Twitter)?*
   - Best times: Monday, Tuesday, Wednesday, Friday and Saturday 9 a.m.
   - Best days: Tuesday and Wednesday
   - Worst day: Sunday

4. *What are the best times to post on TikTok?*
   - Best times: Tuesday 2 p.m.–3 p.m., Wednesday and Thursday 1 p.m.–3 p.m.
   - Best days: Wednesday and Thursday
   - Worst day: Sunday

5. *What are the best times to post on LinkedIn?*
   - Best times: Tuesday 10 a.m.–noon
   - Best days: Wednesday and Thursday
   - Worst days: Saturday and Sunday[29]

Maxwell Iskiev, market research analyst for the HubSpot blog, identified the three best times per channel in his article, "The HubSpot Blog's 2022 Social Media Marketing Report: Data from 310 Marketers." Generally, the best time is six to nine in the evening, Eastern Standard Time, for all platforms.

- Facebook: 9 a.m.–12 p.m.
- YouTube: 3 p.m.–6 p.m.
- X (formerly Twitter): 9 a.m.–3 p.m.
- Instagram: 12 p.m.–6 p.m.
- LinkedIn: 9 a.m.–3 p.m.
- TikTok: 3 p.m.–6 p.m.[30]

He also reported social content marketers' platform usage as follows:

- 62% prefer Facebook
- 54% choose YouTube
- 49% use Instagram and see higher return on investment (ROI)
- 52% turn to TikTok[31]

Using a quick chart to develop content

As you learn to develop content, get in the habit of checking all of the "boxes" to make sure everything is covered. This includes referring to Useful Info 2.9 as your guide. Keep it handy, and refer to it before you post social media comments, videos, blogs, podcasts, etc. Remember, your goal is to not only direct, but also enhance the customer journey experience. Lead them in a creative and informative way to your specific next-step destination.

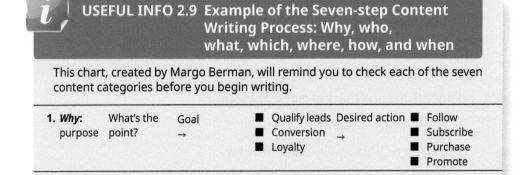

i USEFUL INFO 2.9　**Example of the Seven-step Content Writing Process: Why, who, what, which, where, how, and when**

This chart, created by Margo Berman, will remind you to check each of the seven content categories before you begin writing.

| 1. **Why:** purpose | What's the point? | Goal → | ■ Qualify leads ■ Conversion ■ Loyalty | Desired action → | ■ Follow ■ Subscribe ■ Purchase ■ Promote |

2. **Who:** audience	Who's the audience?	Persona	Target segment	Content community	Niche
3. **What:** message	What are you saying?	Branded content	Story/ testimonial	Tutorial	Challenge
4. **Which:** analytics	Which tools will you use?	SEO analytics	Social media analytics	E-commerce analytics	Consumer-insight analytics
5. **Where**: publish	Where will it appear?	Channel/ platform	Channel	Immersive	Mixed reality/ media
6. **How:** format	How are you delivering it?	Audio ■ Podcast ■ Webinar ■ Interactive discussion (Clubhouse)	Video ■ Recorded ■ Streaming ■ Skippable	Written ■ Digital √ Social media √ Email marketing ■ Print	Interactive ■ Immersive √ AR √ VR ■ E-commerce
7. **When:** schedule	When will it post/appear?	Dates	Day times	Frequency	Calendar schedule

Discovering helpful writing tools

When you're looking for some *content writing tools*, in addition to those that you already use, such as spell checkers and grammar references, these popular ones curated by content writer Aakash Kapil will offer other helpful solutions.

1: Cliché Finder

This search-and-destroy tool is on a mission to reveal commonly used clichés, plus words and phrases you repeatedly used in your writing.

2: Idea Flip

Designed for teams who create content in collaboration, it seamlessly functions on all operating systems, devices, and search engines.

3: Thesaurus

The handy reference tool that helps writers find the exact word they want with its suggested synonyms, or find opposite meanings or antonyms.

4: Humaaans (Yes, this is spelled correctly!)

If you want more than 20,000 illustrations on call waiting for your request. Now, your content can not only sound professional, but also look polished.

5: Google Scholar

This presents a vast search of academic and scholarly research that has appeared in peer-reviewed journal articles, theses, dissertations, conference presentations, books, abstracts, and more.

6: Writer

Like a spell-checker, this tool helps you determine if you've inadvertently plagiarized content by comparing your writing, including style, tone, use of grammar, and even spelling, to other published works.

7: Surfer SEO

This tool allows you to search how well keywords you're considering ranked in search results to help you optimize your content for higher SEO performance.

8: Sharethrough

Grade your headlines and improve them by reading the metrics that determine audience response, overall quality, and general impression. You'll also learn what revisions will raise the score you received.

9: Inspectlet

To learn what guests viewed and digested on your website, choose Inspectlet. You'll be able to review actual videos of visitors' actions and behaviors.

10: Focus Keeper

The product name, Focus Keeper, says what it does. It keeps you concentrating on one selected part of a project until a timer alerts you to stop. Then, the program produces an actual chart that details how much you've accomplished.[32]

Checking out a few social media campaigns

It's important to follow social media campaigns to strengthen your writing and critiquing skills. As you work on creating digital messages, review those that you find exciting, so you always have visual references. Here are some campaigns that explain the consumer benefits and brand features to answer the "why buy?" question. Simply stated, each message solves a commonly experienced pain point.

As we will discuss in Chapters 7 and 11, with Coravin, wine lovers can open more than one bottle at a time because the wine-preservation system keeps the wine's integrity for up to four weeks. So, you don't have to wait to celebrate. You can enjoy any wine, whenever you want. The content almost gives consumers permission to indulge. Both start with "Pairs well with…" Look how inviting the posts are: "Made It to Friday Wednesday" (Figure 2.1) and "A Post-Workout Pint of Ice Cream" (Figure 2.2).

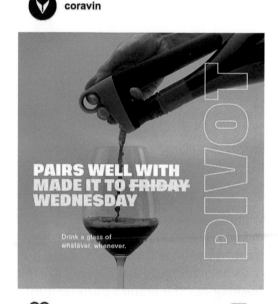

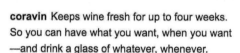

FIGURE 2.1 This "Made It to Friday Wednesday" social media post was created by Young & Laramore for Coravin. Image courtesy of Young & Laramore.

coravin

coravin Keeps wine fresh for up to four weeks. So hey, it's all good—you can drink a glass of whatever, whenever.
#whateverwhenever #coravinpivot

FIGURE 2.2 This "A Post-Workout Pint of Ice Cream" social media post was created by Young & Laramore for Coravin. Image courtesy of Young & Laramore.

For the High & Mighty campaign, the creative team at Young & Laramore selected Facebook and Instagram as the two social media channels to share the product features and consumer benefits of its easy hang-it-up-yourself tools. As you can see in the posts below (Figure 2.3, Figure 2.4, Figure 2.5, Figure 2.6), the play-on-words hashtag has the brand's purpose built into it: #Designed-ToBeStuckup. At first glance, it sounds haughty. Then, once you understand the product connection, you enjoy the whimsy. The other hashtags are also product-centric and benefit-related: #NoTools, #WallHangar, and #Floating-Shelves. Notice how the hashtags relate to the product uses. For taxidermy (Figure 2.4), these hashtags were added: #iFishing and #CatchOfTheDay, targeting that specific audience.

The posts show what makes High & Mighty better compared to the other wall-hanging systems. You can push it into the wall with your thumb and it holds up to 125 pounds (57 kilos). That's impressive!

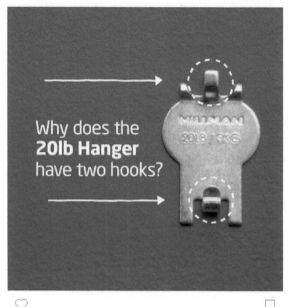

FIGURE 2.3 This "20-pound Hook Hanger" social content post was created by Young & Laramore for High & Mighty. Image courtesy of Young & Laramore.

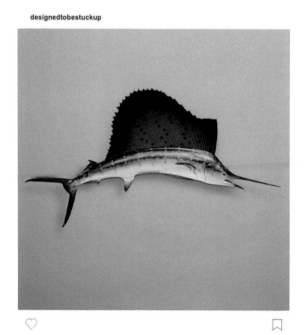

FIGURE 2.4 This "125-pound Taxidermy Fish" social content post was created by Young & Laramore for High & Mighty. Image courtesy of Young & Laramore.

designedtobestuckup

designedtobestuckup Add architectural details to any space in minutes.
@dominomag shows you their take using our 24" beveled bookshelf. Photos by
@codyguilfoyl #SOdomino #notools #floatingshelves #plantsofinstagram

FIGURE 2.5 This "Architectural Details" social content post was created by Young & Laramore for High & Mighty. Image courtesy of Young & Laramore.

designedtobestuckup

Place

designedtobestuckup The secret to the push. Lean the base of the hanger against the wall for better leverage. #wallhanger #howtohang #notools #designedtobestuckup

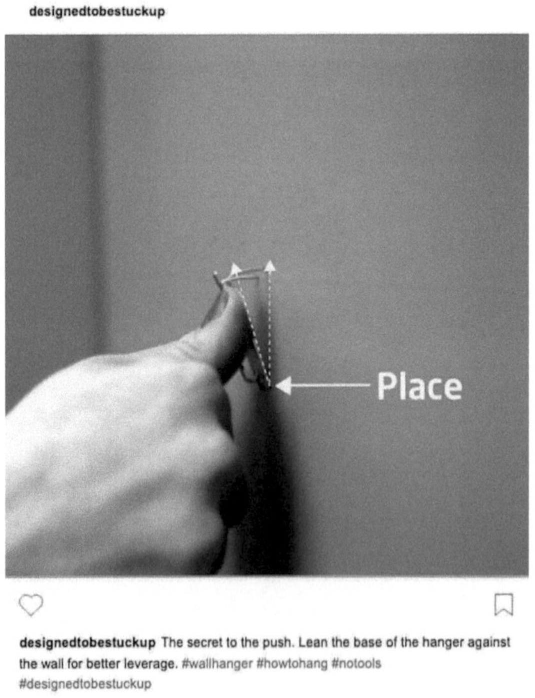

FIGURE 2.6 This "Push" social content post was created by Young & Laramore for High & Mighty. Image courtesy of Young & Laramore.

In the following Paddletek social media campaign, you can see how the copy tells followers exactly what to do to play along. It entices, intrigues, invites, and excites fans, while showcasing the Paddletek brand. If you're one of them, these posts (Figure 2.7, Figure 2.8, Figure 2.9, Figure 2.10) are speaking to you!

Copy: PaddletekPickleBall (Figure 2.7)

- Tag a friend below for a chance to win the new Bantam EX-L. #LetsGoAgain

- Outplay. Outsmart. Outlast. Outdo. #LetsGoAgain

- The come up doesn't come easy. #LetsGoAgain

paddletekpickleball

paddletekpickleball Outplay. Outsmart. Outlast. Outdo. #LetsGoAgain

FIGURE 2.7 This "Paddletek Pickleball" social media post was created by Young & Laramore for Paddletek. Image courtesy of Young & Laramore.

Copy: Bantam EX-L Series (Figure 2.8)

- ▨ Tag a friend below for a chance to win the new Bantam EX-L. #LetsGoAgain

FIGURE 2.8 This "Bantam EX-L" social media post was created by Young & Laramore for Paddletek. Image courtesy of Young & Laramore.

Copy: Phoenix Pro Series (Figure 2.9)

- ▨ Big wins incoming. Explore the new Phoenix series at paddletek.com. #LetsGoAgain
- ▨ Tag a friend below for the chance to win the new Phoenix Pro. #LetsGoAgain

paddletekpickleball

paddletekpickleball Big wins incoming. Explore the new Phoenix series at
paddletek.com. #LetsGoAgain

FIGURE 2.9 This "Phoenix Pro Series" social media post was created by Young &
Laramore for Paddletek. Image courtesy of Young & Laramore.

Copy: Tempest Series (Figure 2.10)

- Control freaks, freak out. Explore the new Tempest series at paddletek.
  com. #LetsGoAgain

Consider the Paddletek engagement techniques as you follow your friends,
brands, and favorite influencers. Observe how the campaign captured fans'
attention and enticed them to engage. Now, look for patterns in posts that
pique your interest. What made them work for you? Apply some of these
formats, templates, or content blueprints for future and/or present clients.
Participate with purpose.

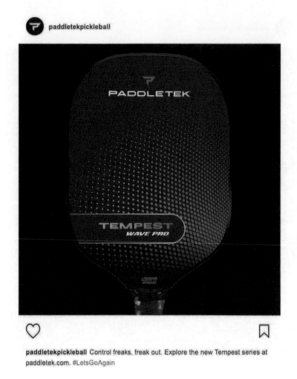

paddletekpickleball

paddletekpickleball Control freaks, freak out. Explore the new Tempest series at paddletek.com. #LetsGoAgain

FIGURE 2.10 This "Tempest Series" social media post was created by Young & Laramore for Paddletek. Image courtesy of Young & Laramore.

Looking at writing SEO copy

Writers today realize they cannot just take printed collateral pieces or broadcast work and apply them online. Writing for the web requires clear and immediate communication with the audience, who, like the radio listener or TV viewer, is just a button or click away from leaving. Surfers are looking for instant information and are impatient if the navigation is slow or the language is confusing. Keeping the visitor on a site long enough to describe the company's services or benefits requires brevity of expression paired with an uncanny insight into consumers' needs. The best way to write engaging online copy is to become the consumer yourself.

Here are a few pointers for writing web copy from Sabina Escalada, senior product manager at Target.

1. *Know your audience* – Develop a "persona," a brief description of a typical buyer.

2. *Less is more* – When writing copy for your home page, think small and begin with the basics. Make sure you include clear benefits of your business in a couple of sentences right up front.

3. *Hook them with your headline* – A good headline is key to attracting reader attention and leading them into the rest of your website copy. It should only be a few words but say a lot about your business.

4. *Create strong support copy* – Once your headline is in place, write a few brief sentences to communicate what your business is all about. . .On your homepage copy, end with a call to action.

5. *Make it well-written* – Make sure that your content is polished and that there are no misspellings or grammatical errors. When people are searching for your business on sites like Google and Yelp, online search engines may rank your site lower in online directories (meaning your business won't be found as easily) if your copy has grammar issues.

6. *Get to know SEO* – With over 90% of customers searching for local businesses online,[33] using the right SEO keywords in your website copy will attract the attention of search engines and help your business rank higher in online directories. The result? More people will find your business. . .To attract more website visitors with SEO keywords, you can also add a blog to your website.

7. *Include an e-commerce store* – Needless to say, having an online store is becoming a necessity for your business and means that your brand is always open and available to your customers...Write product descriptions that are short yet provide all the necessary details and be sure to include a photo with each item.

8. *Track your results* – Free online tracking sites like Google Analytics can show you how many website visitors you are attracting and how long they are staying on each page, so you can see what copy strategies work best for your website and business...You can use this information to determine how to better engage with your audience.[34]

She also added another strong point about writing for the web:

> Good copy is a good sales pitch that offers a solution to your customers' problems.[35]

Engaging with visitors

Each time you check out a site, analyze what worked and why. Notice what you liked or disliked about how the information was presented. Find excellent site examples that serve as copy guides. What would you borrow, and of course, modify? What would you change? Be sure to consider the following:

- The choice of language
- The way the sites were organized
- The images and visual references that supported the copy
- The ease or difficulty of navigation

Did you find everything you were looking for? Could you understand the message of each page? Did the information flow or was it disorganized? If you were writing website copy, how would you modify it?

Any time you write for online or any other platform, think about the visitors before you write your first phrase for a website, blog, or an online article. Ask yourself each of these questions as you're thinking about your content:

- What would you say if the person were in front of you?
- How can you personalize the language?
- Where can you initiate a dialogue (when appropriate)?
- How can you make the content interactive? We will discuss this further in Chapter 4. Think about using:
  1. Questions and answers
  2. Quizzes
  3. Puzzles
  4. Forums
  5. Games
  6. Contests
  7. Comments
  8. Engaging activities (like creative recipes or other how-to tips)

Evaluating the website's tone of voice

How do you want your website to sound? What is the brand or company's personality? Does this site have scientific, medical, or legal advice? Is it a site that explores new technology? Does it present new cocktails or review restaurants? Does it list exciting places to go and famous sites to see? Does it offer tutorials, templates, and other learning tools? You can see how different the copy would be for each of these sites. Just like all copy, you must always decide the following:

- Is it company-appropriate?
- Is it audience-appropriate?
- Is it compelling?
- Is it understandable?
- Is it relevant?
- Is it informative?
- Is it concise?
- Is it persuasive?

Audiences are especially time-conscious. They might be accessing the Internet on a mobile device, not necessarily on their computer. How quickly can they find what they're looking for and how easily is the message received? If key information is buried far (several clicks away) from the main site, they may not bother to search for it.

Digital communication is instant delivery. Any delay is a deterrent. Lengthy, complex sentences are a no-no. Simple, get-to-the-point ones are a go. Less is more. And faster is better. See how easy that was to read? That's the idea. Keep them reading. So, you won't lose their interest.

Examining a humorous site

There's always a fine line when you're creating irreverent copy. It's bound to offend someone somewhere. Then, imagine being brave enough to post it on a website for a client! That takes real courage. That's exactly what The Escape Pod did for Feckin Irish Whiskey. Vinny Warren, founder and creative director of The Escape Pod, being Irish himself, felt it was okay to depict the IRA. The client was nervous, thinking it could be offensive.

Warren defended the copy by saying, "I think people get offended on other people's behalf, sometimes."[36] Warren assured him that anything could be humorous, explaining that he personally said he thought IRA press conferences were hilarious. "And, the constant splitting within the factions was another source of comedy to me."[37] Warren said terrorist and national organizations are always splitting and that there are always internal disputes.

He said the tagline for one of the campaign's posters (Figure 12.27, Figure 12.28, Figure 12.29), which we will discuss in Chapter 12, was

"The Spirit of Irish Rebellion." That became the idea behind the website. Here's how Warren explained the site's creative direction:

> We had a website, which basically looked like an IRA press conference from the 1980s. A guy talking to camera. He's basically announcing that there's been a split within the Feckin Irish Whiskey organization. There are now two separate factions and you should choose which one most reflects your feelings. Then, when you clicked on one of them, you were told that there was a further split within this Feckin Irish community faction, and there are now two new ones. And so, in essence, you keep going and keep going and keep going until it got ridiculous. But, everyone was the same. So, it was a joke on Irish terrorism pretty much, right?
>
> I thought, well I can do that because I'm Irish. We did it and the client looked at it and was nervous about it.[38]

Regardless of what kind of website copy you're writing, whether it's informative, serious, humorous, and so on, ultimately you also want to have some understanding of how to increase traffic through search engine optimization. Now, let's take a look at blogging.

Creating a successful blog

Before you create a blog, choose a topic that speaks to your audience's interests. That way all of your posts will be relevant or "granular." Review this source list of niche topics and see which one best fits the brand. If you're the brand, be just as critical. Here are a few places to look for a topic. Remember to also look at trending influencer topics at the end of the list:

1. *Google Ads Keyword Planner* – Join Google Ads and you'll find research tools to see the number of people searching for certain keywords. There's no need to place an ad.

2. *Google Trends* – This reveals the most popular search terms so you can learn if that topic is generating or losing popularity.

3. *Trending Topic Blog Search* – See who's writing about what. Other blog-trending sources include: ProBlogger, Semrush, Search Engine People, and @whatstrending on Instagram.

4. *Wordtracker* – With a free trial, you can discover which words come up more often in searches and which sites already exist.

5. *Semrush* – Apply its marketing analytics and keyword search for popular topics.

6. *FeedSpot* – Learn which influencers are being read and what they're writing about.

7. *Traackr* – Find out about influencer marketing strategies, success tips, what's happening now in these and other current topics: content and social media marketing.

The HubSpot content team offered this helpful blogging tip:

> *Often, the greatest challenge of blogging is not the actual writing. It's all the other related tasks, let it be brainstorming topics, targeting the right readers, or optimizing posts with the best keywords and calls-to-action. Yet, each of these steps are necessary to be organized, focused, and ultimately, successful.*[39]

Although today's trends are tomorrow's used-to-be-cool ideas, it's important to focus on emerging changes, as indicated below from *Augusta Free Press*. Here are a few to consider when developing content. Before you apply them, check if this is what's happening now.

1. *Include more videos.* People like to see how a product works or how to use it in a new way or even if recorded reviews applaud or criticize it. As the old adage goes, "seeing is believing." Videos can attract or repel a consumer or encourage or dissuade a purchase. Make your video's content by answering any hesitations or objections consumers might have. Have they posted bad experiences with a similar brand? Have they looked for specific solutions to a common issue? Wrap your content around what your viewers want. Turn your attention away from what you're selling into what they're getting. Commonly cited research, including that of Lemon Light, shows that videos increase conversion by 72% and shares by 70%.

2. *Realize that cookies are gone.* Marketers have presented targeted content by tracking consumers' searches and purchases. However, privacy concerns and the GDPR (General Data Protection Regulation) law have driven cookies away. Consumers are able to opt-out of information and can block trackers to try to maintain some degree of control. However, digital content providers will continue to find ways to provide relevant, interest-targeted messages. Watch for these changes and implement those that work for your brand.

3. *Content still rules.* Without question, what you're saying will remain in the foreground. Posting quality, informative information will continue to register high in consumer evaluations. No one has time for fluff or an uninvited sales pitch. People want to be informed, educated, and engaged, as well as entertained. Just being fun isn't enough, unless, of course, your brand is an amusement park or other recreational-driven experience.

4. *Turn to automating processes.* The purpose of data is the application of it for real results. Apply what you learned about audience personas, viewing habits, shopping patterns, engagement modes, and topic-search interests to your campaigns. This will help you create precise and accurate content to reach your targeted segment, achieve your goals, increase brand trust, and build loyalty.

5. *Realize people search with voice and images, too.* How will you rewrite your keywords for these types of searches? When people search aloud, they use more words, or long-tail keywords. So, be sure you lengthen yours to be found more often. They can also search with an uploaded image. Make sure you have clear visuals so that they can find yours when comparing products.[40]

Strategic thinking must be present. It's not just about strong writing. It's always about innovative thinking. It's also about double-checking that you can say "yes" to these questions and points mentioned in Chapter 1, like correct *tone of voice*, relevance, and so on:

■ Does it showcase the firm's *benefits*?

■ Is the message *on-strategy*?

■ Does it keep the visitor reading?

Look at all-new and emerging platforms every opportunity you can. Pay attention to how the messages are presented. Look at the length of content, the kinds of headlines being used for blogs, online articles, websites, and all other media.

Become a student of good digital writers. The best way to learn how to write from a particular platform or channel is to read copy by some masters. Some copywriters who have mastered one medium can easily transfer those skills to another similar one. If you're wondering how long a blog should be, long-form (1,000–3,000 words) is very successful, especially for how-to, lists, or other informative/educational content. However, remember, that consistency is as important as length. If you normally write 250- to 300-word posts, don't suddenly switch to 2,000 words. The change in length confuses your audience. They're expecting a shorter entry.

Writers eager to learn to blog should be aware of which writers are the top content bloggers. Great writers are forever students. So, all serious copywriters should add to their reading list by following top content and copywriting blogs. Sites change frequently. It's your job to keep up. Don't feel overwhelmed. Instead, feel as if you're at a giant candy store with fun, new inventory whenever you return.

As with all platforms, the best thing you can do is jump right in. Replace apprehension with a sense of exploration. Then, think about how you could expand your or your client's digital footprint. The most important thing is to be a dedicated observer. Don't just read social media posts. Analyze them. Don't just visit websites. Scrutinize the copy. Don't just watch YouTube videos. Review them. Don't just sit there. Participate in online discussions. Always ask yourself:

- What other content would work well in this platform or channel?

- How can I repurpose it?

Constantly look for new examples of great content and innovative, digital marketing.

Please see some handy templates in Chapter 3.

> *Where attention goes energy flows. Where intention goes energy flows.* James Redfield, author of The Celestine Vision[41]

Considering blogs for agencies

Vinny Warren, founder and creative director of The Escape Pod, confirms that successful blogs are an open forum rich with interaction. Many agency blogs are used for speaking with their audience, as well as showcasing their work. Warren talked about the kind of writing for the posts on his firm's blog. Unlike bloggers, agency blog writers can talk about whatever they want. Their posts don't have to have a topic or a specific train of thought. One thing they both have in common, though, is the length of time it takes to attract a loyal following.

> *You can be a lot more liberal and lot more indulgent because "Hey, if you're reading our blog, God help you, number one. But, number two, you know it's our blog and it's our forum for what we think." So that's a bit more one-sided in favor of us because no one's forcing you to read it. It's for fun, and it's for promotion, and it's for a lot of things. It doesn't really have a focus.*

Here's one of the reasons I love blogs. It's because they're great for practicing writing. That's a good thing in general, and thinking, and you get to meet new people. But, it's kind of sobering, too, in that you realize you know how hard it is to get an audience online. You know because you're not going to get thousands of people going to your blog. It will take a while. It works slowly.[42]

Here are two handy lists. Refer to the Checklist 2.10 when writing blogs. Use Checklist 2.11 for content writing guidance.

CHECKLIST 2.10 Blog writing checklist

1   Leave out a few points to invite audience in to add their thoughts.
2   Ask a question to encourage participation.
3   Summarize the entire blog series.
4   Create interlinks to all posts in the series.
5   Spread the word about your blog.

CHECKLIST 2.11 Content writing checklist

1   Does the content have a specific purpose?
2   Is the message relevant to the audience?
3   Does it address a pain point?
4   Does it offer a solution to a commonly posted issue?
5   Is it on an audience-appropriate channel or platform?
6   Does the content apply consumer-insight research and/or other analytics?
7   Is it engaging?
8   Is the format the best one to use, for example an image instead of a video?
9   Does it create a response, leading viewers to take the next step?
10 Is the schedule designed for optimal performance?

As quoted in a Smart Insights blog post, James Gurd, e-commerce consultant and owner of Digital Juggler, offered this clear description of social media:

Social is no longer just about conversation and content; it's now an established channel for customer acquisition, remarketing and engaging existing fans/customers to support retention programs."[43]

Content development exercise

Exercise: Applying the content writing process

Part 1 Review the "Seven-step Content Writing Process" chart Useful Info 2.12. The chart was posted earlier in the chapter (Useful Info 2.9) and is repeated below for handy reference.

    a. Choose a brand.

    b. Identify the why, who, what, which, where, how, and when.

    c. Fill in the chart with your answers.

Part 2 Create content that focuses on the purpose (#1) Why are you creating this content? What do you want it to do? Have viewers click for more information or an e-book? Register for an event? Log in to a tutorial? Answer a question or share their opinion in the post?

Part 3 Carefully choose your audience segment (#2). Who are these people? Describe their persona. What is important to them. For example, what are their self-interests? What issues are they trying to solve? What common problems are they facing? Be sure to address that pain and offer a solution. Make sure to state a key benefit and call to action. Would your target audience respond to, engage with, and/or share this content?

Part 4 Decide what you want to say to the brand's audience (#3). Make sure to state a key benefit and call to action. Would your target audience respond to, engage with, and/or share this content?

Part 5 Select the analytics (#4) that will provide insight into your content and/ or later measure the success of your content. For example, you could choose consumer-insight analytics: (1) to write content or (2) to determine the most effective communication channels.

Part 6 Choose two communication channels to reach your audience. Where will you publish (#5)? For example, (1) Instagram and (2) TikTok. Check that these two channels are where the brand's fans absorb content. Are they most likely to be on these channels? If not, change your choices. Where should you be reaching them?

Part 7 How are you going to deliver the message? What's the format (#6)? Are you going to write an Instagram story? Would you create a TikTok challenge or a YouTube video? What would spark a response to this content?

Part 8 Determine when you want this to appear (#7). Do you want this to be a one-time message of an ongoing topic? What would be the best time and how often?

USEFUL INFO 2.12 Seven-step Content Writing Process

This chart, by Margo Berman, shown earlier as Useful Info 2.9, will remind you to check each of the seven content categories before you begin writing content.

1. *Why:* purpose	What's the point?	Goal →	Qualify leads ■ Conversion ■ Loyalty	Desired action →	■ Follow ■ Subscribe ■ Purchase ■ Promote
2. *Who:* audience	Who's the audience?	Persona	Target segment	Content community	Niche
3. *What:* message	What are you saying?	Branded content	Story/ testimonial	Tutorial	Challenge
4. *Which:* analytics	Which tools will you use?	SEO analytics	Social media analytics	E-commerce analytics	Consumer-insight analytics
5. *Where:* publish	Where will it appear?	Channel/ platform	Channel	Immersive	Mixed reality/media
6. *How:* format	How are you delivering it?	Audio ■ Podcast ■ Webinar ■ Interactive discussion (Clubhouse)	Video ■ Recorded ■ Streaming ■ Skippable	Written ■ Digital √ Social media √ Email marketing ■ Print	Interactive ■ Immersive √ AR √ VR ■ E-commerce
7. *When:* schedule	When will it post/ appear?	Dates	Day times	Frequency	Calendar schedule

Notes

1. https://www.web.com/blog/start/website-design/website-copywriting-and-how-it-affects-your-website-performance (accessed February 5, 2022).
2. Benazhir Maratuech, personal correspondence, February 17, 2022.
3. Carolyn Hadlock, personal correspondence, March 16, 2022.
4. https://www.convinceandconvert.com/social-media-strategy/successful-social-media-writing/ (accessed December 16, 2021).
5. https://www.convinceandconvert.com/social-media-strategy/successful-social-media-writing/ (accessed December 16, 2021).
6. https://www.convinceandconvert.com/social-media-strategy/successful-social-media-writing/ (accessed December 16, 2021).
7. https://www.convinceandconvert.com/social-media-strategy/successful-social-media-writing/ (accessed December 16, 2021).
8. https://www.convinceandconvert.com/social-media-strategy/successful-social-media-writing/ (accessed December 8, 2021).
9. Benazhir Maratuech, personal correspondence, February 17, 2022.
10. Benazhir Maratuech, personal correspondence, February 17, 2022.
11. Juan Valente, personal correspondence, February 17, 2022.
12. Juan Valente, personal correspondence, February 17, 2022.
13. Juan Valente, personal correspondence, February 17, 2022.
14. Juan Valente, personal correspondence, February 22, 2022.
15. https://www.wordstream.com/blog/ws/2011/10/19/10-facebook-tips-for-content (accessed February 19, 2022).
16. https://www.forbes.com/sites/robinryan/2019/06/18/17-ways-to-post-on-linkedin-to-get-noticed/?sh=659d027b3a29 (accessed February 21, 2022).
17. https://topdogsocialmedia.com/how-to-write-linkedin-posts/ (accessed June 21, 2022).
18. https://readable.com/readability/flesch-reading-ease-flesch-kincaid-grade-level/ (accessed March 31, 2022).
19. https://business.twitter.com/en/blog/good-copy-tips-writing-effective-tweets.html (accessed February 19, 2024).
20. https://business.twitter.com/en/blog/good-copy-tips-writing-effective-tweets.html (accessed March 31, 2022).
21. Charlie Hopper, personal communication, November 15, 2021.
22. https://www.linkedin.com/pulse/best-5-instagram-marketing-tips-2022-nadira-alo?trk=pulse-article_more-articles_related-content-card (accessed February 21, 2022).
23. https://www.lemonlight.com/blog/video-for-instagram-how-to-choose-between-a-feed-video-a-story-a-reel-and-instagram-live/ (accessed February 17, 2022).
24. https://www.youtube.com/watch?v=6CL-wqxTbtE (accessed March 19, 2022).
25. https://research.com/tutorials/the-best-times-to-post-on-social-media (accessed March 6, 2022).
26. https://digitalmarketersworld.com/best-time-to-post-on-twitter/ (accessed September 20, 2021).

27. https://digitalmarketersworld.com/best-time-day-to-post-on-tiktok/ (accessed October 20, 2022).
28. https://blog.hootsuite.com/experiment-reels-vs-tiktok/ (accessed October 20, 2021).
29. https://sproutsocial.com/insights/best-times-to-post-on-social-media/ (accessed March 5, 2022).
30. https://blog.hubspot.com/marketing/hubspot-blog-social-media-marketing-report (accessed March 9, 2022).
31. https://blog.hubspot.com/marketing/hubspot-blog-social-media-marketing-report (accessed March 9, 2022).
32. https://www.linkedin.com/pulse/top-10-little-known-tools-content-writers-2022-aakash-kapil (accessed February. 21, 2022).
33. https://blog.hubspot.com/marketing/local-seo-stats (accessed December 16, 2021).
34. https://www.web.com/blog/start/website-design/website-copywriting-and-how-it-affects-your-website-performance (accessed February. 5, 2022).
35. https://www.web.com/blog/start/website-design/website-copywriting-and-how-it-affects-your-website-performance (accessed February. 5, 2022).
36. Vinny Warren, personal correspondence, December 14, 2022.
37. Vinny Warren, personal correspondence, December 14, 2022.
38. Vinny Warren, personal correspondence, December 14, 2022.
39. https://offers.hubspot.com/editorial-calendar-templates?utm_campaign=kickback-email&utm_medium=email&utm_content=186820869&utm_source=hs_automation (accessed February 19, 2022).
40. https://augustafreepress.com/5-top-digital-marketing-trends-for-2022/ (accessed December 25, 2021) .
41. https://www.celestinevision.com/2016/06/james-redfield/quotes-by-james-redfield/ (accessed February 19, 2024).
42. Vinny Warren, personal correspondence, December 14, 2022.
43. https://www.smartinsights.com/social-media-marketing/social-media-strategy/understanding-role-organic-paid-social-media/ (accessed February 9, 2022).

3 The Template Word
Visual Engagement for Cross-platform Use

"Twitter is a great proof of concept to see if a writer can write a headline. It's become the modern billboard."

Carolyn Hadlock, Principal and Executive Creative Director at Young & Laramore[1]

The easiest way to stay current is to follow thought leaders who offer marketing insights, shareable content, writing tips, applicable templates, analytic application, and more. Most content marketing companies are eager to share their research once you subscribe. Often, there is no cost to gain access to these useful assets. Others charge a fee. As mentioned in the preceding chapters, some of the go-to resources include these and many other sources. Decide what you need: analytics, content, calendars, design templates, infographics, etc. Then, find the best one for that goal. Search for examples, as new ones continue to appear. Remember to also look for editable templates. So, you can customize them for your marketing needs. Even though many blogs include sponsored links, you may find exactly what you want. Type in what you're looking for and see what appears. You may find free or low-cost ones that work. With the examples changing so frequently, these are just the home links. Type in search phrases, such as "editable social media templates, "free video templates," "infographic templates," "social media calendar templates," and so on. You can use Microsoft templates for your Word and PowerPoint files, as well. Here are just a few to consider:

- *Canva* (https://www.canva.com)
- *CatchUpdates* (https://catchupdates.com)
- *Convince&Convert* (https://www.convinceandconvert.com)
- *CoSchedule* (https://coschedule.com)
- *Creative Market* (https://creativemarket.com)
- *Digital Marketers World* (https://digitalmarketersworld.com)
- *Envato* (https://www.envato.com)
- *HubSpot* (https://www.hubspot.com)
- *Hootsuite* (https://blog.hootsuite.com)
- *Influencer Marketing Hub* (https://influencermarketinghub.com)
- *Marketo* (https://www.marketo.com)
- *Microsoft* (https://templates.office.com)
- *Research* (https://research.com)
- *Sprout Social* (https://sproutsocial.com)

It's helpful to keep a few templates handy as a reference, starting point, or basic template. Feel free to adopt the following for your purposes or use as inspiration. You'll find explanations to guide your decision process.

Applying examples: Facebook, Instagram, LinkedIn, X (formerly Twitter), Pinterest, and Snapchat

As you review these template examples, think about how you could apply them in future posts. Consider which ones would work best for which type of product or service. Are you promoting a podcast, webinar, or tutorial? Are you selling a custom-designed item? Are you inviting people to an event? Think about what you're trying to do and what's the best way to show it.

Take a look at the different types of images you can display. Be sure if you use templates from any website, that you reviewed the correct usage policies. Some allow you to only use the design, but expect you to insert your own visuals, such as photos, charts, and illustrations. Just changing the font or colors may not be fair right of use. Freelance designer, Juan Bermeo, developed these templates to help you get started. Yes, you can reuse them, as long as you give credit to all the artists/illustrators and websites cited below each example. These sources are included for easy reference.

1. *Facebook Live Post*

   Facebook ads are usually arranged as squares with a 1:1 aspect ratio. An aspect ratio describes the numerical relationship between the width and height of an image. It is expressed by two numbers, separated by a colon. The width is the first number, the height is the second number. Unlike standard Facebook posts which are usually more rectangular. This post (Figure 3.1) is an example of a promotional ad for a podcast channel.[2]

2. *Facebook Event*

   Facebook was originally designed for desktop use, which is why most of the ads are oriented horizontally (Figure 3.2). This type of aspect ratio is used in the app version as well.

3. *Instagram Grid*

   An Instagram grid (Figure 3.3) refers to the visual layout of users' content on their Instagram account. A well-designed grid considers all posts as a working ensemble. In other words, posts aren't only chosen for their individual appeal, but by how well they fit into the general aesthetic of their combined style. It's important to establish a consistent visual flow that is easy and pleasing to look at. The grid usually doesn't feature any direct account information like tags or handles. Instead, it creates a visceral, sensory experience that behaves more like an extension of the brand image.[3]

FIGURE 3.1 This "New Episode of RealityRealty.com" Facebook Live social media post was created by Juan Bermeo for Margo Berman. Original Canva template by Amanda of The Rising CEO. Image courtesy of Canva (https://www.canva.com/p/therisingceo/).

Display size – At least 1080 × 1080 pixels. Minimum size 600 × 600 pixels
Aspect ratio – 1.91:1 to 1:1

FIGURE 3.2 This "Glazing 101" Facebook event post was created by Juan Bermeo for Margo Berman. Image courtesy of Chloe Bolton (https://unsplash.com/@crystalmind_design).

Display size (recommended) – 1200 × 630 pixels
Aspect ratio – 1.91:1

FIGURE 3.3 This "Coffee Mug Pottery profile" Instagram grid was created by Juan Bermeo for Margo Berman. Image courtesy of:

1. Gaelle Marcel (https://unsplash.com/@gaellemarcel)
2. Diana Light (https://unsplash.com/@dreamcatchlight)
3. Katja Vogt (https://unsplash.com/@folkmade)
4. Aedrian (https://unsplash.com/@aedrian)
5. Vladimir Gladkov (https://unsplash.com/@vovkapanda)
6. John Forson (https://unsplash.com/@jonforson)

Original Canva template by: Satu Jiwa Design https://www.canva.com/p/satujiwa/

Display size – 1080 × 1080 pixels
Aspect Ratio – 1:1

4. *Instagram Story*

Instagram has a desktop version, but the content is optimized for smartphones. Stories (Figure 3.4), posts, and reels are all oriented vertically for a full-screen experience on a mobile device.[4]

FIGURE 3.4 This "New Vintage Drop promotion" Instagram story was created by Juan Bermeo for Margo Berman. Image courtesy of "Girl With Red Hat" (https://unsplash.com/@girlwithredhat).

Display size – 1080 × 1920 pixels
Aspect Ratio – 9:16

5. *LinkedIn Post*

LinkedIn posts (Figure 3.5) can vary. Videos are usually oriented horizontally, and original image posts are almost always oriented vertically. Display size and ratio will change if the image is generated from a pasted URL. In this case, LinkedIn generated a thumbnail from the attached article URL.[5]

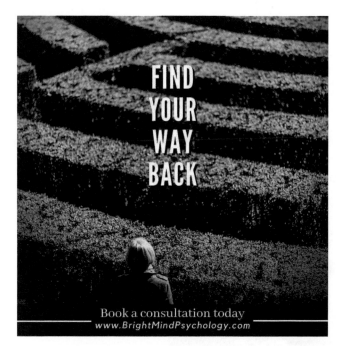

FIGURE 3.5 This "Consultation promotion of Bright Mind Psychology" LinkedIn post was created by Juan Bermeo for Margo Berman. Image courtesy of Maksym Kaharlytskyi (https://unsplash.com/@qwitka).

Display size – 1200 × 627 pixels
Aspect ratio – 1.91:1

6. *X (formerly Twitter) post*

The ideal X display size aligns the image horizontally (Figure 3.6). However, up to four pictures can be included per post. In this case, the first two images will appear as previews, side by side, with an aspect ratio of 7:8.[6]

FIGURE 3.6 This "Happily Ever After Photo promotional banner" X (formerly Twitter) post was created by Juan Bermeo for Margo Berman. Image courtesy of Jonathan Borba (https://unsplash.com/@jonathanborba).

Display size – 1600 × 900 pixels (minimum 600 × 335 pixels)
Aspect ratio (recommended) – Any aspect between 2:1 and 1:1 on desktop; 2:1, 3:4, and 16:9 on mobile

7. *Pinterest Post*

Unlike other social media platforms, where people share daily life content, Pinterest posts (Figure 3.7) are designed for people to "collect" ideas and inspiration. It is usually a more solitary activity meant for people to curate content that aligns with their interests. On average, people will save an image of interest for up to 90 days before acting on it. So, it is common for companies to post both visually appealing images and company information, such as @-handles and websites in the post itself. This lets marketers get their foot in the door early on in the buying process.[7]

FIGURE 3.7 This "Flour Power promotion" Pinterest post was created by Juan Bermeo for Margo Berman. Image courtesy of Miti (https://unsplash.com/@mitifotos).

Original Canva template courtesy of "Go Social Templates."

Display size – 1000 × 1500 pixels
Aspect ratio – 2:3

8. *Snapchat Ad*

Snapchat content, much like Instagram, was designed for mobile devices. Its orientation is vertical to match the phone screen. Snapchat ads (Figure 3.8) are almost exclusively videos, with a swipe-up option that takes the user to a link, usually the company website, a video, or an article.[8]

FIGURE 3.8 This "Vanity Fur: Shop Re-tail" Snapchat Ad was created by Juan Bermeo for Margo Berman. Image courtesy of Karsten Winegeart (https://unsplash.com/@karsten116).

Display size – 1080 × 1920 pixels
Aspect Ratio – 9:16

Modifying video templates: Instagram Reel, YouTube, and TikTok

To perfect your use of video messaging, take the time to notice how successful marketers are using these channels. What are you seeing in Instagram reels? What types of videos are you following on your favorite YouTube channels? Which TikTok challenges and recordings are you participating in or watching? If they're holding your attention, ask yourself what's making you watch these videos in particular? Always picture your target audience and think about what would engage them.

Also, learn about the length used in these channels. Do you need more time, or will a few seconds be enough?

9. *Instagram Reel*

Instagram reels (Figure 3.9) are a type of short video format, up to 60 seconds long. Instagram added the feature in 2020 in response to the growing popularity of TikTok. Reels are heavily shared on Instagram's

FIGURE 3.9 This "New Year's Eve Menu promotion" Instagram reel post was created by Juan Bermeo for Margo Berman. Image courtesy of Roman Odintsov (https://www.pexels.com/@roman-odintsov/) and CottonBro (https://www.pexels.com/@cottonbro/).

Display size – 1080 × 1920 pixels
Aspect Ratio – 9:16

"Explore" page. The organic reach presents a good opportunity for free video ads that feature special offers and promotions.[9]

10. *YouTube Thumbnail*

A YouTube thumbnail (Figure 3.10) is the title image used to identify a video on a search page. It essentially provides a preview of the content, and is, therefore, a user's first impression of the video. A good thumbnail is designed to be enticing and informative. It's supposed to grab a viewer's attention with as few words as possible and with an image that pertains to the video subject matter.[10]

FIGURE 3.10 This "What's the Difference? Light Roast vs Dark Roast" YouTube thumbnail was created by Juan Bermeo for Margo Berman. Image courtesy of Mukul Wadhwa (https://unsplash.com/@mukulwadhwa).

Display size – 1280 × 720 pixels (minimum video resolution for HD, or high definition)
Aspect ratio – 16:9

11. *YouTube Intro*

   It's common for YouTube channels to have recurring intros (Figure 3.11). These introduction sequences are usually animated, or they may include

FIGURE 3.11 This "The Soap Diaries Intro" YouTube video intro frame was created by Juan Bermeo for Margo Berman. Image courtesy of FreeStocks (https://unsplash.com/@ freestocks).

Original Canva template by SXH Designs.
Display size – 1280 × 720 pixels (minimum video resolution for HD, or high definition)
Aspect ratio – 16:9

video content with moving text. The intro "frame" refers to the very last frame of these videos, which conclude with the channel name and call-to-action buttons, such as "Follow," "Like," and "Subscribe."[11]

12. *TikTok End Frame*

TikTok end frames (Figure 3.12) are very similar to YouTube intro frames because they are designed to give viewers a brief, condensed burst of information. TikTok videos are particularly short and the viewers themselves are used to moving through content very quickly. If a creator wants to advertise their own content without paying for ads on the platform, one common way to do this is to include an end frame. These end frames are usually very simple, quick snippets at the end of the video where influencers ask the viewer to follow their account. As the video is shared and reshared, this information helps anchor the content back to its original creator.[12]

FIGURE 3.12 This "Darkroom Chronicles: Follow Me" TikTok end frame was created by Juan Bermeo for Margo Berman. Image courtesy of Annushka Ahuja (https://www.pexels.com/@annushka-ahuja/).

Original Canva template courtesy of Murez Alsyad (https://www.canva.com/p/murezalsyad/).
Display size – 1080 × 1920 pixels
Aspect Ratio – 9:16

Checking the format and content length for each platform and channel

Also, remember to review the content writing templates in Chapter 2 by Nathan Ellering[13] for Convince&Convert. They covered templates for Facebook (Templates 2.2), X (formerly Twitter) (Templates 2.3), LinkedIn (Templates 2.4), and Instagram (Templates 2.5).

Be sure to check the content length, as well, so you won't have to edit down your writing. Nathan Ellering's suggested content lengths from Chapter 2 are given here again, for a quick reference:

1. *Facebook* – 111 characters with no hashtags and one emoji: best results with links, 2nd best with images, and 3rd with text.

2. *X (formerly Twitter)* – 103 characters (including links for best engagement), two hashtags, and one emoji: best engagement with images, 2nd best with text only, 3rd with links.

3. *Instagram* – 241 characters, best posts have 11 hashtags (2nd best have five, 3rd place has ten hashtags) and three emojis: best results with images, 2nd best with videos.

4. *Pinterest* – 215 characters: best results with images.

5. *LinkedIn* – 149 characters, with no hashtags or emojis: best results with links, 2nd best with text, and 3rd with images.[14]

Having templates at your fingertips

With so many accessible, editable, and usable templates, you can keep them on file and apply them as needed. Although there are many reasons to look for and use templates, here's a short list to consider. Templates can:

1. Save time.

2. Help you create a distinctive brand look.

3. Be modified, updated, and repurposed.

4. Inspire new ideas.

5. Become identifiable.

6. Facilitate how you create content.

7. Streamline your design process.

8. Guide your social media scheduling.

9. Impact how you develop your calendars.

10. Become marketing and messaging shortcuts.

Let's review them one by one.

1. *Save time* – If you know what you want to post and have an idea of the look. Now, you can scroll through templates that match your goals. Are you announcing an event? Presenting a webinar? Launching a product? Demonstrating a product's use? Building an audience? Driving web traffic? Selling a service?

2. *Help you create a distinctive brand look* – Use the templates as launchpads for creative designs. What needs to be changed to best represent your brand? What visual can you create to speak on your brand's behalf? What type of visual would be memorable and identifiable? Think about long-term use and application when developing a purpose-driven image.

3. *Be modified, updated, and repurposed* – Why? So, you can extend the use of the look. Focus on designing a recyclable, purpose-directed image. Consider the platform and channel, then, evaluate whether this look works. For example, decide if it would be effective for these or other uses:

   a. *Blog posts*

   b. *Facebook stories*

   c. *Instagram reels*

   d. *Pinterest posts*

   e. *X (formerly Twitter) feeds*

   f. *YouTube videos*

4. *Inspire new ideas* – As you follow content creators and digital design firms, always look for any layout that sparks your curiosity or quickly engages your interest. Could any of them be revised to fit your marketing goals? Become an observer and collector of images and their use in visual design. Be careful that you only reuse and redesign existing templates. You can't just "lift" or steal an idea. However, you can be inspired to create something similar.

5. *Become identifiable* – In addition to creating distinguishable images, remember to select recognizable fonts and a consistent, yet discernable brand voice. Consumers want to feel comfortable and confident in the brand. A familiar look and relatable sound help build a bond and establish a rapport.

6. *Facilitate how you create content* – It's acceptable to use the same content on different platforms. However, you want to rewrite it so it works best in that digital space. No one wants to read the exact same post, word-for-word.

7. *Streamline your design process* – It's helpful to design several layouts with related messages so you can sprinkle seeds across multiple platforms and grow your audience. That way you can pull out modifiable templates and reuse as needed.

8. *Guide your social media scheduling* – Content schedulers can keep you organized. They can serve as reminders or be set up to release the content automatically. You can instantly monitor or revise the content with minimal effort.

9. *Impact how you develop your calendars* – Social media calendars are easy to find. Pick one that works for you and keep your posts listed in one place. You'll know where, what, and when you're sharing content. Calendars offer a handy reference tool to keep you focused on what you need to do to best manage your content.

10. *Become marketing and messaging shortcuts* – The whole point of templates is to do all the above and ultimately condense lengthy processes into manageable tasks. They can feel like your go-to, digital assistants.

Examining social media video templates

Social media videos can catapult a new product into the marketplace and create instant brand awareness. Siggi's yogurt is an excellent example of successful results, as explained on the Tom & Eric 911 agency website: (www.tomanderic911.com):

> *We pitched and won the first-ever branding effort for Siggi's, one of America's fastest growing yogurts. These five digital content spots which capture the simple truth about the brand, appeared on Facebook, Instagram, and YouTube. Each got an average of 600,000 views on YouTube within the first two weeks.*[15]

Tom Amico, co-founder and creative director/art director of Tom & Eric 911, discussed the Siggi's campaign explaining:

> It was the first time they did advertising. Basically, it was to help them sell their company to a French yogurt (company) for some ridiculous amount of money. That's sometimes how it works. They sometimes get more credibility as marketers by doing that. We did three or four spots.[16]

When asked why he chose to use :15 (15-second) videos when developing the campaign, he stated:

> Part of it had to do with [the fact that] they never advertised before. They had a small budget. We wanted to keep things very simple. We choose a table top surface and basically just a hand. Each 15-second spot kind of focuses on one compelling copy point. They had three or four things to talk about. Mostly that they're less sweet. Don't have a lot of sugar. Simple ingredients. The founder started making Siggi's yogurt at a street market in Union Square in New York. There was the Icelandic factor; the nature of the guy who first made the yogurt, is still making the yogurt; the simple part of the story; and the not a lot of sugar.
>
> So, we hit each of these points. One point per spot. So, it's not a bad way to teach students to be single-minded in their approach to advertising.[17]

Here are three of the video templates in storyboard (Figure 3.13, Figure 3.14, Figure 3.15) and script formats (Scripts and Examples 3.1, Scripts and Examples 3.2). Notice how clearly the videos demonstrate the unique selling points of: (1) less sugar, (2) simple ingredients, and (3) fewer ingredients. With so many consumers checking the backs of packages for products ingredients, shoppers could quickly see the Siggi's difference. Unlike many yogurts, Siggi's was created by a consumer who was looking for a product that he couldn't find on the shelves. Refer to these templates as examples when you create social and traditional media videos.

Focusing on video and TV storyboard formats

SIGGI (VO): Unlike some other yogurts, we make ours with not a lot of sugar.

SIGGI (VO): Leaving room for a bit more yogurt.

SFX: TAP OF PRODUCT HITTING TABLE.

SIGGI (VO): Siggi's. Simple ingredients, not a lot of sugar.

FIGURE 3.13 This "Sugar Flick" :15 TV storyboard was created by Tom & Eric 911 for Siggi's. Image courtesy of Tom & Eric 911.

SIGGI (VO): When I moved here from Iceland, I felt most yogurts had too much sugar in them. So I made my own.

SIGGI (VO): And then I made some more.

SIGGI (VO): Simple ingredients, not a lot of sugar.

SIGGI (VO): Siggi's. Half the ingredients. Less sugar and more protein than leading yogurts.

FIGURE 3.14 This "Half the Ingredients" :15 video storyboard was created by Tom & Eric 911 for Siggi's. Image courtesy of Tom & Eric 911.

SIGGI (VO): Our yogurt is made with 25% less sugar and a few simple ingredients.

SIGGI (VO): In fact, you can count the ingredient in most every cup on one hand.

SIGGI (VO): Unlike some other yogurts.

SIGGI (VO): Siggi's. Simple ingredients, and not a lot of sugar.

FIGURE 3.15 This "Simple Ingredients" :15 video storyboard was created by Tom & Eric 911 for Siggi's. Image courtesy of Tom & Eric 911.

SCRIPTS AND EXAMPLES 3.1 Siggi's yogurt video, two-column script: "Not a Lot of Sugar" (see also Scripts and Examples 7.3)

VIDEO	AUDIO	
BEIGE SCREEN WITH TEXT: When I moved here from Iceland, I felt most yogurts had too much sugar in them. So, I made my own.	SIGGI:	When I moved here from Iceland, I felt most yogurts had too much sugar in them.
PHOTO OF SIGGI AT YOGURT STAND.	SIGGI:	So, I made my own.
HAND PLACES YOGURT ON TABLE. TEXT ABOVE YOGURT: And then I made some more.	SIGGI:	And then I made some more.
HAND TURNS CONTAINER TWICE.		
BEAUTY SHOT TEXT ABOVE YOGURT: Simple ingredients, not a lot of sugar.	VO:	Simple ingredients, not a lot of sugar.

(This "Not a Lot of Sugar" :15, two-column video script was created by Tom & Eric 911 for Siggi's yogurt. Script courtesy of Tom & Eric 911.)

SCRIPTS AND EXAMPLES 3.2 Siggi's yogurt video, one-column script: "Not a Lot of Sugar" (see also Scripts and Examples 7.4)

SUPER: When I moved here from Iceland, I felt most yogurts had too much sugar in them. So, I made my own.

SIGGI: *When I moved here from Iceland, I felt most yogurts had too much sugar in them. So, I made my own.*

          Hand places yogurt container on table.

SIGGI: *And then I made some more.*

          Hand turns yogurt around.

SIGGI: *Simple ingredients, not a lot of sugar.*

          Siggi turns product around.

SIGGI: *Simple ingredients, not a lot of sugar.*

(This "Not a Lot of Sugar" :15 video script was created by Tom & Eric 911 for Siggi's yogurt. Script courtesy of Tom & Eric 911.)

Selecting appropriate visuals

For all types of content, regardless of platform or channel, it's important to design or select images that are appropriate for the audience, brand, and use. The usual seven questions apply: (1) *Why* are you sharing it (*What's* the purpose/relevance)? (2) *Who's* being reached? (3) *What's* being said? (4) *Which* analytics will be useful? (5) *Where* is it being consumed/published? (6) *How* are you presenting the content (audio/video/print)? (7) *When* is it scheduled to run/be read? If you're discussing winter-related issues, for instance, showing sunny images would not be suitable.

You can also validate the image choices by double-checking them against the seven Ps for content development to help you: (1) *Plan* the strategy, audience, and message. (2) *Prepare* the post with pain point issues and solutions. (3) *Pinpoint the Persona* to see a mental picture of the individual viewers. (4) *Produce* audience-responsive content. (5) *Persuade* the audience how the problem will be solved. (6) *Publish* the post and repurpose the content. (7) *Promote* the fans' loyalty and advocacy.

Also, ask these questions. Does the image clearly:

- Reflect the audience?
- Represent the brand?
- Suit the social media channel?
- Relate to the common problem?
- Show a solution?
- Encourage followers to share the content?
- Remind them why they're fans?
- Recruit new followers?
- Develop brand advocates?

Ultimately, do these visuals speak on behalf of the brand?

Creating a look to fit the brand

As you've heard many times before, a picture is worth a thousand words. Keep that in mind when selecting images. These will portray the brand and become its voice. Next, consider the overall design of the content. Try various fonts and sizes. Consider the placement of the images and text. Remember to emphasize what's most important when developing the visual hierarchy. Sometimes the message is so important that no visuals are needed. In that case, pay particular attention to how you set the text. You might want a bold font on a white or light background or a small font to draw the reader in.

To help you create a specific, identifiable look, decide where the message will be seen. Then, study posts and videos in those channels or examine promotional messages for podcasts, tutorials, webinars, or experiential events. The point is, relevant references can spark creative solutions. They're guided inspirations to be tweaked to fit your content.

Ask the same key questions we just discussed when determining the brand's look. Does it not only fit the audience, brand, and message, but also fit the strategic direction and deliver a quickly digestible visual statement?

Revising and applying template examples

See how you can take an existing template and modify it for your purpose. Review each element one at a time, including: colors, fonts, images, and each of their positions. Double-check that you're using the correct size for each post. We examined these earlier in this chapter. Then, check that the specs (size specifications) are still correct. Examine new digital channels and learn their requirements. As we will repeat later on, become and remain a student. Stay on top of current media.

Now, make the changes to transform the template into an applicable one. Take a good look at the core message, visuals, and overall layout.

Looking over a few types of social media ads

As you work on social media messages, you'll find there are many more types of ads, in addition to these below, such as specific ones for Pinterest, X (formerly Twitter), YouTube, Snapchat, etc.[18] With technology changing so frequently, it's necessary for you to be a voracious reader and forever student. Follow Hootsuite, Smart Blogger, HubSpot, Convince&Convert, DreamGrow, Sprout Social, WordStream, and other social media marketing blogs. Here is a smattering of social media ads you could create.

Analyzing types of Facebook ads

Carousel Ads – Swipe to see (1) several items or videos, (2) brand features, and (3) take-action choices

Collection Ads – Present multiple products in a grid as small visuals or videos under a larger image, to avoid swiping

Image Ads – Establish name recognition and raise web traffic with one key visual

Messenger Ads – Show up just like a one-on-one, personal Facebook Messenger connection

Slideshow Ads – Look like videos, but with non-animated visuals with captions

Story Ads – Appear as long as the ad runs, not just for 24 hours like a regular Story, with images or videos to encourage take-action-now response

Playable Ads – Let the consumer try the game or app before installing it

Video Ads – Demonstrate industry savvy, increase conversions, and drive sales

Studying types of Instagram ads

In addition to the ones mentioned above: Carousel, Collection, Image, Messenger.

IGTV Ads – Appear as 15-second, non-skip videos when users click on IGTV videos

Reels Ads – Show up as short-form videos, for example, to demonstrate product use

Influencer Ads – Feature influencer for brand credibility and product endorsements

Checking out types of LinkedIn ads

Sponsored Content – Use visuals, videos, or non-video carousel ads

Sponsored Messaging – Present (1) several take-action choices (Conversion Ads) or (2) have one offer and response mechanism (Message Ads)

Text Ads – Use only words, not images

Dynamic Ads (in sidebar) – Tailor to targeted users as (1) Spotlight Ads to highlight products, (2) Job Ads to fuel applicant interest, or (3) Content Ads to generate leads with relevant content

Take a look at the list in Useful Info 3.3 when you create social media ads. Comparisons like these can help you determine where to post them.

USEFUL INFO 3.3 Some types of ads: A handy list

Use this as a general guide when deciding which ads to create and where to place them.

Some types of ads: A handy List by Margo Berman

	FACEBOOK	INSTAGRAM	LINKEDIN	PINTEREST	SNAPCHAT
App-Install	√			√	
Carousel	√	√	√ Without video		
Collection		√		√ Mobile only	√
Commercials					√
Filter					√
Image (single)	√	√	√		√
IGTV		√			
Influencer		√			
Lens AR Experience					√
Messenger (FB) Messaging (LI)	√	√	√		
Playable	√				
Reels		√			
Shopping	√	√		√	√
Sidebar (dynamic)			√		
Slideshow	√				
Story	√				√
Text			√		
Video	√		√		

Saying more in less space

Edit, edit, and edit again. Learn to say what you want and not embellish. Get to the point and get out. No one has time to try to understand what you're saying. It must be instantly absorbed. Remove every superfluous word. Then, reread your content. Can you reduce it more or have you deleted too much? Is it no longer clear? Show it to people who are unfamiliar with the brand or promotion. Can they grasp the message? Or, do you need to explain it? If it's not instantly comprehended, rewrite it. Even if you think it's obvious. It's not. Let others be the judge. You might be too close to it to realize it's vague.

Make it a habit to notice small-space writing in social and traditional media. Look at brief posts, outdoor signage, even restaurant table tents promoting special items. Pay attention to the power of concise writing. Then, practice it in content, presentations, and everything you write.

When you need a reminder, use Checklist 3.4 as a template writing reference. Double-check that your content and visuals fit the chosen template and the brand's identity.

 CHECKLIST 3.4 Template writing checklist

1 Is the content featured in the layout?
2 Did you check the content length for that channel?
3 Is the content short enough?
4 Does it create a response?
5 Does it embody the brand's voice?
6 Is it immediately understood?
7 Does it show a pain point?
8 Does it offer a solution?
9 Can you repurpose the content and the template?
10 Do the visuals support the content and the brand?

To help stay inspired and create memorable content, look for a fresh way of seeing the ordinary. Children often offer insights that adults can easily miss. Or, they can blurt out a surprising remark on a famous campaign. The duck from Aflac Insurance is an example from Tom Amico, creative director and founder of Tom & Eric 911:

> *A friend of mine, who was about five when he saw the duck for the first time said, "Oh wow. They trained a duck how to say 'Aflac'."*[19]

Stay alert and curious. Challenge yourself to find innovative concepts and unexpected views. You might be amazed at what sparks your next brilliant idea.

Visual format exercises

Exercise 1: Designing a customized, repurposable template

Part 1   Choose a product or brand for your message. Then, select an existing template from those in this chapter or others you've found.

    a. Picture your persona. (Imagine a specific audience member.)

    b. Determine why your content is relevant.

    c. Select the format, for example, a social media post or video.

    d. Choose the channel: X, TikTok, YouTube, etc.

    e. Find or design appropriate visuals.

Part 2   Write your content with the correct word count. Be sure you use the appropriate voice for the audience and brand. Review the Template writing checklist (Checklist 3.4). Design a template that you can apply elsewhere.

Part 3   Repurpose the message and template for a different format or channel. For example, if you created a video storyboard for TikTok, now write a social media post for Instagram. Be sure you create a consistent look that reinforces the core content and main strategy.

Exercise 2: Find two more reusable templates

Search for two more template examples. Revise them to work for the same or a different product or brand. What can you do to make it more exciting, so others will respond to it or share it? What new visuals could you choose? What different fonts could you select? What other similar design could you create? Now, create one more template that keeps a consistent tone and look.

Notes

1. Carolyn Hadlock, personal correspondence, March 16, 2022.
2. Juan Bermeo, personal correspondence, June 6, 2022.
3. Juan Bermeo, personal correspondence, June 6, 2022.
4. Juan Bermeo, personal correspondence, June 6, 2022.
5. Juan Bermeo, personal correspondence, June 6, 2022.
6. Juan Bermeo, personal correspondence, June 6, 2022.
7. Juan Bermeo, personal correspondence, June 6, 2022.
8. Juan Bermeo, personal correspondence, June 6, 2022.

9. Juan Bermeo, personal correspondence, June 6, 2022.
10. Juan Bermeo, personal correspondence, June 6, 2022.
11. Juan Bermeo, personal correspondence, June 6, 2022.
12. Juan Bermeo, personal correspondence, June 6, 2022.
13. https://www.convinceandconvert.com/social-media-strategy/successful-social-media-writing/ (accessed December 16, 2021).
14. https://www.convinceandconvert.com/social-media-strategy/successful-social-media-writing/ (accessed December 8, 2021).
15. https://www.tomanderic911.com/siggis (accessed April 16, 2022).
16. Tom Amico, personal correspondence, April 20, 2022.
17. Tom Amico, personal correspondence, April 20, 2022.
18. https://smartblogger.com/social-media-advertising/ (accessed March 9, 2023).
19. Tom Amico, personal correspondence, April 20, 2022.

4 The Experiential Word
Immersive, MR (Mixed Reality), and Interactive Engagement

"Why should a brand exist? What purpose does it serve? Where is its heart? This is a craft of careful identification and distillation. Our work shares three common principles: Simplicity, Clarity, Allure."

Scott Buckley, Founder/Principal, Buckstarter[1]

Content and Copywriting: The Complete Toolkit for Strategic Marketing,
Second Edition. Margo Berman.
© 2024 Margo Berman. Published 2024 by John Wiley & Sons Ltd.
Companion website: www.wiley.com/go/contentandcopywriting

Audience engagement has moved miles from the VCRs, which became affordable by 1985, followed by DVDs in the late 1990s. That is when people discovered that they could control what they saw. They could pause, rewind, and fast forward movies, not just passively watch them on TV or in movie theaters. What this constituted for the viewer was active interaction. They could take a break and come back to where they stopped the video.

Today, people can interact on multiple devices, channels, and platforms; via myriad engagement practices; and within diverse digital ecosystems that connect products, platforms, and partnerships. For example, they can collaborate via Zoom, a software product; collaborate using a workplace platform, such as Slack; create layouts using Canva, a software design tool; search and shop from a link, button, or QR code via different devices, on various social media channels, such as Instagram; and communicate through traditional broadcast media channels and on many platforms to search, sell, and/or share, including Google, Apple, and Amazon. You'll notice that rather than confusing consumers with labels, many products, tools, and platforms describe how they work and what they do. Marketers will use this type of language to show the benefits:

- A single place for files, messages, and teamwork (Slack)

- A simple way to have meetings with handy tools (Zoom)

- A library of templates to design layouts with illustration and font choices, animation, and size options (Canva)

- An immersive way to experience art (experiential events, such as Seismique)

- A virtual, multisensory museum visit (websites, apps, games, channels, on-site LED installations)

- A fast way to find answers (Quora and Google)

People can use different, interactive channels and platforms (from social and traditional to experiential media) to participate in polls, reviews, and challenges; enjoy immersive experiences; play with a brand through gamification; and more. This is especially important to turn viewers into participants. For instance, using interactive TV spots can help change audience behaviors and guide them away from ignoring commercials, muting the sound, or fast-forwarding through commercials. Some videos let viewers choose which clips to view, ask them to answer preference questions, invite them to click for more information, use a QR code to subscribe to a streaming service, or do something else.

With social media, consumers became influencers with name recognition and persuasive opinions who encouraged followers to participate with them, each other, and the brands. Then, the commercialization of social media sites allowed consumers to shop directly from links on influencer, marketing, and brand posts.

One-sided marketing, as mentioned earlier, became dialogues, which led to more engagement, interaction, and finally full-content immersion through different types of experiential campaigns. These invite consumers to enjoy exciting, entertaining experiences. These are not just fun, they're also relevant because they're designed around followers' and customers' preferences. These personalized, audience-driven interactions also lead to the following benefits: (1) attentive interaction, (2) brand awareness and recall, (3) message retention, (4) data gathering, (5) audience insights, and ultimately, (6) purchases. We will now discuss different types of engagement. These can be created in digital environments or as live events, sometimes called "IRL," meaning *in real life*. Augmented reality environments are also referred to as "AR ecosystems."

Examining types of interactive campaigns

As technology advances, marketers will be able to use even more robust, immersive vehicles. Some of the most popular ones are:[2]

1. Apps

2. Branded games

3. Social media channels

4. Interactive videos

5. Virtual (VR), augmented (AR), and mixed reality (MR)

Other applications include these types of interactive ads:[3]

6. Digital ads

7. Playable ads

8. Lead ads

9. Geo ads

10. Display ads

11. Mobile ads (quizzes, polls, etc.)

12. TV spots

13. Print ads (magazine)

Live events and interactive, out-of-home ads offer opportunities to connect with on-site audiences:[4]

14. Kiosks

15. Pop-up stores

16. Special events, such as festivals

17. Product-introduction or launch parties

18. Art installations

Now, let's look at these experiential marketing techniques, one by one. Use these as idea generators and realize there are always more to examine.

1. *Apps* – Consumers gravitate to useful, problem-solving, and easy-to-use tools. This is why apps that fit right into people's everyday lives, such as fitness, health, and even language-learning apps, are popular. The information is always within reach or even on a wearable device. Kia America introduced its EV6 (electric vehicle model) and "Robo Dog" in a Super Bowl commercial. Then, it created its first NFT (non-fungible token), which secured ownership rights to Robo Dog as an app, with proceeds benefitting Petfinder Foundation. People could interact with the "doggie" and share their AR experience with others. What a fun way to entertain, engage, and reinforce the brand's message, while also supporting a worthy cause: dogs in need of a home!

   Another example is McDonald's "Star Hunt" in Saudi Arabia. Using AR-embedded technology in the app, consumers could search the desert sky and see colorful constellations appear with free offers. They'd hunt in The McFries Belt, McSundae Nebula, and the Big Maccer to receive coupons for pickup or delivery. What made it most exciting was that in that region of the world, there were no restaurants open late at night. Yet, most people were active after sunset to avoid the daytime heat. McDonald's only advertised at night, when people became delighted stargazers who could find free, in-the-sky offers of their favorite items. The campaign boasted a 1,900% return on investment and a 12% increase in sales.[5]

2. *Branded games* – When brands integrate gamification, they introduce fun into the user experience, so people enjoy engaging. Whether the game is a self-improvement, product tutorial, or learning system, consumers will eagerly and repeatedly interact. One example of a learning tool, which became part of educational classes on democracy, was "Build the Vote" by Sid Lee, a Canadian ad agency, and Minecraft, a popular 3D virtual cross-platform video gaming world. Written in the language teens use when speaking to each other, the game demystified the voting process. With cartoon-style illustrations, it demonstrated how to vote with step-by-step instructions. The lighthearted images made the serious topic digestible. By making it easy to understand, young voters could

familiarize themselves with the voting process before the election. It was so successful, it garnered 362 million impressions, an 85% conversion rate, and more than 100 global press articles.[6]

3. *Social media channels* – Without question, this is an interactive communication that people frequently access. Although, it was once a way to just share exciting moments of your life, it quickly grew into a digital ecosystem of its own, embracing personal and branded content, and often blending the two. With the ability to specifically target interested communities of consumers, brands can promote new products, offer quick how-to videos, link to e-commerce sites, and more. Without question, new channels and types of engagement will continue to populate.

4. *Interactive videos* – With these videos, audiences can interact and participate, rather than just passively watch. The brand or product can use these in different ways, including: develop content with multiple story endings; escort users on interesting journeys (Netflix's *Call of the Wild,* where people can choose which animal to see and whether to answer that animal's Facetime call); participate in making story character choices in clothing or makeup (Maybelline New York); and even show how donations can make a difference (*Mended Little Hearts*). Three reasons marketers use interactive videos are that they:

   a. Are popular

   b. Have higher interaction rates

   c. Allow for trackable results by measuring audience actions

5. *Virtual, augmented, and mixed reality (interactive technology)* – These campaigns are designed to instantly immerse, inspire, and engage audiences. Here are a few examples:

   a. *Pepsi Max "Bus Shelter"* – This campaign generated 4.6 million views in a week by creating optical illusions at only one London location on Oxford Street. People waiting for buses saw shocking, lifelike videos. Was that a weird creature coming out of a hole that just grabbed someone on the sidewalk? Did they actually see a huge lion run by? Was there a massive robot coming towards them? Are UFOs really flying overhead? Designers mixed cameras on the side of one designated bus shelter with pre-recorded, special-effects videos. These needed to be visible anytime, day or night. This complex setup would be difficult to duplicate in bus shelters all around the city. So, the campaign successfully stuck with just one location.

   b. *BBC Earth* – Again, a bus shelter was the selected site for an augmented reality experience in Oslo. Videos of fun, scary, and beautiful animals popped up right next to unsuspecting commuters. A massive snake slid down the side. A playful penguin marched right next to them. Although they looked real, people soon realized that they were projected videos. However, that didn't stop them from interacting with them and trying to touch the snake or mimic the penguin's walk. The campaign brought awareness of the beauty of Earth and importance of its preservation.

   c. *KFC Gold Hunt AR Experience* – To celebrate its 50th or golden anniversary in South Africa, KFC created Golden Buckets with hidden, 24-carat real-gold tokens. Eager consumers could register their devices on the app, turn on the location setting, and find the participating KFC stores on a map. Then, once they were close enough, they would see the Golden Buckets in augmented reality. If they were lucky, they could find the gold! Both these hashtags generated excitement: #KFCTurns50 and #KFCRealGold.

6. *Digital ads* – These include all kinds of messages, even weather-sensitive, out-of-home ads such as temperature-related apparel messages suggesting anything from bathing suits and umbrellas to snow boots. Digital ads[7] can be customized. They offer ways to improve effectiveness and enhance engagement. Here are two examples.

7. *Playable ads* – Fanta created an interactive kiosk with a touch-screen game. People could touch the screen when they saw an image repeatedly pop up. It was similar to playing a Whac-A-Mole game.

8. *Lead ads* – To improve effectiveness, these allow you to collect data about possible customers who clicked on an ad. Place them where your targeted audience consumes content.

Breaking out from the list, we've already discussed some of these types of ads in Chapter 1, which you probably already knew. The less familiar ones, in Group 2, have a description to explain how they strengthen the consumer-brand relationship.

   a. Group 1 – Popular Choices

      i. *Facebook*

     ii. *Google*

    iii. *YouTube*

    iv. *Bing*

     v. *Amazon*

    vi. *Instagram*

   vii. *TikTok*

viii. *LinkedIn*

ix. *X (formerly Twitter)*

x. *Snapchat*

b. Group 2 – Useful Tools

i. *Taboola* – Provides current ad experiences based on how consumers behave with customizable formats

ii. *BidVertiser* – Allows ads to appear in a specific geographic area

iii. *RevContent* – Offers seamless ad integration that doesn't disrupt the user experience

iv. *BuySellAds* – Enables marketers to display ads to targeted audiences for direct sales

v. *AdRoll* – Offers companies a single platform for social media, email, and display ads to be more competitive

In reviewing myriad techniques for experiential campaigns, you'll find that all engagement is based on strategy, supported by well-thought-out tactics. That is the key to sustained consumer interaction. One more example is the "Fact Avalanche" online tool, created by Sid Lee, to fight against climate-change misinformation in Canada. It alerted subscribers on their preferred platform, including email, text, or Slack, whenever false statements were made. They could find out the truth from a library of scientific articles. Then, they could post the facts in response to the climate-change deniers. The campaign generated a 300% increase in Instagram followers, 25 million organic impressions, and the inclusion of the app on the Slack channels of 100 Canadian companies.[8]

> *I believe that "risky" work is rarely risky at all, that people are longing for honesty and authenticity from corporate communications, and most of all, that engaging story-driven, emotionally rich work almost always leads to terrific results.* Craig Miller, Creative Director/Copywriter, Craig Miller Creative[9]

Be sure to review all types of ads so you have an arsenal of options as starting points. Although there are many more, and some fit into more than one category, let's continue the list.

9. *Geo ads* – Designed to appear in a specific geographic location, such as in a pedestrian or commercial setting to catch consumers on the go. (See BidVertiser listed as "Group 2, ii".)

10. *Display ads* – These push content to consumers who weren't looking for this information.

11. *Mobile ads* – These are also push ads that can include ways to engage the audience with action steps, such as QR codes. However, if consumers opted to receive ads from the brand, they turn into pull ads.

12. *TV spots* – Once strictly push ads, now TV spots engage the audience. These types of interactive spots allow viewers to choose the (1) length, (2) theme, and (3) language they prefer. Many of these include QR codes to websites, product offers, and links to more information. TV commercials have become as short as a few seconds to one-minute spots and longer for special events, such as the Super Bowl.

13. *Print ads* (magazine and out-of-home) – These have moved from flat messages into print that includes (1) scent, (2) sound, (3) pop-up features, and (4) interactive components, such as virtual "drinkable" straws. Expect new technology to continue transforming this medium.

14. *Kiosks* – These can be located in malls, conferences, or in other places where people can learn more about the product via interactions, such as challenges, games, and mini tutorials.

15. *Pop-up stores* – Even if you never noticed it, think about the pop-up stores you may have visited, including holiday-based temporary shops for Christmas and Halloween. Now, add technology, where customers can virtually decorate a tree or try on costumes. One fun example is the pop-up store set up by BarkBox in Manhattan. Given outfits with RFID tracking devices to wear, doggies went on a shopping expedition and could play with any of the toys. Their owners could see which ones they preferred and order them at the e-commerce site: BarkBox.[10]

16. *Special events* – You can choose what works best for your brand: festivals, concerts, workshops, sporting events, and more. One exciting example was by Chipotle when it created a virtual reality illusion of a sporting event. Projected images of a life-size Zamboni machine pushed a gigantic burrito bowl and a massive fork onto a Stanley Cup quarterfinal game. As fans waited for the two teams, St. Louis Blues versus the Colorado Avalanche, to continue battling after a break, the live announcer, Alan Roach, narrated while the burrito crashed through the ice, followed by a huge, gloved hand which came up and grabbed the bowl, then returned for the fork. The audience was shocked and delighted by the 45-second stunt. It actually looked as if it were really happening and not a 3D projection (*CGI* or computer-generated imagery). What a brilliant way to seize the moment and shock the audience with an unforgettable experience.[11]

17. *Product-intro parties* – Create an unexpected, interruptive event, such as interactions with models during a fashion show. People could use an app to virtually change the outfits and see more designs that the models could wear. For example, the audience could vote for the specific outfit

they wanted to see. Then, it would be projected onto the models as they strutted the catwalk or within the event. The different designs could be displayed on a large screen for everyone to enjoy.

18. *Art installations* – These are oversized objects that appear in everyday or ambient settings. Two examples are sculptures of giant, lifelike cheeseburgers and ice cream cones sprawled across sidewalks as if they fell from the sky. They promoted the movie, *Cloudy with a Chance of Meatballs*. These hard-to-miss installations were an exciting way to promote the film.

As always, keep informed on emerging, creative applications. Look for exciting, ambient messages, where you least expect them. Even if they're not interactive, they can be exciting and engage the senses with surprise.

Playing with the audience

Just creating relevant, targeted content isn't enough to get noticed. People are looking for experiences that surprise, entertain, and delight them. Novelty wears off quickly unless it's so unique that it gets shared, expands the reach, and increases engagement. For example, museums that developed augmented reality experiences then created exhibits that toured the world. Many more people discovered an appreciation for art through the two-story projections created in the "Beyond Van Gogh: The Immersive Experience" exhibitions. Designed by Mathieu St-Arnaud, creative director, the spectacular images allowed visitors to walk through enormous replicas of the paintings and see the images come to life in multisensory ways. Imagine strolling in a virtual forest of Van Gogh images! Even watching the creation of a visually immersive, 360-degree animation is exciting. For example, to demonstrate the Google Tilt Brush tool, web series *Art Attack in VR* paired up with VR Scout and asked 3D artist George Peaslee to recreate the famous 1889 Van Gogh painting, *The Starry Night*. George had the image saved on Tilt Brush and used several tools to draw the three-dimensional painting. For the sky, he used the coarse bristle brush and switched to the flat marker tool to create the town. He wanted to replicate the impressionistic style in brush strokes and texture. It's fascinating to watch him create the work. See this one on the YouTube, *Art Attack in VR* channel, season two, episode two.

Another video (season two, episode three) captures George recreating the well-known George Seurat 1884 painting, *A Sunday Afternoon on La Grande Jatte*. As with *The Starry Night* VR work, he used the bristle brush for the background and changed to the 2.5D tool for the fine details, as with the pipe. He explained that although VR drawing was done in 3D, detailed figures were drawn in 2D. Using a picture of the original work, George was able to check that the proportions matched Seurat's painting.

Although George was wearing VR glasses, viewers don't need them to see what he did. They can move through the image, fly over the painting, and become immersed in it. You, too, can view it on YouTube without any special virtual reality glasses. You see the sky and trees move, as you watch the town go by as if you're walking through the painting. One of the house doors creeks opens. You go inside, move through the "Aries Room," and finally peer through a window that opens with sound as the sky moves in the background. It's magical!

If you're also an artist, as well as a writer, take a look at how VR allows artists to work in the metaverse with the VR Art Gallery Metaverse interviews. See the one with host Paul Barron interviewing Roger Haas, ArtMeta founder/CEO, and Alissa Alekseeva, head of marketing. Or follow them at #Metaverse to see what else the tech team is discussing.

You can even try your hand in creating experiential art.[12] If you're curious, visit YouTube and check out these and other VR apps and tools that allow you to paint and sculpt in 3D formats:

1. *Oculus Quest 2* and VR art apps, such as Color Space, like a VR coloring book

2. *Tilt Brush* by Google and *Painting VR*[13]

3. *Kingspray Graffiti*, which uses Oculus Quest 2 and Rift platforms

4. *Gravity Sketch* to sculpt and create 3D objects

5. *SculptrVR* to collaborate with friends and design sculptures in VR

6. *Let's Create! Pottery VR* to design homemade ceramics

Companies today are using immersive and interactive tools to target specific audiences to showcase existing and introduce new products. One app example is the Brine "Shoot. Score. Repeat." lacrosse game (Figure 4.1, Figure 4.2, Figure 4.3). It allowed Brine equipment fans to improve their shooting technique by practicing virtually. The first app, "Shootout," was so popular that two more followed: "Hotshot" and "Shootout 2." Here are some insights shared by the creative team at Young & Laramore who developed the marketing campaign. The :75 (75-second) video showed all the app's features and promised to be fun to use. It was! Be sure to pay attention to how many app downloads the digital campaign generated: 70,000. To speak directly to the players, the headline spoke about their passion and the video depicted the high-powered action:

Laxers just want to play

So we let them do just that. We worked with Brine to build excitement for their lacrosse gear through Shootout – a mobile app where players can practice their shooting reflexes and compete with friends, all while using virtual Brine gear.

Within the first three weeks, Shootout had been downloaded 70,000 times, quickly becoming the #1 lacrosse game in the App Store. Fans loved it so much, we worked with Brine to release two sequels: Hotshot and Shootout 2. And as more and more players practiced their shots, Brine's brand awareness and loyalty shot up.[14]

FIGURE 4.1 This "Shoot. Score. Repeat" :75 video screengrab was created by Young & Laramore for Brine. Image courtesy of Young & Laramore.

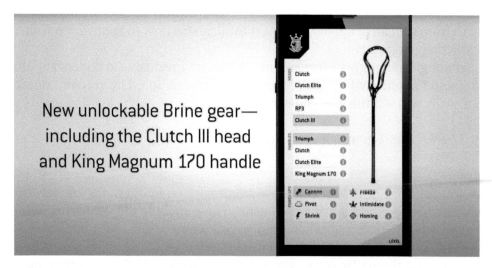

FIGURE 4.2 This "Shoot. Score. Repeat." :75 video screengrab was created by Young & Laramore for Brine. Image courtesy of Young & Laramore.

FIGURE 4.3 This "Shoot, Score. Repeat" :75 video screengrab was created by Young & Laramore for Brine. Image courtesy of Young & Laramore.

There are always new technology advances to enhance apps, so continue to search for and experiment with them. After exploring how some of these work from a creative application, next think about how to apply them from a marketing perspective.

Although you might be focused on content, it's invaluable to understand the way your audience will visually receive the information. The graphic context can easily redirect the way you express your ideas.

> *Technology is a tool, not a weapon. Peter Sena II, Founder and Chief Technology Officer, Digital Surgeons*[15]

As you consider how you would use immersive technology, let's review the basic audience-tailored principles again. These include the why, who, what, which, where, how, and when, and so on, we've discussed in Useful Info 2.9. Why do they care? Who is interested? What would excite them? Where can you find them? How can you get them involved? When are they most engaged in that platform/medium? With any of the augmented, virtual, or mixed-reality experiences, you want to answer why you're choosing any of these. As discussed under "Examining types of interactive campaigns" and "Playing with the audience," you could be taking the audience on a:

1. Virtual tour of:
   a. Real-estate home listings
   b. Museum exhibitions

2. Training tutorial of:
   a. Software applications
   b. Social media management
   c. Medical equipment
   d. Robotic tool functions
   e. AR-enabled website design (WebAR)
   f. Tools for cross-platform design to connect headsets, websites, and smartphones

3. Home improvement lesson of:
   a. Color choices
   b. Furniture placement
   c. Renovation design

4. Product demonstration of:
   a. Digital environments, such as the metaverse
   b. Mixed reality and alternate realities
   c. Augmented reality features on mobile devices
   d. Smart glasses paired with smartphones
   e. AR/VR headsets
   f. AR "see-through" glasses

Revisiting ways to engage

Although, we discussed this earlier, here's a quick refresher. Remember to ask yourself how you can interact with the target. Would any of these work for the brand, message, and audience?

- Creative activities, such as painting with Tilt Brush
- Engaging challenges, puzzles, and quizzes
- Enticing, brand-centric games
- Live stunts and events
- Exciting contests and fun polls
- Product tutorials and education tools
- Immersive experiences and installations

Set a goal to learn about the different formats that explore user experience and interface in immersive and experiential environments, including AR and VR as well as interconnected, extended reality, or MR, which blends AR and VR, as in smart glasses.

As with all media, the best thing you can do is jump right in. Replace apprehension with a sense of exploration. Then, think about how you could expand your own or your client's digital footprint. The most important thing is to be a dedicated observer. Don't just read social media posts. Analyze them. Don't just visit websites. Scrutinize the copy. Don't just watch YouTube videos. Review them. Don't just sit there. Participate in online discussions. Always ask yourself:

- What kind of clients would work well using an experiential campaign?

- How can I create an app to work in a new way?

- Which campaigns, events, technologies, or templates could I use?

Constantly look for new examples of great content and innovative digital marketing. Even older campaigns may still be applicable. Be open-minded and receptive. Pay attention to campaigns that have survived the life cycle of their peers.

Ask yourself how often you participate in interactive campaigns. How frequently do you engage in branded games or respond to TikTok challenges? The best way to build your toolkit is to join in on all social, digital, interactive, and immersive experiences. Then, you'll be able to create them yourself.

Be sure to check out the Wheat Thins "@CrunchisCalling" X (formerly Twitter) campaign. Wheat Thins followed consumers who posted about the product. When fans posted that they couldn't believe Wheat Thins was really following them, some of them received a free box from "The Crunch is Calling" Wheat Thins truck. Some people thought the whole campaign was a hoax and even posted:

> *Hey @CrunchisCalling I think the Wheat Thins commercials are UBER FAKE. How do they find these people?*[16]

Wheat Thins answered doubters with visits, free samples, and video crews to record the naysayers' surprise. Next, it tweeted their reactions. The fun-packed social media campaign rewarded fans and nonbelievers alike with boxes of Wheat Thins.

As you become more adept at developing interactive social media and virtual campaigns, you'll appreciate how consumer engagement extends a brand's impact. Later, you'll see how ASICS spoke directly to its audience through the ingenious "New York City Marathon" interactive campaign. You'll find out how Domino's not only revamped its entire pizza formula, but also created a fun, interactive campaign, "Pizza Holdouts," to spread the message. You'll discover why the innovative Burger King campaigns "Whopper Freakout" and "Whopper Virgins" went viral.

Carefully notice how each social media channel can be used to support the other. For example, you can use an Instagram story to promote a product, which can link to an e-commerce site. Or, use an app that plays off a TV commercial, like the Kia Robo Dog. Or, even create apps that transform how people use them, as in the examples below. The app:

- Fits a specific region, such as McDonald's "Star Hunt" in Saudi Arabia.

- Lets people see perfectly scaled IKEA furniture in their own space, then put it in a shopping cart for pick up or delivery through IKEA Kreativ.

- Entertains consumers with projected 3D images, such as flying dinosaurs, into their living spaces right from their sofas with StealthTech, an AR/MR technology, embedded in immersive Lovesac furniture.

- Allows consumers to see the paint in a room before choosing a color, as in the Behr ColorSmart app.

- Prints digital photos, so consumers can create personalized scrapbooks, calendaring, gifts, and more.

You could also examine how companies, such as a French postal agency, created immersive games as virtual job simulations or workplace events to recruit and retain employees. Think about ways you can design interactions across channels and platforms to repurpose content and reinforce brand edutainment.

You can never underestimate the importance of engaging the consumer or employee to strengthen the emotional bond to the brand. Information and entertainment are key. The direction you choose depends, again, on your brand and audience.

> *Have a one-on-one conversation with someone. Having a one-on-one conversation entails having your point of view on the world.*
> Sheena Brady, Commercial Director/Creative Director[17]

Asking: What's the point of interaction?

Before you create any interactive element, you must completely understand the ultimate objective. What do you want the audience to do? Why are you engaging their participation? Is it for any of these reasons?

- Learn about a company.
- Claim a free reward.

- Challenge the consumer.

- Entertain the audience.

- Show how a product fits in their lives.

- Solve a problem, like redecorating or refurnishing.

You get the point. Think of interactivity as the old "call to action." Let the audience understand what action to take and show them why they should want to get involved. Here are a few fun sites that became viral because everyone enjoyed playing and sharing.

You've probably created sendables. These are messages, videos, and fill-in-the-blank animations or characters that you can create and share with friends. If you haven't "Elfed Yourself" yet (www.elfyourself.com), you're one of the few people who hasn't joined in the OfficeMax fun. So many millions of people have that the campaign went viral. Besides sendables, you can print and share photos via Snapfish and other apps.

One engaging way to remind consumers about the brand was an experiential, live-event activation, "Schlage Key to Strong Challenge" by Young & Laramore (Y&L) for Schlage locks (Figure 4.4, Figure 4.5). This "find-the-key-and-win-$5,000" challenge sent participants around town to locate a house key. Why? To unlock a guy who was locked in a house for six days. Get him out and unlock $5,000. How much fun is that? The prize was enticing enough to get people scurrying to find "the" key. One lucky person succeeded. The case study video script appears later in Chapter 7. Here are campaign insights found on the agency's website:

No one spends much time thinking about locks

When Schlage locks first reached out to us, they were struggling to keep their brand top-of-mind. After all, people only buy new locks an average of once every seven years. Y&L helped reposition and re-launch the brand. Nationally, sales shot through the roof, but there was one hold-out: sales were flagging in Seattle.

Our Approach:

Lock a guy in a house, then hide the key.

We needed to get people's attention on a limited budget. So, we thought out of the box. Or, rather, in it. We hired an aspiring comedian and locked him in a tiny house in the middle of Seattle's busiest shopping center. Then we sent people on the hunt to find the key and let him out, combining social, digital, experiential and retail in one tiny-but-massive activation.[18]

FIGURE 4.4 This "Locked in a House" experiential activation was created by Young & Laramore for Schlage. Image courtesy of Young & Laramore.

FIGURE 4.5 This "Locked in a House" experiential activation and social media campaign was created by Young & Laramore for Schlage. Image courtesy of Young & Laramore.

Thinking more about interactivity

Whether you're asking your audience to participate in AR experiences like the election-learning tool, "Build the Vote," or the KFC hunt-for-gold "Golden Bucket," focus on writing impossible-to-ignore invitations. Vinny Warren, founder and creative director of The Escape Pod emphasized that the concept, and not necessarily the writing, triggers a response:

> *I think it's more of a case of, not necessarily writing, as it is thinking. If you want people to interact with something, that's tough. It's tougher to get someone to literally interact with something than it is to get someone to watch a video. If you truly want to get someone to interact with something, then that something has to be very attractive and appealing. So it's not necessarily how you write it. It's what's the idea? Is it something that's exciting or not? If it isn't you're just open to a battle.*[19]

What's important to retain is how the campaign considers the consumers' experience preferences. Do they prefer to watch a video? Listen to a podcast or join in on Clubhouse? Dive into an immersive experience? Or watch from the sidelines? How do they consume content? Are they (1) visual, (2) auditory, or (3) kinesthetic (experiential)? These three neurolinguistic terms describe the primary ways people absorb information, which will be discussed in Chapter 9. If you always focus on the message's recipient, you'll drive your point home faster. As with all types of engagement, the challenge is to create innovative ways to interact and build brand loyalty.

Just look at how the McDonald's "Star Hunt" app spoke to the consumers. The language was clear and concise. Participants knew how to play with the brand and receive rewards. For example:

- ▪ "Find your prize & win. Scan the sky."
- ▪ "Congratulations. Your offer has been stored in your wallet. Go to deals."
- ▪ "Congratulations. You found the Big Maccer. Redeem now."[20]

When using AR technology, pay attention to the directions. If they're too complicated, no one wants to play along. People want the fun without the learning curve.

Using interactivity for social causes

When the beautiful Boston waterfront was threatened with overdevelopment, opponents turned to social media to get the word out. Activists engaged with concerned citizens by alerting them to the imminent negative impact to their beloved harbor. Soon, people were posting comments and sharing other followers' posts. Here are a few examples (Figure 4.6, Figure 4.7, Figure 4.8) that demonstrate how a small-space social media message can have a powerful impact.

People's comments showed a full understanding of the magnitude of the proposed development project and included these posts:

- "Nooooo there's def effects of climate change, and building that building is just not smart for the structure of the Long Wharf."

- "By stopping a building that would not save Boston waterfront. It's way bigger than that and you all know this!!!"

FIGURE 4.6 This "The Waterfront Needs You" landing page was created by DeVito/Verdi for Save Boston's Waterfront. Image courtesy of DeVito/Verdi.

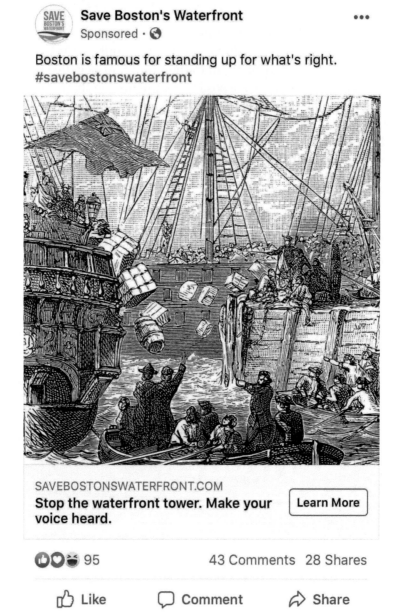

FIGURE 4.7 This "Tea Party" Instagram ad was created by DeVito/Verdi for Save Boston's Waterfront. Image courtesy of DeVito/Verdi.

What's interesting is how the campaign harkened back to the Boston Tea Party when locals protested against being bullied into taxation without representation. Now, their fight was to have a voice, or be represented, in city planning.

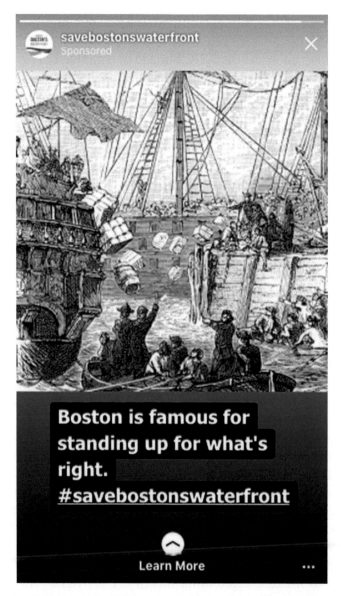

FIGURE 4.8 This "Standing Up for What's Right" Instagram story ad was created by DeVito/Verdi for Save Boston's Waterfront. Image courtesy of DeVito/Verdi.

Finding other ways to use interactivity

As you're working on different creative assignments or client projects, think about how you could extend the message to include an experiential component. Consider how you might modify the campaign and use the element of surprise. Where could you engage the audience in an unexpected way?

Take a quick look ahead at the ASICS image in Chapter 12 (Figure 12.18). We'll discuss the campaign in more detail again in Chapter 14. The creative team at Vitro wanted to connect to the New York City Marathon runners in a unique way. They developed the "Support Your Marathoner" website (www. supportyourmarathoner.com), where people could create a personal video and/ or text message to motivate their loved ones during the grueling 26.2 miles. The New York Road Runners club promoted the site, as did bloggers and other runners using social media like Facebook.

Instead of just being the standard sponsor, the week preceding the marathon, ASICS set up special stands where people could record their messages. Runners would read the message on huge LED screens set along the course. "Trigger chips" were set on RFID tags given to every runner to place on the top of their shoes. As the marathoners ran across sensors on the road, their trigger chips sent their personalized message to the screen, so they could see their unique note of encouragement as they were running. The response was amazing. People from 17 countries sent messages in all media, from printed words and still photos to videos, to 7,000 runners. Once again, a company used consumer-created content to develop relevant messages to a very special and targeted audience. With the name "ASICS" displayed along the course, 45,000 runners were reminded of a brand that sold something they would need: running shoes.

There are many other excellent interactive campaigns. Some help charitable causes in new ways. One such is the UNICEF "Tap Project." The long-running, grassroots campaign started in 2007 in New York City restaurants and continued until 2016. Restaurant patrons were used to receiving a free glass of tap water. When they were asked to add one dollar to their bill as a donation to help bring drinkable water to areas of the world without clean water, almost everyone said, "of course." This free, word-of-mouth campaign spread and soon vending machines selling "Dirty Water" allowed people to make a $1.00 donation to the UNICEF "Tap Project." Celebrity spokespeople like Mario Lopez and Sarah Jessica Parker got on board. Corporations made donations and advertising and other agencies volunteered their time and talent.

> So it really does start at the beginning with defining the
> essence of what the project is about. *Matt Ziselman, Creative*
> *Director, Sapient*[21]

It's inspiring to review a highly creative interactive campaign from 2005 by DDB London and Tribal DDB: "Monopoly Live" (Figure 4.9). It was a standout that still shows the power of gamification, even without an app. The game celebrated the seventieth anniversary of Monopoly, using the first-ever updated version of London properties as they exist today. It was the first time that cabs were fitted with GPS devices and functioned like Monopoly pieces traveling in real time around London.[22]

FIGURE 4.9 This "Monopoly Live" website image was created by Tribal DDB for Monopoly. Image courtesy of Tribal DDB.

With so many people in the target audience already familiar with and owners of Monopoly, the challenge was to get them to buy a new version of an all-time-favorite game. Consumers could register free on the campaign website and select how they should spend their £15 million Monopoly play money. Here is an overview of the campaign as a case study.

Background

This was the "first interactive, real-time, life-size Monopoly game using GPS-transmitter-fitted cabs, functioning like Monopoly pieces, throughout the streets of London."[23]

Campaign objectives

1. To spark sales of the new Monopoly game

2. To increase core value of the Monopoly game

3. To reignite people's passion for Monopoly and appeal to a new, younger generation of consumers[24]

Target audience

The traditional target for Monopoly is moms with kids aged 8–13 years, although due to the modern appeal of the updated game, we also targeted teens, and people in their 20s and 30s.[25]

Strategy

We decided the best way for people to rediscover Monopoly and experience the updated board was to actually play it! So, we turned London into a life-size, real-time Monopoly board by creating a true-to-life, interactive version of Monopoly. Eighteen black cabs, fitted with GPS transmitters and liveried in Monopoly colours, acted as the real-life playing pieces.

Taking this approach allowed the communication to resonate much more strongly, as consumers could familiarize themselves with the changes to the new Monopoly board over a period of days, in their own time, rather than having these changes communicated to them in the seconds of a TV ad.[26]

Execution

The 18 Monopoly-branded taxis were fitted with a GPS transmitter using top-of-the-range security technology, so that their location was known at all times.

As the taxis went about their normal day, picking up and dropping off passengers, players would pay out rent as their cabs passed properties they didn't own, and receive rent when other cabs passed their properties. The grand prize was winning your mortgage paid for a year, and there were also daily and weekly prizes to play for.

There was also an SMS element to the game allowing people to SMS for bonus cash, which deepened their involvement with the game.[27]

Media

The media involved ranged from online marketing to TV, radio, and public relations.

Results

- *Monopoly was the* **best-selling** *board game of 2005*

- *At campaign launch,* **sales of Monopoly were up 200%** *[from] the same period of the previous year*

- *Demand for the game was so great that Hasbro* **sold out** *of the limited edition game two weeks before Christmas!*

- *Monopoly Live bolstered Hasbro's CRM database by over* **100,000** *names*

- *Over* **1 million people** *visited the site;* **200,000 people** *played the game and, on average, played three times over the 4 weeks the campaign was live*

- **45,000** *text messages were sent*

- *Shortlisted for* **Cannes Titanium Lion**, *winner of* **Gold Media Lion**, *and winner of* **2 IPA Effectiveness Awards**[28] (IPA, Institute of Practitioners in Advertising, is the UK's top association for advertising, media and marketing communications agencies.)

This campaign, although not a copy-centric one, is a perfect example of how to reenergize buying interest in a beloved brand that most already owned. By adding consumer engagement via digital interactivity the updated Monopoly game generated renewed appeal.

There are many interactive campaigns today once you start looking for them. Some, you may have already discovered. So, make a mental note when you see them. Think about what other products or companies would be able to participate in interactive campaigns. Some interactive campaigns are so much fun, they become viral and create buzz.

Discovering how to create buzz

If you're trying to understand exactly what goes viral, pay attention to what you repost, share, or link to on social media. Most likely, you loved it and couldn't wait for someone else to see it, hear it, experience it, or chat about it. Become a better observer the next time you become an interactive participant. Notice examples of campaigns that created buzz. Be sure you look into the Freestyle Coke machine commercial. It introduced the vending machine that offered customizable drinks. The stunt offered free sodas, giant sub sandwiches, little floral bouquets, and more, coming out of the Coke machine to the delight of unsuspecting college students.

It's helpful to review outstanding viral campaigns of the past. You'll see that the following ones are still as exciting as they were years ago. Let's take a look at a few of the Whopper campaigns. Rob Reilly, global chief creative officer at WPP, offered these comments when he was partner and worldwide chief creative officer at Crispin Porter + Bogusky. Reilly explained the creative process behind the viral phenomenon for Burger King with the "Whopper Freakout" campaign. The agency wanted to say the Whopper was number one without sounding boastful. Reilly stated no one likes a "chest pounder." Exactly, how do you show that people really preferred the Whopper and make it sound authentic?

> So that's where the essence of Whopper Freakout was born: Well, what if you had consumers saying it? But the problem with that is: Well sure, the consumers got paid. You know, you asked them a question. We started peeling away the layers of why something was going to be perceived as right or wrong, or what was going to work. So, then it was: What if we did the opposite? What if we took the thing they loved and took it away? Would people actually care?[29]

That strategy, as we discuss in Chapter 6, is the *deprivation strategy* (#35): having people miss something they once had, as in the first "Got Milk" commercials. The idea behind "Whopper Freakout" was to record people's real reactions when they were told that the Whopper was no longer on the menu. The reactions were hilarious. Being created for an online viewer, the video didn't have the time restraints as for standard TV spots. Here the story could be told in 7.5 minutes, not in under 30 seconds.

The video, which got two million hits, quickly created consumer interest. People soon created their own versions and posted them on YouTube. Another Burger King viral campaign you should look at is "Whopper Virgins". An entire team of videographers and cooks searched the world to find people who had never had a hamburger. They wanted to create a "real taste test" and have these fast-food virgins compare the Burger King Whopper to a McDonald's burger. When you watch the video, you see all the preparation it took. Looking at people in native costumes attempt to eat a Whopper for the first time is very funny. Most had to be coached into using two hands and taking a big bite. Once again, consumers created their own YouTube parodies, which added viral fuel to the fire.

For the Domino's "Pizza Holdouts" campaign, the pizza chain admitted on camera that it had received negative feedback about its product line. It decided to change the entire formula, ingredient by ingredient. To convince consumers that it had really created a new recipe and to attract people who had never tried the new "inspired" Domino's Pizza, it created a no-holds-barred multimedia campaign that went viral. It selected three "holdouts" and persuaded these consumers to call Domino's by putting their names on giant billboards, trucks, and signage with a call to action. Cameras were standing by to capture their surprise when they saw messages specifically and singularly targeting them. Of course, each of them ordered a pizza and naturally cameras caught their positive reactions. Friends were invited to vote for their favorite holdouts on Facebook.

Nike, on the other hand, knew it had a loyal, almost fanatical, fan base called "Sneakerheads." Many of these devout loyalists would sit on the sidewalk for days on end waiting for the release of a new Nike sneaker model, especially when the new arrivals were limited editions. Some had as many as 300 pairs and were still collecting more. To recognize them, Nike created an entire website in their honor and continued to produce sneakers with the cool factor. This only strengthened the already deep emotional bond consumers had with the brand.

Apple also created one cool product after another and spoke directly to its audience through its humorous, now classic "Mac versus PC" (also called the "Get a Mac") campaign that showed the benefits of Mac (strategy #1) with *product demonstration* (strategy #7), *product comparison* (#8), *humor* (#25), and *continuing characters* (#41) strategies. (Take a moment to review the list of strategies in Chapter 6, so you can identify the techniques being used.) Pay attention to the copy when you listen to the spots. Notice the laid back, casual *tone of voice* of Mac and the stiff delivery of the PC. Observe how Mac introduced each new product with spots that showed consumers how easy it would be to use the new technology, implying a short learning curve because of Mac's intuitive design.

Each of the above-mentioned campaigns deserves your attention. Write yourself a note so you remember to review them and see why they were imaginative and effective. Realize that the campaigns' concepts in all of these examples are what created the response. Big, entertaining ideas, not just great copy, create reactions. Wonderful writing won't rescue a poor idea. Sometimes straightforward copy with consumer benefits and clear product demonstrations, as in the Apple new product introductions, are all that's needed for a response. Dissect every campaign you see. As you read industry news look for campaigns that spark ideas.

Creating irresistible, Interactive marketing

Make it a point to analyze campaigns, videos, images, and so on that you receive and pass along. Think about what captured your attention. Consider how you would create messages that are engaging and interactive. In looking at how to create campaigns that go viral, consider the following list:

1. Develop an irresistible idea. Ask:

   - Can you make it interactive?

   - Does it reflect your audience's perspective?

   - Can you use humor?

   - Would being irreverent fit the brand?

2. Highlight the brand's benefit. Ask:

   ▪ How does it help the audience?

   ▪ What problem does it solve?

   ▪ How user-friendly is it?

   ▪ Can you get consumers to create brand-related content (develop videos, comment on blogs, post, or shoot commercials about the brand)?

3. Understand why you're creating this message. Ask:

   ▪ Can you make it relevant to the audience?

   ▪ Does it reflect the brand's image?

   ▪ Does it reach a new audience?

   ▪ Does it showcase something unique or new?

As you become more familiar with current and past viral campaigns, be sure to see this unique commercial for its visual creativity: "LED Sheep" – aptly nicknamed "Extreme Shepherding." Created for Samsung, it generated 13 million views. Although, this is not an example of viral writing, the creativity behind the campaign drove users to immediately share it with everyone they could. The object was to show the brilliance of Samsung's LED TVs. This viral video can still be found on YouTube. Just look for "LED Sheep Viral Video" or "Extreme Sheep LED Art." You'll find that even now, it's nothing short of absolutely amazing. Just to come up with the idea of creating images with sheep in LED-adorned jackets driven by herding dogs directed by expert Welsh shepherds is mindboggling. The sheep are masterfully herded by "extreme shepherding" into mesmerizing, moving images, most with lights on the back of the sheep to create a:

▪ Video game

▪ Mosaic-light display of the Mona Lisa

▪ Series of fireworks displaying as sheep bursting out in different directions

You'll instantly see why the campaign went viral. The images were aired on BBC, ABC's *Good Morning America*, Digg.com (front page), Sky News, ITV News, and other media outlets. Best of all, each video closes with a call to action to visit Samsung's LED TV website. So, the creators drove traffic to the client.

Check out unexpected videos, VR experiences, AR/MR events, and IRL (in real time) stunts from all over the globe. Once you've passed an amazing video to a friend, who's passed it to a friend, you can easily see how they can quickly circle the world. Because of this instant global effect, campaigns, such as the UNICEF Tap Project, can influence millions and even change lives.

> *So I think the interactive world inherently has very different requirements in terms of messaging. It's a totally different animal than print. But at the same time, to me – and this is how I have always felt – a story is a story.* Matt Ziselman, Creative Director, Sapient[30]

After viewing some of the above-mentioned campaigns, you could think about creating messages that can go viral. To have a better idea of the kinds of campaigns that generate buzz, go to YouTube and type in the words "Viral Video Ads." Examine a few and see if any of them spark ideas for your current assignments or clients.

Today, many messages actually avoid sounding like advertising. Brands can offer interactive tutorials, experiential events, or engage in challenges. Many have their own online community and speak to the audience in the *vernacular*, or everyday language. Sometimes, if consumers aren't happy with the brand, they answer back, not necessarily as a quiet complaint.

Understanding when buzz goes wrong

Consumers use the Internet to vent or create parodies. They may want to share a frustrating experience, point out brand flaws, or get satisfaction instead of being dismissed by a company representative. Brands must be aware of the possible repercussions of their actions. Disgruntled customers today don't just tell their friends. They tell the world. Although the following story is mentioned in Chapter 5, it's worth sharing here because of its relevance. An original song about a Taylor guitar damaged by United Airlines handlers became a YouTube video hit when it was performed by the injured party: Canadian Dave Carroll and other members of the Sons of Maxwell band. The negative press damaged the airline's reputation. You can still see the "United Breaks Guitars" story and video on YouTube with more than 22 million views.

You've probably already seen consumer-created parodies of commercials and political issues on YouTube, www.jibjab.com, and www.funnyordie.com. The point is if you have an online presence, be prepared for an online response. It could range from admiration to possible assault. This is why most large firms have specialists who track consumer comments by listening in on blogs, posts, videos, and so on.

As a marketer, it's not just about creating inspiring content, videos, live installations, and edutainment. It's about connecting with your audience at multiple *touchpoints* and engaging them with interactivity that's rewarding.

> *What can this campaign do to get attention? Rather than what kind of ad can I do for Dominos?* Craig Miller, Creative Director, Craig Miller Creative[31]

Interactive content develops a consumer-facing culture to engage audiences with brands. They can be invited to show their loyalty as brand advocates in many ways, including via TikTok challenge participation, shares, and reviews. As you develop these types of campaigns, consider the following:

1. Know the creative goal.
2. Decide the ultimate experience.
3. Show the audience how the technology works.
4. Keep the experiential campaigns on course; being creative isn't enough.
5. Expand the interactions for myriad channels and platforms.
6. Create device-appropriate interactions.
7. Interrupt and surprise your target where they are: virtually and IRL.
8. Make it unique and exciting.

In Advice from the Pros 4.1, Peter Sena II presents three effective, digital writing tips that are instantly applicable.

 ADVICE FROM THE PROS 4.1 Three digital writing tips from Peter Sena II

1 Online writing is a digital storybook, where brands should focus on telling stories and creating experiences that fit their audiences.

2 Writing successful copy online is all about filtering out the noise and tuning into the channel.

3 Digital content has to focus on developing a meaningful connection with the consumer. Without engagement you could just as easily use *lorum ipsum* (*"Greeked in"* or fake language) as your content.[32]

Messages read differently in different venues. What sounds natural in one medium may sound awkward in another. Consider where your audience is encountering the message. If you plan on reaching the same audience in a different channel or platform, think about how the message "translates."

Charlie Hopper, principal at Young & Laramore explained, "You can't think of the writing without thinking of how and where and when people will encounter it. The web has made it very relevant, but it's all in context."[33] He continued:

> *You have to think about what order people are reading it, where they're entering it, where they're exiting, what little stations you give them to get in and out, and that's why the design is very relevant. Because like it or not, your writing is part of a great deluge of words and thoughts and images, not even just in an advertising context, in any context these days. Even if you send an e-mail, don't send a long e-mail. Break it up. Put a little bit up at the top and introduce it with something relevant and deliver your message and get it out.*[34]
>
> *Tweet. Learning to be relevant and humorous and interesting (and retweetable!) in 280 characters is a great exercise. Besides, it's a fun way to meet strangers without having to make eye contact or think about how you're dressed.* Charlie Hopper, Principal, Young & Laramore[35]

Using apps to solve problems

For years, IKEA has designed fun, unexpected campaigns that thrilled audiences with unexpected rewards. For example, in the fall of 2009, to promote its new store in Malmö, Sweden, IKEA used Facebook's popular function "the Tag" to create a viral campaign via social media. The "IKEA Facebook Tag" campaign developed a Facebook page for store manager Gordon Gustavsson. It displayed 12 rooms decorated with IKEA furnishings in his photo album. The first person to "tag" an item won it for free. People all over the world begged for new pictures to be uploaded so they could try again if they missed out the first time. People showed off what they won on their profile pages. The word spread via newsfeeds and links people sent to their friends and followers. The word about free IKEA products spread quickly.

In 2022, it launched an app using AI and VR technology, IKEA Kreativ, to allow consumers to see IKEA furniture in their homes. In addition to virtually browsing showrooms to consider galleries of design ideas, they could see how perfectly scaled 3D images would look in their own rooms. They could see if the sofa was too small or the bookshelf was too big. Then, they could select what worked, save the items, and pick them up at the store or arrange for delivery. It made the problem of proportional accuracy nonexistent. In other words, it found the pain point and offered a quick fix.

Designing games to recruit, train, and retain staff

Recruiting games aren't new. In the early 2000s, the New Zealand Army created a highly successful and affordable game as a recruiting tool. Today, companies are using interactive recruiting more frequently and in novel ways. For example, in the hospitality industry, Marriott International developed an online game as a recruiting tool. Based on different aspects of hotel service, the game allowed prospective employees to see how specific areas worked. So, they could "work" in the kitchen and discover that there weren't enough croutons for the Caesar salad, or that the budget was too tight to replace a nonworking oven. The virtual challenges let recruits see how they would measure up as they solve various problems. They also learned how a particular department operated to see if they were interested in pursuing a career there.

In the pharmaceutical field, the Siemens AG unit bought the game *Plantville* because it empowered players to act as managers for different companies, including a bottling plant, a vitamin manufacturer, or a train-building facility.

Other games that focus on time-management assignments would be particularly suitable as a recruiting or training tool for hair, nail, or tanning salons; event planning businesses; fitness or yoga centers; design studios; and other service-focused entities.[36]

In addition to recruiting and training, gamification can also be used for retention. In 2021, Formaposte, a postal service in France introduced Jeu Facteur Academy to reduce staff attrition. The app allowed curious, prospective employees to see what a postal worker's daily life included. Those who found the job exciting applied. Instead of losing workers, Formaposte easily retained them, converting the dropout rate to 8% from 25%.[37] Why? Because new employees could experience the job before applying for it.

As you start developing interactive experiences, don't limit yourself to what has been done. Think about how you can continue, as well as innovate new kinds of consumer engagement. Refer to the Interactive writing checklist (Checklist 4.2) to perfect your writing skills to further engage the audience.

CHECKLIST 4.2 Interactive writing checklist

To become familiar with immersive and experiential technology here are several steps that will increase your digital concepting and writing skills. Take a moment and review this list:

1 Plunge into immersive technology.

   a Learn by doing. Become a participant.

   b Deconstruct what enticed you to participate.

   c Analyze the relationship between the interactivity and the brand.

2 Become an investigative reporter.

   a Speak to the innovators. Ask digital creative talent about their work.

   b Collect resources and AR/VR/MR examples.

   c Dig for innovative answers. Be tireless in your pursuit of novel knowledge.

3 Study must-share, immersive engagement.

   a Look at the technology.

   b Consider new uses and applications.

   c Create, don't wait for new ideas.

Reviewing experiential writing

Enough cannot be said about stretching your creative, strategic, and immersive-focused skills. Look beyond everyday use of each medium and think about how you could apply it in a novel way. Also consider how you could connect one channel or platform to another, engage the audience, and create interactivity. Every campaign and each piece of content has to solve a marketing challenge and fulfill a creative direction. It has to be easy to understand and hard to forget. Also, look at the most mundane assignments and strive to find breakthrough ideas that deliver targeted messages in a unique way. That's the beauty of technology. There are fewer executional limitations. That allows you to free your mind and think like a child. Let your work be unpredictable. Unanticipated. Unexpected. Go on. Be bold. Be outrageous. Even be irreverent. Don't say, "Oh, that can't be done." Instead say, "Here's a great idea. Let's figure out how to do."

Be sure to review the Experiential writing checklist (Checklist 4.3) to stay on track when developing campaigns that include exciting, experiential components.

CHECKLIST 4.3 Experiential writing checklist

1 Review successful experiential campaigns.

2 Collect those that intrigued you.

3 Look for a unique way to engage the audience.

4 Check that the experience fits the brand and target.

5 Consider how you integrate experiences into products, such as technology-embedded furniture.

6 Offer incentives for consumers to share it.

7 Use branded games as inspirations.

8 Ask how AI and immersive technology can solve a consumer's problem.

9 Focus on making all interactions consumer-facing and user-friendly.

10 Be sure to integrate brand's end goals into all engagement.

Creative experiential strategy and writing exercises

Exercise 1: What experiential strategy could you develop for a local business?

Choose your favorite gym, pizza shop, restaurant, or discount chain. Let your audience be college students. Then, plan an unexpected and entertaining experience. How would you execute it? For example, could any of these work?

- A live, interactive installation to complete in teams playing against fitness buffs, athletes, or virtual participants.

- A mixed-reality experience to participate in a live sporting event, such as playing against a superstar athlete in your favorite sport? Win an Olympic 100 metres gold medal, outshoot a basketball player, score a hole-in-one on the golf course, etc.

- Create an AR app for a pizza shop. If they discover a slice in designated locations, such as a popular park, sports arena, pedestrian-only retail center, etc., they can get a coupon and claim it.

- An app to make the weirdest sandwich combination.

Exercise 2: Find one experiential campaign that you loved or shared.

- ▪ What was so compelling about it?

- ▪ How could you modify it for a brand you love?

- ▪ How would you get the word out?

- ▪ Create one social media post, one interactive video, and one YouTube video or TikTok challenge to promote it.

Notes

1. https://buckstarter.com/ (accessed May 4, 2022).
2. https://rockcontent.com/blog/interactive-media/ (accessed June 1, 2022).
3. https://instapage.com/blog/interactive-ads (accessed May 18, 2022).
4. https://www.masterclass.com/articles/experiential-marketing#5-types-of-experiential-marketing (accessed June 3, 2022).
5. https://www.saadialkouatli.com/work/starhunt/ (accessed May 1, 2022).
6. https://sidlee.com/en/work/rock-the-vote/2020/build-the-vote (accessed October 11, 2022).
7. https://www.adamenfroy.com/advertising-platforms (accessed June 17, 2022).
8. https://sidlee.com/en/work/protect-our-winters/2019/fact-avalanche (accessed June 23, 2022).
9. Craig Miller, personal correspondence, April 18, 2022.
10. https://blog.hubspot.com/marketing/creative-pop-up-events (accessed June 3, 2022).
11. https://musebycl.io/sports/chipotle-smashed-through-ice-stanley-cup-quarterfinal (accessed May 27, 2022).
12. https://www.oculus.com/blog/unleash-your-creativity-through-vr-art/ (accessed May 25, 2022).
13. https://www.oculus.com/experiences/quest/3106117596158066/?intern_source=blog&intern_content=unleash-your-creativity-through-vr-art (accessed May 25, 2022).
14. https://yandl.com/brands/brine/mobile-games (accessed September 16, 2022).
15. Peter Sena II, personal communication, February 1, 2011.
16. https://theescapepod.com/work/wheat-thins/ (accessed December 8, 2022).
17. Sheena Brady, personal communication, December 3, 2022.
18. https://yandl.com/case-studies/sg-2020 (accessed August 8, 2022).
19. Vinny Warren, personal communication, December 16, 2022.
20. https://play.google.com/store/apps/details?id=com.starhunt.app (accessed May 1, 2022).
21. Matt Ziselman, personal communication, January 30, 2009.
22. Grace Wright, personal communication, February 12, 2009.

23. Grace Wright, personal communication, February 12, 2009.
24. Grace Wright, personal communication, February 12, 2009.
25. Grace Wright, personal communication, February 12, 2009.
26. Grace Wright, personal communication, February 12, 2009.
27. Grace Wright, personal communication, February 12, 2009.
28. Grace Wright, personal communication, February 12, 2009.
29. Rob Reilly, personal communication, December 15, 2008.
30. Matt Ziselman, personal communication, January 30, 2009.
31. Craig Miller, personal correspondence, April 18, 2022.
32. Peter Sena II, personal communication, November 10, 2022.
33. Charlie Hopper, personal communication, November 15, 2021.
34. Charlie Hopper, personal communication, November 15, 2021.
35. Charlie Hopper, personal communication, November 15, 2021.
36. Alexandra Berzon, "Enough With 'Call of Duty,' Answer the Call in Room 417," *Wall Street Journal*, June 6, 2011, B1, B7.
37. https://www.spiceworks.com/hr/recruitment-onboarding/articles/gamification-in-recruitment-all-you-need-to-know/ (accessed October 29, 2022).

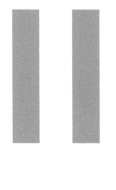

Copywriting for Three Platforms: 1) Video, 2) Audio, 3) Print, plus Cross-platform Campaigns

5 The Persuasive Word

Strategy ABCs: Audience, Benefits, and Creative Briefs

"Having a clear vision of what it is that you are heading for, and know it when you see it and dismiss it when you don't see it, is really, really important. Just think from the outset about what it is that you're writing because writing is not an accident."

Benazhir Maratuech, Director, Social Media, VML[1]

In this chapter, you'll examine a campaign's creative starting point: the strategy. You'll take an up-close look at the creative brief, which acts as the campaign's directional guide. You'll analyze the structure and function of the creative brief; see how it drives the strategy; and find out how it's based on several key aspects, including market research, consumer insights, specific objectives, and product positioning.

You'll also learn how to create effective media intersections, or the best places for your message to collide with the consumer. In no time, you'll grasp how to use these "collision venues" or *touchpoints* to change or reinforce

Content and Copywriting: The Complete Toolkit for Strategic Marketing,
Second Edition. Margo Berman.
© 2024 Margo Berman. Published 2024 by John Wiley & Sons Ltd.
Companion website: www.wiley.com/go/contentandcopywriting

consumers' impression of the brand. You'll see how selecting the right tactics (specific distribution vehicles, like online ads or mobile messages) help propel your message to the targeted audience.

In addition, you'll realize that creating a two-way conversation with consumers can result in an unexpected backlash. That happens when consumers share their feelings (good and bad) about the brand. You'll quickly recognize that being able to analyze your audience through various means like VALS will help you create authentic and credible messages.

You'll soon comprehend the difference between primary and secondary audiences, be able to identify them, and know why you need to consider both. You'll gain insight into why some agencies copy test (ask consumers their opinion of ad messages) and some still conduct focus groups, surveys, mall interceptions, and other means of consumer research, discussed later in the chapter. Finally, you'll be reminded of the importance of focusing on the benefit in your main idea. So, let's start looking at strategy right now.

Thinking about strategy first

Every advertising campaign needs a specific objective, a clear message, a target audience, and a *strategy*. The strategy is the overall creative direction of a campaign, which is determined by the account and creative teams. They work together to develop an underlying solution that addresses a specific consumer benefit or need, clarifies the product or service, or solves a brand's marketing challenge. The strategy acts like a compass and allows the agency to double-check that the campaign direction is on-course. For example, if the agreed-upon strategy was to show the whitening power of a detergent and the ad talked about a special two-for-one offer, then the message was off-strategy. It should be highlighting the whitening ability, not the price.

How does each agency decide the strategy? First, it conducts research to gain consumer insights. What does the audience want or need? How can this product deliver a solution? What is the benefit or reward for the consumer to make this purchase? The agency team looks to answer these and other questions and to gain a deeper understanding of consumers and how they think. What they value? What's important to them? What solution the product offers? Why should they choose this product and not another?

The agency team uses the creative brief to answer these and other specific questions in order to develop a Creative Strategy Statement to steer the campaign. The account team always thinks about the big picture, concentrates on the overall strategic direction, and looks for long-term creative solutions in its messaging. To gain greater insight into the creative-problem-solving process, we'll start by examining the elements of a *creative brief*. Then, we'll see how it serves as an outline for the campaign *strategy*, or basic creative destination.

But, before we get to the brief, we should take a look at how much of this strategic thinking has been changed over the years by technology and consumer behavior. Starting in 1900, when N.W. Ayer first introduced campaigns to fulfill the advertisers' marketing objectives,[2] agencies used to work in this way:

1. Brief
2. Creative strategy
3. Concept
4. Execution

First, the brief was created based on client input, market research, consumer insights, advertising objectives, product positioning (in the mind of the consumer), competitors, product's uniqueness, tactics, main message, and so on. Then, the strategy was created based on the brief, a main concept was developed from the strategy, and the concept was executed. Today, marketers are thinking about the execution as they're creating the brief. Why?

Because the advertising isn't just about the concept; it's also about where the message and consumer intersect. These *media intersections* are *touchpoints*, which we discussed earlier. As a reminder, these are places where the campaign messages are seen by the target. Another key point is that consumers now participate in delivering the brand's message. They do this through consumer-created content and user-generated content. The difference between these two is that user-generated content are messages developed by people who use the product, not just the general public. With so many people involved in social media, like Facebook, LinkedIn, X (formerly Twitter), and Instagram, consumers can continue a dialog between themselves and the brand. Or, they can initiate an open conversation among members of their online community.

Consumers can share their opinions, photos, videos, and even their own impression of the brand through self-created commercials. This puts the power of selling a brand's message in the hands of the consumer, without anyone's permission. Marketers must be careful because once a negative impression is circulated online, it's difficult to change it. Advertisers have to protect their brands' images. There are several ways they attempt to do this. Notice the word "attempt," because it's not that simple to achieve. First, they need to constantly monitor their social media sites. Second, they need to immediately address consumer complaints. Third, they need to be willing to face harsh criticism in a graceful and responsive way.

Now, unhappy consumers can create damaging user-generated content. One unforgettable 2008 United Airlines incident was globally publicized online. While the band Sons of Maxwell was on tour, the musicians witnessed the careless handling of their $3,500 guitar by the United Airlines' baggage crew. After several unsuccessful attempts to have the airline resolve the problem, the band created a video detailing the event. It posted it on YouTube where it instantly went viral. Unlike years ago, companies today that are nonresponsive to customer complaints have to face irate, public backlash. Consumers are no longer going to sit idly by when they can broadcast their poor customer service complaints. Smart marketers are wise to address problems immediately. Most likely, that would be any brand's best corporate strategy.

Taking that one step forward, Crispin Porter + Bogusky, once named "Agency of the Decade" by *Advertising Age*, usually starts with the end in mind: press coverage. Creative talents must write a jaw-dropping press release before they begin any creative conceptualization. They must present what the press will write about.

Then, they have to find a way to make that happen. The campaign's "big idea" must transcend medium and format. It must be so powerful it cannot be ignored. In thinking about the reaction to their work, their strategic thinking teams include cognitive anthropologists (account managers), creatives, digital technologists (developers), and anyone else who would like to work on the campaign. It's a collaborative effort in which everyone shares ownership, with credit lists of possibly 75 people.

Now, let's get back to the function and format of the brief, which is more commonly used at agencies, and how that guides the strategic direction.

Examining the brief: An up-close look

Although agencies differ in their brief formats, most include the same key information. The templates (Templates 5.1, Templates 5.2) may be used for your briefs. These force you to determine the audience, product competitors, consumer opinions, product uniqueness, and other critical areas.

We will look at the basic or shorter brief (Templates 5.1) and the more expanded, detailed brief (Templates 5.2).

You can see there are only eight parts to this shorter, basic brief. This will give you a good start in your overall thinking. However, before you can begin outlining your creative direction, you should go through and complete the longer brief (Templates 5.2). Be sure to answer every one of the questions and fill in each answer specifically.

The brief is a series of questions that need to be carefully answered before developing a solid campaign strategy. First, you need to fully understand all the terminology. Next, we'll examine some of the words used in Templates 5.2.

The brand is advertising to say something to (VERB – persuade, convince, inform, educate) the audience (SPECIFIC CONSUMERS) that this (PRODUCT, SERVICE, OR BRAND) will (STATE THE BENEFIT) because (FEATURES THAT EXPLAIN WHY AUDIENCE SHOULD BELIEVE IT. THIS ACTS AS A SUPPORT STATEMENT).

TEMPLATES 5.1 The shorter creative brief

1 What is the *brand's character* or personality?

2 Why does the brand *want to advertise*?

3 Who is the *audience*?

4 What do they (audience members) *currently think*?

5 What do you *want them to think*?

6 *Why should they buy* this product/service?

7 What is the *big message* you want them to know?

8 What *kinds of tactics* (specific ad/promotional techniques) do you want to use? For example, do you want to use interactive components, out-of-home messages, print ads, transit (buses, subways, taxis, etc.), social media, immersive technology, direct mail, or other vehicles?

TEMPLATES 5.2 The creative brief

1 Why does the brand *want to advertise*? What does it want to accomplish? (Use this template.)

Creative Strategy Statement template

To_____ _____ that_____ will_____ because _____
  (verb)   (audience)   (brand) (benefit)   (support statement / reason why)

Example

To convince fastidious moms that Tide will get out the toughest stains because of its enzyme-fighting formula.

2 Who is the *audience*?

  a *Demographics* – Provides insight into audience by their age, income, education, gender, occupation (employment status), etc.

  b *Psychographics* – Examines how audience lives. Think lifestyle, attitude, personality, behavior (like brand loyalty), and value (what's important to them). (VALS and OBSERVATIONAL RESEARCH. See section on "Gaining deeper audience insight through VALS and observational research.")

    c *Geographics* – Explores where (location and kind of setting: urban, suburban, rural) audience lives.

3 Who are the *brand's competitors*?

4 What do they (audience members) *currently think* (about the brand)?

5 What do you *want them to think* (about the brand)? (FOCUS ON CONSUMER BENEFIT. What the product does for the end user.)

6 *Why should they buy* this brand (product or service)? Clearly answer: "WHY BUY?"

7 What is the *big message* you want them to know? (THINK SLOGAN.)

8 Determine what the *brand's positioning* is. Do you want consumers to say it's safe, cool, fun, reliable, etc.? (WHAT IS THE BRAND KNOWN FOR?)

9 What is the brand's *USP*? (UNIQUE SELLING POINT OR PROPOSITION?) What separates this brand from its competitors?

10 What is the *brand's character* or personality?

    a What kind of personality does the brand have?

    b Who would the brand be as a famous person?

    c Who would that famous person be in relation to the consumer? (A coach, friend, uncle, sister, neighbor, dad?)

    d How would that person (friend, brother, boss) speak to the consumer? How would a coach speak to team members? CHOOSE AN ADJECTIVE. A coach would be authoritative, encouraging, concerned, etc. This is the brand's *TONE OF VOICE*. (Use it in #11.)

11 What is the *tone of voice*? (HOW YOU SPEAK TO YOUR AUDIENCE: Choose an adjective. Refer to #10d.)

12 Who's speaking. What's the *point of view*? Which of the following?

    a The Brand: *Self-serving* – "We're number one."

    b The Consumer: *Testimonial* – "It really worked!"

    c The Conscience: *Emotional Blackmail* – "What happens if I don't do it?"

    d The Brand Icon: *Brand Stand* – "Magically Delicious!" (Keebler Elves)

13 What *kinds of tactics* (specific ad/promotional techniques) do you want to use? For example, do you want to use viral marketing, interactive online components, ambient messages, print ads, transit (buses, subways, taxis, etc.), new media, direct mail, or other vehicles?

14 Think about what kind of campaign will *generate press* and *create buzz*.

The creative strategy, as shown in Templates 5.2 is a deceptively simple formula that explains the broad direction of the campaign. Although it looks like an easy-to-develop sentence, the challenge is to write it in the most descriptive and accurate language, specifically relating to the brand. Just fill in the blanks. Use the capped words in parentheses as explanatory guides.

The point here is to explain in detail why the brand is advertising; however, you don't want to just say "to increase sales" or "to build awareness" because that could apply to any brand. Those statements are too general. This is where you want to differentiate your brand from any other. You must answer this general question in a very specific way: What do you want this campaign to do for the brand? Don't just rush in with the first obvious answer. Look deeper into the audience profile you'll outline before proceeding. Who are they? Why are you targeting them? What benefit will they derive from this product or service? What features explain why they should pick this brand and not one of its competitors?

The trick to writing a great brief is in drilling down the information. Think of it as if you're a chef and you're reducing the ingredients in a pan to create a sauce. You must reduce the information down to its core essence. This one sentence must act like a one-line review if this were a restaurant. Then, the campaign or "menu" is what will attract diners to taste the food or brand.

Gaining deeper audience insight through VALS and observational research

Two other important terms appeared in Templates 5.2 under "Who is the *audience*," in section 2b, "Psychographics." These were *VALS* and *observational research*. VALS connects consumer personality traits to future purchasing behaviors. VALS stands for Values, Attitudes, and Lifestyles and was created in the 1970s by SRI International, a research company, in Menlo, California. VALS market segmentation places audiences into easy-to-refer-to, shopping-prediction categories. Observational research is a method of collecting consumer information by seeing targeted audiences firsthand in a natural, everyday setting like at home rather than learning about them through their answers in a focus group. So, instead of asking them what magazines they read, researchers can see them usually lying around their homes. This sidesteps a common consumer desire to impress others in the focus group or tell researchers what they think they want to hear.

> *We use the creative brief all the time. Carolyn Hadlock, Principal, Executive Creative Director, Young & Laramore*[2]

These are just two of many ways to analyze audiences. There are target groups by age-group titles. Some of the dates vary depending on the source, but you can get a quick idea of the various target groups here. These labels include the Baby Boomers (born between 1946 and 1964); the Generation X or "Gen X" (born between 1965 and 1976); the Gen Y or "Millennials," "Gen M,"

"Generation Next," or "Generation Y" (born between 1977 and 1994); the Gen Z or "Net Generation," "Internet Generation," "Digital Natives," or the "Verge Generation" (born between 1995 and 2002); and "Generation Alpha," or the "New Silent Generation" (born between 2002–2020). These groups have an attitudinal likeness or similar perspective. Even though it's unfair to categorize any individual, researchers will create a one-word nickname, or short expression, to act as a short cut to identify a group. For example, the Baby Boomers are the "never get old" group. Gen X are "independent." Gen Y are team players. Gen Z are "digital savvy." Generation Alpha believes each person is "unique."

There are also ethnic groups, which you reach through their cultural similarities. Plus, there are interest target groups, which you speak to through their common interests, like technology buffs, wine lovers, conscientious environmentalists, and so on.

VALS, on the other hand, allows marketers to predict consumers' future shopping behavior by considering different buying motivational categories based on consumer attitudes and values. The first VALS, or VALS 1, which explored consumers' lifestyles and buying motivations, was later refined to reflect consumers' ability to pay for products they desired. The revised VALS, or VALS 2, blended demographics into the mix and considered income, education, and health. VALS 2 answered the question of the strength of consumers' buying power. Today, all the categories are used to reflect different audience's lifestyles, buying motivations, and purchasing power. Let's compare the two different VALS, one after the other, as they are so clearly explained in *Ads, Fads and Consumer Culture*.[3] After this, we'll compare these to VALS 3 (Useful Info 5.3).

VALS 1: From lowest to highest income

Group I: Need-driven consumers – Financially challenged.

1. *Survivors* – People on low incomes and older people, those scraping by.
2. *Sustainers* – Young and clever with a desire to succeed.

Group II: Outer-directed consumers – Representative in attitude, geography, and financial status as "Middle America;" concerned about other people's opinions of them; want to leave a positive impression.

3. *Belongers* – Conservative traditionalists, who long for yesterday, and stick to what's tried and true, rather than experimenting with something new.
4. *Emulators* – Eager, status-driven, and competitive, these are up-and-comers on the path to financial success.

5. *Achievers* – Have reached their financial and material goals, community leaders.

Group III: Inner-directed consumers – Make purchases from their own desires, not to impress others.

6. *I-Am-Me's* – Young, self-focused freethinkers who do their own thing.

7. *Experientials* – More individualistic naturalists who seek self-improvement and personal growth.

8. *Societally conscious* – Environmentalists interested in global conservation and consumer product protection.

9. *Integrateds* – Self-assured and confident, less responsive to advertising messages, may be unintentional trendspotters because of their good taste.

VALS 2

Starting at the lowest income group, and moving to the highest, we start with the Strugglers (Survivors in VALS 1) and end up with the Actualizers (Integrateds in VALS 1). Now there are only eight categories as follows:

1. *Strugglers* – Lowest income, those barely surviving financially.

2. *Makers* – High energy, lower income group who enjoy constructing things.

3. *Strivers* – Emulating Achievers without the income or skill set.

4. *Believers* – Like Fulfilleds with a lower income, conservatives who prefer name brands.

5. *Experiencers* – Avid shoppers, risk takers who relish unusual, novel, even whacky, items.

6. *Achievers* – Accomplished and structured, goal-oriented consumers whose purchases reflect their status.

7. *Fulfilled* – Financially stable, who value durable, functional products, and are receptive to new ideas.

8. *Actualizers* – Wealthy individuals who reached their personal goals, their purchases reflect their sophisticated taste.

VALS 3

A third VALS segmentation also breaks consumers into eight categories (with some different labels) and three groups. At the bottom of the financial ladder are the Survivors with limited resources and little creative innovation. In the top group are the opposite. These are Innovators with deep resources who are highly innovative. In the middle are these six groups that represent the primary buying motivations based on their (1) ideals, (2) achievements, and need for (3) self-expression. In each of the middle groups (numbers 2–7) are low- and high-income subsets. For example, the "Ideals" group has Thinkers (higher income) and Believers (lower income).

Group I: Survivors – Lowest income and lowest ability to innovate.

1. *Survivors* – Reluctant, brand-loyal shoppers, focus on needs not wants.

Group II: Ideals – Idealistic, inspired by moral principles and beliefs.

2. *Thinkers* – Informed and analytical, educated consumers who seek new knowledge, value structure, and appreciate durability (higher income).

3. *Believers* – Brand-loyal, predictable, conservative shoppers with deep moral values, a preference for anything familiar, strong community, and religious alliances (lower income).

Group III: Achievement – Goal-oriented, motivated by accomplishments.

4. *Achievers* – Committed to success and family values, driven by career and family goals, seek prestigious products that reflect social status, conservative, and risk averse (higher income).

5. *Strivers* – Status purchases demonstrate their need for approval, lack job skills to advance in the marketplace, have jobs not career positions (lower income).

Group IV: Self-expression – Stimulated by expressing themselves.

6. *Experiencers* – Young impulsive shoppers looking for the cool factor, attracted by novel and quirky items (higher income).

7. *Makers* – Enjoy being self-sufficient and making or building things themselves, more impressed with getting their money's worth than status purchases or luxury products (lower income).

Group V: Innovators – Highest income and ability to innovate.

8. *Innovators* – Strong self-image, upscale leaders, sophisticated shoppers.

The point of considering VALS categories before you begin writing is to try to actually picture your audience. To see them as people with specific lifestyles, attitudes, and different values, so you can speak to them in a way that singles them out. You want the readers or viewers to feel as if you're talking directly to them. Even if you don't have the category titles perfectly in your mind, you can at least have a strong sense of the audience's way of life. Always remember to remind yourself of your audience when looking at a brief and beginning every assignment.

In thinking about the audience, Teddy Brown, executive creative director at Planet Propaganda, explained that Taco Bell talks to a psychographic, not a demographic. He said:

> *So, it's really more about what this audience believes more than necessarily who they are. It's quite a broad target in general, so we spend more time talking about how this target audience acts and how they live their lives, than we do if they're male or female.*[4]

Review all the observational research and internalize the consumer insights provided to you by the account team. Ask questions to the account and research teams if you need audience clarification. The more clearly you understand your audience, the more effective your message will be. Writing just to explain product features won't drive anyone to make a purchase. But, writing to show what those features mean and how they can solve a problem or improve someone's life will. Ask yourself when you're about to create an ad in any product category what has or would compel you to buy it. Pay attention, whenever you buy anything, to your decision process. If you were skeptical at first, what did you see, hear, or read that swayed you?

It's this kind of thinking that is the backbone of the brief. It forces you to examine various aspects of marketing and fully understand the product's overall advertising goals, competitors, consumer beliefs, tactics, as well as its character, *tone of voice*, uniqueness, and main message. You need to consider everything when you're developing the campaign's direction and creative strategy.

---

i | **USEFUL INFO 5.3 VALS comparison by Margo Berman, starting with highest incomes on top**

The categories in all caps do not line up with VALS 1 groups. Subgroups are in italics. Notice that VALS 2 has no subgroups.

VALS 1	VALS 2	VALS 3	CAMPAIGNS
		High Resources and High Innovation	
9. Integrateds	8. Actualizers	8. Innovators	*Charitable causes, new approaches*
	7. FULFILLED		

VALS 1	VALS 2	VALS 3	CAMPAIGNS
Inner-directed		*Self-expression*	
8. Societally conscious			*Eco-friendly campaigns*
7. Experientials			*Sky diving, hiking,*
6. I-Am-Me's	6. Experiencers	7. Experiencers	*biking, exploring, etc.*
	5. MAKERS	6. MAKERS	*The Home Depot, Lowe's*
Outer-directed		*Achievement*	
5. Achievers	4. Achievers	5. Achievers	*Luxury items: Gucci, Dior*
4. Emulators	3. Strivers	4. Strivers	*Designers for less, T.J.Maxx, Marshalls*
3. Belongers			*Tried-and-true, reliable brands*
Need-driven		*Ideals-driven (higher income)*	
2. Sustainers	2. Believers	3. Thinkers	*Designers at deeper discounts: outlet malls*
1. Survivors	1. Strugglers	2. Believers (lower income)	*Walmart, Costco*
		Low Resources and Low Innovation	
		1. Survivors	*Goodwill, thrift shops*

Sheena Brady, commercial director/creative director, explained how important the brief is in reaching client objectives this way:

> *I think what the brief is, is what the client is trying to do. So that's going to have a direct impact on the work. Then we, as creative people, find the best way of creatively solving that problem. Without a brief, there's no way of knowing whether we're doing our job for the client.*[5]

Understanding secondary audience versus primary audience

In addition to the primary target who eventually buys the product, another audience should also be considered. This secondary audience is made up of the people who influence the primary audience. Those are the people who make the purchase and use the product. The secondary audience could be a friend, relative, business associate, mentor, or anyone who affects the buyers' purchasing decisions. According to Larry Percy, there are five different groups of people who influence purchasing decisions. They fall into the following "purchasing role" categories:

1. *Initiator:* person who first suggests buying the product or trying the service.

2. *Influencer:* someone who encourages or dissuades the buyer.

3. *Decider:* the actual person who makes the final decision on purchasing selections.

4. *Buyer:* the shopper who buys the item.

5. *User:* the person who ultimately uses the item or service.[6]

When creating a campaign, it's helpful to think about how the *tone of voice* could also speak to these groups, so they're impacted by the message. Also, when you're working on new product introductions, think about whether your audience members are early or late adapters. If they're the type of people who would wait online for hours to be one of the first consumers to buy the latest Nike or high-tech gadget, then you might entice them with a be-the-first-to-own kind of message. If they're late adapters, the people who wait until all the bugs are out of a new computer, a smartphone, a software, and so on, you might talk humorously about how this model has been "bug-proofed" with a digital exterminator.

Delving into consumer insights

There's more to understanding the consumer than psychographic VALS categories, primary and secondary audiences, and purchasing roles. There are also insights gleaned from observational and other types of consumer research. Here's a short list of some types of advertising-based research.

Focus groups provide information gathered from small groups of people placed together to review products and evaluate campaigns. Sometimes, one person dominates and drives the discussion, thereby "tainting" or influencing the opinion of others in the group.

Pre-testing (or *copy testing*) allows copy to be tested before it's released in an ad campaign. Subjects are asked to comment on myriad ad messages. Some questions might include:

1. Whether they'd seen comparable ads and/or would consider buying the product (overall ad appeal)?
2. What the audience's overall impressions were (general impressions)?
3. What they liked or disliked about the ad, whether it seemed to be cohesive or confusing (ad consistency)?
4. Whether they responded to the ad in an emotional way (ad emotional effect)?
5. How they might use the product (usage effect)?
6. Whether they'd talk to others about the ad?

Their responses are used to predict ad performance in these and other areas: (1) audience attention, (2) brand awareness, (3) purchase motivation, (4) emotional response, (5) ad recall, and (6) clarity of message.

Post-testing (or *ad-tracking*) evaluates the brand's performance by monitoring these and other results from the advertising campaign: (1) product/brand sales, (2) brand name recognition, (3) top-of-mind awareness, (4) unaided advertising awareness, (5) aided advertising message recall, (6) aided and unaided brand awareness, (7) brand preference (loyalty), (8) product adoption (usage), and (9) consumer opinion.

Mall interception reveals consumer opinions as they're going about their normal mall shopping. People are stopped randomly and asked to answer some questions.

Surveys indicate how consumers feel about the questions asked. Survey questions are designed to glean specific consumer insights. Often very lengthy surveys offer free products to the participants.

Digital anthropology shows consumers' online behavior, including which sites they visit, how long they stay; what items are purchased; which articles, podcasts, vodcasts are viewed and shared; and so on. Marketers are looking to understand how to communicate with online communities through "tribalization" studies.

Multiplatform (or *cross-platform*) *research* tracks which media consumers prefer to consume: television, radio, print, online, digital, and so on, and helps advertisers evaluate which platforms are the most effective communication vehicles.

Observational research (or *ethnography*) is conducted at consumers' natural settings, as they go about their everyday routines. The idea is to watch them in their own environment. It's easy to see the books or magazines they read. The kind of décor they prefer. The types of electronic gadgets they use. The brands they prefer, and so on. Understanding consumers' lifestyle is more than statistics. It's having a visual reference, an actual image of these people, so they're three-dimensionally real to the writer.

You also want to know how they feel about the brand and its competitors. Not only if they use it, but also if they do, why? And if not, why not? What do they really think about the product? If they don't like it, why not? What exactly don't they like about it? Having more insight into how consumers make buying decisions gives you more firing power so you'll hit your target with relevant messages. Think of your client's product as "your product." It will make your creative approach more personal. Ask yourself if you can answer these questions:

1. What do they like about "your product" (the one you're advertising)?
2. What do they like better about its competition?
3. What can you say to persuade them to choose "your product" the next time?
4. What haven't you mentioned before that could sway their decision?
5. How can you show them their personal benefits?
6. What need does it fulfill?
7. How does it enhance their lifestyle?
8. How can you differentiate "your product" in their eyes?

Most importantly, think like the consumer. Write that in big letters next to your computer. Before you create any promotional message, answer this: What would you need to hear to take action?

Realizing the importance of a benefit

There's no point in creating a vague campaign. The target audience wants to know why they should make a purchase. They need to find out how this brand will improve their lives, solve a problem, address a specific need, and so on. They don't have time to decipher a complicated message. Put a spotlight on your benefit or W-I-I-F-M ("What's in it for me?") and place it center stage.

The reason Apple sold so many iPhones and iPads is that the advertising shows how easy they are to use and how they can simplify owners' lives. All of the messages answer consumers' objections to learning new technology by demonstrating them in use. The ads don't just say, "Here's a cool new gadget." They make consumers feel confident that the devices are user-friendly and promise a quick-to-integrate learning curve. They remove any hesitancy consumers might have about using a new device.

Try to understand what problem your product or service solves or how it fits into your target audience's lifestyle. If you don't know why they should buy it or order it, your message will be meaningless and ineffective. You must give them an indisputable reason to buy. At the same time, your creative solution must also realize the brand's objectives for advertising. Remember, you want to avoid common reasons such as generating traffic or increasing name recognition. These two goals are not definitive enough. You should be able to encapsulate the campaign message in a short phrase. Think about famous slogans and how they zero in on one sticky idea. It's important to showcase product features; just don't forget to explain how they ultimately help the audience.

For example, Taco Bell's campaigns are usually product-focused and sometimes use exaggeration to drive home a product feature. In the "Volcano Nachos" spot, an actor's face was flaming and smoke was coming out of him to show the product was hotter than other menu items. The "Grande Quesadilla" spot showed a young, pregnant woman boarding a bus. Climbing on board right after her is a young guy with an equally big belly who makes a remark suggesting that she must have enjoyed her Taco Bell lunch as much as he did. The product promises to satisfy your hunger. Brown explained Taco Bell strategies like this:

> The thing with our product is "that new news drives the whole category." So, it must be newsworthy. It's always solving some sort of consumer need or problem. The point of difference is that our product stands out and is celebrated.
>
> The difference between brand marketing and product marketing is that our work is always food-centric. It's the product that inspires the brief, but the story is always centered around the food. In that bus stop spot it's all about the main message. I'm looking at a brief here that states: "the quesadilla that actually fills you up."[7]

Whenever you create a message, you must consider the target audience. See them as three-dimensional people, not just a general group with certain characteristics or identified by a VALS, demographic, psychographic, or cultural category. How would you speak to them one on one? What do they value? What would be your *tone of voice*? Your *point of view*? What would be the main benefit most important to them? If you begin by focusing on who's receiving your message, you'll be able to tell them what you want to in the most relevant way. In the next chapter, we'll talk about the strategies behind message development.

Creative strategy exercises

Exercise 1: Deconstructing the thinking behind the message

Part 1   Examine one long-running, multimedia campaign like CareerBuilder. com "Monkeys," Coke "Polar Bears," E-Trade "Talking Babies," Energizer "Bunny," and so on.

- a. Identify the main idea in the campaign.
- b. Decide the primary audience.
- c. Determine the key benefit.
- d. Analyze the main message.
- e. Identify the *tone of voice*.

Part 2   Now create another ad in the campaign, targeting the same audience, using the same *tone of voice*, and main campaign message. What other medium could you introduce? Could you create a new place to place a message to reach the audience? Could you use an ambient ad?

Part 3   Create a message for a different audience by using the same basic strategy. Where else would you run this message to reach this audience? How would you change the *tone of voice*?

Exercise 2: Where have you seen new messages?

Can you think of a new place to advertise besides luggage carousels, manhole covers, telephone wires, escalator steps, elevators, store floors, sidewalks, taxi tops, shopping bags, subway hand straps, and online? Think beyond traditional media. Consider an interactive vehicle, such as a billboard, a TV spot, an app, a live event, or a game.

Notes

1. Benazhir Maratuech, personal communication, February 17, 2022.
2. Carolyn Hadlock, personal communication, March 16, 2022.
3. Arthur Asa Berger, *Ads, Fads, and Consumer Culture: Advertising's Impact on American Character and Society* (Lanham, MD: Rowman & Littlefield, 2000), 84–89.

4. Teddy Brown, personal communication, December 14, 2022.
5. Sheena Brady, personal communication, December 3, 2022.
6. Larry Percy, *Strategies for Implementing Integrated Marketing Communications* (Oxford, UK: Butterworth-Heinemann, 2008), 252.
7. Teddy Brown, personal communication, December 14, 2022.

6 The Strategic Word
Strategy Categories

"I would say strategy is the art of planning creative solutions to reach a goal or overcome obstacles. It's the big picture at first but the beauty of it is in the details. A good strategy must always be accompanied by carefully crafted tactics because it's the life cycle of any project. Beginning and end."

Benazhir Maratuech, Director, Social Media, VML[1]

When you start working on creative solutions, you want them to be on-strategy and on-target. To do that, you'll need to constantly reexamine your concepts and double-check that you haven't veered off course. In this chapter, you'll learn how strategic thinking maximizes the impact of each message. This is especially true when the selected touchpoint is particularly relevant

Content and Copywriting: The Complete Toolkit for Strategic Marketing,
Second Edition. Margo Berman.
© 2024 Margo Berman. Published 2024 by John Wiley & Sons Ltd.
Companion website: www.wiley.com/go/contentandcopywriting

to that audience. That means if your target is online, you as a writer should have a clear understanding of what's important to your audience (what they value), how they access the Internet, and what they need to hear to respond to your ad.

In the following pages, you'll start to think about developing a strategy that specifically targets your audience. You'll first consider the six basic strategy categories. Then, you'll explore the 50 different strategies you can add to your creative toolkit. These include strategies (strategic-based concepts) that highlight the consumer, product, and savings, plus messages that deliver emotions, stories (storytelling), and interactivity (or audience engagement).

You'll also discover, or possibly review, common needs that are divided into easy-to-refer-to categories and charts by Jib Fowles, Abraham Maslow, and others. In addition, you'll investigate different types of product positioning. You'll begin to consider how to clearly position your brand "in the mind of the consumer." So, consumers perceive the brand as you want them to.

You'll be reminded to (1) feature the *unique selling point* (USP), so your target knows what makes your brand different from its competitors, (2) create a sticky main message (*slogan*), (3) develop a distinctive and appropriate *tone of voice*, (4) consider competitors' messages, and (5) be selective about your *tactics*. Now, we'll begin by examining the relationship between strategic thinking and relevant *touchpoints*.

Using strategic thinking strengthens each touchpoint

Be sure you think through all the questions in the brief for even a one-time promotion. Remember every consumer touchpoint can be a breakthrough to that consumer. Touchpoints are every place your audience sees your ad. These include out-of-home messages, online banner and interactive ads, TVs spots, floor and shelf talkers, print ads, social media posts, escalator steps, and so on.

So, where do you begin with your strategic thinking after you've examined the brief, reviewed the media vehicles, considered audience touchpoints, studied consumer insights, and analyzed current audience trends? You must consider where and how you'll be speaking to your audience. Knowing where your message will intersect with the consumer's life is critically important. This is how VALS can help because it focuses on the psychographic profile of the audience: how they live their lives. Also, think about the audience's demographics. Then, think about the most effective campaign touchpoints. For example, for an interactive text messaging campaign, you'd consider a younger, more connected audience who might be I-Am-Me's or Experientials. For a do-it-yourself, home improvement campaign, you'd consider Makers and maybe also Innovators who had sufficient income to purchase the exact materials they want to create what they imagine.

In thinking about your strategy, today you must evaluate your audience's possible participation. An interactive dialogue on a blog or social media channel would not be approached the same way as a traditional, one-way TV message. For example, an out-of-home advertising communication could include an audience directive. It could tell viewers to dial a number and text a message, download a free, mp3 song, or grab a photo of a moving menu item to get it free at a nearby fast-food place. The last one is what McDonald's did on a London billboard. The interaction was both fun and rewarding, especially for surprised consumers.

It has become more and more clear that interactivity and engagement strengthen consumers' bond with a brand. The more vested the target market is, the more loyalty the audience feels toward that brand. However, here's one note of caution. You don't want to create interactivity for its own sake. You want it to reward the participant. After people are engaged, they must discover a benefit, be entertained, or at least have fun in the process.

When we discussed interactivity in Chapter 4, we looked at some of the most successful uses of audience engagement. For now, realize that every message must be relevant and resonate with authenticity. Gimmicks insult the audience. People don't have time for useless information and resent having their energy wasted. Your creative strategy, regardless of where it is executed, should zoom in to the needs of that particular audience and make those people feel as if they're having a personal, one-on-one conversation with the brand.

Now, we'll examine different types of strategies that you can consider using when you're developing your next campaign.

Analyzing types of strategies

There are many ways to portray the product and address the audience. What you want to do is create a message with legs, one that can keep going and *spin out* or work across all platforms. Think back on some campaigns you've seen that have become ingrained in your memory. Then, examine the strategies below and see which one(s) they fit into. Some brands use several strategies at the same time. This is because each strategy targets a different market or drives the audience to take a different action. Let's look at a few of these.

First there's PEDIGREE® the brand that used three separate strategies:

1. *Charity or cause-related strategy* with its "Adoption Drive: Dogs Rule" campaign and its "Help Us Help Dogs" line.

2. *Quality strategy* with its healthy ingredients message and humorous, anthropomorphic campaign.

3. *Benefit strategy* with its reminder of how dogs enhance our lives campaign and its "We Love Dogs" slogan.

Each strategy had its own goal. In the first, the cause-related strategy, PEDI-GREE® wanted people to go to their local pet shelter and adopt, as well as to buy PEDIGREE® dog food because a portion of the proceeds went to aiding shelter dogs find homes. For the second quality strategy, it told dog owners to feed their pets PEDIGREE® because of the healthy ingredients. In the third benefit strategy, it reminded dog lovers how their pets were an integral part of their lives and reminded them about the joy of "pet parenting."

Taco Bell also used two strategies concurrently. These were messages that addressed (1) *abundance* and products that featured (2) *value*. With the *abundance strategy*, Taco Bell presented larger, more filling menu items like the Grande Quesadilla. For the *value strategy*, it featured items at special savings. Most of these are shown on TV and then posted on-site in the windows of the restaurant on large, colorful posters. Each strategy targets a different group. The abundance strategy is talking to those with a larger appetite. The value strategy is singling out the consumer looking for savings, like the coupon shopper. Taco Bell directly asked consumers, "Why pay more?" in an earlier campaign slogan. (Read more about Taco Bell in Chapters 5, 7, 10, and 13.)

According to Teddy Brown, who once led the creative for the Taco Bell account, value advertising is critically important in a down economy:

> *The advertising is becoming more scrutinized, and we could see where this year (2009) was taking us. So, we took a look at all of our work that was going to run in the back half of the year. We wanted to make sure that it was strong enough and retail-focused enough. It's very difficult in this climate when there's this sort of notion that America's on sale.*[2]

He added that copywriters on the Taco Bell account write 1,000 TV commercials each year. Yes, 1,000. Two hundred are tested. That means they're shown to consumers for their opinion of and reaction to the spots. Finally, 40 are actually aired. Most brands don't require the development of such an inordinately high number of scripts; however, Taco Bell wants to find the most effective spots and testing is one way to do so.[3]

Most brands focus on one strategy for each campaign. As a copywriter, you would benefit from identifying the strategy behind every campaign you encounter. This will strengthen your analytical skills and heighten your creative awareness. Make it a habit to actively evaluate all messages, so you can identify the (1) target audience, (2) campaign strategy, and (3) *universal truth*. In Chapter 7, we will discuss universal truths in detail, and review them again in Chapters 11, 12, 13, and 14. However, let us clarify the term here. A universal truth is an instantly understood statement that is accepted as fact regardless of gender, age, or nationality. Here are a few examples: (1) Hard work pays off. (2) Never underestimate your opponent. (3) He who owns the gold rules the world. (4) You can't concentrate when you're hungry. Each time you hear or see an advertising message, look for the universal truth. Because it helps to quickly deliver the underlying meaning, making the ad more relevant to the audience.

Now, let's take a look at the strategy list. It will give you a library of strategic directions before you begin any creative assignment.

> *Positioning is an organized system for finding windows in the mind.*
> Al Ries and Jack Trout[4]

Keeping a handy reference list of strategies

As you review the list, realize that new strategies can be added at any time. If you find another category, add it to this list. Remember, the strategy you choose should be so easy to understand that it can be reduced down to a few words as shown in the next few sections. It should be so simple that the moment you see the definition, you understand the strategy. Take a few moments to log onto YouTube and view as many of the spots as possible. That will give you an instantly applicable frame of reference.

Notice that the 50 strategies fit into six basic categories: (1) *Consumer-focused*, which are campaigns that show the W-I-I-F-Ms or how the consumer benefits from using the product; (2) *Product-focused*, which are campaigns that showcase the product's features; (3) *Savings as the Star*, which are campaigns that emphasize price; (4) *Emotional Approach*, which are campaigns that involve consumers' emotions; (5) *Storytelling*, which are campaigns that tell the audience about the product in a story; and (6) *Audience Engagement*, which are campaigns that encourage consumer participation.

Consumer-focused

1. *Benefit strategy* – This explains how the product will help you. It highlights your W-I-I-F-M and answers your question "What's in it for me?" like the iPhone and iPad campaigns. They all show how the devices make consumers' lives easier whatever they're doing: phoning, texting, or surfing the Internet; storing images, music, and files; reading books,

researching online, or evaluating information; sharing images, and so on. The benefit could even be social status, a sense of individuality, or even a whatever-makes-you-feel-good or cool benefit.

2. *Before-and-after strategy* – This illustrates the difference the product makes, like Jenny Craig or Weight Watchers campaigns.

3. *Picture yourself strategy* – This shows you what result you can expect from the product, like cosmetic surgery, Peloton, or Bowflex campaigns.

Product-focused

4. *Feature strategy* – This shows an important product feature and then should relate it to your needs. So, if the feature is durability that means you won't have to replace it soon.

5. *Abundance (quantity) strategy* – This demonstrates that consumers will have a wide selection of items or receive a large portion of something, like a super-sized meal.

6. *Quality strategy* – This illustrates the excellence, claiming superiority to other brands. A few examples would be Neiman Marcus, W Hotels, Rolls-Royce, and De Beers.

7. *Product-demonstration strategy* – This exemplifies the product's results, like detergents, deodorants, stain removers, or Breathe Right nasal strips.

8. *Product comparison strategy* – This places two competitors in a head-to-head competition, like the "Mac versus PC" campaign's "Crash" commercial. (Be sure to see several of these spots on YouTube.)

9. *Testimonial strategy* – This allows people to explain what they like about the product, like the "Beautiful" Stanley Steemer spot. If a celebrity is delivering the testimonial, it's called a "celebrity endorsement," like Jessica Simpson for Proactiv or Michael Phelps for Talkspace. If celebrities only talk about the brand, they are part of a *celebrity spokesperson* campaign.

10. *Icon strategy* – This uses an iconic character in the campaign, like Nabisco's Keebler Elves, the Charmin Bears, or the Brawny Man.

11. *Information strategy* – This explains the product in detail like pharmaceutical ads or Colgate Total toothpaste's announcement that bacteria are building up in your mouth right now.

12. *Uniqueness strategy* – This shows what's different about this product than its competitors, like the Crest 3D Whitestrips.

13. *Product as hero strategy* – This places the product center stage, like the "Absolut Perfection" campaign, with the bottle artistically portrayed, or Coke's "Open Happiness" campaign.

14. *Come from behind strategy* – This asks for the audience's empathy, like Avis's classic "We're Number 2. We Try Harder." campaign.

15. *Brand-centric strategy* – This focuses on the brand, its features, and how it works in consumers' lives, like Google's "Parisian Love" spot.

16. *Product-centric strategy* – This focuses on a specific product, like Taco Bell menu item spots. (See more in Chapters 5, 7, 10, and 13.)

17. *Company history strategy* – This reminds the audience of a firm's long-standing tradition, like "With a Name Like Smucker's, It's Got to Be Good."

18. *Company's founder or corporate leader strategy* – This presents the company message from the voice of one of its owners or business leaders, like Perdue Chicken's Frank Perdue, Orville Redenbacher's popcorn with his namesake, or Chrysler's Lee Iacocca and his famous, timeless campaign line "If you Can Find a Better Car Buy It." This also integrates a *challenge strategy*. Even long after KFC founder, Colonel Harland Sanders, passed away, actors portrayed him in commercials. That showed how closely he was tied to the brand's identity.

19. *Performance strategy* – This epitomizes the product's commitment to top-level performance like Nike's dedication to enhancing every athlete's performance or Ford's "Built Ford Tough" (since 1979).

20. *Positioning in the marketplace strategy* – This depicts the brand's placement in the industry. It could relate to one aspect such as sales, safety, or customer service.

21. *Stamp of approval strategy* – This states that experts have approved the product, like the Sensodyne statement: "Nine out of 10 dentists recommend it for patients with tooth sensitivity."

22. *One-word strategy* – This identifies the brand with one memorable word, like Disney's "Magic" or Macy's "Believe."

Savings as the Star

23. *Value strategy* – This promises the audience they got a great deal, leading them to believe they received more than they paid for, like two-for-one dining or BOGO (Buy one. Get one).

24. *Makes sense strategy* – This explains why the product is a logical choice, like a fuel-efficient car model rather than a gas-guzzler.

Emotional Approach

25. *Humor strategy* – This approaches the audience in a comedic manner, like Tide To Go's "Talking Stain" campaign. (Be sure to watch it on YouTube, if you haven't seen it.)

26. *Honesty strategy* – This tells consumers the real, unfiltered information, like the anti-smoking Truth® campaign's "Body Bag" spot that depicted 1,200 body bags on a sidewalk to visually depict the number of people who die daily from smoking. This spot is also an example of the *shock strategy* (strategy #33).

27. *Anthropomorphism strategy* – This shows animals with human emotions, like the many Budweiser Super Bowl spots. One example is "Hank," the Clydesdale horse that wanted to make the hitch team and was "trained" by a Dalmatian for a year with *Rocky* music in the background.

28. *Role reversal strategy* – This places a character in an unexpected role, like Doritos "Keep Your Hands Off My Mama," the E-Trade "Babies" as the financial experts, or the Mrs. Paul's "Whole Fillet" commercial with the little girl demanding an answer to these "grown-up" questions about another brand's fish sticks: "You feed me minced? You ever catch a minced fish?"

29. *Exaggeration strategy* – This obviously inflates the real benefits of the product, like the For Eyes campaign with inflated promises like claiming the eyeglasses can speak French ("French"), or they can shoot laser beams ("Laser"), or they can make an older lady see her senior-citizen husband as a young man ("Husband").

30. *Challenge strategy* – This invites the audience into a product test, like the "Activia 14-Day Challenge" or "You Can Do It, Nicorette Can Help" campaign, inviting people to quit smoking; or the Dove Beauty Bar "Discover the Truth about Soap" promotion, enticing women to see for themselves the residue other soaps leave behind.

31. *Emotional blackmail strategy* – This makes consumers feel insecure as if they'd feel guilty if they didn't use the product, like all-natural pet food brands.

32. *Temptation strategy* – This promises irresistibility for consumers, like the "Axe Effect" TV spots.

33. *Shock strategy* – This surprises the audience in some way. It can be positive (Domino's Pizza "Hold Out" campaign), negative (Balenciaga with Kids Holding Bondage-clad Teddy Bears), or controversial (Pepsi with Kendall Jenner who seemed to trivialize protests).

34. *Playful strategy* – This is a lighthearted way to present the product, like the Coke animated "Beautiful" commercial.

35. *Deprivation strategy* – This exemplifies what life would be like without the product, like the earliest "Got Milk" campaign. (See the "Got Milk" commercials "Aaron Burr," "Body Cast," and "Heaven or Hell" on YouTube.)

36. *Sexy strategy* – This portrays the brand or the consumer in a sexually enticing manner, like the Doritos TV spots that showed girls who craved a chip so much that they licked the last crumbs off guys' faces once they saw the empty bag.

37. *Parody strategy* – This pokes fun at a trend, culture, or creative direction, like the AT&T "Award Ceremony" with Mila Kunis and Demi Moore.

38. *Letting off steam strategy* – This allows actors to vent in a fun way, like the Allstate "Mayhem Hashtag Challenge" spot.

Storytelling

39. *Mini movie or "vignette" strategy* – This presents a little story, like the De Beers "I Do" story-of-our-lives spot.

40. *Continuing story strategy* –This is a campaign with an ongoing storyline, like the Budweiser "Lizards," which followed up after the "Frogs" campaign.

41. *Continuing characters strategy* – This establishes one character and continues using him or her, like the Progressive Insurance's quirky character Flo, played by Stephanie Courtney, or the Geico Gecko.

42. *Breaking news strategy* – This exploits news that relates to the product, like the Candy Crush Soda "Saga" introduction spot.

43. *Green strategy* – This spotlights the ecological consciousness of the brand, like the World Wildlife Fund spot "We Are All Connected." It showed hanging, string sculptures from fish, butterflies, elephants, and birds to a family of people. Each sculpture was connected by a string to another with a simple message: Every creature counts. Although this is a *cause-related strategy* (#49), environmental issues have become so important, they merit a separate category.

44. *Futuristic strategy* – This places the product benefits in the future, like the Audi "Future is an Attitude" commercial.

45. *Reposition the brand strategy* – This is used when the product has been modernized, upgraded, or reengineered to appeal to a different or reappeal to the same audience.

Audience Engagement

46. *Interactive strategy* – This engages the audience, like the launch of Citizens Bank's first New York location with a 10-day immersive, multimedia experience to reflect it had grasped life as a New Yorker: "The Living Portrait of NYC."

47. *Social media strategy* – This uses social media to connect to the audience like the Coors Light Biodegradable Bodega, as a pop-up store in Brooklyn, New York via Instagram. While the brand demonstrated its commitment to reduce the use of plastics, it offered prizes to engaged consumers.

48. *Fill-in-the-blank strategy* – This invites the audience to figure out some part of the message like the Guinness Beer "Gu_ _ _ess Who" headline above the brand logo.

49. *Charity or cause-related strategy* – This heightens consumers' charitable consciousness, like the RED "Fight AIDS in Africa" multibrand campaign with HBO, Hallmark, Starbucks, and other sponsors; the American Express annual Christmas drive "Charge Against Hunger" (since 1994); the UNICEF "Tap Project" to provide pure water in 100 countries; and the Susan G. Komen "Cure Breast Cancer," commonly called "Pink," campaign. The Anti-Advertising Agency wanted to point out how excessive out-of-home advertising had become, so they created several *anti-advertising campaigns*. Ambient communication, placed over existing posters, and other out-of-home ads, reminded consumers that they didn't need the items being advertised. This group even blacked-out existing ads, fully covering them, and replacing them with a new statement: the word "Graffiti" stenciled. This new message

labeled the original ads as graffiti. For example, "Graffiti" was placed over flat screens in the "Light Criticism" campaign.

50. *Pop culture strategy* – This lets the brand reflect a cultural behavior or create a popular phrase that becomes integrated into everyday language, like the classic Budweiser's "Whassup!" or Wendy's "Where's the Beef?" slogans.

Before you keep reading, can you imagine other campaigns and decide which strategies they used? Think back to a spot or promotion you really enjoyed. Now, ask yourself what you liked about it and what *strategy* and *universal truth* it depicted. Do you think you were the primary targeted audience? If the campaign resonated as authentic for you, and you instantly connected to it, you probably were. Have you noticed that some commercials use several strategies in one campaign? For example, the E-Trade "Talking Baby" spots use a continuing character, exaggeration, humor, and little vignettes (mini movies).

Can you sum up the message in a phrase or a word? If so, you just clarified product positioning in the mind of the consumer. Here are two examples: "Save. Buy in Bulk." for Costco or "expensive" for Rolls-Royce. This positioning, as opposed to other kinds of positioning, relies on the consumer's opinion of the brand. If your opinion is not what the advertiser wants you to think, new messages will be developed to create a different positioning statement. There are more than two types of *positioning*.

Evaluating strategies and needs

The most sophisticated marketers know that the more detailed the audience information, the more accurate the creative direction. Understanding the three audience components – demographics, psychographics, and geographics – is one part of the puzzle. Looking at the different strategies is another. Considering consumers' basic needs is yet another. You're probably already familiar with Maslow's commonly known Hierarchy of Needs (Figure 6.1). Perhaps you may know about Jib Fowles's list of Advertising's 15 Basic Appeals,[5] based on more than 25 Social Motives as listed in *Explorations in Personality* by Henry A. Murray in 1938.[6] The 70th edition was published in 2007. If he were still alive, there would probably have been even more updated versions.

Advertisers use consumer needs in many ways. Products demonstrate how they satisfy different needs. Here are a few examples using Abraham Maslow's Hierarchy of Needs:

1. *Physical* needs with food and beverages.
2. *Safety* needs with insurance or alarm systems.

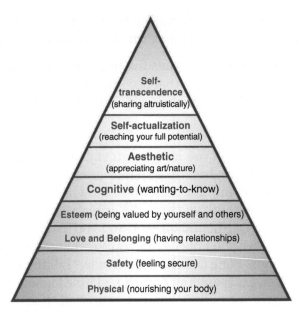

FIGURE 6.1 This Maslow's "Hierarchy of Needs" chart was created by M2 Design. Image courtesy of M2 Design.

3. *Love and Belonging* needs with Facebook fan pages.

4. *Esteem* needs with luxury products and designer brands like Gucci.

5. *Cognitive* needs with advice like Butterball's Thanksgiving Day turkey cooking tips.

6. *Aesthetic* needs with art and home decorating classes.

7. *Self-actualization* needs with self-growth courses.

8. *Self-transcendence* needs with mentoring programs like Big Brothers Big Sisters.

It's crucial that you absorb the various strategies, motivations, and needs lists and then apply them in your strategic thinking. Look at the table (Figure 6.2) and see how the strategies align with the lists of motivational appeals and needs. Now, consider what products, services, or brands could use the strategies to answer specific consumer needs. For example, when could you use a product-demonstration strategy? What need(s) could that fulfill? Okay, let's consider a color-safe detergent. You could demonstrate how it gets stains out without fading (safety need) the garment's color. The campaign shows both

BERMAN **Strategies that Relate to** **Fowles's Appeals & Maslow's Needs** **(Brand examples)**	JIB FOWLES **Advertising's 15 Basic Appeals** **(Buying Motivations)**	MASLOW **Hierarchy of Needs**
1. *Sexy strategy* (#36) (Victoria's Secret)	1. *Need for sex* – according to Fowles this may be too overt and may distract the audience's attention from focusing on the product. Back in the early 1980s, only 2% of the ads used this approach.	**HELPING INFORMATION** **(#1 Physical & #2 Safety)** 1) *Physiological needs*: basic drive for survival, hunger, thirst, bodily comforts, etc.– ALSO ALIGNS WITH APPEALS #15 - FOWLES
2. *Interactive strategy* (#46) 3. *Social media strategy* (#47) 4. *Pop culture strategy* (#50) **(www.GetTheGlass.com – Milk)** **(Bahamasair Interactive Campaign)**	2. *Need for affiliation* – wanting to socialize. Can be used in a positive or negative way. Showing you how to gain friends or reminding you that you could lose them without this product.	**ENLIGHTENING INFORMATION** **(#3 Love and Belonging)** 3) *Belongingness and love needs*: desire to join, connect with, and be accepted by others
5. *Charity, cause–related strategy* (#49) **(www.RedCampaign.org – fighting AIDS in Africa)**	3. *Need to nurture* – people's natural parental and protective urge	
6. *Information strategy* (#11) **(www.Butterball.com – recipes/info, Google)**	4. *Need for guidance* – looking to be advised and cared for	**(#4 Esteem, #5 Cognitive, & #6 Aesthetic)** 5) *Cognitive needs*: aspire to gain information for clarification (Part of Empowering information)
7. *Letting off steam strategy* (#38) **(https://blog.12min.com/united -breaks-guitars-pdf/ – customer service complaints)**	5. *Need to aggress* – seeking vengeance when you feel wronged	
8. *Celebrity spokesperson strategy* (#9) **(Valerie Bertinelli for Jenny Craig or Jennifer Hudson for Weight Watchers)**	6. *Need to achieve* – striving to accomplish something very difficult 7. *Need to dominate* – wanting to control your environment	4) *Esteem needs*: hope for accomplishment, recognition, competence, and appreciation
9. *Positioning in the marketplace strategy* (#20) **("Avis. We're Number 2")**		
10. *Company history strategy* (#17) **(Barbie's 50th Anniversary)**	8. *Need for prominence* – wanting recognition and social status	7) *Self–actualization needs*: wish to gain self-fulfillment, reach your potential and do what you're born to do
11. *Quality strategy* (#6) **(Tiffany–little blue box)**	9. *Need for attention* – hoping people will notice us	
12. *Before and after strategy* (#2) **(cosmetic surgery – https://straxaesthetics.com)**		
13. *Picture yourself strategy* (#3) **(anti–wrinkle creams like Retinol Night Cream)**	10. *Need for autonomy* – wanting to be unique 11. *Need to escape* – desiring adventure	
14. *Uniqueness strategy* (#12) **(Benihana)**		
15. *Feature strategy* (#4) **(iPhone apps – Apple)**	12. *Need to feel safe* – wanting to feel safe and unthreatened	2) *Safety needs*: long to stay out of harm's way and avoid danger
16. *Emotional blackmail strategy* (#31) **("There's a Lot Riding on Your Tires." Michelin)**	13. *Need for aesthetic sensations* – desiring to experience art, music and other kinds of beauty	6) *Aesthetic needs*: want to have order, organization, beauty and experience joy in arts and nature
17 *Performance strategy* (#19) **("Just Do It." Nike)**	14. *Need to satisfy curiosity* – wanting to know accurate and detailed information supported by data	
18. *Product demonstration strategy* (#7) **(Proactiv)**		
19. *Testimonial strategy* (#9) **(Carol's Daughter)**	15. *Physical needs* – Fowles includes sex in this category (item #1) and biological needs like sleeping, eating, drinking, and reproducing	1) *Physical needs*: basic drive for survival, hunger, thirst, bodily comforts, etc.
20. *Benefit strategy* (#1) **(Colgate Total Plus Whitening Toothpaste)**		

FIGURE 6.2 This "Strategies–Motivations–Needs" chart, created by Margo Berman, shows how various Berman's Advertising Strategy Categories line up with Fowles' 15 Basic Appeals and Maslow's Hierarchy of Needs. It presents a quick cross-reference for consumer insight and acts as a tool for strategic thinking. Source for Jib Fowles: Jib Fowles, "Advertising 15 Basic Appeals," *Et Cetera*, Vol. 39.3 (1982): pp. 273–290.

the cleaning power and the color protection qualities of the detergent. People want clean, not faded clothes.

There are other categories of needs, as well. You could consider the Institute for Management Excellence, which suggested that there were nine basic human needs:

1. Security

2. Adventure

3. Freedom

4. Exchange

5. Power

6. Expansion

7. Acceptance

8. Community

9. Expression

You can see how most of these fit into Fowles's list. For example, the institute's #2 "adventure" would be Fowles's #11 "need to escape," and #3 "freedom" could correlate to #10 "need for autonomy." You don't have to know every single category ever created; you just have to know the needs your audience have that your product/service/brand satisfies. Think of the strategies, motivations, and needs chart (Figure 6.1) as a guide to creative thinking and an easy-to-refer-to, problem-solving method. Notice that not all the strategies are listed, just the ones that correlated to specific needs.

If all these needs confuse you, you can think about the four basic or buying motivations, which group several of Fowles's and Maslow's into just these four categories. This might simplify your creative process. These four groups are as follows:

1. *Biogenic needs* – basic requirements for survival: food, water, rest, procreation, and so on.

2. *Psychogenic needs* – needs based on cultural pressures like status, power, affiliation, and so on.

3. *Utilitarian needs* – desire for useful and functional solutions in products or services.

4. *Hedonic needs* – yearning for pleasure, experiences, and excitement.

This shortened version enables you to think of creating campaigns that appeal to consumers' physical, psychological, functional, and pleasure needs. You can easily see how a beer, spa, or exotic resort commercial would go under hedonic needs. Home gyms would fit under utilitarian needs. Cosmetics, social networking sites, and designer clothes would fit under psychogenic needs. Restaurants would fit under biogenic needs.

Consumer needs are what drive their spending. They're the motivations behind the actual purchase. Here it is interesting to note that some of the motivations actually create a psychological conflict in consumers. For example, if they're torn between two good choices, like two equally wonderful vacations, this is called "Approach–Approach Conflict." If the conflict drives people to resolve existing conflicts between their beliefs or their behaviors, like they're against the death penalty but feel conflicted about the severity of the punishment when a child was murdered, it's called "Cognitive Dissonance Reduction." If they have a conflict between reaching a goal and the behavior modification required to reach it, like dieting, it's called "Approach–Avoidance Conflict." If consumers have to decide between two unpleasant choices, like buying a new car or repairing an old one, it's called "Avoidance–Avoidance Conflict."

Once you realize all advertisements want to change or reinforce behavior, it will help you think about how you want the audience to respond and what you want them to do. For example, if they hardly use the product (inertia involvement), you want to increase their purchase, so they move toward more purchases (flow state or high involvement). If they're already fans, you want them to become fanatics (cult-like involvement). You don't just want people to know about your product; you want them to begin to get involved and actually "sell" your product to their friends. This is the highest form of product involvement because it embraces engagement, interactivity, and advocacy, which increases the consumers' relationship with the brand.

Then, after you consider strategies and needs, you should look at the different kinds of product positioning. For copywriting, the one you want to focus on is the first one: positioning in the mind of the consumer, discussed next.

Applying different types of positioning

Most advertisers want to create an impression in the consumer's mind. This kind of positioning is called "positioning in the mind of the consumer." Earlier, we also discussed *sales-related positioning*. But those are not the only ones. By knowing the brand's different positioning, you could choose to feature one in a campaign. For example, Cadillac used to be your grandfather's car. However, it was *repositioned* to be a cooler car both for the individual and the family.

Likewise, you could emphasize the brand's number rating in customer service or safety, as Subaru did years ago. Review the list below and think about how any of these could be integrated into your campaign message.

Here is a list of the various types of positioning.

1. *Positioning in the mind of the consumer* – What the consumer currently thinks about the product/brand. This is critical when developing your message. If consumers have the right impression, you want to reinforce that. If not, you want to change their opinion.

2. *Positioning in sales* – What place does this product/brand hold in relation to sales: first place, second place like Avis, and so on?

3. *Positioning in real estate* – Where the product sits in stores: eye-level shelves, at the front of the store (in bookstores), end caps (facing out at the end of the isle), freestanding displays (separated island with product), and so on. The placement of products is directly linked to the selling power of the brand.

4. *Positioning in the media* – What media vehicles are used for the ad message: TV, radio, Internet, out-of-home, transit, mobile, and so on.

5. *Positioning in the medium* – Where the ads are placed in a specific medium, like surrounding the news on TV, morning or afternoon drive time for radio, banner ads on sites targeting a specific audience, key billboards for out-of-home, inside subways for transit, and so on.

6. *Positioning in the marketplace* – Where is the product sold: globally, nationally, or regionally.

7. *Positioning in performance* – Where consumers rate the brand through customer service and safety awards.

8. *Positioning on the Internet* – What is the size of the brand's digital footprint? This is especially important for small businesses, entrepreneurs, and solo-preneurs.

9. *Repositioning of the brand* – What is the new way you want to present the brand's image? Just because it used to be old-fashioned doesn't mean it can't get an image facelift. Brands can reengineer the styling, performance, or technology of one product or the entire line of products to regain a previous market or target a new audience, as in Cadillac. This can also be used as a strategy (#45).

You must consider the brand's current position in each of these categories and decide if you want to showcase that in your message. You've seen car commercials that boast about their customer service awards or safety ratings. If the car's been recognized as the safest in the automotive industry, you may want to share that information with the consumer. If you realized your audience listens to the radio in different dayparts (specific blocks of times in a 24-hour cycle, as discussed in Chapter 8), you would schedule your commercials during those segments. Positioning awareness and emphasis is key for all marketing.

Besides positioning, you should be 100% clear on what differentiates your product or brand from the competitors. Let's focus now on the USP, or *unique selling proposition* (or position).

Inventing the USP: Selling uniqueness

The target audience needs to know why they should pick your brand, product, or service. You must be able to answer the following: How is your beer different? What makes your exercise equipment more effective? Why is your pizza better? Strong brands do that. Think about Papa John's slogan "Better ingredients. Better pizza," which simply states what distinguishes its pizza compared to everyone else's.

Think about Bayer aspirin's slogan "Take it for pain. Take it for life." As soon as research proved that an aspirin could actually save a heart-attack victim's life if taken immediately when the symptoms appear, Bayer claimed that benefit. By being the first to state Bayer can save your life, it made people believe only Bayer aspirin had this power. Some people today don't realize that any aspirin, not ibuprofen, can offer the same benefit.

Just as mp3 players existed before iPods, Apple showed people how easily they could carry their favorite songs with them. By being the first to clarify why consumers needed the product, Apple became the first successful mp3 player brand by popularizing the technology.

Not being first isn't as important as being the first to clearly state the unique selling proposition. Clarity is key. That's how the main message sums up the point in an easy-to-remember or "sticky" slogan.

Creating the main message: Campaign slogans

What's one of the stickiest slogans you know? "Just do it." Right? That's because it doesn't tell you what sport to do. Just to be sure you go out and exercise. The brand's promise is to help improve your performance in any sport because it has shoes specially designed for different activities: walking, hiking, running, and so on.

When you're thinking of a slogan, think about all the ones that are stuck in your head. Those are sticky. Think of messages that are short. To the point. And instantly understood. They're the battle cry of the brand. They're unique, original, and fresh. Be sure you check in Chapter 10 for slogan techniques as you develop your ideas.

You want consumers to not only remember your slogan, but also to remember the brand. Slogans that could apply to any other brand need to be reexamined. Of course, you could say "Just do it" could work for another brand. Just realize Nike's ability to drive home the message in multiple formats, multiple media, and without interruption. That doesn't take away from the power of the message. It was strong to begin with and a big-budget campaign only enhanced its impact.

Deciding the *tone of voice*

Although we'll discuss *tone of voice* in greater detail in Chapters 5 and 9, to better understand how it fits into the brief, we need to look at it for a moment. The *tone of voice* is the way you speak to your audience. Is the message going to be delivered in a serious or other *tone of voice*? Think about an adjective. What would be the best way for the brand or product to talk to the audience? Should it be playful? Authoritative? Informative? Intimidating? Friendly? It's not what the message is saying, it's the way it's presented. It's not the media vehicles. Those are *tactics*, which we'll discuss last. Now, we'll look at the product's competitors in the marketplace.

Considering competitors

Why do you need to know your competitors? First, you can understand what they're doing to reach your audience. What is their message and where are they reaching your customers? Next, you can think about how you can differentiate your brand, so your audience picks yours.

Designing tactics

When you think about advertising vehicles, don't just make a list of media outlets. Evaluate which media are the most likely places your message will intersect with your audience. Are your audience members involved in social media? Do they like to play online games? Do they watch sports live, streaming, on TV, or on mobile devices? By understanding how your audience gets information, engages in discussions, and uses technology, you'll be better equipped to select target-relevant avenues where you can capture your audience's attention. You want to implement the creative direction in a relevant and effective way. Your main goal is to develop an on-target and on-strategy message. Here's what Charlie Hopper, principal at Young & Laramore, suggests when you're thinking through writing for various media vehicles (Advice from the Pros 6.1).

> **ADVICE FROM THE PROS 6.1 Charlie Hopper's writing for specific media tips**
>
> We feel pretty strongly that we start with where people are going to encounter it. Then, you can absolutely surprise and delight them that you know where they are. That gives you the chance to really craft the piece to be appropriate to its medium.
>
> There's a little green light that goes on in a person that knows it's a manhole cover or it's sitting on a gas pump. It isn't just the slogan. It somehow acknowledges where you come across it. That's why your first question, as a writer, ought to be: Where will people be seeing this?
>
> "Oh, it's an outdoor board, so it should be seven words." Now we have all the different ways to getting at people. In the old days, there were outdoor things that were innovative. But, now you've got online as a whole new world, and you've got cell phones ringing in people's pockets, and you've got all the different technologies for outdoor that you didn't used to have, or things that stick on to stuff.[7]

Notice how writers today are thinking about the medium first to be sure the message will work wherever the audience will see it. You can't just write a TV spot and hope you can turn it into a billboard, a branded game, or an interactive experience. You need to plan the message as you're creating the campaign. You need to be thinking backward: from the *touchpoint* to the message.

Final creative direction checklist

Enough cannot be said about strategy. Every piece of copy has to be aligned with a predetermined creative direction and must clearly support it. The overall message must reflect that objective. For example, if the campaign is for Jif peanut butter where the slogan (tagline or main theme line) is "Choosy moms choose Jif," but the copy talks about price, the message would be off-strategy. All copywriters must recheck the final copy against the initial strategy to be sure the message delivered is the one originally intended. Double-check your creative solution against this list:

1. Did you *create an on-strategy campaign* that reflected the Creative Strategy Statement objectives?

2. Did you clearly *identify the psychographic profile of the audience?*

3. Did you develop an *on-target message,* one that speaks directly to that particular target audience in a relevant and authentic way?

4. Did your message properly *reflect the brand's image?*

5. Did your concept allow for multiple executions, so it *can "spin out"?*

6. Did your solution clearly *highlight the main consumer benefit?*

7. Did your audience walk away with a message that *reinforced or changed their beliefs* about the brand, product, or service?

8. Did you *correctly position or reposition the product* in the mind of the consumer?

9. Did you *answer the consumer's question: "Why buy?"*

10. Did you clearly *project the brand's USP?*

11. Did you succinctly *state the big idea* that will drive the slogan?

12. Did your concept *illustrate the brand's personality?*

13. Did you *use the appropriate tone of voice* for the brand and the audience?

14. Did your tactics *reach the appropriate touchpoints* for the right audience?

15. Did you create a campaign that *would create buzz?*

Creative strategy exercises

Exercise 1: How can you use traditional media in a new, unexpected way?

For example, placing a gigantic comb in power lines to demonstrate how a detangling product unsnarls unruly hair. Search for edgy and/or innovative ads and look at some exciting examples of new media. What can you come up with that's unique and surprisingly effective?

Exercise 2: Write two briefs and think about your creative direction

1. Select a product (client) and a short creative brief. (See Chapter 5, Templates 5.1, or the list here.) Short creative brief example:

   ▪ What is the *brand's character* or personality?

   ▪ Why does the brand *want to advertise?*

- Who is the *audience*?
- What do they (audience members) *currently think*?
- What do you *want them to think*?
- *Why should they buy* this product/service?
- What is the *big message* you want them to know?
- What *kind of tactics* (specific ad/promotional techniques) do you want to use?

   For example, do you want to use viral marketing, interactive online components, out-of-home messages, print ads, transit (buses, subways, taxis, etc.), experiential media, direct mail, games, or other vehicles?

2. Using the same product (client), expand the brief into a longer one. Remember to describe your audience using the appropriate VALS, such as Belongers, Emulators, Achievers, and so on. (See Chapter 5.)

3. List the *touchpoints* where you'd reach your audience.

4. Consider competitors' campaigns. How could yours stand out?

5. Review the six categories of 50 strategies.

6. Select the one that would work best for this "client."

7. Decide how that strategy could become a campaign that would *spin out* to different *touchpoints* (media).

8. Be sure you've considered *consumer benefits*.

9. Think about a campaign direction.

10. Double-check that your campaign is *on strategy* based on your Creative Strategy Statement (#1) from your brief.

Notes

1. Benazhir Maratuech, personal communication, October 23, 2022.
2. Teddy Brown, personal communication, October 26, 2009.
3. Teddy Brown, personal communication, October 26, 2009.
4. Al Ries and Jack Trout, *Positioning: The Battle for Your Mind* (New York: McGraw-Hill, 2000), 21.
5. Jib Fowles, "Advertising 15 Basic Appeals," *Et Cetera* 39.3 (1982): 273–290.
6. Henry A. Murray, *Explorations in Personality*, 70th ed. (New York: Oxford University Press, 2007).
7. Charlie Hopper, personal communication, November 26, 2021.

7 The Animated Word
TV, Interactive Spots, and Video Scripts

"Be single-minded and try to stuff the turkey with much stuffing."
Tom Amico, Co-Founder of Tom & Eric 911[1]

In this section, you'll scrutinize the art of writing for TV so you can increase your proficiency. You'll investigate "The Three Rs" and "The Five Rs," delve deeper into universal truths to see how they're used in TV, compare different kinds of script formats, and inspect various storyboards.

You'll also learn to identify different types of commercials, including the talking head, continuing characters, reason why, and more. You'll become familiar with the basic rules for TV writing, like writing for both the eye and the ear. Plus, you'll hear firsthand about TV writing tips from several successful copywriters, including Tom Amico, who created copy for the Aflac Duck, and Vinny Warren, best known for the Budweiser "Whassup!" campaign.

Finally, you'll have access to a list of commonly used industry terms at the end of the chapter. Now, let's find out the secrets to great TV writing.

Scrutinizing television writing: What's the secret?

If you want to be a better TV writer, watch more terrific commercials and videos. Become an active viewer, a clever deconstructionist, an insightful analyzer, and a discerning critic. The next time you see a great commercial, dissect it. Ask yourself why it hit you so hard. What captured your attention? What resonated with you? Most likely, you were the primary target because the spot caused a response and you unconsciously connected to the message.

I expanded "The Three Rs" of successful campaigns – *Messages that are RELEVANT and RESONATE with authenticity are REMEMBERED* – to "The Five Rs" shown in Tips and Rules 7.1: *Only RELEVANT content that RESONATES with authenticity gets REMEMBERED, RESPONDED to, and RETOLD.* Apply all the "Rs" and your writing will speak directly to your audience in a meaningful way and create a reaction.

These types of powerful, targeted communications get in under consumers' radar and are referred to as "BLT" or "below-the-line" messages. They're so perfectly constructed they penetrate past consumers' shields that block out unwanted advertising communications. They speak directly to the audience

TIPS AND RULES 7.1
The five Rs

Only RELEVANT content that RESONATES with authenticity gets REMEMBERED, RESPONDED to, and RETOLD.

in the consumer's language. They get delivered before the shields go up. They sneak in, invisible to the radar detectors.

How do creative teams create these kinds of campaigns? They start with gaining consumer insight and having a clear understanding of the audience. They go beyond demographics (age, gender, income, education, etc.), geographics (residence location), and psychographics (overall lifestyle). They also lock in on where the audience prefers to absorb content. It's not enough to know how old the audience is and what they earn. Marketers want to get inside the mind of these consumers so they can position the brand in a way that singles them out and specifically targets them. The next time you see a spot and you react strongly to it, be sure you allow yourself time to reflect and answer what pulled you in. Was it the visual(s)? The language? The message? The humor? Always remember to analyze every ad that interrupts your day-to-day activities and gets you to stop, read, look, listen, or respond.

Analyzing TV writing: Where to begin

When writing for TV, as with radio, start in the middle of the action. Don't write a prologue or introduction. Begin with act two, as if you were creating a play. This will immediately engage the audience's attention because something is already happening. They don't need to know the preceding scene. Remember, you're writing to the senses. Your dialogue needs to sound conversational. You need to write in little bites or phrases. Not lengthy sentences. Just like this. Watch your use of language. If you don't say "however" in your everyday speech, you can't include that word in TV or radio. Read out loud. If you're stumbling, you're not writing naturally. If your writing sounds as if you're reading from a brochure, it's too stiff. Also, with TV, if you show it, you may not need to say it.

If the spot has someone speaking to the camera, as in the Laurel Road spot "Freudian Slip: Dental School" (Figure 7.1), viewers feel as if the actor is speaking to them, in a one-on-one conversation. It has a personal, intimate feel to it. For example, if it starts with "Look, I think it's ridiculous," that line has a real-life, conversational tone. If it also includes usual small talk and naturally repeated phrases, such as "mmmm," or "ummms," it is more natural. You can also see this language in the "Freudian Slip: Law School" spot (Figure 7.2). When you include everyday speech, you make the writing sound as if someone were actually talking to a friend, not reading a script.

The dentist, when discussing the patient's plaque build-up changes the words to "loan build-up." You'll see in each of the Laurel Road scripts, the Freudian slip is evident and yet humorous. The lawyer, meaning to say, "I

Laurel Road
Freudian Slip - Dentist
:15

Open on a shot from a dental patient's POV looking up at the dentist.

Dentist: **Mmmm. Seems like you've got some Loan build-up in the back there.**

Patient: **Whahhaaa?**

Dentist: **Yeah, those loans really build up, don't they? (He gets more intense) You can make payments. You can floss. But they just keep building and building.**

Super/VO: **Can't get your student loan off your mind?**

Logo/VO: **Laurel Road. Refinance your student loans and you could save thousands.**

FIGURE 7.1 This "Freudian Slip: Dental School" video storyboard was created by DeVito/Verdi for Laurel Road. Image courtesy of DeVito/Verdi.

Laurel Road
Freudian Slip - Lawyer
:15

Open in a courtroom...

Defense Lawyer: Well, clearly the witness is lying --"

Our lawyer bursts up out of his chair.

Lawyer: **I'm in debt your honor!!**

SILENCE. Judge stares at him.

Judge: **You mean, you object.**

Lawyer: **Oh, ummm, that too. But I'm also in debt.**

Super/VO: **Can't get your student loan off your mind?**

Logo/VO: **Laurel Road. Refinance your student loans and you could save thousands.**

FIGURE 7.2 This "Freudian Slip: Law School" video storyboard was created by DeVito/Verdi for Laurel Road. Image courtesy of DeVito/Verdi.

object," instead states, "I'm in your debt." The fact the words rhyme makes it even funnier. The closing line, "Can't get your student loan off your mind?," speaks to a universal truth that many college graduates have experienced: the pain of student debt long after graduation. These conversational phrases and social references showed insight into the consumer's everyday speech and day-to-day challenges. It talked in an honest and empathetic tone of voice that reflected true angst.

It's actually a universal truth: "Debt is stress." It's not often that an actual common complaint is stated so clearly. But, that's the genius behind the copy in this entire campaign. It sided with the consumers' complaints and offered a solution. It spoke directly to the consumers' concerns in their own language, free from typical loan-related ad copy.

Likewise, in the "Freudian Slip: Medical School" spot (Figure 7.3), the doctors are so distracted, they replace the word "bone" for "loan." Again, the rhyme drives home the message. Memorable campaigns exemplify fun, yet offer strategic problem-solving solutions. Notice how each spot in the campaign reiterates the pain point and then provides a much-needed solution: a Laurel Road debt-reduction loan.

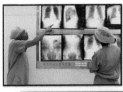

Laurel Road
Freudian Slip - Doctor
:15

Doctor is in a room with two other doctors pointing to various x-rays and bones. The two other doctors are watching.

Doctor: **So I believe there is a hairline fracture on this loan right here.**

The other two doctors look at each other.

Doctor: **Then there's another loan here.... a broken loan here. (MORE INTENSE) The big loans connected to the... even bigger loan.**

Super/VO: **Can't get your student loan off your mind?**

Logo/VO: **Laurel Road. Refinance your student loans and you could save thousands.**

FIGURE 7.3 This "Freudian Slip: Medical School" video storyboard was created by DeVito/Verdi for Laurel Road. Image courtesy of DeVito/Verdi.

You can see how commercials that resonate with authenticity are those that address a universal truth. Most often these are just implied rather than stated. However, they're understood at a subconscious level, even if they can't be restated perfectly. There may be several similar underlying universal truths, as well. It doesn't matter which one you choose as long as it has the same message.

Applying universal truths to common goals

As soon as possible, get into the habit of dissecting every TV commercial. Look for the universal truth and then restate it in everyday speech. For example, Sheena Brady, commercial director/creative director, explained the importance of integrating consumer thinking this way:

> Most of my experience comes from trying to find a universal human insight that works across many cultures. But depending on what you're doing, you might need to tailor it. For example, soccer isn't as well known in the States and it is very established in Europe. You would speak to it differently. But for the most part, what I work on is I try to find a universal truth that is relatable to a lot of people.
>
> We all want love, and family, and compassion towards others. There are certain inherent qualities that are across the board whether you're Puerto Rican, or you're German. Most of my work has been focused on finding those truths that we can all relate to.[2]

She went on to explain her writing process before she develops her message and said that the brief is the starting point rather than what she called "blue-sky thinking." She added:

> You know what you are trying to solve and you can then have the fun and the freedom of solving for that in an interesting way.[3]

TV and video spots can also exemplify one common goal that's a universal truth: Healthy eating is good for you. One campaign, Siggi's yogurt, describes how the creator of the brand, Siggi Hilmarsson, came to the United States from

Iceland and started his brand. When he couldn't find any yogurt with less sugar and more flavor, he invented Siggi's yogurt. It was a healthier yogurt from his grandmother's recipe. Then, he introduced it by selling it at a Manhattan's farmer's market in Union Square.

The universal truth, "less is more," is particularly applicable here. Each spot highlighted the consumer benefits – less sugar, fewer ingredients, and more protein – in a direct and relatable way. But, how did he introduce a new product? He simply opened a street stand, met the consumers one by one, and described his new product. He told his story and stuck to core differences in his yogurt. Then, using social media, he offered short, :15 (15-second) videos (Scripts and Examples 7.2, Scripts and Examples 7.3, Scripts and Examples 7.4) that ran on the YouTube channels for the brand and Icelandair, the Icelandic airline, to share the message.

The campaign writer, Tom Amico, said he agreed with the quoted line in the script:

> *"Simple ingredients, not a lot of sugar." That would also be my philosophy for copywriters as words to live and persuade by.*
> Tom Amico, Creative Director/Writer, Tom & Eric 911[4]

Notice that the video scripts examples have different formats. You'll see that there are several ways to present a script to clients. Notice that "Not a Lot of Sugar" is the same script. One has one column and the second uses two: Video and Audio.

In the first example (Scripts and Examples 7.2), Siggi introduced himself and explained what made his yogurt different. The delivery was simple, honest, and to-the-point. There were no advertising gimmicks, no fluff, no slick production, and no fake celebrity endorsements. Consumers today realize these are paid sponsors and question their sincerity. Siggi erased all doubt and presented an honest, believable story. He even said "more proud" instead of "prouder" (Scripts and Examples 7.2) because that was the way he spoke. The truth in Siggi's commercials was both palpable and credible.

1. "Proud of the Back," one-column (Scripts and Examples 7.2)
2. "Not a Lot of Sugar," two-columns (Scripts and Examples 7.3)
3. "Not a Lot of Sugar," one-column (Scripts and Examples 7.4)

SCRIPTS AND EXAMPLES 7.2 Siggi's yogurt TV, one-column script: "Proud of the Back"

CLIENT:	SIGGI'S YOGURT
JOB:	:15 TV (one-column)
TITLE:	"Proud of the Back"
DATE:	12/16/22

VIDEO:	SIGGI HILMARSSON SPEAKING.
	ONE HAND HOLDS THE FRONT OF PRODUCT.
SUPER:	SIGGI HILMARSSON, FOUNDER OF SIGGI'S YOGURT
SIGGI:	My name is on the front. But, I'm more proud of the back.
VIDEO:	SIGGI TURNS PRODUCT AROUND.
SIGGI:	Siggi's. Half the ingredients, less sugar and more protein than leading yogurts.
SUPER:	HALF THE INGREDIENTS, 40% LESS SUGAR, AND 50% MORE PROTEIN THAN LEADING YOGURTS.*
(DISCLAIMER)	*at least 40% less sugar than the average of the top 3 leading fruit yogurt brands; at least 50% more protein than the average of the top 3 leading fruit yogurt brands; at least 50% less ingredients than the average of the top 3 leading fruit yogurt brands.
VO:	Siggi's. Only available at Woolworth's.** (**Location changes to Whole Foods, in the US)

(This "Proud of the Back" :15 TV spot was created by Tom & Eric 911 for Siggi's yogurt. Script courtesy of Tom & Eric 911.)

SCRIPTS AND EXAMPLES 7.3 Siggi's yogurt TV, two-column video-audio script: "Not a Lot of Sugar"

CLIENT:	SIGGI'S YOGURT
JOB:	:15 TV (two-column)
TITLE:	"Not a Lot of Sugar"
DATE:	12/16/22

VIDEO:	AUDIO
BEIGE SCREEN WITH TEXT: When I moved here from Iceland, I felt most yogurts had too much sugar in them. So, I made my own.	SIGGI: When I moved here from Iceland, I felt most yogurts had too much sugar in them.
PHOTO OF SIGGI AT YOGURT STAND.	SIGGI: So, I made my own.
HAND PLACES YOGURT ON TABLE.	SIGGI: And then I made some more.
TEXT ABOVE YOGURT: And then I made some more.	
HAND TURNS CONTAINER TWICE.	VO: Simple ingredients, not a lot of sugar.
BEAUTY SHOT	
TEXT ABOVE YOGURT: Simple ingredients, not a lot of sugar.	

(This "Not a Lot of Sugar" :15 TV spot was created by Tom & Eric 911 for Siggi's yogurt. Script courtesy of Tom & Eric 911.)

SCRIPTS AND EXAMPLES 7.4 Siggi's yogurt, :15 video/TV one-column script with italics: "Not a Lot of Sugar"

CLIENT: SIGGI'S YOGURT
JOB: :15 video/TV (one-column with italics)
TITLE: "Not a Lot of Sugar"
DATE: 12/16/22

BEIGE SCREEN WITH TEXT:

> When I moved here from Iceland, I felt most yogurts had too much sugar in them. So, I made my own.
>
> Photo of Siggi at yogurt stand.

SIGGI: *When I moved here from Iceland, I felt most yogurts had too much sugar in them. So, I made my own.*

> Hand places yogurt container on table.

SIGGI: *And then I made some more.*
         Hand turns yogurt around.

VO: *Simple ingredients, not a lot of sugar.*

(This "Not a Lot of Sugar" :15 TV spot was created by Tom & Eric 911 for Siggi's yogurt. Script courtesy of Tom & Eric 911.)

Discovering more about universal truths

Notice how strong campaigns express what many people feel. In the following Johnson & Johnson "Having a Baby Changes Everything" campaign, the entire premise is based on that undeniable, universal truth: Once you have children, your life changes and priorities shift. What once was a fun, boys' night out becomes an enchanting boys' night in, as shown in the "Frogs" spot (Figure 7.4).

Another spot, "Hats" (Figure 7.5), showed how a mom who used to primp for hours to look beautiful, now enjoys the simple pleasure of looking silly and wearing funny hats just to amuse her baby.

You can see how each of the spots (Figure 7.4, Figure 7.5, Figure 7.6) showed the parents' perspective with unaffected empathy and genuine candor. They portrayed what it was really like to have a baby, depicting the experience accurately. Parents everywhere could quickly identify with the heart-warming scenarios.

Just look how the "Short and Bald" storyboard (Figure 7.6) depicts a mother's love. It humorously talked about how she used to be attracted to the tall, dark, handsome type. Now, her tiny, short, and bald baby has won her over and completely captured her heart.

When asked how the campaign was created, Andrew Langer, chief creative officer at Roberts + Langer, said:

> The creative brief has to drive the idea. It always comes first. The single-minded proposition was to show that Johnson & Johnson understands and values the relationship between parents and their baby.[5]

He explained how the campaign was built on a universal theme, as follows:

> The sequence was brief, idea, execution. Everything else followed.
>   The strategy is universal. The execution changed to fit the market. It had to be real and honest wherever it ran. It was always shot in black and white which gave it a documentary quality and added to the reality.[6]

FIGURE 7.4 This "Frogs" :30 TV spot was created by Roberts + Langer for Johnson & Johnson. Storyboard courtesy of Roberts + Langer and Johnson & Johnson.

Langer then described how strategic thinking drove the core campaign message:

> The strategic idea that helped form the campaign is based on a reality of being a parent. Your whole life you're the center of the universe. You decide what you do, what color your car is, what movies you watch, what you eat, who you see. Everything is centered around you. And maybe you fall in love and say we're doing this together, but it's still really about you. You are the center of your universe. And then you have a baby and the center of the universe moves from you to your baby. You give up rock and roll for rock-a-bye baby. Things that were important for you are no longer important unless they're important for the baby. Therefore, "Having a baby changes everything."[7]

FIGURE 7.5 This "Hats" :30 TV spot was created by Roberts + Langer for Johnson & Johnson. Storyboard courtesy of Roberts + Langer and Johnson & Johnson.

The question that marketers always want to know is if the campaign is effective. According to Langer, this one was because it "increased already-high equity."[8] That is often the case when a universal truth is used correctly. The audience connects both to the message and the brand. It establishes a trustworthy relationship and natural loyalty.

FIGURE 7.6 This "Short and Bald" :30 TV spot was created by Roberts + Langer for Johnson & Johnson. Storyboard courtesy of Roberts + Langer and Johnson & Johnson.

What you really want is to entice the audience to at least listen to what you have to say. Charlie Hopper, principal at Young & Laramore, explained that you need to offer the audience something new, maybe even tease them into paying attention because they might actually want to hear this. He recognizes that most people are trying to avoid advertising, as much as insurance salespeople.

You're not teasing them in order to just torture them or be
obscure. But, you're teasing them a little bit with something to
say, "You would be interested in this if you would give it half
a second."
      The audience is trying to eject from everything you write,
like James Bond's car. Your reader is trying to get away
from you.[9]

Remember, when choosing universal truths, you're looking for a familiar expression that is commonly accepted as true. It crosses cultural, geographic, and generational barriers. It's universally adopted; although it may be modified slightly in different languages, it still carries the same idea.

Sheena Brady, commercial director/creative director, emphasized the importance of finding a universal truth that transcended cultural barriers. She further explained that campaigns would be modified to fit the consumers' frame of reference. For instance, football is more popular in America than soccer. These sports preferences are just the reverse in Europe and other parts of the world, like South America, for example. She also said:

If you have a voice that is in everything from your label to your
messaging in the Internet, or the piece that you send out, and it's
all consistent, it really gives people a sense of who you are, It's very
singularly focused. It's very integrated and people get a sense of what
you stand for as a brand.[10]

She continued:

You have to take the kind of brand attributes, the kind of things that
make a soda a soda, or a running shoe a running shoe, and you
have to tailor that. But, the idea of a one-on-one communication
with someone, that doesn't change.[11]

Also, when reviewing commercials, be sure to compare script and storyboard formats. See how storyboards highlight ("billboard") the action in the spots. They allow clients to simultaneously see the spot visually, while reading the actors' lines. Few storyboards can capture every single frame. The point of the storyboard is to portray the main points in as few frames (and boards) as possible. One presentation board per spot would be ideal. Some spots may require more than one board. Ultimately, strive to have as few as possible. This will help you eliminate depicting unnecessary frames.

Speaking from the consumer's perspective

The one challenge almost everyone faces is time management. So, a campaign that speaks to that concern will be heard. One example is the Pet Supplies Plus campaign, which we'll discuss in Chapter 12, when we look at in-store displays (Figure 12.15, Figure 12.16, Figure 12.17), that show adorable pet images with playful headlines. One display shows a cat with a pensive stare, as if to concur with the message: "You can leave empty-handed. But we don't recommend it." Another stated, "Oversized is overrated." and showed a close-up of a cute guinea pig.

The campaign challenges the bigger-is-better idea behind big-box chain pet supermarkets. Are they really more convenient? Having a great deal of inventory on the floor means wading through the aisles is time-consuming. Shoppers can't easily dash in, find what they want, and check out. Young & Laramore created these TV spots that make consumers think twice and discover the joys of not-so-massive stores. In the first one, "Waiting" (Figure 7.7), two dogs are anxiously waiting for their treats. One gets it quickly and the other is kept waiting, just as consumers have to do when they're waiting in line to check out. Be sure to read the copy in Scripts and Examples 7.5.

"Waiting"

FIGURE 7.7 These "Waiting" :30 TV storyboard screengrabs were created by Young & Laramore for Pet Supplies Plus. Courtesy of Young & Laramore.

SCRIPTS AND EXAMPLES 7.5 Pet Supplies Plus, :30 TV script: "Waiting"

VISUAL:	*Open on two dogs sitting next to each other, in between our spokesperson who is holding dog treats out above their heads.*
	One side of the screen reads Pet Supplies Plus. The other side of the screen reads petgoliath.com
	Dogs look at the treats expectantly.
VO:	*Pet Supplies Plus stores are small by choice,*
VO:	*which means you get in and out quickly without the wait.*
	PSP dog is given his treat. He eats it and runs off happily.
VO:	*If only we could say the same for shopping at big box stores.*
	Big box dog is still waiting for his treat. He whines and begs for the treat, but the spokesperson doesn't give it to him.
VO:	*Ah-ah, not yet, Moose.*
Super:	*Plus – everything you need.*
	Big box dog sighs and pouts.
Super:	*Minus – waiting to get it.*
	Art card / rotating tagline:
	Pet Supplies Plus. Minus long lines.
	Pet Supplies Plus. Minus winding aisles.
	Pet Supplies Plus. Minus keeping you waiting.
	Pet Supplies Plus. Minus the hassle.

(This "Waiting" :30 TV script was created by Young & Laramore for Pet Supplies Plus. Script courtesy of Young & Laramore.)

In the next :30 spot, "Big Box vs. Small Box" (Figure 7.8), two dogs are each in shallow boxes filled with colorful ping-pong balls. They're challenged to find a toy hidden among the balls. The doggie searching in a box representing Pet Supplies Plus, finds it quickly. The other dog is hopelessly searching, imitating frustrated shoppers hunting for their items in a giant pet store. The unstated question is: How much time do you really want to spend meandering through "miles" of products to find what you need? The clear copy is found in Scripts and Examples 7.6. Take a moment to enjoy it.

FIGURE 7.8 This "Big Box vs. Small Box" :30 TV screenshot was created by Young & Laramore for Pet Supplies Plus. Image courtesy of Young & Laramore.

SCRIPTS AND EXAMPLES 7.6 Pet Supplies Plus, :30 TV script: "Big Box vs. Small Box"

VISUAL: *We're in a white room with two shallow boxes (Think kiddie pool depth.) on the floor. There is a small box filled with green ping-pong balls, and a large box is filled with blue and red balls.*

A flag near the green box reads "Pet Supplies Plus." A flag near the blue box reads "Pet Goliath."

VO: *This box is small like Pet Supplies Plus. This one is large like a big box store.*

VO: *In each, Stu, (Hi Stu.) has carefully hidden a toy.*

VO: *Question is which dog will find it first.*

Two dogs enter from either side of the screen and dive into their respective boxes.

Both dogs dig for toys. Ping-pong balls fly everywhere. Some fall out and bounce on the floor.

The dog in the small box retrieves the toy.

Spokesperson holds up that dog's leg/paw victoriously. He's clearly naming the dog in the small box the winner.

VO: *Sings/makes "triumphant" trumpet noise*

Dog in big box is still digging then gives up; a photo backdrop of the interior of a Pet Supplies Plus unrolls behind scene.

VO: *Tada! Moose. No you were so close.*

Super: *Plus – an easy-to-navigate store.*

Super: *Minus – making you work for what you need.*

Pet Supplies Plus. (Rotating end tag) Minus the hassle.

(This "Big Box vs. Small Box" :30 TV script was created by Young & Laramore for Pet Supplies Plus. Script courtesy of Young & Laramore.)

The social media content video scripts (Scripts and Examples 7.7, Scripts and Examples 7.8) reinforce the benefits with closing lines that state, "Oversized is overrated." (Figure 7.9) and "Less searching. More shopping." (Figure 7.10). The entire campaign reminds shoppers of the hassle of big-store shopping and the joy of quickly darting in and out to get what they want without the headache. Take your time to read and appreciate the benefit-rich scripts.

 SCRIPTS AND EXAMPLES 7.7 Pet Supplies Plus, social content video: "Oversized is Overrated."

Dog runs in and attempts to pick up log-like stick.
Art Card: Oversized is overrated.

(This "Oversized is Overrated." social media content video script was created by Young & Laramore for Pet Supplies Plus. Script courtesy of Young & Laramore.)

 SCRIPTS AND EXAMPLES 7.8 Pet Supplies Plus, social content video: "Less Searching. More Shopping."

Dog runs across screen, back and forth a few times.
Art Card: Less searching. More shopping.

(This "Less searching. More shopping." social media content video script was created by Young & Laramore for Pet Supplies Plus. Script courtesy of Young & Laramore.)

FIGURE 7.9 This "Oversized is Overrated." social content video was created by Young & Laramore for Pet Supplies Plus. Image courtesy of Young & Laramore.

FIGURE 7.10 This "Less Searching. More Shopping." social content video was created by Young & Laramore for Pet Supplies Plus. Image courtesy of Young & Laramore.

Seeing how exaggeration, humor, and strong copy drive home benefits

Some commercials use overt exaggeration to feature consumer key product selling points and/or clear consumer benefits. You'll find that some spots incorporate exaggerations. These are often what make spots so funny. Take a look at the Super Bowl "Beer Closet" spot for Heineken. It featured a group of women screaming with delight as the lady of the house showed off her massive closet to her friends. Then, the women heard men shouting from downstairs as her partner proudly showed his buddies his trophy: a Heineken-filled, walk-in closet. It exaggerated this universal truth: Women love enormous, personal closets. But, it cleverly flipped the concept and showed men's love of beer, celebrated by a huge, walk-in, stocked only with their favorite brand: Heineken. So, the exaggeration really worked.

Taco Bell used humorous exaggeration in several of its commercials. One spot, Taco Bell's "Grande Quesadilla," showed a pregnant girl struggling to get on the bus and waddling down the aisle because of her big belly. She sat down next to a young guy with an extended stomach. He turns to her, looks at her belly and says, "Grande Quesadilla?" assuming she was overstuffed like he was, missing the obvious. The announcer says, "So filling, it's like you're eating for two," emphasizing the *abundance* strategy discussed in Chapter 6. The closing line restated the brand's clever *play-on-words* slogan (#4 technique in Chapter 10): "Think outside the bun."

The use of exaggeration and humor, and descriptive, mouth-watering copy drives home the product-centric TV messages. You can see how the writers strive to make an item sound scrumptious through their use of language.

It's not just about naming the products and listing the ingredients. It's about making consumers almost taste the items as they hear them being described. You actually want to arouse consumers' appetites and tempt their taste buds.

Realizing a great tip for TV spot length

As you watch commercials, pay careful attention to the writing. You'll learn how to create tighter (more concise) spots by having exceptionally well-written references. Sometimes new writers wonder how much copy should be in a 30-second spot. Kevin Moriarty, former vice president and creative director at Leo Burnett, said that a previous creative director gave him some great advice when he worked at BBDO in New York. He told Moriarty to keep his 30-second TV spots to 70 words or less. When Moriarty presented him with a 71-word script that he thought was perfect, the CD told him to keep working until he could eliminate one word. He struggled with this editing assignment, asking:

> How important could it be? And he made me do it. But, it made me think ever since about that. I went to the award books from the previous year and I went through every award-winning commercial and none of them were more than 70 words. In fact, most of them were a lot less than that. So there really was something there.[12]

Moriarty's desire to better understand his creative director's TV word-length rule drove him to closely examine commercials in award annuals. He sat and counted the number of words in each award-winning TV spot. How many writers would have had the initiative to disprove or confirm this unwritten rule? He found out that all the winning spots were 70 words or less.[13] Just as billboards should be as few words as possible, preferably around seven to ten words or less, TV spots also have a word count that makes them most effective. The next time you're writing a 30-second spot, try keeping it under 70 words. Then, ask yourself if the spot seems "tighter," more succinct, more focused?

Investigating ways to present TV ideas

After you examine the word count, you need to think about how you're going to present your idea to the client. Each agency has its own presentation techniques. Some use storyboards. Others show scripts. And others create stories. Sara Rose, an executive creative director/writer, said that sometimes she doesn't write copy for global clients. She said, "We tend to *not have* dialogue in that ad, and that doesn't mean that there isn't writing involved."

It means that she and her former creative partner, group creative director/ art director Lea Ladera, would write a story and a script to communicate the basic idea in a client presentation. She said, "What we're doing is trying to get them to understand what message we're trying to create and what our vision is."[14] The creative team writes this out in a few paragraphs. Sometimes it requires a little longer explanation.

She went on to clarify that a lot of people are under the misconception that writers only write and art directors only design. The truth is that together they create a story and a larger concept behind it. She elaborated on this point:

> I like to think that what I do is that I'm a conceptual person who specializes in writing and my art director is a conceptual person who specializes in art direction. Our titles don't necessarily limit what our contributions are to a project.[15]

For TV spots, copywriters and art directors write a script and a short story about what takes place. As a team, they're drawing a picture in the minds of their clients. They need to convey an idea in a visual way. They need to make the idea understood by everyone: both the visual and non-visual clients.

Likewise, a concept for a global client needs to be grasped by audiences around the world. The idea must be instantly understood without a need for explanation.

When asked who handles what when working on a TV spot, Rose said that when it comes to production, each team is different. In her partnership with Ladera, Rose usually handled the music, sound, and final mixing of the commercials. It's important to realize that oftentimes the writers' work isn't finished when they complete the copy. They may need to edit the spot, before they go into the studio to produce it. They're usually expected to handle words and sound in commercials. They must read every script out loud with a stop-watch and remember to count a slow "one–two" for each sound effect to ensure accurate script length before going into production.

Learning from beloved Super Bowl spots

The best way to improve your TV writing skills is to examine excellent commercials, both new and old. Guard yourself against being a marketing ageist. Celebrate creativity everywhere you find it, regardless of its time stamp. Brilliant ideas will always be just that: brilliant and inspiring. At least familiarize yourself with the *Advertising Age* list: "Top 20 Super Bowl Ads Ever" on YouTube. Also, immerse yourself in award-winning spots in annual award competitions and review top-ranked Super Bowl spots each year.

Take a few minutes to view the spots. See if you can deconstruct them to determine why they created such a strong response in viewers. Try to determine what was it that created the most prized result: "talk value," also known as "buzz," "water-cooler chatter," or "social media comments." When a commercial causes people to talk about it and they remember the advertiser, the spot raises awareness, heightens brand recognition, and strengthens retention.

For example, Apple's "1984" spot, which introduced the Apple Macintosh personal computer, aired one time during the Super Bowl of that year and is often ranked as the number one commercial in Top 20 Super Bowl Ads Ever list. Can you understand why it claimed first place? Part of its success was its literary reference to George Orwell's *1984*, a book often seen on high school reading lists. Many students grew up believing that the government, "Big Brother," would monitor, supervise, and control everyone's life. The spot showed a female athlete tossing a brass-headed hammer through a large screen as a breakthrough moment that defied this kind of control, explaining in the copy why "1984 won't be like 1984."

Look at the monster.com spot "When I Grow Up" and notice the intelligent copy that lets young children describe what their career goals might be if they grew up without sports. Here's one line: "When I grow up I want to file all day long." Of course, no one wants that job. That's what makes the message so compelling. How many people settle for a job they hate because they believe they can't succeed? Although not stated, playing sports can help build self-esteem and confidence, enabling children to seek more satisfying jobs. The universal truth is people settle for less because they think they can't achieve more. Sports challenge kids to try harder and give them a vehicle to stretch their self-limiting beliefs.

Although universal truths are a powerful way to connect to the audience, selecting the right type of commercial is another decision to help drive home the message.

Identifying types of TV commercials

As you can see in Useful Info 7.9, there are many kinds of TV formats. Think of these as packages that contain and then deliver the concept. You're probably already familiar with many of these. You may not have known what the spots were called, but if you've watched TV, you've seen them. Think back. Do you recall viewing any *product demonstrations* (examples of how products work), *testimonials* (people talking about products they use), *talking heads* (actors talking into the camera, shot from the chest up), and *vignettes* (mini plays)? Look over the list in Useful Info 7.9 and see how many other examples you've already watched.

The sooner you're able to identify the kind of spots you're seeing, the quicker you'll develop a library of TV commercial references. Ask yourself what spots used *animation*? Which campaigns used *continuing characters*? What other brands have instantly recognizable *icons*? Have you seen other spots that don't fit into any of these categories? If so, start making an ongoing list of new categories. See how many more you can find.

USEFUL INFO 7.9 Some popular types of TV spots

1   *Demonstration* (like detergent spots, including Tide "Talking Stain" spot)

2   *Testimonials* (like the L'Oréal "Because you're worth it," spots)

3   *Talking Head* (like a news anchor delivering the news, as in the Hasbro "Mr. Potato Head" spots)

4   *Slice-of-Life* or *Vignette* (a little story like a TV episode where product solves problem, like the three Google "Parisian Love" spots)

5   *Lifestyle* (how product fits into someone's lifestyle like a minivan packed with kids, dogs, and sports gear. It's not a story, just a snapshot. This is like the Tacori diamond ring commercial "Cupid's Arrow.")

6   *Animation* (like the Keebler Elves "Magic Middles Cookies," Petco "Holiday Tails," or the Coke "Beautiful" spots)

7   *Jingles* (like the Christmas spots by De Beers, such as "Falling for You," or the Meow Mix "Cats Ask for Them by Name" spots with cats singing "Meow" with subtitles describing what they're saying)

8   *Visual as Hero* (Coke "It's Mine")

9   *Humor* (like the Heineken "Beer Closet" spot)

10 *Continuing Characters* (like the "Mac versus PC" or Flo in the Progressive Insurance spots)

11 *Reason Why* (like the De Beers "A Diamond is Forever" commercials)

12 *Emotion* (like the Thai Life Insurance commercials, such as "Unsung Hero" and "Garbage Man")

13 *Before and After* (like weight-loss programs, often with a "split screen")

14 *Anthropomorphism* (when animals take on human emotion, like the Budweiser Clydesdale "American Dream" spot)

15 *Emotional Blackmail* (makes you feel guilty for not using the product, like the Johnson's baby shampoo "No More Tears" commercials)

16 *Consumer-Created Content* (like the Doritos "Anti-bark Collar" commercial)

17 *Truth* (like the Dove "Real Beauty" and the "Truth" anti-smoking campaigns, including the "Tobacco Kills" spot)

18 *Celebrity Spokesperson* (like these actors in Allstate Insurance spots: Dean Winters as the "Mayhem" character and Dennis Haysbert as the general spokesperson)

19 *Celebrity Endorsements* (like the weight-loss commercial for Weight Watchers with Jennifer Hudson in the "Me Power" spot)

20 *Sexy* (like the Budweiser spots with beauty shots of the beer dripping down the glass to the lyrics of the "You Sexy Thing")

21 *Cultural Impact* (like the Budweiser "Whassup!" or Wendy's classic "Where's the Beef?" spots)

22 *Role Reversal* (like the E-Trade "Talking Baby" campaign and the Doritos "Keep Your Hands off My Mama" spots)

23 *Holiday Greeting* (a few classics: Hershey's Kisses as bells playing "Wish You a Merry Christmas" and the Budweiser Clydesdales retro-style "Holiday Greetings" spots)

24 *Product Icons* (like the classic Coca-Cola "Polar Bears" campaign, the famous Keebler "Elves" and "Energizer Bunny" campaigns)

25 *Product as Graphic Visual* (like the product-launch spots for the Nike swoosh-branding campaign and Apple's iPod white ear bud cords against a silhouetted image)

26 *Visual as Benefit* (like the Axe deodorant and hair product campaigns that promise to create animal magnetism, such as "Axe Effect" spots)

27 *Public Service Announcement* (how it focuses on a particular cause or charitable organization, usually created pro bono – without creative and/or production fees – by the agency, production house, or broadcast station, like the Mothers Against Drunk Driving (MADD) campaign, such as the "Drinking and Driving" spot)

Writing TV scripts

After reviewing the list did you notice how the visual drives home the message? The next time you're writing for TV, think visually. Try to let an image move the story or action along. How can your idea be projected in a visually compelling way? What graphics could stop the viewer? What scenarios could draw the audience in? What characters could become part of everyday culture? Consider all the commercials you loved. What part did the visual play? Here are a few other examples, in addition to the above-mentioned ones: milk mustache (California Milk Processor Board), Clydesdales and Dalmatians (Budweiser), cool guy versus geek (Apple), the bottle (Coke "Open Happiness"). What other images or characters can you name?

Next, think about production. Will this idea be executable or is it so complex, it would require an entire film cast and crew? If that's in the budget, fine. If not, how else could you get this message across? If you're struggling to execute your idea, remember some of the most powerful commercials are simple. Here's one example. For a public service campaign promoting AIDS prevention, the script used two actors, one indoor location (setting), one scene, three frames, and four superimposed words. Take a moment and see if you can come up with an idea. Any luck? Okay. Here's how the spot went.

> *Frame one (scene one)*: A young couple are holding hands while walking toward double doors in a beautiful hotel room. The doors open, a luxurious king-size bed appears. They walk through the doors.

> *Frame two*: Fade to black. White text appears in two parts, one line at a time. BANG! BANG! YOU'RE DEAD!

> *Frame three*: Logo of AIDS prevention association

So simple. So clear. So unforgettable. So affordable. It didn't lecture or preach. It just demonstrated the risk of careless behavior. One reckless moment of passion could cost you your life. It doesn't get more direct than that.

Simplicity can sometimes create a stronger response than a complicated, expensive shoot. Even fascinating, high-tech imagery doesn't have to produce high-impact reactions. How many times have you marveled at the visual techniques in a spot, but couldn't remember the product? That spot could have represented tens or hundreds of thousands, possibly even millions of dollars spent with no brand recognition. Always keep in mind that you want the viewer to not only to remember the spot, but also to recall the brand.

TIPS AND RULES 7.10
Basic TV writing rules for scripts

1 *Concepting*
   - Review the brief, product/brand research, and consumer insight.
   - Think about the audience. See them three-dimensionally, as real people, not a list of statistical data. Which *VALS category* or categories would they fit into?
   - Analyze the Creative Strategy Statement to determine the strategic creative direction.
   - Reread Chapter 5. Examine the handy list of strategies in Chapter 6. What strategy would work for this brand? Think about choosing one, or blending several strategies, before deciding.
   - Consider the *brand personality* and how best to depict it.
   - Think visually.
   - Think about the kinds of talent you will be *casting*, so you have their voices and images in your mind.
   - Decide what kind of programs or channels the spot would air on. Are they skewed to a particular type of audience?

2 *Writing*

- Write for the ear and eye.
- Imagine the finished spot.
- Tell a complete story.
- Present an instantly comprehensible version of the spot in script or story-board format.
- Grab viewers' attention.
- Have on- and/or off-camera actor(s) in mind from the beginning. *On-camera* actors appear in a scene or frame. *Off-camera* actors are heard as "voice only" talent.
- Start with act two. Jump right into the action.
- As in radio, use contractions like "you're" and "they're."
- Use *vernacular* (everyday speech like "gotta" and "gonna") when appropriate for the brand.
- Write in phrases, the way you speak, not in full sentences.
- Make dialogues sound natural and conversational.
- Consider various TV formats like *product comparison, animation, testimonial, vignette, product demonstration* (before and after), *celebrity spokesperson*, etc.
- Write around the setting like on location or in the studio.
- Allow a few seconds of time for visual effects like: *morphs, slow dissolves, page turns, scrolls* or *crawls, fades to black.*
- Count aloud, slowly "one, two" for a full two seconds for each sound effect and music cut.
- Remember to use the appropriate *tone of voice* for the brand.
- Analyze the pace of a celebrity's delivery if one is being cast in the commercial. Write to that specific talent's rhythm.
- Ask yourself if you want to close with a super, logo, sig, wrap up, button, and/or call to action.
- Read all scripts aloud for correct timing and copy flow.
- Time your spot with a stopwatch and allow one second of silence at the end to ensure the ending won't be cut off, so a :30 is :29 closing with a *beauty shot, logo,* and possibly a *fade-to-black* close.

3 *Formatting*

- Set up two columns, left side for video directions, right side for audio (music, sound effects, spoken lines). Music, sound effects, and actors create an aligned middle (third) column. (See TV script format in Templates 7.12.)
- Double space between "frames" (separate visual ideas and scenes).
- Use single space within each "*frame.*"
- Break key ideas into selected frames.
- Make sure frames move the story along.

- Decide and indicate where music comes in and out.
- Determine where to place *supers* (superimposed words like easy-to-remember phone number, website, other information).
- Break lines correctly for *voiceover* and on-camera talent.
- Think about what sound effects to use and where to place them.
- Use industry standard abbreviations and terminology like *SFX* and *CU*.
- Say client name at least twice and *superimpose* it at least once.

4 *Production*
- Consider production while you're writing. What *camera angles*, shooting techniques, and visual effects will enhance the spot?
- Think about the kind of "read" you want (how the actors should interpret the script when they read their lines).
- Select key frames to create the storyboard. Not every image will be shown.
- Select appropriate music cuts and decide where they post (are inserted).
- Select the most accurate sound effects and insert them in the appropriate places in the spot.
- Decide where to place supers on the screen. Do you want any information crawling along the bottom of the spot or scrolling down from the top of the screen?
- Choose where you might include a beauty shot (close-up) of the product.
- Consider post-production modifications like scene edits, visual effects, music posts, and sound levels.
- Remember when producing:
    - Listen to sound levels.
    - Determine if you need to color correct a frame because of a lighting or other issue.
    - Watch for picture safety, so you don't place any supers too close to the screen edges.
- Select key frames to use as *"screengrabs"* or *"screenshots"* as images that represent the main action or concept in the spot.

See the list of basic rules for writing TV scripts (Tips and Rules 7.10). Review them each time you start to create a commercial. They will help guide you toward developing successful commercials.

Absorbing key copywriting tips

Nothing replaces experience and the wisdom of seasoned writers. Sometimes, just reading a few tips will help you grasp the specific writing techniques needed for great TV copy. Look at these tips from copywriting masters,

Tom Amico, Sara Rose, and Vinny Warren. Amico is co-founder and creative director/writer at Tom & Eric 911. When he was at the Kaplan Thaler Group, he was co-creator of the Aflac Duck with Eric David, creative director/art director. Sara Rose, is an executive creative director/writer, who developed cross-channel campaigns for Target, including the "Holiday Odyssey." Vinny Warren is the founder and creative director of The Escape Pod and one of the creators of the Budweiser "Whassup!" campaign while at DDB. Here are some important points that will fine-tune your writing.

Tom Amico's tips (Tom & Eric 911, formerly at Kaplan Thaler Group)

Tip 1. Make sure your writing has attitude. When we created the Aflac Duck campaign, we made sure the client bought into the fact that we didn't want a cute cuddly *spokesanimal*. A little attitude goes a long way in copywriting, and too much attitude is sometimes, well, just too much attitude and a turn-off. But a little can be just the right amount.

Tip 2. Saturate yourself with great advertising from around the world. The best work is coming from all over. Brazil. Iceland. Singapore. Thailand. Because they are havens for the hottest art direction, the writing is kept to a minimum. If the story can best be told in pictures (visually), be a good enough writer to leave the writing out.

Tip 3. Three words: "Kills Bugs Dead." Your English teacher might say it's redundant. The Raid client might have said we don't want to say "dead" let alone "kill" and dead in our theme line. But writing doesn't get any more succinct or to the point than "Kills Bugs Dead." Plus, it's persuasive and tells me everything I need to know about the product.

Tip 4. Read *Catcher in the Rye*, *Catch-22*, and *The World According to Garp*. They are not necessarily the best-written books, but any page you open to, the writing is engaging enough for you to want to read more. Any place in a block of copy you write or on a script, should have the same power.[16]

Sara Rose's tips (executive creative director/writer)

Tip 1. Well, I read this somewhere once and it always helped me, is that you need to sort of throw out your first 20 or so ideas. Write them on your first day ever working on a project because that's when you just get the bad stuff out, for lack of a better word. The most obvious solutions to a problem usually come out first. There are exceptions to that rule. You just can't be too self-satisfied with yourself. So that's a big thing. I'm never exactly happy with everything I do. I'm always willing and open to continue to work on it until I get it right.

Tip 2. Don't overwrite. A lot of people really, really overwrite. You need to learn how to make an impact with the fewest words possible. And that's even in a dialogue spot.

Tip 3. You have to be hard on yourself. You have to be really, really hard on yourself. Whenever Lea and I do a project and we work on a script, or work on an Internet idea, before we even show it internally, we talk to each other and say, "Is this something that I would want to produce? Is this something I would want to spend a lot of time on? Do I feel good enough about it? Do I feel proud of it? Could it be better?" And if we say, "Oh no, I don't really think I would be happy if it was produced," then we just don't show it. But that also means trashing 90% of our ideas. I think you have to be really hard on yourself.

I think that some young writers, juniors, think everything that they come up with is going to be amazing. There are some people where that's the case. But I think for a lot of people, you have to be hard on yourself.[17]

Vinny Warren's tips just on screenwriting (The Escape Pod)

If you're talking about TV, film, video, or whatever it is, there's an old saying if you ever saw it, it was: You write film three times. You write it when you write it. You write it when you shoot it. And, you write it when you edit it. That's the truth, right? You start out with a script when you present it, or when you sell it. That, of course, is done in isolation because you have no idea what the filming is going to be like, who is going to be directing it, any of that stuff. You have no idea of that.

Then, when you get into filming it, things will change. You think, "Oh, I was thinking of it this way, but now that I thought about it more, in reality in terms of shooting, it'll change a bit, and the words will change, and things will change." Like for example, the Budweiser "The Out-of-towner" spot [https://www.youtube.com/watch?v=_UAzkmv50o0]. The script that we presented was radically different than what we shot. It had to be because the words had to change to suit this actor who wasn't terribly experienced. So, if we had adhered to the original script, it would have been insane because it wouldn't have worked.

Then, of course, you rewrite it again when you edit it, by virtue of what you choose to go on the film. So, that's the way I look at writing for film. When you start out, you have no idea of this. You can't. That's something you've got to experience. When you start out everyone has the same idea. It's basically, "You get to shoot exactly what's on my page from my script because it's perfect and brilliant and I've thought about it," which is exactly wrong. When you go about it, then you realize, "Oh no, hang on, that's not right."

Then, you get more open and then, of course, that predisposes that you have the freedom to do it. When we came back to Anheuser-Busch with our "The Out-of-towner" idea they weren't going, "Wait a minute. That's not the script you sold us." But, that was the general idea we sold them. And, it was funny. That's all they cared about.[18]

Just for clarification, "The Out-of-towner" spot has a guy from Texas in a cowboy hat in a bar in New York. Everyone who comes in casually says, "Hi, how ya doin'" as a standard greeting. The out-of-towner thinks people are really asking him how he is. So, he answers each person with the same response, drawn out in his Texan drawl, "Thanks for asking. I'm doin' just fine. I just got in today. My brother-in-law just picked me up from the airport. Mighty fine airport you got here. The people here are real friendly." Obviously, the out-of-towner doesn't understand that no one really cares and that's just how everyone says hi. It's a very comical scene. Try to watch it so you can hear how humorous his repetitive response is and how it's another example of exaggeration.

Creating interactive TV spots

Today, viewers have choices. They can select an interactive 30-second spot or view several minutes of commercials. If they hit the okay button, they may be prompted to use the arrows to select the topic. For example, for a travel-related spot, they might be asked what kind of trip they'd prefer: a mountain adventure, an island retreat, or a city exploration. Then, information about that specific type of journey would appear. The reward would be one short spot instead of having to sit through several minutes of commercials.

Viewers can also click to make purchases, find out more about credit card benefits, and so on. Many spots include a QR code that direct viewers to websites with opted-in content. Marketers know that consumers who click through are interested in the product or offer. This is a great advantage to any budget because it's money well spent or a great ROI (as you know, return of investment).

Another option is to create a series of interconnected spots. For example, Acura introduced the Type S performance cars with four one-minute episodes to target a younger car buyer. The episodes followed a teenager whose uncle was teaching her how to drive so she could outdrive a competitor, who regularly zoomed around the racetrack. According to Acura's VP and brand officer Jon Ikeda, the brand wanted to emphasize "fun," and in so doing, aimed to open the floor to younger buyers who were more connected to social media. "The one-minute spots lend themselves better to digital platforms and social media," stated Ikeda, referencing how his own son doesn't watch TV.[19] They also include a Spanish-language voiceover to appeal to Spanish-speaking audiences, with the aim of building a "multicultural base," Ikeda said.

Other even shorter, three-second spots, or *blipverts* were created to run during the Sundance Film Festival. However, the event was moved to online because of the COVID-19 pandemic.

The question now is how can you get a relevant point across to an already distracted audience in the least amount of time possible?

Casting TV talent

Just as in radio, you should think about the kind of talent you want as you're writing the spot. Are you looking for an *announcer*, an *actor*, or a *character actor*? What's the difference? Announcers can present a dramatic or straightforward read. Think of one-voice retail commercials or trailers for movies you've seen. They're often voiced by announcers. These voice talents don't act a part; they deliver the information about the film or brand. Actors, on the other hand, are cast for various types of spot, including vignettes, lifestyle spots with dialogue, or other commercials with scenes. Character actors are selected for their ability to create different and authentic-sounding regional accents and specific personalities or professions.

Try to hear the kind of read you want before you start casting. Be sure you see the talent live or on a video demo (demonstration or "demo" tape). This way you can cast the actor(s) with the appropriate look and delivery and see how well they take direction. If you're casting for a spot with a family, you may need to spend extra time to find actors who are playing various family members. You may want them to resemble each other and look related. Or, you may want to show a culturally diverse family. At the casting audition, ask the talents to read the script so you can hear their style of delivery. If you hire a casting agent, be sure you can view a few additional talents, even if she or he has selected the key actors. In case there's a last-minute cancellation, you will have some other talent options.

Becoming familiar with TV terminology

Now let's examine how important it is to speak the lingo. If you're at a shoot, casting talent or finalizing the spot in post-production, people around you are going to expect you to understand what they're saying and to use the industry language and common TV terms (Useful Info 7.11). If you want to refilm a scene, you'd say, "Let's retake that shot," or "Let's reshoot that scene." If you wanted to superimpose words on the screen in *post-production*, you'd want to check for screen safety. If you need to fix the actor's collar, you'd need to call out "*wardrobe*" to alert the wardrobe person. Take some time to completely familiarize yourself with all the words listed in Useful Info 7.11. Then, when you're on the set, you'll be comfortable with the language of TV writing and production.

Pay attention to how each frame is single-spaced, but is separated from the next frame by a double space. This format (Templates 7.12) helps the actors and the camera crew to see the spot in a progression of actions. The more spots you view in a campaign, the more you'll understand how to create spots that relate to each other. Look for excellent visual references that you can keep in mind when you're writing.

---

i USEFUL INFO 7.11 Common TV terms

Animation	Cartoon-like images for special communication (Aflac Duck)
ASCAP	American Society of Composers, Authors and Publishers (organization that provides licenses and royalties for members' performances)
Beauty shot	Close-up of the product by itself
Blipvert	Commercials that run for three seconds or less
Camera angle	Position of camera in relation to the subject (object, person, or scene) when filming or photographing
Camera person	Films all the scenes and beauty shots
Casting agent	Person who auditions and selects the talent
Chyron	Character generator that creates the supers (on-screen text)
Clap board	Chalkboard used to identify the "take" number for post-production (camera assistant holds the clap board up to be filmed, announces the take number, and closes the hinged top bar, producing a "clap")
Color bars	Striped bar of test colors that precedes the commercial and is used as a reference point to allow for color adjustments to ensure playback will match recorded spot

Crawl	Words or images move along the screen horizontally, like a baby crawling across the floor
CU	Close-up, camera is near object or actor
Demo	DVD or digital demonstration of talent's range of abilities or production house's samples of best commercials
Director	Person in charge of supervising the production
Dissolve	One image fades as another one comes up, if done very slowly, it's called a "slow dissolve"
Dolly	Camera is mounted on a small truck that smoothly moves across tracks to follow action in scene and carries the camera crew and director
ECU	Extreme close-up, camera is right beside object or actor
Flow	How smoothly and effortlessly the copy reads
Frame	One scene or shot in the commercial
Freeze frame	Action is completely stopped
Gaffer	Head electrician who oversees lighting apparatus
Grip	Carpenter who builds and repairs the set during production
Hair stylist	Person who styles the actors' hair for the shoot
Humor	Uses comedy for entertainment and retention
Icon	Drives brand recognition (Geico's Gecko)
In sync	Soundtrack and actors' mouth movements (sound and action) are synchronized
Insert	(1) Image showing a specific detail is inserted on screen, sometimes in a box; (2) another shot is inserted into the spot
Interactive	Commercial allows viewer to interact by using buttons on TV remotes, tablets, mobile phones, or other devices
Key frame	A single, instantly recognized image from a spot
Lifestyle	Shows product in everyday use (like minivans or SUVs)
Makeup artist	Person who applies and checks actors' makeup throughout the shoot (person may also be the hair stylist on the set)
Morph	When one image slowly becomes (blends into) another
MS	Medium shot of scene (camera's not close or far away)
Music	Helps reinforce the message like an auditory punctuation mark

Music post	Where the music comes in and punctuates the spot
OS	Overhead shot
PA	Production assistant (handles details of the shoot)
Page turn	An effect that changes one scene to another, resembling someone turning a page in a book
Pan	Camera moves slowly to give a wider (panoramic) view
Picture safety	During post-production, check that images and text within a preset area on the screen will appear on at-home TVs (the "safe zone")
Post-production	Finalizing the spot (putting the scenes together, editing out superfluous copy or images, correcting colors, adding music, superimposing text, etc.)
Pre-production	Everything that needs to get done before filming (casting, booking studio, choosing location or studio, creating props, hiring production team and caterers, attaining script approval, etc.)
Product	Features product advantages and how it works (detergents)
Product comparison	Highlights product's advantage (spot removers)
Props	Objects on the set to help create the scene (lounge chairs, seashells, sand for a beach scene)
Public service	Illustrates a charitable cause or organization, usually created pro bono – without creative and/or production fees – to showcase a need to the public
Quick cut	One image is replaced by another, without a transition
SAG-AFTRA	Screen Actors Guild/American Federation of Television and Radio Artists (union that represents performing talent: actors, singers, dancers, and broadcast announcers)
Screenshot (screengrab)	Key image from one TV frame
Scroll	Words or image move vertically from the top down or from the bottom up
Sex appeal	To make products seem sexy, to create the cool factor (Axe), or to include sexy celebrities for attention
SFX	Special effects designed to create an illusion
Shoot	Production of a TV spot or infomercial

Slice of life	Emotional sell (Hallmark)
Slo-mo	Slow motion (of camera)
Snipe	Type on the bottom of the screen like promos for TV shows
Split screen	Screen is divided with side-by-side images, usually for a comparison
Spokesperson	Creates awareness (Dennis Haysbert for Allstate Insurance)
Storyboard	A visual representation of a spot that shows the action and spoken lines in a frame-by-frame portrayal
Super	Superimpose text or image on screen
Tags	Closing lines that are recorded and inserted at the end of a spot to announce different locations, sale dates, and special offers
Take	A specific shot in a commercial, numbered and recorded on the clap board for future reference
Talent release	A written agreement with a talent as legal proof of payment, indicating a buyout that is signed by the talent, stating the amount paid, client name, title of spot, date of spot, name and location of studio
Talk value	Spots that generate consumer conversations about them
Talking head	Focuses attention on what's being said about product
Testimonial	People talk about the product to establish credibility
Tone	1,000 hertz tone plays before commercial as a pretest for audio track levels
Union signatory	Authorized union representative who completes, signs, and sends in paperwork for each spot using union talent
Union talent	Actors who are union members of SAG-AFTRA
Vignette	Presents a little story like a short play
Voiceover (VO)	Off-camera actor
Wardrobe	Person in charge of selecting (styling) and maintaining the actors' clothing during filming
Wipe	Image is swept off screen as if it's wiped away
Wrap	The word to describe the completion of a spot, "That's a wrap"

TEMPLATES 7.12 Basic TV copy format

Remember only double space between frames. Also, allow the music, sound effects, and actor names to create an aligned column between "Video" and "Audio."

VIDEO	↓	AUDIO
MS SUPER MODEL ON	SUPER MODEL:	Humming along to song.
HAMMOCK AT OCEAN	MUSIC:	ROMANTIC BRAZILIAN UP AND UNDER
	SFX:	(OCEAN WAVES)
CUTE GUY WALKS BY	GUY:	Room for two?
	SUPER MODEL:	Maybe. . . that depends.
	SFX:	(SEAGULLS)
	GUY:	On what?

Looking at video scripts

When you watch videos that interest you, think about the construction of the scripts. Did you notice how tightly written they were? How simply and clearly did they state the message? Whether it's for a social media post, a website, a YouTube video, or for another platform, focus on any similarities. Scripts and Examples 7.13 is a case study video script by Young & Laramore for an experiential activation for Schlage locks, as discussed in Chapter 4. The live event locked a young man in a house for six days. Participants followed scavenger-hunt-like clues to find the key and let him out. What was the impetus to play along? A $5,000 prize! The video script succinctly explains the engaging activation.

SCRIPTS AND EXAMPLES 7.13 Schlage, case study video script: "Locked in a House"

Most consumers don't think about locks. So, we forced them to with Schlage Key to Strong Challenge. We put up a tiny house in an outdoor mall in Seattle. Then we locked a stranger inside. "Hi, I'm Joshua Downs and in about 30 minutes, I'm going to be locked in this house right here for six days."

We hid one key and left clues in Seattle's "strongest" spots. The activation drove traffic to Schlage's website and retail outlets. Josh says, "This downtown pier is getting a new Ferris wheel. But, it's already got one ride that stays on the ground."

One contestant goes to a coffee shop and hoping to land the final clue, asks the barista, "What's the strongest cup you've got?" She gets the cup with the key in it and wins $5,000.

And Joshua got the taste of sweet, sweet freedom.

(This "Locked in a House" case study video script was created by Young & Laramore for Schlage. Script courtesy of Young & Laramore.)

Another Young & Laramore website video describes the exciting features of a Brine app that helps lacrosse fans improve their playing skills. (We examined this campaign before in Chapter 4.) Look how the script pulls you in (Scripts and Examples 7.14). If you're a Brine gear loyalist, you'll listen to the script as the video demonstrates the features.

 SCRIPTS AND EXAMPLES 7.14 Brine, video script: "Video Shootout"

The original flick lacrosse game is back. And this time, it's packing some serious heat. Seven all-new levels with 3D environments and defenders. New unlockable Brine gear – including the Clutch III head and King Magnum 170 handle. Six new Power-Ups:

Cannon

Pivot

Freeze

Shrink

Homing

Intimidate

Get it now at Shootout.Brine.com.

(This "Video Shootout" video script was created by Young & Laramore for Brine. Script courtesy of Young & Laramore.)

The social media campaign for High & Mighty (Figure 7.11, Figure 7.12, Figure 7.13) demonstrates why this reliable and easy wall-hanging system works. The scripts here speak from the picture's perspective, using personification for wall hangings (Scripts and Examples 7.15), anthropomorphism for the cat in the photo (Scripts and Examples 7.16), and the bulldog shelf holder (Scripts and Examples 7.17). The Young & Laramore scripts talk about the benefits to make consumers quickly understand how the product works and why they should use it.

 SCRIPTS AND EXAMPLES 7.15 High & Mighty, social media content video script: "Ascent"

Visual: "Ascent" *"I'd love to see the top again. There's nothing like the air at six feet."* *The image shows mountain climbers in gear in winter. The voiceover leads listeners to believe this is about the climb. It's about the hang.*

Script: *Base Camp. Day 378. Conditions still aren't right to make the climb. At this point, it feels like we might never make it up there. I've done what I can but I'm startin' to lose the morale of the group. And I have my suspicions the twins are planning something. Joke's on them, I'd welcome a mutiny at this point. Anything to see the top again. There's nothing like the air at six feet.*

(This "Ascent" social media content video script was created by Young & Laramore for High & Mighty. Script courtesy of Young & Laramore.)

FIGURE 7.11 This "Ascent" social content video was created by Young & Laramore for High & Mighty. Image courtesy of Young & Laramore.

SCRIPTS AND EXAMPLES 7.16 High & Mighty, social media content video script: "Fat Cat"

Visual: "Fat Cat" *The cat sitting inside a broken frame on the floor talks about getting its adorable pet-table figure, just to be sitting on the ground. Closing line: Hanging shouldn't be this hard.*

Script: *I told them this wasn't going to work out. I mean, look at me. You think a sticker was going to be able to hold all of this furry figure. Get. It. Together. I didn't work this hard to get this adorably pet-able body just to be stuck on the ground.*

(This "Fat Cat" social media content video script was created by Young & Laramore for High & Mighty. Script courtesy of Young & Laramore.)

FIGURE 7.12 This "Fat Cat" social content video was created by Young & Laramore for High & Mighty. Image courtesy of Young & Laramore.

 SCRIPTS AND EXAMPLES 7.17 High & Mighty, social media content video script: "Gravity"

Visual: "Gravity" *Bulldog book end on lower side of an uneven bookshelf, "I think about gravity a lot." Closing line: Hanging shouldn't be this hard.*

Script: *Did you know that the gravity on Mars is almost 60 percent less than it is on Earth. So, if something weighed oh, let's say, 20 pounds it would only weigh 8 pounds on Mars. I think about gravity a lot.*

(This "Gravity" social media content video script was created by Young & Laramore for High & Mighty. Script courtesy of Young & Laramore.)

FIGURE 7.13 This "Gravity" social content video was created by Young & Laramore for High & Mighty. Image courtesy of Young & Laramore.

Here are a few more social media content video scripts that continue the Coravin "Whatever Whenever" campaign, which was examined in Chapter 2 and will be discussed again in Chapter 11. The content clearly demonstrated how the wine-saving product worked and how it solved a specific consumer pain point: the challenge of choosing only one wine. Now, they can choose to open as many bottles as they want because this system can preserve their favorite wines for four weeks. So, why choose? They can open whatever they want whenever they want. You can see how every social media content video script (Scripts and Examples 7.18, Scripts and Examples 7.19, Scripts and Examples 7.20) and screenshot (Figure 7.14, Figure 7.15, Figure 7.16) reinforces the core concept. The scripts are direct and memorable. They demonstrate The Five Rs: If the message is RELEVANT and RESONATES with authenticity, it will be REMEMBERED, RESPONDED to, and RETOLD (Tips and Rules 7.1).

 SCRIPTS AND EXAMPLES 7.18 Coravin, social media content video script: "Engagement Announcement"

SCRIPT: *"Pairs well with. . .the fifth new engagement announcement on your feed this week. Pivot. Any bottle lasts up to four weeks. So drink a glass of whatever, whenever."*

(This "Engagement Announcement" video content script was created by Young & Laramore for Coravin. Script courtesy of Young & Laramore.)

FIGURE 7.14 This "Engagement Announcement" video was created by Young & Laramore for Coravin. Image courtesy of Young & Laramore.

SCRIPTS AND EXAMPLES 7.19   Coravin, social media content video script: "White Goes with Fish"

SCRIPT: *"Pairs well with. . .you want a red with the salmon, but your date is stuck on 'white goes with fish.' Drink whatever you want. Open two bottles."*

(This "White Goes with Fish" video content script was created by Young & Laramore for Coravin. Script courtesy of Young & Laramore.)

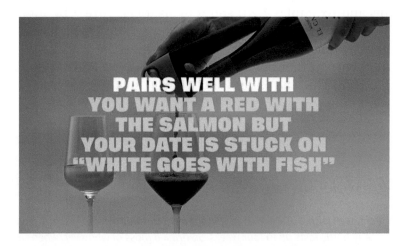

FIGURE 7.15 This "White Goes with Fish" video was created by Young & Laramore for Coravin. Image courtesy of Young & Laramore.

SCRIPTS AND EXAMPLES 7.20 Coravin, social media content video script: "Vintage Aesthetic"

SCRIPT: *"Pairs well with. . .seeing the clothes you wore in high school described as a 'vintage aesthetic.' Pivot. Any bottle lasts up to four weeks. So drink a glass of whatever, whenever."*

(This "Vintage Aesthetic" video content script was created by Young & Laramore for Coravin. Script courtesy of Young & Laramore.)

FIGURE 7.16 This "Vintage Aesthetic" video was created by Young & Laramore for Coravin. Image courtesy of Young & Laramore.

Learn to look at TV spots and videos as short bites of information. With these communication vehicles, you engage more of the senses, not just sight and hearing, but also touch, with the addition of interaction. Consider what else you can do to enhance the viewers' experience. How can you strengthen the power of brand-created video with consumer loyalty?

Creative TV exercises

Exercise 1: Watch two interactive TV spots

What techniques did they use: QR codes, use arrows to choose your content, click OK for more information, set a program reminder, or something else?

Which would you have chosen? How would you change the options for a different brand? For example, what would you use for a:

    a. Travel destination?

    b. Car manufacturer?

    c. New TV series?

    d. Program reminder?

    e. Fitness equipment?

    f. Low-calorie beer brand?

    g. Link to an app?

Exercise 2: Choose one of your favorite TV spots

You can go to YouTube to view a few fun commercials. Take a look at some famous ones that aired on the Super Bowl, including the Budweiser Clydesdales and/or puppies. Be sure to see the consumer-created Doritos' "Crash the Super Bowl" spots. Winners won $1 million!

How could you creatively extend the campaign. For example, would you use continuing characters in new scenarios, spin off the same theme, create interactions with the audience, or something else?

Exercise 3: Write a 30-second TV spot to spin out the campaign using the same strategy of the main campaign

Be sure you create a campaign and use the same talent, characters, visuals, music, typography for supers, and placement of elements. Consider what sound effects would place the listener in the same scene.

Now write the same commercial as a 10- or 15-second spot. What copy could you eliminate and still deliver the same message?

Exercise 4: Find one TV spot that uses one of these techniques

    a. Unusual visual

    b. Compelling sound effects

    c. Humor

    d. Vignette

Exercise 5: Write a humorous :30 radio spot and a :30 TV spot

The TV spot should be for an unusual flavor of Jones soda like the following:

a. Turkey and gravy

b. Broccoli and cheese

c. String bean casserole

d. Pumpkin pie

Go to the Jones Soda website or Wikipedia list for more information about the flavors.

Exercise 6: Write a TV spot, blipvert, and social media video for iClean Dog Wash

Part 1 To start, just write three strong paragraphs.

Write a convincing :30 TV spot and two under-two-second blipverts for iClean Dog Wash. It's an automatic, coin-operated doggie wash. Think of it as a car wash for your pet: a self-contained grooming station with a deep tub, hose, and blow dryer. It can shampoo, blow dry, and de-flea dogs in under 10 minutes. It's a safe and easier way to wash your pet.

You can use any technique like product demonstration, testimonial, celebrity spokesperson (can be a canine film star), vignette, product comparison, or slice of life. It's your choice.

Part 2 Now write a social media video to explain and promote it.

Part 3 Which channels would you choose: Instagram, X (formerly Twitter), Pinterest, YouTube, or elsewhere?

Exercise 7: Review the "top Super Bowl ads ever" on YouTube

Pick your favorite spot. Why did this one resonate with you? Why was it ranked so high? What made this spot work? What was the strongest part of the spot: (1) the concept, (2) the visual treatment, (3) the excellent copy, or (4) the combination of all these?

Notes

1. Tom Amico, personal correspondence, April 20, 2022.
2. Sheena Brady, personal communication, December 3, 2022.
3. Sheena Brady, personal communication, December 3, 2022.
4. Tom Amico, personal correspondence, April 20, 2022.
5. Andrew Langer, personal communication, January 6, 2012.
6. Andrew Langer, personal communication, January 6, 2012.
7. Andrew Langer, personal communication, January 6, 2012.
8. Andrew Langer, personal communication, January 6, 2012.
9. Charlie Hopper, personal communication, November 26, 2021.
10. Sheena Brady, personal communication, December 3, 2022.
11. Sheena Brady, personal communication, December 3, 2022.
12. Kevin Moriarty, personal communication, August 24, 2009.
13. Kevin Moriarty, personal communication, August 24, 2009.
14. Sara Rose, personal communication, November 29, 2022.
15. Sara Rose, personal communication, November 29, 2022.
16. Tom Amico, personal communication, June 30, 2009.
17. Sara Rose, personal communication, November 29, 2022.
18. Vinny Warren, personal communication, December 14, 2022.
19. https://mag.adage.com/2022/01/22/how-acura-is-using-anime-to-appeal-to-younger-generations/content.html (accessed February 2, 2022).

8

The Spoken Word
Radio Script Writing and Formats

"Become your target and then write to convince yourself."

Andrew Langer, Former Executive
Creative Director, BBDO Worldwide[1]

You know what a radio spot sounds like. You're familiar with the format. You may even listen to the radio in your daily commute. But, do you really listen? When you hear a spot you particularly like, have you ever thought about what makes that spot work?

In this chapter, we'll talk about radio spots. We'll cover: (1) the main radio script format that is double-spaced, all caps, and breaks each line at the end of

Content and Copywriting: The Complete Toolkit for Strategic Marketing,
Second Edition. Margo Berman.
© 2024 Margo Berman. Published 2024 by John Wiley & Sons Ltd.
Companion website: www.wiley.com/go/contentandcopywriting

a phrase; (2) other script formats; and (3) some radio "rules," such as leaving two seconds for sound effects and music cuts, plus using ellipses to "billboard" or emphasize a word or phrase. We'll remind you to think about production while you're writing, including the talent, delivery, sound effects, and music you'll use; writing for the ear, not the eye as in print, TV, social, or interactive media; casting, booking, and directing talent; creating scripts for specific celebrities; targeting different radio *dayparts* (times the spots air on radio); applying handy radio writing tips; and listening for great radio spots to use as references.

Becoming a radio aficionado

Starting today, you're going to do that with every great radio spot you hear. You're going to analyze what you like about it and why it works. You'll deconstruct spots the second you hear them. Identify spots that catch your attention. Group them in your mind: lousy ones, so-so ones, good ones, and great ones. What makes the difference? Is it the overall concept? The music? The talent? The sound effects? Does it sound natural to the ear or forced? Radio, like TV and video, is an oral medium, meaning the lines will be said aloud, not read silently by the consumer. So, scripts that include dialogues need to sound casual, the way people actually speak in their everyday conversations.

Okay, how many times have you heard a contrived dialogue like this one on the air?

ASHLEY:	Oh, Jessica. I love your hair. What is the name of your hair salon?
JESSICA:	I go to Great Hair at 120 Catalina Drive.
ASHLEY:	Where is that?
JESSICA:	That is at the northeast corner of 8th Street and 4th Avenue.

What's wrong with this script? Well, people just wouldn't talk like that. They'd use contractions, like "what's," not "what is." They probably wouldn't give the exact addresses. Okay, at this very moment, stop reading. Ask yourself: Do you know the exact address of your hair salon, or drycleaner, or bank? No. You just need to know what shopping center they're in or what intersection they're near. Just to get started, let's look at a more conversational version of this spot. This time, Ashley and Jessica would sound more like this:

ASHLEY: Oh, Jessica. Your hair looks great. Who does it?

JESSICA: Brad at Great Hair. They're great, and right nearby. You know, on Catalina Drive.

ASHLEY: Oh, across from the mall?

JESSICA: Yeah, on the corner of 8th.

Of course, grammatically, you'd want to say, "Brad at Great Hair. HE'S great." But, we mix our subjects up when we speak. First, Jessica's talking about Brad at Great Hair. Then, she switches to the salon. Instead of saying, "It's great and right nearby," she used "THEY." Of course, it's incorrect. But, that's how we speak. Most of us say "they" when we're talking about a company. Grammatically, it's wrong, but it's perfect for broadcast.

The more relaxed the language is, the more it sounds like a real conversation. Writing in the vernacular is crucial. Notice the useful tips that focus on writing for the ear (Tips and Rules 8.1).

TIPS AND RULES 8.1
How to write for the ear

- Take listeners on a journey.
- Paint pictures so listeners can imagine the scenario.
- Place them in a setting with
  - sound effects
  - dialogue
  - ambient, random conversations
  - music
  - environmental noise (glasses in a restaurant, seagulls at the ocean)
- Make dialogues sound natural and conversational.
- Close with a clear statement, wrap up, button, or call to action.
- Read aloud.
- Let other people read the script aloud. If they stumble, rewrite those lines.

Let's take a moment and hear what some of the radio greats have to say about writing for this medium.

Learning some radio tips from the masters

Many great advertising giants knew how to create unforgettable messages in all media, including radio. Some writers think it's the most difficult medium because there's no visual component. Others think it's the most exciting because it taps into the listeners' imagination. David Ogilvy found that a research study identified four main factors needed in radio spots. These were:[2]

1. *Identify your brand early in the commercial.*
2. *Identify it often.*
3. *Promise the listener a benefit early in the commercial.*
4. *Repeat it often.*

Then, he promptly added that 90% of commercials don't do any of these things, but they still work. How many times have you heard a commercial and didn't know what it was for until the very end? Some of the most interesting spots keep you waiting the same way a blind headline works in print: You don't know who's advertising until you read the entire ad.

Instead of just listening to what the research said, he came up with his own checklist of eight steps when writing great radio spots. These were:[3]

1. *Get people to listen.*
2. *Surprise them.*
3. *Arouse their curiosity.*
4. *Wake them up.*
5. *Once they are awake, talk to them as one human being to another.*
6. *Involve them.*
7. *Charm them.*
8. *Make them laugh.*

The truth is, the second list is as applicable now as it was in 1983 when Ogilvy wrote it. Today, marketers are looking to engage the audience with a brand. Involving them (#6 above) creates an emotional attachment to the brand's product line, such as the ever-evolving series of Apple iPads, iPhones, and Apple Watches.

When learning to write for a specific medium, read articles and books. Listen to podcasts and radio spots. Watch TV commercials and YouTube videos. Absorb content everywhere you find it. Then, apply it to today's vehicles and audiences. For example, in *How to Advertise,* Kenneth Roman and Jane Mass explain that radio can target a niche audience in a local market, making it a versatile medium. With so many types of music and so many different groups listening to their favorite formats, radio can speak to people with the same musical taste, reaching a certain community. Even if many people listen to music on various devices, some still turn on the radio while driving. Roman and Mass offer 10 tips for radio writing that would be extremely helpful to the novice and seasoned professional alike. These are still applicable today:[4]

1. *Focus on one idea.*

2. *Think about the program environment.*

3. *Don't splinter your efforts. (Use the same music for TV, for example.)*

4. *Stretch the listener's imagination.*

5. *Register your brand name.*

6. *Use the strength of music.*

7. *Advertise promotions.*

8. *Listen to the commercial in context.*

9. *Make it topical and timely. (Advertise ice cream in the summer when it's hot, for instance.)*

10. *Talk one-to-one.*

When looking at these, pay particular attention to listening to the commercial in context (#8). In other words, how does this spot sound on your car radio or in the office. When producing a spot, be sure to listen to it on several different types of speakers to check that the music is audible, yet not too loud. Don't stop there. Also consider how the music in the spot works with the music on the station. If your spot includes classical music, it will stand out when played on stations with contrasting music like reggae, indie, hip hop, jazz, or Top 40 hits, or other formats.

Just as we discussed car products for morning and afternoon drive times, think about advertising seasonal products (#9) just before the season starts, like showcasing snowblowers in the fall, or featuring lawn seeds in late winter.

Some advertisers, who are not sponsors of the Olympic Games, wrap their commercials before and after the full schedule of events is aired. The idea is to make audience members think they actually were the official sponsors.

Again, the tenth tip reminds writers to speak to listeners as if you were talking to a friend. Be personal and create an open dialogue. The warmer the message, the more comfortable the listener.

Each of these suggestions is an invaluable insight into writing powerful radio scripts. Keep them handy when you're writing radio. You can never have enough tips when you're writing to the ear.

Now, let's look at a few examples (Script 1, Script 2, Script 3, Script 4, Templates 8.2) created by Young & Laramore. Notice how naturally these Trane radio spots move along. Examine how the scripts are written in a block of type, a nonradio format. Look at how the length is shown as ":30" for a 30-second spot.

Observe how conversational the scripts sound. Instead of saying "you are," the writers used the contraction "you're." That's because we almost always use contractions when to speak. Pay attention to the use of parallel construction in "testing, retesting, engineering, and reengineering" in the "Right There with You" spot. Study the phrase "drop, slam, shake, silence" in the "Torture Test" script. Can you see how both lines are rhythmic and easy to imagine? The closing line, which is also the brand's slogan, uses a *play on words* (technique #4 in Chapter 10): "It's hard to stop a Trane." When you hear it, you're thinking "train." Then, you connect the power and force of a train with the brand name "Trane." It's an "Oh, I get it" instant reaction.

SCRIPT 1   Trane "We Run Together" campaign, :30 radio script: "While You're Running"

While you're taking your kids to the school bus in the rain, we're drenching a highly sophisticated Trane cooling and heating unit with five inches of water an hour. While you're applying SPF 60 within a high of 97, we're subjecting Trane systems to temperatures north of 120 degrees Fahrenheit.

While you're doing whatever it is you do, we're testing, retesting, engineering, and reengineering to keep up with you. We run together. It's hard to stop a Trane.

(This "While You're Running" :30 radio script was created by Young & Laramore for Trane. Script courtesy of Young & Laramore.)

Script 2 is another spot from the "We Run Together" campaign. Remember, with radio, everything has to be imagined. Descriptive words help listeners picture the scene. So, verbs, such as "punishing" and "dumping" conjure up images that listeners see. The scene is created with phrases, such as "hiding your face behind the two-inch collar of your jacket" and "waiting out a Little League rain delay." These are actions parents of baseball enthusiasts have experienced. That makes the copy relatable.

SCRIPT 2 Trane "We Run Together" campaign, :30 radio script: "Right There with You"

While you're hiding your face behind the two-inch collar of your jacket, we're punishing a Trane heat pump at zero degrees. While you're waiting out a Little League rain delay, we're dumping five inches an hour on a Trane air conditioner that's still running.

While you're doing whatever it is you do, we're testing, retesting, engineering, and reengineering to keep up with you. We run together. It's hard to stop a Trane.

(*This "Right There with You" :30 radio script was created by Young & Laramore for Trane. Script courtesy of Young & Laramore.*)

In the "Tested to the Extreme" campaign, writers again used parallel construction and imagery. Consumers can imagine the extreme testing that Trane heating and cooling products endure. Take a look at Script 3 and Script 4 and you'll immediately see how the copy ignites the listener's imagination.

SCRIPT 3 Trane "Tested to the Extreme" campaign, :30 radio script: "Torture Test"

Inside the Trane testing facility, our heating and cooling products go through endless torture tests to ensure they can run through anything.

And when we say torture, we don't take that lightly. We drop them, slam them against a wall, shake them, and then expect them to run without an extra decibel in our anechoic sound chamber.

Without fail.

Drop Slam Shake Silence

Drop Slam Shake Silence

And there's no end in sight. We test. So it runs.

That's why it's hard to stop a Trane.

(*This "Torture Test" :30 radio script was created by Young & Laramore for Trane. Script courtesy of Young & Laramore.*)

SCRIPT 4 Trane "Tested to the Extreme" campaign, :30 radio script: "Hot Cold"

Inside the Trane testing facility, our heating and cooling products are put through 16 weeks of extreme temperature fluctuations to simulate 5 years of wear and tear. But these aren't just seasonal shifts. Inside the lab, it fluctuates between 150 degrees one day to subzero temperatures and layers of snow the next.

Then back to hot. Then back to cold.

Then hot

And cold

Hot Cold Hot Cold Hot Cold

And we didn't even get through the first month. We test. So it runs.

That's why it's hard to stop a Trane.

(This "Hot Cold" :30 radio script was created by Young & Laramore for Trane. Script courtesy of Young & Laramore.)

Many radio scripts use the format preferred in radio stations: two columns, all caps, and double-spaced. The two-line spacing allows the voiceover talent to jot down reminders to themselves between the lines. The same script, "Hot Cold," would be written in grouped phrases, the way the announcer would read the script. The format would look like Templates 8.2.

TEMPLATES 8.2 Standard radio format, Trane script: "Tested to the Extreme" (Script 4)

CLIENT:	TRANE
JOB:	:30 Radio
TITLE:	"Hot Cold"
ANNCR:	INSIDE THE TRANE TESTING FACILITY,
	OUR HEATING AND COOLING PRODUCTS
	ARE PUT THROUGH 16 WEEKS
	OF EXTREME TEMPERATURE FLUCTUATIONS
	TO SIMULATE 5 YEARS OF WEAR AND TEAR.
	BUT THESE AREN'T JUST SEASONAL SHIFTS.
	INSIDE THE LAB, IT FLUCTUATES BETWEEN 150 DEGREES

ONE DAY TO SUBZERO TEMPERATURES

AND LAYERS OF SNOW THE NEXT.

THEN BACK TO HOT. THEN BACK TO COLD.

THEN HOT

AND COLD

HOT COLD HOT COLD HOT COLD

AND WE DIDN'T EVEN GET THROUGH THE FIRST MONTH.

WE TEST. SO IT RUNS.

THAT'S WHY IT'S HARD TO STOP A TRANE.

(This "Hot Cold" :30 radio script was created by Young & Laramore for Trane. Script courtesy of Young & Laramore.)

When you hear a Trane commercial, you can easily put yourself there, whether it's a baseball game or the testing facility. That's because the writing is so vivid.

Now, let's look at a few more important points you should consider when you write for radio. For the body of the script, review the list in Tips and Rules 8.3.

TIPS AND RULES 8.3
Basic radio writing rules

For the body of the script, just use:

- All caps.
- Double spacing.
- Two columns.
- Contractions like "we're" not "we are".
- Everyday phrases like "you're kidding," "no way," or "that's ridiculous" (not words that work better in print, like "moreover" and "therefore").
- Conversational style, especially in dialogues.
- Phrases instead of full sentences.
- As many complete phrases as possible on each line of the script.
- Dashes to spell something out like this: *P-L-A-Y.*

- Narrow, half-inch margins on right and left side to allow more script per page.

- Easy-to-remember phone numbers only (and repeat three times).

- Two full seconds for every sound effect and music cut.

- The client name at least three times.

- Short, simple phrases.

- Three dots before (and sometimes after) a word to "billboard" (emphasize) it, like this: *Remember. . . friends drive you home or call a cab*. Use these dots sparingly.

- Italics to emphasize a single word.

- Repeated letters to drag a word out like this: *GRRRRRRROW* UP, ALREADY!

- A stopwatch to be sure you don't exceed, even by a second, the length of the spot. A 30-second spot is not 30.5 seconds.

- The same page for a talent. Don't break a talent's lines at the bottom of the page and continue it on a second page.

Like this:
ASHLEY: I CAN'T BELIEVE SHE SAID THAT. THAT WAS SO MEAN. I THOUGHT
          SHE WAS A FRIEND.
Not like this:
ASHLEY: I CAN'T BELIEVE SHE SAID THAT. THAT WAS SO MEAN.
(*Script continues on next page*)
ASHLEY: I THOUGHT SHE WAS A FRIEND.

Observing a few more radio writing "rules"

When writing for radio, you also need to know the correct length of time. For length, a 60-second spot can run to 60, but not a second longer. Some people write 59.5 seconds, just to be sure. If the spot runs past 60 seconds, even by a half of a second, it can get cut off at the end by the DJ, a show host, or an automated system that's preset to 60 seconds or 30 seconds for shorter spots.

As mentioned earlier, radio scripts have a specific format that is used at radio stations, recording studios, and production companies. This format is universally accepted as are these basic rules for writing radio spots.

You must also realize that it's important to write using a specific format or template that's common in the radio industry. Now, let's look at a commonly used script format.

Applying basic radio copy format

Before we go any further, scripts should have an identifying section at the top, for easy client and agency reference. Some agencies only use a double space between speakers. Also, it should be in two columns and in all caps like this:

CLIENT:	SUPER HAIR
JOB:	:15 Radio
TITLE:	"Great Hair"
DATE:	INSERT DATE (Some agencies also add the "RECORDED DATE.")
ASHLEY:	HEY, JESSICA! LOVE YOUR HAIR. WHERE'D YA GO?
JESSICA:	BRAD AT SUPER HAIR. THEY'RE GREAT. RIGHT NEAR BY. YOU KNOW, ON CATALINA.
ASHLEY:	OH, ACROSS FROM THE MALL?
JESSICA:	YEAH, ON THE CORNER OF 8TH.

Aside from the format, notice how it's written: in phrases, not sentences. Also look at the use of vernacular, or everyday speech: *"hey"* and *"yeah."* This is the way friends speak to each other, in little bites of information. Instead of *"Where'd ya go?"* Ashley could have also asked, *"Who did your hair?"* or *"Who does it?"* That's still conversational. Ashley could have said, *"Where's that?"* if she didn't know it was *"across from the mall."* Or she could have asked, *"Where's it at?"* even if that's incorrect English. Why? Because people use that phrase. Remember writing for radio is not about proper grammar. It's about real communication when there's dialogue. Listeners have to imagine the relationship, the setting, and the scene.

If you're writing a one-voice spot, the copy can be just as natural sounding, enticing, and engaging. Think about the kind of talent you want for this spot. If you can, cast a voiceover talent with a unique voice that would help capture the listener's attention. One-voice spots can be dramatic, like an auditory film trailer; or, compassionate, like a public service announcement trying to raise funds and awareness for a needy cause; or humorous, like someone talking herself out of eating a dessert when she's on a diet.

Now, let's take a more detailed look at basic radio format.

Finding out more about radio format

The two columns make it easy to see who's speaking and what's being said. The left column identifies the actor speaking, plus it indicates where to place the music and sound effects. The top of the page includes all the file information. That's the only part of the script that's set single-spaced. Right from the very beginning, get in the habit of using clients' names, dates, job numbers, script length, and edit version number. That way, you won't have any unidentified scripts sitting around without full client information.

You might ask why the script is in all caps and double-spaced. Even though caps are usually harder to read for radio announcers and voiceover talents, caps are a commonly used format. As mentioned earlier, the double spacing between the lines makes sense because it lets the talents make personal notes. Many radio stations use this format, but some agencies don't.

Break lines in phrases means that you start a new line at the beginning of a phrase. Try to fit as many phrases on a line as possible, so the script doesn't run past two pages. Here's an example:

Like this:

BRIAN: BRAD, I CAN'T BELIEVE YOU DIDN'T TELL ME.
              WHY DIDN'T YOU SAY ANYTHING?

Not like this:

BRIAN: BRAD, I CAN'T BELIEVE YOU DIDN'T TELL ME. WHY DIDN'T
              YOU SAY ANYTHING?

Can you see the difference? It's more natural to keep *"Why didn't you say anything?"* on the same line, rather then, breaking after *"Why didn't..."* That chops the sentence up and leaves an unfinished phrase. You wouldn't say, *"Why didn't."* You would say, *"Why didn't you."* Read aloud to hear where to best break the line.

The reason to break lines in phrases is that it reflects the talent's natural rhythm, making for a smoother read. To have the talent highlight or "billboard" a word or phrase, you can use three dots, but use them sparingly. Once or twice in a spot is fine. You may find the three dots at the end of the spot, just before the client's slogan or name. The three dots look like an ellipsis, but they don't indicate an omission. To spotlight a single word, use italics.

Now, let's take a look at an example of a preferred radio format to use as a template (Templates 8.4).

After mastering radio formats, next you should be familiar with the short-hand that's used in scripts. There is a quick overview of some of the most common radio and broadcast terminology in Useful Info 8.5. Keep this list handy when you're writing for radio or booking the studio and talent.

TEMPLATES 8.4 Standard radio format

DATE:	05/15/23
CLIENT:	Ticket Fighters
JOB #:	TF-6502
RE:	:60 Radio Spot – "No Points"

JUAN: I CAN'T BELIEVE HE GAVE ME A TICKET.

LINDSEY: WELL, YOU DIDN'T HAVE TO FLOOR IT AT THE LIGHT.

JUAN: I DIDN'T KNOW HE WAS A COP.

LINDSEY: I TOLD YOU THEY WERE GIVING TICKETS ALL WEEK.

JUAN: WHAT A PAIN!

ANNCR: DON'T GO TO COURT. GIVE YOUR TICKET TO THE TICKET FIGHTERS.

SFX: (LOUD PUNCH)

ANNCR: THEY GO TO COURT.

SFX: (GAVEL)

ANNCR: SO, YOU DON'T HAVE TO. WITH A 95% SUCCESS RATE, YOU COULD AVOID POINTS ON YOUR LICENSE AND MIGHT ONLY GO TO TRAFFIC SCHOOL, DEPENDING ON YOUR DRIVING RECORD.

ANNCR: THE TICKET FIGHTERS. 888-4-TICKET. THAT'S 888-4-TICKET.

LINDSEY: (TEASINGLY) STUDY UP IN SCHOOL, JUAN!

JUAN: (SARCASTICALLY) NICE!

ANNCR: GOTTA TICKET? CALL 888-4-TICKET AND LET THE TICKET FIGHTERS. . .

SFX: (LOUD PUNCH)

ANNCR: REDUCE THE PAIN.

JUAN: I REALLY HATE TRAFFIC SCHOOL.

LINDSEY: WHO DOESN'T?

JUAN: BUT IT BEATS POINTS ON MY LICENSE.

LINDSEY: YA GOTTA POINT, JUAN! (LAUGHS) ONLY KIDDING!

JUAN: FUNNY, REAL FUNNY!

USEFUL INFO 8.5 Common radio terms

Air-ready	A completed, fully produced spot that's ready to be aired on a radio station.
Airtimes	Specific schedule of times the spot will run.
ANNCR	Announcer.
ASCAP	American Society of Composers, Authors and Publishers. Organization that protects the rights (intellectual property) of musical artists.
Billboard	To emphasize a word or phrase. Indicate by using three dots. . . like this.
BMI	Broadcast Music Incorporated – Where businesses, agencies, studios, etc. obtain a license to play or use recorded music and avoid copyright infringement.
Book the studio	To schedule a time and day to record your spot in a recording studio.
Book the talent	To hire a voiceover talent or actor.
Button	A clever closing line that may refer back to something mentioned earlier in the script.
Buyout	To pay a one-time fee to a nonunion talent, allowing unlimited use of the recorded spot.
Call to action	A reminder to the listener to do something: go to a website, visit a store, call for an appointment, etc.
Cast the talent	To audition various talents for a spot and then select the actor(s).
Character voice	An actor who can create a distinctive personality, speech pattern, or regional accent, like a Southern farmer, New York gangster, "mad" scientist, cowboy, diva, snob, sweet old lady, wise guy, or even a quirky, cartoon-like character.
Check or ride levels	To adjust the volume of voices, effects, and music during production.
Copyright	Music, lyrics, recorded sound effects, and other intellectual property (creative works) are protected from being copied (plagiarism and piracy) or played (copyright infringement) without consent and/or compensation.
Copyright infringement	Inappropriate use of copyrighted material without permission from the work's creator.

Dayparts	How the stations divide up specific segments of time.
Morning drive	6 a.m. to 10 a.m.
Midday	10 a.m. to 4 p.m.
Afternoon drive	4 p.m. to 7 p.m. (some stations start at 3 p.m.).
Evening	7 p.m. to midnight.
Overnight	Midnight to 6 a.m.
Demo (talent)	Digital MP3 (audio) and/or MP4 (video) recording used to showcase the talent's voice and/or image for future bookings.
Echo	Add an effect, like an echo, behind the voice.
Filter	Used as a special effect to create a muffled sound, or to replicate talking on the phone.
Flight	Pre-arranged radio schedule detailing how many spots will air at what time and on which stations.
Intellectual property	Creative work including, but limited to music, lyrics, novels, plays, books, screenplays, TV shows, etc.
Levels	The volume of the different tracks containing voices, effects, and music.
Library	Digital collection of compiled selections of sound effects.
Line reading	Saying a line in the script to the talent, demonstrating how you want the line read.
Live announce	Radio host reads spot live on the air.
Mic	Microphone.
Mix	The combining of each voice, music cut, and sound effect into a final spot.
Music cuts	Short, edited selections of music.
Music fades	Music gradually fades away.
Music post	The way the music hits in a certain place to emphasize copy point or set a mood.
Negotiate rates	Media buyers work with radio stations to get lower rates and/or special packages.
Nonunion talent	An actor who does not belong to a union (SAG-AFTRA, see later in list).
Phone patch	To direct the talent in another studio via a telephone connection.

Producer	Person who goes into the recording studio, supervises the production, and directs the talent and recording engineer.
PSA	Public service announcement – a commercial for a social or charitable cause, non- or not-for-profit organization, or other community service entity that is usually given free airtime and may be created pro bono (without creative and/or production fees) by an agency, production house, recording studio, or radio station.
Punch in	To insert a corrected, new line to fit into a specific amount of time.
Radio buy	The agreed-upon on-air schedule for radio spots, including dayparts: morning/afternoon drive, midday, evening, and overnight "flights".
Rate card	A sheet listing the cost of radio spots during dayparts.
Recording engineer	Someone who records the voiceover talent(s), music, and sound effects, adjusts levels, and creates the fully produced, final spot so that it's air-ready.
Remote broadcast	When a radio station broadcasts live from an advertiser's site, outside the station.
ROS	Run of station – spots aired randomly between 6 a.m. and midnight.
SAG-AFTRA	Screen Actors Guild/American Federation of Television and Radio Artists - a labor union for film, TV, and radio.
Scale	The going union rate for talent per market, per 13-week cycle.
SFX	Sound effects.
Signatory	An authorized union representative who can handle and submit the required paperwork for booking union talents.
Tag	A specific ending on the spot that advertises a certain location, event, or date.
Track	The individual channel that separately records each voice, music cut, and sound effect.
Union talent	Actors who are members of SAG-AFTRA (see above in list).
Up and out	Music comes in and cuts right out (of the spot).
Up and under	Music comes in and remains playing (under the spot).
VO	Voiceover.
Wild line readings	To have the talent read the same line several different ways, one "read" after another, so you have many versions as options for your final, completed spot.

Thinking about production from the start

Before you start writing, while you're developing the overall concept and main message of the spot, you need to focus on the entire production, including talent, sound effects, and music. You should remind yourself to leave at least two seconds for each sound effect. Count a slow ONE–TWO for timing when you're reading aloud. Remember to also leave time for music. At least two or three seconds per music cut, depending on how the music will *post* or punctuate the spot. Be sure to listen carefully to more radio spots. Pay attention to what music is used. Notice whether it's the same music throughout the spot or whether there are different cuts (short selections) of music. Listen to how and where the music comes in and/or out.

Remember, you must paint a picture. Radio, often called "theater of the mind," must appeal to the listeners' imagination. They must be able to picture what is being stated, feel what is being portrayed, then hear and absorb what is being said. So, they can imagine the scene.

Consider where the spot is taking place. Realize that everywhere you are has ambient noise. For example, in a plane there are many sounds: the hum of the engine, the whir of the air conditioning, people sneezing, babies crying, people typing on their laptops, etc. In a restaurant, there are plates, glasses, and silverware clinking; people talking; background music; and the popping of wine bottles and champagne being opened. On the beach, there are the sounds of waves breaking on the shore, seagulls, volleyballs being hit, and kids squealing and splashing in the water. Listen everywhere you are. Close your eyes. Then, ask yourself what sounds put you where you are? Are these sounds distinctive and instantly identifiable, like the clicking of a pen or the sizzling of meat on a grill? If not, replace them with more easily recognizable effects.

As you're writing the spot, consider the music. What kind of music would work? Do you want several different cuts (selections) of music? Or, should the spot not have music, just voice and sound effects? Now, ask yourself where would you place sound effects? Should you start with an attention-catching sound, like kids arguing, a car engine revving, or a bee buzzing? Interrupt the spot with an unexpected noise like a helicopter's blades whirling? Close the spot with an effect like a closing door? Of course, the sound effect has to work. You don't want to just get the listener's attention with a distinct sound or even word that doesn't have anything to do with the spot.

If a spot started with a loud "Ouch!" but the topic was a dental office, it would be completely inappropriate because of the common fear of going to the dentist. Yes, it caught the audience's attention, but then it focused on everyone's trepidations. Including a sound effect just to have an effect is never the right solution. As mentioned earlier, leave at least a full two seconds for each sound effect. Always read every spot aloud and allow enough time for music and sound effects to register in the listeners' minds. Decide if you would need to add a filter to one of the voices in a dialogue to replicate a phone conversation. If one voice sounds muted, it's as if you're listening personally to someone on the other end of the phone line.

One other sound effect to consider is white noise, or natural room noise. Just listen to the sound in the room you're in right now. If you're home, you might have the TV on, a heater or air conditioner might be running, the dishwasher or washing machine might be on in the background. If you're in an office, you might hear the clicking of someone typing on a computer keyboard, or someone on the phone, or someone making copies. If you're in an elegant restaurant, not a fast-food spot, you might hear silverware on a plate, corks being popped, quiet conversations, footsteps, servers announcing menu specials, or any other familiar restaurant sounds. The point is, there's almost always ambient noise everywhere. So, creating a radio spot with no background noise, could either sound unnatural, or could stand out because of its stark background, like an all-white room.

Next, explore possible vocal talents. Who should voice the spot?

Using union and nonunion talent, music, and sound effects

As you're creating the spot, hear the talent's voice or voices in your mind. What kind of voice do you have in mind? Determine if you want to use local colloquialisms like "Fuggetabout it," "Who ya kiddin'?" or "Ya talkin' to me?" for a New York audience.

Does the actor have to portray someone with a distinctly different voice? Do you hear an accent or a regional dialect? Do you imagine a high or low voice? A character voice (see Useful Info 8.5)? A dramatically powerful voice? A rich, resonating voice? A heavenly voice? Are you imagining a guy- or girl-next-door voice? A celebrity with an instantly recognizable and/or distinctive voice?

Every time you watch TV or see a movie, listen to the exact timbre (tone quality and depth) of the actors' voices. Can you recognize any of them with your eyes closed? Can you pick out actors just by hearing their voices without seeing them on the screen? If so, do those actors have distinctive voices? For example, can you hear the voice of Owen Wilson or Robert De Niro? What about Whoopi Goldberg or Keira Knightley? Or Brad Pitt or Chris Pine? Or how about Jennifer Lopez or Reese Witherspoon? Do you see how you can actually hear their voices because they have a unique sound?

Replay different actors in your mind whenever you're writing a script so you can determine what kind of voice to cast, especially if you're not using a celebrity. Listen to voiceover demo MP3s from both union and nonunion talent. Look at digital demos or MP4s of actors in your budget. All serious voiceover talents and actors will present each agency with their demo reels. If you've heard of some talents and don't have their demos, contact them or their agents and request one.

Be open-minded. You might find an undiscovered talent who isn't seasoned, but would be perfect. Audition voiceover talents and actors you haven't worked with before to be sure they are right for your spot. If at all possible, participate in the process of casting the talent. If you're using union talent, be sure you've arranged for a *union signatory* to be on-site at the recording session. Most recording studios have signatories on staff. Be sure you double-check that. Union talents are paid for each geographic market and in 13-week increments. This means you cannot replay any commercial after the initial 13-week run without paying the talent for the next cycle.

If you're using nonunion talent, remember to bring two copies of a talent release detailing the time, date, studio name and location, client name, job number and title of the spot, as well as the name of the talent with the amount that was paid. This is a legal document that verifies the nonunion talent was financially compensated in full. (You could also use an electronically signed file.) If your release states that you have unlimited use of the talent's voice, that arrangement is called a "buyout." This means you can replay the commercial in any market for as long as you wish without paying the nonunion talent any additional fees. If you book union and nonunion talent in the same commercial, the nonunion talent must be paid union fees, called "union scale."

Just as you need to pay for talent, you need to remember to include music and sound effects charges in the budget. Even though as a writer, you may not be involved in budgetary discussions, you must still be cost-conscious when you're working on a small account or for a mom-and-pop establishment. In this case, you need to be cognizant of the fact that each music cut or selection is a separate fee that must be paid to cover the music rights. Just because you paid for a song or musical work doesn't mean you can use the music in a commercial spot. Only if you wrote and recorded the music yourself are you free to use it. If you included other singers or musicians on your recording, they must be financially compensated and must sign a talent release to protect you in any unexpected legal disputes.

Likewise, sound effects selected from a studio library or from a collection of recorded effects, such as a digital download (like WAV or MP3 formats), need to be paid for to avoid copyright infringement. Recording studio owners and engineers can give you the current pricing for music and sound effects cuts so you have a frame of reference as you're conceptualizing the spot.

Always know that you must pay for and have the proper authorization if you want to use any part of any recording. Let's say you want to use a hit song. If it's on the charts listed in *Billboard* magazine, it's expensive. Therefore, unless you're working with a client that can afford tens, or even hundreds of thousands of dollars, chances are you won't be using a chart-topping artist or song. You might consider using local artists and giving their work exposure for a more affordable fee.

If you're looking to develop custom music, the more specific you can be when working with the composer, the quicker the process. You might hire a jingle writer, or contemporary composer, or rap producer if there's a singularly unique musical sound you want to create. Don't limit your thinking to just jingles. Any musical phrase can punctuate a spot and act like a sound logo. For example, the three notes that musically represent the General Electric Corporation are the same as those in the corporate name: G, E, and C. Your custom music needs to be completed before you enter the recording studio. So, it can be integrated into the spot. If you're involved in producing radio commercials, it's critical that you know how to work with the engineer and the talent so you execute the spot exactly as you imagined it. Now, let's discuss some aspects of the production process.

Working with and directing the talent

It's one thing to write the spot. It's another to produce it. The best writers/ directors have an extremely clear picture of what the spot should sound like. They can hear the finished spot with the correct inflection and emphasis long before they enter the recording studio. This is why it's vitally important to know the following:

1. How to *work with talent.*

2. How to tell the recording engineer *exactly where the sound effects and music should post.*

3. How the *completed spot should sound.* He or she needs to know what you want and not be left guessing what you had in mind.

Likewise, working with voiceover talents requires that you can give them an accurate *line reading*, so they know the delivery or "read" you want. By acting out every spot aloud, you will hear when a line sounds awkward. You may want to record yourself reading the script on your phone or a digital tape recorder. That way, you'll be able to rewrite any lines that don't work well before the studio clock starts ticking the dollars away. You should be able to hand your script to people you've just met and they should be able to read it flawlessly the first time. They don't even have to be familiar with the campaign or the product. Well-written spots just flow. There are no clumsy lines or stiff phrases. They're written the way people speak. The easier your scripts are to read, the faster they'll be read and the better they'll sound. Great writing is a time and budget saver.

Now, back to directing the talent. This is a skill worth learning. You can't walk into the studio and say, "Oh, you're a professional. Read it the way you want." It's okay to allow voiceover talents to deliver several interpretations, but you must always know the end result you're seeking. You could email or text your digitally recorded line readings to the talent pre-production to give the talent an idea of the delivery you want. This could save some studio time. Sometimes, talents will offer some excellent conceptual ideas or various character portrayals you may not have considered. Be willing to listen to alternative suggestions and be ready to accept other "reads." A fresh perspective can transform a good spot into a terrific one.

It usually takes most talents a few run-throughs to get the gist of how the spot should be read. Make the talent as comfortable as possible and encourage early exploration. Just remember you're the guide, so don't wander too far away from the approved creative direction.

Award-winning radio writers and producers like Joy Golden, who was president of Joy Radio in Manhattan, explain that getting the results you want from the talent requires that you have them imagine that they're actually in the setting, not in the studio. Here's what Joy Golden said:

> *The key to making a good radio commercial is to know how to direct the people... What I often do, especially with some of the new people, is set up a visual scenario for them. I'll say, "You're a husband and a wife in bed, right? And, it's early in the morning, and he's feeling lousy and she's feeling ___." I'll give them a whole physical and personality scenario, so they can perform, in their minds, in a setting that isn't so audio. Because I want a bigger thing to come out... In the studio, most of the time it requires ten, twelve, fifteen takes for the talent to get it right, especially if it's a monologue. We do and we redo and we redo.*[5]

Dick Orkin, remembered as a celebrated radio specialist, along with other voiceover talents including his brother, Sandy Orkin, and Christine Coyle founded Radio Ranch, an award-winning, full-facility recording studio. Visitors to the company's website can hear many of their famous and funny commercials. Some of the spots are listed as outrageous and you may question how they ever aired. Take a listen and see if you can determine what makes these spots such award winners. Be sure to notice how each one is set in a particular place that you can quickly imagine. Pay attention to the way the scripts are read and to the line readings and talents' voices. Also, be particularly observant of how conversational and engaging these spots are.

Understanding radio dayparts

If you know what the *radio buy* might be, you could write certain versions for certain times of the day, called "dayparts." For instance, if your spot is for a nightclub, you might consider talking to listeners during afternoon drive time (4 p.m. to 7 p.m.) to remind them about your club as they're making their evening plans. If it's for a bank or financial institution, you may want to remind listeners about your competitive car or home loans during morning or afternoon drive time. So, they can think about your rates to and from work. You might have a special offer that tells listeners to say they heard about your loans on a certain station.

If you have a popular, local radio celebrity on a particular station, you could also incorporate a few "live announcements." The fan base will pay attention when their favorite radio personality says something. If the message is offered as a relaxed, conversation-like read, as if the on-air personality were chatting with you, the audience, it will sound like a celebrity endorsement. Other live spots can be aired when you arrange *live radio remotes*. These are shows aired on-site from advertisers' locations. People can stop by and visit the "show" as it airs because these often take place on weekends.

With radio, you can speak to the audience while they're driving. So, any car-related messages are particularly relevant, like specials on tires, car repairs, tune-ups, car washes, car rentals, and so on. When writing radio, consider what messages would be particularly effective if you were behind the wheel. During rush hour, while drivers are frustrated sitting in traffic, a spot that discussed the convenience of using a train, metro rail, tram, trolley, or carpool lane might make commuters think about other transportation options. A spot that said this kind of message could really resonate.

ANNCR:	RIGHT NOW, YOU COULD BE CATCHING UP ON E-MAIL OR TAKING A NAP INSTEAD OF...
SFX:	(TRAFFIC NOISES, HORNS HONKING, DRIVERS SHOUTING)
BILL:	HEY, BUDDY, WAKE UP! THE TRAFFIC'S MOVIN'!
ANNCR:	SITTING BEHIND THE WHEEL. TAKE THE TRI-RAIL TRAM AND TAKE A BREAK.
SFX:	(SNORING)
ANNCR:	YOU EARNED IT. YOU'VE BEEN WORKIN' HARD ALL DAY.
SFX:	(PHONES RINGING)

WOMAN:	(FRANTICALLY) HEY, BILL! IT'S BOB. NOW HE NEEDS THE REPORT IN AN HOUR!
ANNCR:	WORKS OVER... UNLESS YOU'RE STUCK IN TRAFFIC.
SFX:	(SIRENS, CARS HONKING)
ANNCR:	THEN YOU'RE WORKIN'... JUST TO GET AWAY FROM WORK. TRY THE TRI-RAIL TRAM.
SFX:	(TRAIN MOVES ON TRACKS. DOORS OPEN, COMMUTERS CHATTING.)
ANNCR:	TRI-RAIL. TRAM IT TOMORROW!
SFX:	(TRAIN MOVES ON TRACKS. DOORS OPEN.)
ANNCR:	TRI-RAIL TRAM. TURN RUSH HOUR INTO HUSH HOUR.
SFX:	(SNORING)

Exploring examples of great radio scripts

DeVito/Verdi has created many attention-grabbing scripts. Several radio campaigns for clients like Mount Sinai Medical Center and the National Thoroughbred Racing Association (NTRA) stand out. The way Script 5 and Script 6 immediately draw the listener in show how personal and intimately conversational radio writing can be.

As you read each script, pay attention to how the writer draws you in right away. It helps to think of radio writing as if you're writing a play, but without the first act. Just jump right into act two and you'll put the audience in the center of the action. Radio is so short, you won't have the time to set up the scene. There are no prologues, no intros, no preludes. That's why you need to get going from the start. See how each of these spots makes you keep reading, the same way they made the listener keep listening.

Also see how these scripts veer away from traditional radio format and are written in blocks of text, in upper case and lower case. But, notice how they use all caps for the actor's character name. Each agency determines its own way of writing scripts, although radio stations tend to use the same format: double-spaced, all caps, and lines grouped into phrases.

In the spot by DeVito/Verdi, "Two-Year-Old," notice how each line repeats with two different actors. The haunting repetitions draw the readers in. The topic is serious: "Patricia Puia was born deaf in Romania." As the script continues, the second echoed phrase slowly changes, moving the listener from sadness to hopefulness. Examine how the last repeated line talks about the child after successful cochlear implant surgery. She's a typical two-year old: "She can hear, but she doesn't listen." The gradual changes allow the listener to see the words in pictures, playing to radio's often-dubbed "theater of the mind." We will see these scripts, "Two-Year-Old" (Script 5) and "Father" (Script 6) again in Chapter 14 (Scripts and Examples 14.2, Scripts and Examples 14.3) when they appear as part of a cross-platform campaign.

 SCRIPT 5 Mount Sinai, :60 radio script: "Two-Year-Old"

MAN 1:	Two-year-old Patricia Puia was born deaf in Romania.
MAN 2:	Two-year-old Patricia Puia was born deaf in Romania.
MAN 1:	Her life was lived in silence.
MAN 2:	Her life was lived in silence.
MAN 1:	She had never heard a lullaby or the voice of another human being.
MAN 2:	She had never heard a lullaby or the voice of another human being.
MAN 1:	Her parents were told nothing could be done.
MAN 2:	Her parents were told that Mount Sinai in New York could restore Patricia's hearing.
MAN 1:	Patricia's parents were filled with despair.
MAN 2:	Patricia underwent cochlear implant surgery.
MAN 1:	Patricia withdrew into a shell.
MAN 2:	Patricia was able to hear for the very first time.
MAN 1:	Life has been difficult for Patricia and her parents.
MAN 2:	Life for Patricia is that of a typical two-year-old. She can hear, but she doesn't listen.
WOMAN:	Which hospital you choose can make all the difference in the world. Mount Sinai. Another day. Another breakthrough. For more information call 1-800-MD-SINAI.

(This "Two-Year-Old" :60 radio spot was created by DeVito/Verdi for Mount Sinai. Script courtesy of DeVito/Verdi.)

 SCRIPT 6 Mount Sinai, :60 radio script: "Father"

MAN 1:	Sixty-four-year-old Norman Lewis suffered from Alzheimer's Disease.
MAN 2:	Sixty-four-year-old Norman Lewis suffered from Alzheimer's Disease.
MAN 1:	His children suffered with him.
MAN 2:	His children suffered with him.

MAN 1:	His condition grew progressively worse.
MAN 2:	His condition grew progressively worse.
MAN 1:	His speech in particular had badly deteriorated.
MAN 2:	His speech in particular had badly deteriorated.
MAN 1:	No treatment was available.
MAN 2:	He was treated with a new drug developed by a team of doctors at Mount Sinai.
MAN 1:	He could barely speak.
MAN 2:	He began speaking in full paragraphs.
MAN 1:	His family found they could no longer communicate with him.
MAN 2:	His family found they could now communicate with him.
MAN 1:	His children felt as if they had lost their father.
MAN 2:	His children were thrilled to have their father back.
WOMAN:	Which hospital you choose can make all the difference in the world. Mount Sinai. Another day. Another breakthrough. For more information call 1-800-MD-SINAI.

(This "Father" :60 radio spot was created by DeVito/Verdi for Mount Sinai. Script courtesy of DeVito/Verdi.)

In the National Thoroughbred Racing Association "We Bet You Love It" campaign, the next five spots (Script 7, Script 8, Script 9, Script 10, Script 11) have been some of the most celebrated, award-winning radio commercials in the industry. The DeVito/Verdi copywriters ingeniously tied together unique thoroughbred horses' names to create hilarious scripts. Anyone who has ever heard a racetrack announcer can picture the horses passing each other. But, funnier than that is how their names tell a story when intertwined the way they were. All the horses' names are in caps and bolded for easy reference. Take a moment to read through the scripts or, better yet, listen to them either on YouTube or the agency's website (www.devitoverdi.com).

Pay special attention to the time on these spots. The numbers ":40/:20" mean the body of the spots is 40 seconds long. The ":20" means each spot allows for a local racetrack to insert 20 seconds at the end. This is called a "tag." One spot, "Karate Class" (Script 10), has a :42/:18 label. That means the commercial is two seconds longer and the tag is two seconds shorter. Tags affordably allow for customization. They can be used to change a location, a date, a period of time, and so on. These variations enable campaign consistency while easily allowing for specific changes. It's both a time-saving and cost-efficient solution, commonly used in the industry. You've probably heard many national car-manufacturer spots with tags for the local dealers.

SCRIPT 7 NTRA, :40/:20 radio script: "Dinner Date"

NTRA - AS PRODUCED

RADIO :40/:20

"DINNER DATE"

ANNCR: And they're off. Out of the gate is **DINNER DATE. DINNER DATE** starts strong. But here comes **NO RESERVATION**, followed by **HOURS OF WAITING**. Now **IDLE CHIT-CHAT** is making a move. But **IDLE CHIT-CHAT** is no match for **AWKWARD SILENCE**. It's **IDLE CHIT-CHAT**. It's **AWKWARD SILENCE**. And here comes **TABLE BY THE KITCHEN** and **SNOOTY WAITER** followed by **UNDERCOOKED CHICKEN**. I don't believe it, out of nowhere comes **DECLINED CREDIT CARD** and **UTTER HUMILIATION**. As they come down the stretch, **FIRST BASE** is nowhere in sight. And finally it's, **PECK ON THE CHEEK** and **LET'S JUST BE FRIENDS**.

VO: For a better time, go to the track.

   National Thoroughbred Racing. We bet you love it.

(This "Dinner Date" :40/:20 radio spot was created by DeVito/Verdi for NTRA (National Thoroughbred Racing Association). Script courtesy of DeVito/Verdi.)

 SCRIPT 8 NTRA, :40/:20 radio script: "Guy's Night Out"

NTRA - AS PRODUCED

RADIO :40/:20

"GUY'S NIGHT OUT"

ANNCR: And they're off. Out of the gate is **LOCAL BAR** and **GUY'S NIGHT OUT**. Here comes **ONE TOO MANY BEERS** and **LIQUID COURAGE**. **LIQUID COURAGE** makes a move on **BEAUTIFUL GIRL**. But **BEAUTIFUL GIRL** pulls away. And here comes **FLATTERY**, but **FLATTERY's** going nowhere. Oh no, here comes **CHEESY PICK-UP LINE. CHEESY PICK-UP LINE** is immediately followed by **GET A LIFE, YOU'RE A CREEP** and **IN YOUR DREAMS**. And down the home stretch, it's **BRUISED EGO, LAUGHING FRIENDS**, and the favorite, **SHE WASN'T MY TYPE ANYWAY**.

VO: For a better time, go to the track.

   National Thoroughbred Racing. We bet you love it.

(This "Guy's Night Out" :40/:20 radio spot was created by DeVito/Verdi for NTRA (National Thoroughbred Racing Association). Script courtesy of DeVito/Verdi.)

SCRIPT 9 NTRA, :40/:20 radio script: "Yoga"

NTRA

Radio :40/:20

"YOGA"

ANNCR: And they're off. Out of the gate it's **YOGA CLASS** with **DEEP BREATHING** and **MEDITATION**. Now coming around the outside of **FOREHEAD** is **LEFT-FOOT**. It's **LEFT-FOOT** in front of **FOREHEAD**. It's **FOREHEAD** in front of **PELVIS**. It's **PELVIS** in front of **EYE SOCKET**. It's **EYE SOCKET** in front of **FAMILY JEWELS**. How the heck did **EYE SOCKET** get in front of **FAMILY JEWELS**? And here comes **DEEP BREATHING** again with **INNER PEACE**. But wait, from out of nowhere it's **SILENT BUT DEADLY**. **SILENT BUT DEADLY** is all over **YOGA CLASS**. **DEEP BREATHING** has stopped in its tracks. And **YOGA CLASS** isn't gonna last long. And in the end it's **GASPING FOR AIR, LIGHT A MATCH** and **SO MUCH FOR SERENITY**.

ANNCR: For a better time, go to the track.

National Thoroughbred Racing. We bet you love it.

(This "Yoga" :40/:20 radio spot was created by DeVito/Verdi for NTRA (National Thoroughbred Racing Association). Script courtesy of DeVito/Verdi.)

SCRIPT 10 NTRA, :42/:18 radio script: "Karate Class"

NTRA - AS RECORDED

RADIO :42/:18

"KARATE CLASS" - REVISED - CLIENT VERSION

ANNCR: And they're off. Out of the gate it's **KARATE CLASS** and **KARATE CLASS** is off to a nice start with **WHITE BELT** and **HIYA**. But wait, here comes **SENSEI** with **THIRD DEGREE BLACK BELT** and **MERCY IS FOR THE WEAK**. And now it's **SENSEI** with **FIVE FINGER LOTUS PUNCH**. But here comes **WAX ON WAX OFF**. But **WAX ON WAX OFF** is no match for **NAGASAKI NOSE BREAKER**. And what's this? From out of nowhere it's **KICK TO THE YING YANG** right between **THE CHOPSTICKS** and **THE DUMPLINGS**! And **KICK TO THE YING YANG** is really digging in! And in the end, it's **HOLD ONTO YOUR EGGROLL, GET ME SOME ICE** and **BIG TROUBLE IN LITTLE CHINA**.

ANNCR: For a better time, go to the track.

National Thoroughbred Racing. We bet you love it.

(This "Karate Class" :42/:18 radio spot was created by DeVito/Verdi for NTRA (National Thoroughbred Racing Association). Script courtesy of DeVito/Verdi.)

SCRIPT 11 NTRA, :40/:20 radio script: "Walk the Dog"

NTRA - AS PRODUCED

RADIO :40/:20

"WALK THE DOG"

ANNCR: And they're off. Out of the gate it's **GET UP EARLY** and **WALK THE DOG**. Here comes **DO THE LAUNDRY, WASH THE DISHES** and **TAKE OUT THE TRASH**. Out of nowhere comes **CALL FROM MOM** with **YOU NEVER CALL** followed by **NAGGING** and **GUILT TRIP**. It's **NAGGING** it's **GUILT TRIP**. It's **GUILT TRIP** it's **NAGGING**, and **NAGGING** is relentless. But wait, it looks like **WALK THE DOG** has a little left in him. Now it's **WALK THE DOG** followed by **WATCH TV**. It's **WATCH TV** all alone. But here comes **TAKE A NAP**. Wait a minute, I don't believe it. It's **CALL FROM MOM**, she just won't go away. And in the end it's **ANOTHER BORING SATURDAY**.

VO: For a better time, go to the track.

    National Thoroughbred Racing. We bet you love it.

(This "Walk The Dog" :40/:20 radio spot was created by DeVito/Verdi for NTRA (National Thoroughbred Racing Association). Script courtesy of DeVito/Verdi.)

Notice the script format for this spot. It uses upper case and lower case, not all caps. As mentioned earlier, the reason was to point out the names in caps of the thoroughbred horses in the race. Agencies differ on their script formats. Learn which one your agency uses and adopt it consistently, so all your script formats are uniform. Also pay attention to the use of vernacular contractions like "they're" in the phrase "and *they're* off" as the race begins.

It's always useful to look at classic radio commercials that reached celebrity status. One of the most celebrated radio commercials ran from 1985 to 1990 and was the campaign for Fromageries Bel's The Laughing Cow brand cheese. TBWA New York asked Joy Golden to create a campaign to boost sales. The spots used "heavy ethnic" talent: a female actor with a Valley Girl dialect (a regional California teenage sound at that time). There were several spots created as a series. So, radio listeners could follow the story. The three spots (Script 12, #1, #2, #3), using the Valley Girl accent, featured a budding romance that blossomed into marriage. It started with the Valley Girl being stopped by the highway patrolman, "Highway" (Script 12, #1), and ended up with his asking her to marry him, "Proposal" (Script 12, #3). Golden offered tips to help you write funny radio spots (Advice from the Pros 8.6). She also explained how she created the humor in The Laughing Cow series like this:

> *The story of The Laughing Cow cheese commercials is one of miscommunication. Is the product a cow or a piece of cheese? Two spend 60 seconds attempting to solve this important question. And their dialogue is what forms the basis of the humor that ran on the radio for 5 years in many different spots. Finding the right actors to carry this off was a huge challenge. As a matter of fact all radio casting is a huge challenge. Great film or theater actors don't necessarily have the vocal genius to translate characters for a strictly audio medium. They don't have the rhythm, the timing, the quirkiness. Radio is like music. Obviously, you can't see it. So what you hear is the whole show. And with comedy radio, if the script is funny, an actor better laugh before he or she does the first take. If he doesn't, it's goodbye Murray.*[6]

Sales increased by a staggering 52% after advertising in six markets over only 13 weeks. Script 12 showcases those famously successful, award-winning spots.[7]

 SCRIPT 12 The Laughing Cow "Valley Girl" radio campaign

VALLEY GIRL #1: "HIGHWAY"

VALLEY GIRL:
Like I was driving down the freeway, ok
and this totally gorgoso highway patrolman stops me.
I said like wow there's wheels on your motorcycle and
wheels on my car. That's really kharmoso. He said
you were speeding. I said have to get my little round
Laughing Cow in the red net bag into the fridge, ok. He said
where's the cow? I said in the trunk, ok. He said you're not
authorized to carry livestock. I said officer that is
like really heavy. The Laughing Cow isn't a real
cow, ok. It's like cheese, ok. Mild Mini Bonbel. Nippy Mini
Babybel. And new Mini Gouda. You know like really
awesome and naturelle. Five delicious round cheeses

in little net bags.
Each one wrapped in wax with a cute little zip thing. He
said open the trunk. I said ok. He said you need a key. I
mean this guy was totally brilliant ok. I said so you want a little
Laughing Cow. So he said ok. So I said ok. So we said ok.
So then he asked me for my license. And I said when can I
see you again. He was so totally freaked like he
dropped the cheese
and bit the ticket.
And so now it's two weeks and he never called.

VALLEY GIRL #2: "COUNTING SHOES"

VALLEY GIRL:
Okay, so like I was sitting here
eating a little round Laughing Cow
in a red net bag
and counting how many pairs of shoes I owned
when the phone rang. I said like hello.
And this deep voice said like hi.
And then like I totally freaked.
I said this isn't the highway patrolman?
He said yes it is. I said no it isn't.
He said yes it is. So I said really?
Then he said like what're you doing.
I said eating a little Laughing Cow and counting my
shoes. He said got any extras?
I said they're too small for you.
He said that's ok, I eat twenty of them.
I said even the suede ones?
He said oh no. I said officer, why don't you come over
and have The Laughing Cow
instead.
Mild Mini Bonbel. Nippy Mini Babybel.
And Mini Gouda.
You know like really awesome and naturelle.
Six delicious cheeses in little net bags.
Each one wrapped in wax
with a cute little zip thing.
He said what's your address?
I mean talk about an inquisitive mind, right?
I said you want crackers, too? He said ok.
So I said ok. So ok, ok?
So *then* I said what should we do
after we eat the cheese.
He said I'll watch you count your shoes.
I mean like
I've had heavy relationships before, but this is intense.

VALLEY GIRL #3: "PROPOSAL"

VALLEY GIRL:

So like hold on to your nail tips – ok – you're not going
to believe this –the gorgoso highway patrolman
asked me to marry him.
I mean talk about matching white shoes and bag, ok?
I am like totally freaked. Because like who would have guessed
that this hunkola who stopped me for speeding when I had the
little round Laughing Cow in the red net bag in my trunk
would be my groomoso for life, ok? Can you see this wedding
with like real Frenchola champagne and trays of Laughing Cow
cheeses in little red net bags everywhere? Mild Mini Bonbel.
Nippy Mini Babybel. And mellow Mini Gouda, too.
Like really awesome and naturelle. And me in flowing lace for days.
Anyhow it happened when we were eating Laughing Cow cheese
for lunch and talking about how many grains of sand are on the
beach because we are both like really deep. Then like all of a sudden
he said you want to get married? I said ok. So he said ok. So ok, ok.
So then he gave me a little round diamond ring in a red net bag.
And I said officer that is like so intensely sentimental. And he said
he couldn't find wrapping paper with cows on it. I mean talk
about romance. This is like movietown, USA.

(*These Laughing Cow Cheese :60 radio commercials were written and produced
by Joy Golden for Fromageries Bel. The Laughing Cow, Bonbel and Mini Babybel
are registered trademarks of Fromageries Bel. Script courtesy of Joy Golden and
Fromageries Bel.*)

 ADVICE FROM THE PROS 8.6 Joy Golden's 10 secrets for creating successful comedy radio commercials

1 You must have worked for at least 147 agencies without ever writing a radio commercial.

2 You must have worked for at least 147 agencies, none of which let you be funny.

3 You must have spent 38 years writing small-space, black-and-white douche ads.

4 You must have a moderately unraveled family. An Aunt Yetta who can chew celery without making noise is a help.

5 You must have had 20 years of intense therapy with a shrink who slept through the last 10.

6 You must be a card-carrying hypochondriac at all times.

7 You must have been at a dentist who does Groucho Marx imitations.

8 You must have a lawyer who wants to give it all up and be a voiceover.

9 You must have an Uncle Sy who says "Explain to me again what it is you do for a living."

10 You must love to write and produce radio commercials better than sex, or death-by-chocolate ice cream. Well, maybe not better than ice cream.[8]

What gave these commercials celebrity status was the use of distinctive, regional accents like the Valley Girl mentioned earlier. The combination of a female voice presented as a specific character in a vignette paired with a particularly identifiable accent gave the campaign an instantly recognizable sound, increasing brand awareness.

One award-winning radio campaign, hailed as having some of the greatest radio spots ever created, in addition to the NTRA spots already discussed, has more than 100 variations. The first two spots in the campaign were "Mr. Footlong" and "Mr. Toupee." The Bud Light "Real Men of Genius" was developed in 1999 by Bob Winter when he was a copywriter at DDB, before joining Leo Burnett. The announcer was Peter Stacker and the singer is Dave Bickler, formerly with Survivor, who mimics the announcer. The composers, Sam Struyk and Sandy Torano, were from Scandal Music in Chicago. The spots pay tribute to many ordinary, yet annoying, characters most people have encountered, comically addressed as "Real American Heroes." One salutes "Mr. Bumper Sticker Writer" and attributes to him the ridiculous line "You can't hug with nuclear arms." The singer echoes back, "I need a hug now!" You'll find the full scripts online, as well. Be sure you take the time to listen to these spots on YouTube under the "Bud Light Real Men of Genius." Here are the actual titles to use when you're searching for these commercials:

1. "Mr. Cargo Pants Designer"

2. "Mr. Centerfold Picture Retoucher"

3. "Mr. Over-Zealous Foulball Catcher"

Writing radio tips

Charlie Hopper, principal at Young & Laramore, offered the helpful tips in Advice from the Pros 8.7. He discussed writing backward, that is writing with the medium, the talent, and the production in mind. He explained how writers need to understand casting talent and the production process in order to get the exact read and sound they have in mind. His comments are highly useful and easily applicable (Advice from the Pros 8.7). Read through them and refer to them the next time you're writing for radio.

 ADVICE FROM THE PROS 8.7 Charlie Hopper's tips for writing for radio

The Process

Starting with the production and working backward, you gotta know that you're going to be changing the script in there [the studio] at some point. So you gotta know how to walk in with the script written the right way. You gotta read it out loud at your desk, and not rush it because you want it to fit. That happens to every writer, and I sit here, as the creative director, having done it and having learned my lesson the hard way, I keep telling the writers as they're writing, "You've gotta make it shorter. Make it shorter. Make it shorter." They start off and they don't want that to be true. They think you're just being mean and you want them to cut out a joke or something. You get into the recording session and it just doesn't fit. Then, you end up writing on the spot. Maybe you're good at that and maybe you're not. It's stressful and everybody's waiting and you're burning the studio time. You gotta rewrite it right there and then. It just isn't working because you didn't read it slowly enough with a stopwatch.

The Script

Certain radio ads are simply 60 seconds of a guy talking. Others have sound effects, so you end up having to make it easy for the guy to read it. That's the key. I feel like sometimes I can manipulate and save time in the studio by typing it a certain way, so the guy reads it the way I want it right off the top. He gets the spot. He knows how he fits in the spot and isn't trying to guess what you want.

You can indicate the sound effects within the block. Or you can break it up and put it into blocks, and you can decide if you want to do each block individually when you're recording him. Or whether you want to do the body of the spot and punch him back in. I'm famous in the radio circles around here for belaboring my talents because I believe in two things.

The Direction of Talent

Your first takes are your freshest. Your announcer is going to have a little twinkle in his eye and a little sparkle in his tone that you can't quite put your finger on, but it's there in the first five takes.

The second thing I "believe" in: that you learn things about your script as you go and you have to stay spontaneous and open to change. The problem is, in those first five takes, you're learning things about your script, like "Oh, it's too long. That joke isn't funny. That phrase isn't as pronounceable as I thought it was, or whatever." You're learning stuff like that. Maybe they're hitting a word wrong and calling caramel, CAR-MEL, CARA-MEL. You're not supposed to do it that way. Little things like that. Then, what happens is I get those first takes for their *esprit*, but then we've belabored everything after that. So, I get all the little nuances the way I want them if I'm working with somebody who isn't automatically getting it.

If you're working with someone great, they get all those nuances, those little twists and turns, that you want them to take that you can't necessarily direct because it's too much for them to hold in their head. A really good voice talent does that. By and large, the level that most people are working, they don't get to work with the real voice talents. They don't get to work with Dan Castellaneta [the voice of Homer Simpson]. They get to work with some random guy from a talent agency who's pretty good. He's got good pipes, but he's not that good of an artist or a performer that he gets all those little ins and outs.

The Production

That's when you have to go in and punch in all these little phrases. You need to really work with your engineer and bond with him so that he knows, "Okay, that pause after that word was right on this take and wrong on that take. But, the latter take is best overall. So, we'll take the pause from the earlier take and cut it into this other one."

You end up really having the ability to control the result. Radio is a writer's solo flight. Radio is the writer's chance to really make something. That's the funny thing about being a writer. We don't actually ever make anything. We're always an interim step. We've gotta be on it. We have to be ready to kill a widow [one word hanging alone at the end of a paragraph on top of a page] and rewrite it so it fits the space better. And, "Oh my gosh, I wrote too much. Let me go edit that." Let's make sure that when I'm on set [for TV spots] and the announcer's not reading it right, let me get that in the director's head so that he isn't burning a bunch of film with the wrong read because I know we need to do it this other way.

The Writer's in Charge

The writer has all these duties, including sharing responsibility for the overall look and concept of anything you're involved with, but as far as actually physically making something, radio is your only real chance. I get a weird, sweaty feeling going in to do radio because as a writer I so seldom make a final product. Writers make an interim product, but don't finish off the layouts and send them to production like the art directors do. Writers don't finish up the final edit the way the editors do. Writers are usually just commenting the whole time. Radio is the exception where the writer has to go, "Yes, we're done," and that's the fun part. That's the hard part: deciding you're done.

You can always make something better, but you have to stop at some point. There's actually a good quote that I like from Roger Miller, the guy who wrote *King of the Road*: "Half of art is knowing when to stop." You just have to know where we have to stop. We gotta move on. That's hard to know for the writer some- times because he doesn't usually do that. He usually relies on his editor, or his art director, or creative director or client or someone else to say, "Okay, that's good. We're going to go with that." The writer can say, "That's good. Let's go with that," but then he's not physically finishing it. Radio is your chance to do that.

Starting with the production and working backward, you gotta know that you're going to be changing the script in there [the studio] at some point. So you gotta know how to walk in with the script written the right way. You gotta read it out loud at your desk, and not rush it because you want it to fit. That happens to every writer, and I sit here, as the creative director, having done it and having learned my lesson the hard way.

Then, you've gotta know how Pro Tools works. You don't actually have to touch Pro Tools, but to some degree your engineer is going to be doing what you say. You've gotta know that you can cut in that word from the other take here. You can take that phrase out; it's not necessary. We've already released the talent, but now we want this pause to be longer over here. So, we have to take this phrase out, and you say, "Okay, you could take that out," or "Oh, you couldn't take that out because he blends those words together." "Oh, he went on for a half an hour about this."

But, about typing the script, we're kind of loose about that because we're going to get in there and roll up our sleeves. We just want to do whatever's going to make it work.[9]

Reviewing radio: The wrap up

Remember when writing for radio, you only have one sense: hearing. So, everything you create has to be instantly understood aurally. You can't expect anyone to know it's snowing unless a voiceover talent mentions it. You can't see clouds, but you can hear plane engines. If you're setting a scene, use sound effects and/or music to portray that setting, like island music playing, palm fronds rustling, ocean waves breaking, and seagulls "talking." Think produc- tion right from the start. Do I want one voice or more? Do I want to depict a story or deliver a message? Do I want a strong or soft delivery by the talent? Do I want several different music cuts or one uninterrupted music bed? Am I casting an actor or a character voice? What else will help sell the product or tell the brand's message? Radio has been called "theater of the mind" for years because everything that happens must be projected through sound alone.

Close your eyes and listen to every sound you hear. Can you tell where you are? Do you hear the hum of a computer-cooling fan, the typing of someone at a keyboard, the ringing of a phone, or the sound of people chatting? Each sound you hear around you helps define where you are. Think about this when you're writing radio scripts. Always ask yourself: Can I tell where this is taking place?

Then ask: Does my copy sound natural, like real people speaking? Or, does it sound awkward or "forced," like people talking about the product in an unnatural way? For example: "Maria, did you see the new gym on the corner? It has weights and treadmills, and yoga classes. It's awesome." Maria answers, "No, I haven't. Gee, that sounds great." People don't usually tell friends a list of features as an announcer would. We just don't talk like that.

Finally, be sure you read all your scripts aloud. Rewrite any place that causes you to stumble. Don't worry about what's wrong in the script. Just revise it so it flows more easily.

Radio is a challenging, yet exciting medium. Don't let it scare you. Jump right in and speak the lines as you're writing them. This will help you find your own natural voice.

Creative radio exercises

1. Work in teams of two or individually.

2. Choose one of your favorite Super Bowl spots. Usually, you can remember these easily, making the decision faster. Or, you can go to YouTube and look for the top 10 of the year.

3. How could you extend the campaign creatively?

4. Write a 30-second radio spot to continue the campaign and "marry" into the strategy of the TV spot by using the same talent, characters, creative approach, music, and sound effects. Consider what sound effects would place the listener in the same scene.

5. Now write the same commercial as a 10-second spot. Think about what you can edit out yet still get the message across.

6. Next, ask: Would this product work for another audience? If so, choose one. Then, rewrite the spots to speak directly to this new consumer group.

Notes

1. Andrew Langer, personal communication, January 6, 2012.
2. David Ogilvy, *Ogilvy on Advertising* (New York: Vintage Books, 1985), 113.
3. Ogilvy, *Ogilvy on Advertising*, 113–114.
4. Kenneth Roman and Jane Mass, *How to Advertise*, 3rd ed. (New York: Thomas Duane Books, 2003), 126–130.
5. Joy Golden, personal communication, July 28, 2010.
6. Joy Golden, personal communication, July 28, 2010.
7. Pete Schulberg and Bob Schulberg, *Radio Advertising: The Authoritative Handbook*, 2nd ed. (Chicago: NTC Business Books, 1996), 155–156.
8. Joy Golden, personal communication, July 28, 2010.
9. Charlie Hopper, personal communication, November 26, 2021.

9 The Chosen Word
Copywriting Techniques

"The overall point is that you can't think of the writing without thinking of how and where and when people will encounter it."
Charlie Hopper, Principal, Young & Laramore[1]

As you read through this chapter, you'll accumulate your personal arsenal of writing tools. You'll soon discover the appropriate use of the vernacular and realize when it's acceptable to digress from stringent grammatical rules to deliver a more conversational style. The goal is to create copy that sounds as if you're talking to your best friend. You want readers to feel as if you're having a personal conversation with them. Great copy mirrors the spoken word. It's a skill you can learn through easy-to-apply techniques and by reading aloud. Be sure you review the list of writing tips in this chapter to use as a guide. Remember that copy that talks about serious topics like healthcare, medical procedures, or insurance, normally veers away from a casual *tone of voice*.

Content and Copywriting: The Complete Toolkit for Strategic Marketing, Second Edition. Margo Berman.
© 2024 Margo Berman. Published 2024 by John Wiley & Sons Ltd.
Companion website: www.wiley.com/go/contentandcopywriting

Normally, but not always. Think about the Aflac Duck and how he speaks like an everyday person and not an insurance salesperson. If your campaign creates a whimsical character in a usually solemn, complex, or informative product category or service, then it's okay to use a lighthearted creative direction.

After you examine the following library of writing techniques, you'll see how idea development, execution, and production across all platforms, specifically apply to the verbal message. Let the *creative brief* guide you as you think about your audience and advertising objective (Creative Strategy Statement). Before you create advertising copy, be sure to think about conceptual messaging, *tone of voice* (how you speak to the audience), and *point of view* (who's speaking). While you're writing, you'll know when to implement *ABA* (referring back to the headline [that's the first "A"] in the closing line [that's the second "A"] after the body copy [that's the "B"]), parallel construction (repeating a phrase, word, or part of speech, like "no salt, no sugar, no calories"), and weave (connecting one main idea from the headline throughout the copy). These are discussed again later in the chapter. Let's start with the development of a strong message.

Developing a strong message with legs

Once you review the brief and have a strong sense of your audience, competition, tactics, and overall direction from your Creative Strategy Statement, you'll want to establish a message that can stand up in all media, platforms, and touchpoints. It's equally important for it to work in a predetermined medium, as it is to be media neutral and work in a new, unexpected, or experiential medium. The campaign concept needs to be so big it transcends the media. That's when you know you have a powerful idea.

Think about when the M&M'S campaign launched new colors. People could vote for their favorites. Create M&M'S characters in their likeness. And order customized M&M'S with their own messages on the outside. The idea of engaging the audience in different ways worked equally well everywhere: from print to TV and online. However, no one could have expected any controversy after the green M&M'S changed shoes from knee-high boots to sneakers, or the brown ones from stilettos to lower heels, or the orange ones left the shoelaces untied, or after the brand introduced a purple character to celebrate successful women. The marketing team's goal was to make the M&M'S characters more relevant to a younger audience and to be more inclusive. Unfortunately, others thought otherwise and took offense for different reasons. One was that the candies became too urban and alienated other audiences. For example, Tucker Carlson, a Fox News host, inappropriately labeled them "Woke M&M'S."[2]

So, as you're thinking through your messaging, be sure to look at the intended media. Will your message *spin out*, that is, will it translate easily into any promotional vehicle? Does it have "legs," meaning will it have longevity like the character-based slogan *"Snap! Crackle! Pop!"* of Kellogg's® Rice Krispies®?

What you're looking for is the big idea that doesn't have constraints. Like a chameleon, it can take on any backdrop and blend in perfectly. It's flexible, malleable, and translatable. It's a message that can be *transcreated* (recreated in other languages) and still retain its core idea. Did you realize that the McDonald's slogan, "I'm lovin' it," was originally created in Germany? Yet, it's relevant to the American market. The message is conversational and uses vernacular or everyday speech like "lovin'" instead of "loving." The way, or the verbal manner, that the message is delivered is called the "tone of voice."

Determining the tone of voice

This is how you speak to your audience. Think about adjectives. Should the message sound whimsical, authoritative, informative, concerned, lighthearted, mysterious, friendly, cool, trendy, sophisticated, or something else? If you were discussing open-heart surgery, you wouldn't want to sound too casual. You're talking about a potentially life-threatening surgical procedure to repair a serious condition. No one wants to hear a funny message when you're discussing this kind of topic. They want to be reassured, not joked with. Choosing the right *tone of voice* for the product and the audience is crucial to a successful campaign.

Take your time when you're thinking through the *tone of voice*. One good idea is to think of the brand as a famous celebrity. It has to be someone your audience would immediately know. Then, consider who that celebrity would be if he or she were in the consumer's life. Would that person be a friend, sister, mentor, neighbor, teacher, coach, or someone else? The more you see this celebrity as someone who could be part of the consumer's life, the more accurate the message will be. Just look back at the difference between the PC geek and the Mac guy who was cool. You instantly see the cool guy as your friend, your buddy. So how would that buddy speak to you? He'd be casual, cool, and friendly. Precisely the way the Mac guy was portrayed.

Now, select an adjective that depicts how your brand would speak to the consumer, the same way the Mac guy sounds "cool." For example, if you had an ultra-expensive luxury brand, you might think of adjectives like "sophisticated," "polished," "refined." These would create an elegant *tone of voice*. However, regardless of how chic the product is, "chic," although it's an adjective, can't be a *tone of voice*. Here's the rule of thumb: Ask yourself to speak in a "chic" *tone of voice*. If you can't, then it's an ill-fitting adjective for tone.

However, you could speak in a sophisticated, polished, or refined manner, or *tone of voice*. These would be appropriate adjectives for the "voice" of the campaign.

This is an extremely useful mental exercise that you should include in your message development. After you've decided your *tone of voice*, now you determine your *point of view*, namely who's delivering the campaign message?

Finding the point of view

There are several points of view. Choose the one that best supports your strategy. Ask yourself who will speak on the brand's behalf? Whose voice will be heard? Will it be the company that talks about its consumer service, performance, or safety ratings? Will it be a consumer who states a testimonial, singing praises? Will it be the consumer's conscience that warns consumers what could happen if they don't use the product? Or will it be the brand speaking for itself? Here's a short list explaining these four *points of view*:

1. *Self-serving* – The brand/product/company boasts about its achievements and awards. The consumer is not delivering the message. For example, "You can't drive a safer car," or "We're number one in customer service." It's all about the brand. Yes, the benefit is mentioned, but it's told to, not stated by, the consumer. It's a promise of quality and a guarantee of performance that the brand makes to its audience. One recognized example, created in 1965, is the famous slogan for Hebrew National (all-beef cold cuts and hotdogs): "We answer to a higher authority."

2. *Testimonial* – Product users rave about the product. They eagerly share what they love about it and enthusiastically talk about how it improved their lives. Comments like "I tried every diet and none of them worked. Look at me now! I lost 50 pounds and kept it off. And, so can you." Because she's a real person and not a superstar with a fitness trainer and personal chef, she's more relatable. If a celebrity is speaking, not a consumer, that campaign is called a "celebrity endorsement." Here are a few examples: (1) Ashton Kutcher and Mila Kunis for Cheetos, (2) Queen Latifah for the CoverGirl "Easy, Breezy, Beautiful" and her own "Queen Collective" campaigns, and (3) Jennifer Hudson for Weight Watchers. If a celebrity talks only about the product but doesn't claim usage, that star is a celebrity spokesperson, like Carly Foulkes or Catherine Zeta-Jones for the T-Mobile campaign.

3. *Emotional Blackmail* – The consumers' conscience is warning them of a potential problem they could avoid by using the product. One example

would be the "Hertz? Not Exactly" campaign, which warned if you rented from another company, you'd be missing all that Hertz promises as the number one car company rental. Another great example of emotional blackmail was the Tide To Go "Talking Stain" campaign. It's worth a moment to see it on YouTube. The stain on the young interviewee's shirt is talking and drowning him out. So, the potential employer is distracted and can only hear the stain's voice. If only the applicant had used Tide To Go, the problem would have been averted!

4. *Brand Stand* – The brand takes a stand in its own voice with a distinct personality convincing consumers to buy. For example, go to www.elfyourself.com and discover how much fun OfficeMax created in its "Elf Yourself" campaign. People could upload their image or their pet's image and create animated elves. The interactive campaign has returned for another playful year.

Writing the way you speak

Writing copy for ads is not like writing a scientific article or term paper. You're not delivering a deep lecture or making a formal speech. Instead, you're having a conversation. You're chatting with the consumer. So just how friendly should you be? This is where knowing your audience and your brand's *tone of voice* is crucial. Your language needs to both speak to the audience and properly represent the brand and its message. If either one is wrong, there's a disconnect between the brand and the consumer. If your message is *off-target,* it's incorrect for the audience. If it's *off-strategy,* it's going in the wrong creative direction.

1. *Use vernacular when it fits* – So, when do you use vernacular, or everyday, informal speech? When it's appropriate. That casual *tone of voice* works perfectly for its audience of young, carefree college-aged guys, as depicted in Budweiser's "Whassup?" campaign or its "Beer House" 2010 Super Bowl spot. Remember there are degrees of casual. You would have to decide whether to use texting with its abbreviated spelling, or a relaxed tone with "gonna" or "woulda," or, a cultural or regional dialect. For instance, would writing using idiomatic expressions like "ma'am," "ya'll," or "fuggetaboutit" from Texas, the deep South, or New York enhance the message and target a specific audience? Ultimately, the *tone of voice* you choose and the delivery mechanism, such as vernacular or regional expressions, are crucial in establishing a credible link with your consumer.

2. *Choose simple, easy-to-grasp language* – Whatever you write, use simple, easy-to-grasp language. Avoid complex words, insiders' jargon, and

"techie" terminology. Unless you're writing to a specific market that naturally uses those types or terms, leave them out. Don't you hate reading something that's supposed to explain how to use a product and you can't understand it? Many product manuals have been simplified. So, consumers can quickly understand the directions.

3. *Write in phrases, not lengthy sentences* – Shorter is usually better. See how easy it is? Just keep it short. The way you speak. Next time you're at a café, in the park, at a train station, listen. Pay attention to how people often don't even finish their thoughts or use one-word sentences. Get it? Great.

4. *Write in a conversational style* – Actually picture your consumers. What do they look like? How would they dress? How would you talk to them? Then, just say what you want to say aloud. That's how you'll hear your own voice and natural delivery. Use it. But, this time write it.

5. *Read your copy out loud* – After you've written it. Read it again out loud. Are you stumbling anywhere? Does it sound stiff or awkward or unnatural? If so, restate it and rewrite it the way you said it.

6. *Use punctuation to guide the reader's pace and focus* – Stop and start the reader with short sentences and periods. Like this. See?

7. *Choose active, not passive voice* – Keep the action alive by using straightforward writing, such as the active subject-followed-by-the-verb sentence construction. So, you'd say, "That guy SNAPPED a photo," not "The photo WAS SNAPPED by that guy."

8. *Weave* – Use the main idea throughout the copy. So, if your headline talks about "Creating Buzz," you would weave "buzz" in interesting ways in the copy.

9. *Consider parallel construction* – This is a specific kind of phrasing or wording that you've heard or read many times: "To be or not to be." "It's not just coffee. It's Starbucks." "No salt. No sugar. No calories." "Get it? Got it? Good." It could just be the same word or part of speech used *over* and *over* and *over* or like this: here, there, and everywhere.

10. *Apply ABA format* – Often used in many of the arts, this structure repeats the headline's main idea in the closing line of the copy. The first "A" refers to the headline. "B" refers to the body copy. The last "A" refers to the last line of copy. So, if the headline used Maxwell House's slogan "Good to the last drop," the closing line could read, "One sip and you'll know why it's good to the last drop." The closing line doesn't have to repeat the headline word-for-word, just embody the concept.

11. *Use connectors* – These are words that tie each sentence or paragraph to the next, like "and," "so," "the truth is," "naturally," etc. Think of them as little stepping stones that create a path that leads the reader through the woods.

12. *Start writing in the middle* – This means don't have a long intro. Jump right into your message or you might lose your reader.

13. *Think about alliteration* – This is another technique you're familiar with: "Sally sells seashells by the seashore," "Monday Madness," "Fabulous Fun Fridays," "Ho, Ho, Ho!" for the holidays.

14. *Use a button* – This is a clever closing line that does *not* refer back to the headline. It can be a pun or a witty line that makes the reader smile.

15. *Rewrite until it's right* – Don't be satisfied with your first effort. Look the copy over. Is it wordy? Vague? Hard to read? Too complex? Take out superfluous words and unnecessary phrases. Then, reread it. Does it need more editing? Be honest!

16. *Know when to break grammatical rules* – In advertising copy, it's okay to start a sentence with because. Why? Because it works. You can end a sentence with a preposition because that's the way we naturally speak: "Who'd you sent the letter TO?" sounds better to the ear than "To whom did you send the letter?" even though the second one is proper English. You want to connect to the audience, not sound stuffy and affected. Some slogans use incorrect spelling or improper English. That's fine in this kind of writing. When Apple used this tagline, "Think Different," grammarians were upset, saying it should have used an adverb "Think differently." What Apple claimed was that "different" was a noun, not modifying the verb "think." Likewise, Toyota deliberately used the wrong spelling in the slogan "Toyota Everyday." Saatchi & Saatchi Advertising developed the slogan. It should have read "Toyota Every Day," because everyday, as one word, is an adjective modifying a noun like everyday routine. But you'd say, he goes to that restaurant every day. The reason the agency creatives wrote "every day" as one word was for two reasons. First, they wanted the audience to read the slogan like a verbal logo. Second, people would absorb the slogan faster if there were only two words to digest. Hence, "Toyota Everyday."[3] Even Leo Burnett, the advertising legend, agreed that "ain't" could be used if it precisely expressed the point. Here's a much-quoted Burnett comment using "ain't":

A good basic selling idea, involvement and relevancy, of course, are as important as ever, but in the advertising din of today, unless you make yourself noticed and believed, you ain't got nothin'.[4]

Writing to your audience

In Chapter 5, we spent a lot of time talking about the different types of audience categories (VALS). The reason for this was to prepare you to think about your audience as a living, breathing human being, not a statistic. You want to get inside the mind of your consumers and know how they think. What's important to them. What they value. And, how they live their lives. Numbers are one thing. But, seeing your product from their *point of view* is everything. Probably the most important tip is to "Think like the consumer." Write down that phrase in big letters and post it on your computer. You won't go wrong – off strategy or off target – if you remember this point.

Always ask yourself what you would want to hear to take action. What would motivate you to make that purchase? To order that service? To hire that company? Sign up for special offers? Then, select a *tone of voice* that sounds natural for the brand and right for the audience. Write a message that will interrupt your target wherever they are.

1. *Catch their attention with a compelling headline.* What could you say that would be intrusive? Actually make them stop what they're doing at that precise moment in time and hear what you're saying. Keep working until you find an interruptive or disruptive message. For example, this message was on the top of a double-decker bus in London: "For people in high places." The advertiser was *The Economist,* a financial publication. Only those people, who worked in tall buildings, usually where financial institutions had offices, could see the ad.

2. *Show the benefits up front.* No one wants to wade through miles of copy to find out what's in it for them? People want to know the answer to "Why buy?" immediately. Place the benefits in the headline or subhead so they'll read on.

3. *Select a familiar tone of voice.* Be sure your tone is correct for both the brand and the consumer. How conversational or casual is appropriate? You will know this if you have insight into your brand's personality and your consumer's core (or key) values.

4. *Include relevant copy points.* Tell consumers how the product will fit into their lives, solve a specific problem, or fill a need. This is where the copy has a chance to further explain the *consumer benefits* and the product features. Is the product lighter, faster, safer? What features prove these points?

5. *Determine VALS language.* If you're speaking to "Makers," you should be talking about how simple it is to build this bookcase or to customize this deck. They enjoy the process of construction and like to celebrate their creativity.

6. *Consider regional dialects.* Should you use them? Do they reflect the tone of a regional brand or a specific audience? Do they catch the target's attention? Do they present the brand in an acceptably humorous way without being offensive?

7. *Connect directly using NLP.* NLP, *neurolinguistic programming*, also called "NLC," *neurolinguistic conditioning*, shows the connection between the people's state of mind (mood) and their physical reaction (health). A quick example is the way you cannot smile when you're in the middle of a fight. That expression would be incongruous with your feelings. However, if you wanted to change from angry to calm, something that makes you smile, like a baby's laugh, can help you change your mood. This neurolinguistic link shows the connection between how you feel and how you look. If I told you that you just won a million dollars, you'd smile, sit up straighter and feel great, instantly. That's how quickly your mood can change.

Use this handy "Grammar" copywriting checklist (Checklist 9.1) to help your copy sound more natural, believable, and persuasive.

CHECKLIST 9.1 A quick "Grammar" copywriting checklist

1 *Use slang (vernacular):* gonna, gotta, hey, lemme, 'em, wanna, shoulda, lovin', etc. work for many types of products, like the Kit Kat candy line, "Gimme a break." But, if your client's tone is formal, covers a serious problem, or deals with health, medical, or insurance issues, you need to reconsider.

2 *Put prepositions at the end of the sentence* if that's where they naturally fall. For example: Who's the audience you're talking to? The dangling preposition is fine for ad copy.

3 *Write in fragments.* Not sentences. Like this.

4 *Create short paragraphs.* Even with just one sentence.

5 *Use short sentences.* They read faster.

6 *Use contractions* like we'd, you'd, she'll, not we had, you would, or she will. M&M'S used this headline: "Hey, how'd that get in there?" The image is of an X-ray of an M&M'S with the pretzel inside. Notice the use of "how'd" instead of "how did"?

7 *Sound conversational.* Like you're talking to a friend. (Notice the fragment, starting with "like.")

8 *Make up a new word* so the message is catchier like "Hangry" for a Snickers campaign.

When people want to change their behavior, they model the habits and gestures of successful people. They change their carriage and gait when they walk. They stick their chests out with pride. Just changing your physiology can change how you see yourself. This can lead you to opening yourself up for greater success.

When used in advertising messages, NLP singles out audience members by modeling their patterns of language. There are actually three ways we process information. Most of us are stronger in two of these. They are (1) *kinesthetic* (by touch), (2) *auditory* (by hearing), and (3) *visual* (by sight). People will tell you which one they are by the language they use.

The *kinesthetic* person will make comments like "Feels good to me," "I have a handle on it," and "I need to wrap my brain around it." These are the people who kick the tires and have to feel the interior of a car they're buying.

The *auditory* person will say sentences like, "I like the sound of that," "Sounds good to me," and "Listen up."

The *visual* person will say statements like, "Can you picture it?" "Take a look at this," and "See what I mean?"

Whenever you see a message that uses language like "Listen up," "We see how you feel," or "Sounds too good to be true? Well, it is true," it's talking to the audience in a way that will generate a response from a particular way those people best absorb information, that is in an *kinesthetic, auditory,* and *visual* manner.

When you're writing to an audience and don't have a sense of how they process, it's good to use words to target these three senses: touch, hearing, and sight.

Writing for the medium and the senses

We just discussed writing for three of the senses. With advertising, each medium addresses one or more of these. When writing for a specific medium, think about engaging the senses, how your choice of words can awaken one or more of them.

1. *For print: eye, ear, nose, and hand (touch)* – Print ads can incorporate more senses than sight. Now there are sound chips and scent advertising

that can be added. Think about the Hallmark cards where you can record your own message. That's done with a sound chip. Remember scent strips in perfume ads in magazines? That's scent advertising. Even though most print ads involve only sight, consider adding sound and scent to the medium when appropriate. With print, you're physically holding the message.

2. *For online: eye, ear, and hand* – Online messages can include hearing when there's animation or a video with a soundtrack. If you're creating an online message, you may be working with a strip or narrow ad. For a banner ad, it would be a horizontal strip, and for a skyscraper ad, it would be a vertical strip format. Should you involve a multipanel ad (with same-size boxes) that includes animation and sound effects as the action moves from one scene to another? Or does the ad work well enough by itself without movement and sound? Will it click through to another site?

3. *For radio: ear* – This is the one pure medium. The only sense is hearing. This is why you need to think visually. When writing for this medium, carefully decide the music and sound effects. They will put the listener in the exact setting.

4. *For TV and video: eye and ear* – The next time you watch TV, notice how much of it is enhanced with sound. To prove this, shut the sound off. You immediately feel as if you're missing half the story. Because you are. When writing for this medium, carefully decide the location and visual effects. Then, consider what additional sounds and music can be added to further tell the story.

5. *For ambient: eye, ear, nose, and hand* – Actually, this medium can connect all the senses. As with print advertising, you can use visuals, sounds, and scent. For example, for a fair, you could have a carousel horse going up and down, kids' screams and giggles, and spray the scent of French fries, cinnamon buns, or hot fudge. This could be a 3D billboard, at a bus shelter (within the safety glass), at kiosks in a mall. You could use two or three senses. For example, the back of escalator steps could show people in seats going up the Ferris wheel with the sound of people laughing. The point is to think about your audience's reaction to multiple sensations. Or, you could show people in rollercoaster seats with the sound of a wooden track clicking with each elevating step. Or you could place the message on subway turnstile handles.

6. *For mobile* – Think eye, ear, and hand. Portable devices allow you to create messages while consumers are on the go. They could be shopping or surfing. Using their apps or texting. What kind of message would

you want to receive on your device? Coupons? Invitations to events? Special offers? Think about an older market. Perhaps, they'd like to have medication renewal reminders and senior savings. Don't be judgmental and think they don't use a smartphone, Kindle, or iPad. Look around. You may be surprised to see your grandparents are sending you photos from their phones.

7. *For experiential* – Consider how exciting immersive experiences are. Be sure you're trying out new technology. Then, challenge yourself to see how you can make your campaigns more engaging through augmented reality (AR), virtual reality (VR), mixed reality (MR), gamification, or other emerging, experiential, and audience-enriching applications.

8. *For other touchpoints* – Ask yourself: Where else your consumers are seeing this message? In supermarkets? On shopping carts? On shelves in stores? How can you activate the audience's senses in unexpected ways?

There's already so much writing in the world, nobody is actively interested in reading what YOU have to write, especially if it's on behalf of somebody who's trying to sell them something. Charlie Hopper, Principal, Young & Laramore[5]

Writing for celebrities

This is a skill you will want to develop. Start right this minute and listen carefully to a few famous celebrities. Watch them on TV, YouTube, Hulu, or wherever you can. Do they speak quickly or slowly? Do they have a slight accent, like Kyra Sedgwick, or a slight lisp, like Holly Hunter, or rich vocal tone, like Demi Moore? Do they have a distinctive voice like James Earl Jones or Denzel Washington or Al Pacino? Try to find their cadence, their rhythm, their inflection, and their pace. Then, write for it.

For print – If you're writing a quote as if the celebrity actually said it, you need to write in that star's individual *tone of voice*, using natural phrasing and expressions. Most stars have a manager or agent who needs to approve the copy before allowing it to be used in an ad.

For broadcast – In this case, if the celebrities are delivering the lines you wrote as voiceover talents for radio or on- or off-screen as actors, each phrase must sound authentic, as if that was something they would say. This is where copy length is crucial. If you have a star with a slow delivery, you might only write 15 seconds of copy for a 30-second spot. In this way, you're using the celebrity's normal inflection and pace, for a natural-sounding delivery. When talents appear to be rushing through the script, especially in a testimonial, the commercial loses its credibility.

For the Internet – If stars appear in an online video, they have to sound as if they're speaking to the audience one-on-one. The same rules apply for online copy, even if the audience, and not the talent, is reading the message. Everything has to sound true to the star's style of speech.

The best thing you can do is immerse yourself in the celebrity's speech pattern by watching the star in as many movies, films, TV shows, and so on, to capture the person's vocal mannerisms, idioms, phrasing, and idiosyncrasies. Some stars might pepper their speech with colloquial expressions, like "y'all" or "sugar" if they're from a Southern U.S. state. Or, you might use a phrase or word that would reflect the celebrity's attitude like "winning" for a famous athlete. If that's how they naturally speak, there's no reason not to use those phrases. It makes the star and copy sound genuine.

Finding your own voice: Some tips

Write and rewrite your copy until it sounds natural. Listen to how you speak. Record a few of your conversations, so you can hear your natural delivery. Would your way of speaking work for your client? Do you use too many qualifiers, such as "like," "sort of," "kinda," and so on? If so, edit those out. What other habits do you have that might not work?

Now write a paragraph of copy for the "client." Read it aloud. Does it sound stiff or contrived? Or does it sound like you? Reading aloud helps you find your rhythm and capture it on paper.

You may want to mimic other copywriters to hear how your voice differs. Write another commercial, post a blog, or use another form of communication following the rhythm of another writer. It's not that easy to step into someone else's voice, is it? However, you may need to do that if a copywriter can't get to a recording session and the copy has to be edited. This is a great exercise to help you learn another way to express ideas. Then, when you get back into your own voice, it will be like sliding into a comfy pair of slippers. A perfect fit.

Quick chapter overview

Take a look at Checklist 9.2 before you begin writing. It's a quick reminder to write in an easy-to-grasp manner so your target audience can "get" your message. Remember, less is more. Try to write as succinctly as possible. Create interest and curiosity. Then, get the point across. Think of copywriting as a conversation with the reader. If you read your copy out loud, you may discover sections where you're stumbling. Don't worry about what's wrong with the copy. If you can't read it effortlessly, just rewrite it. Use this "Writing technique tips checklist" to develop powerful copy.

> ### CHECKLIST 9.2 Writing technique tips checklist
>
> 1 Review the Brief.
> 2 Read the Creative Strategy Statement.
> 3 Consider using *ABA* format, *parallel construction, weave, alliteration, connectors*, or a *button*.
> 4 See your audience as three-dimensional people, not as a statistic.
> 5 Create a strong message that can *spin out*.
> 6 Select the appropriate *tone of voice*.
> 7 Decide the campaign's *point of view*: Who's speaking?
>   a The brand (self-serving)?
>   b The consumer (testimonial)?
>   c The conscience (emotional blackmail)?
>   d The brand's unique personality, as an icon like the Aflac Duck (brand stand)?
> 8 Write naturally. Sound conversational.
> 9 *Weave* the main idea of the headline through the copy.
> 10 Read your copy aloud for flow.
> 11 Use familiar *slang* (gotta, getta, etc.), simple language, short phrases, and contractions.

Creative writing exercises

Exercise 1: Creating a consistent message

Part 1 Look at multimedia ads for your local zoo. How did the campaign work for print compared to TV? Look for consistency in language and graphics. Does the website reflect the campaign images and *tone of voice*?

Part 2 Develop another, related message to spin out the campaign. Would you use a different medium like a video, social media post, or live activation? Could you create an interactive, online game or app?

Exercise 2: Using vernacular

Part 1 What kind of "client" could use vernacular in the campaign?

Part 2   Write three headlines in a campaign for different media: out-of-home, bus shelters, magazines, or digital ads. Make sure you use the same writing technique for each.

Part 3   Could this campaign be used for an ambient message? What type and where? For example, could you create lawn signs for parks?

Exercise 3: Write two to three paragraphs of body copy, using one or more of the techniques below

1. *Parallel construction* – For example: "He loves me. He loves me not."

2. *Alliteration* – For example: "Betty Botter bought some butter."

3. *Weave* – Make the copy refer to the headline concept throughout the ad.

4. *Connectors* – Insert words to connect some lines or paragraphs, such as "but," "the best part is," "additionally," and so on.

5. *Button* – Introduce a witty, unexpected closing line.

6. *ABA* – Wrap up the last line of copy by relating back to and reinforcing the headline.

Notes

1. Charlie Hopper, personal communication, November 26, 2021.
2. https://time.com/6249551/m-m-candy-mascots-culture-wars/ (accessed January 28, 2022).
3. Margo Berman, "Teaching Grammar Through Lyrics, Film and Literary Quotes. The Grammar Controversy." *American Society of Business and Behavioral Sciences*, 10 (1998): 67–73.
4. Brainy Quote, www.brainyquote.com/quotes/authors/l/leo_burnett.html (accessed August 12, 2010).
5. Charlie Hopper, personal communication, November 26, 2021.

10 The Sticky Word
Headline and Slogan Techniques

"If a client says to use something we never thought of and it makes that a better ad, we more than welcome it."

William Bernbach, One of the Founders of
Doyle Dane Bernbach (DDB)[1]

In the following pages, you'll walk through various techniques to create unforgettable headlines and slogans. You'll learn the structure of ad copy, including eyebrows, headlines, subheads, body copy, call-to-action wording, closing lines, and slogans. You'll discover specific types of headlines that you can easily refer to when you're concepting, like the celebrity endorsement, the metaphor, or the story.

You'll find out what makes slogans sticky and how to create them using 16 different techniques. Most importantly, you'll recognize the importance

Content and Copywriting: The Complete Toolkit for Strategic Marketing,
Second Edition. Margo Berman.
© 2024 Margo Berman. Published 2024 by John Wiley & Sons Ltd.
Companion website: www.wiley.com/go/contentandcopywriting

of writing in a conversational way and creating a message that's relevant to your audience. In short, you'll begin to think like the consumer. You'll look at how they shop, where they shop, what's important to them. And so on. You'll become a more active listener, a mental-note keeper of natural speech, a collector of great ad examples, a curator of exciting content references, a discoverer of intriguing immersive models, and a more powerful writer.

Best of all, you'll uncover invaluable copy tips from master copywriters, as you did in earlier chapters from content writers. Now, let's take a good look at the construction of copy messages up close.

Devising ad structure: Headlines, subheads, body copy, and slogans

After creating a heart-stopping *headline,* make sure it will work as part of a campaign and not just as a standalone message. This headline needs to be able to work as one in a series of ads, each one related to the next. Remember, you're always looking for a big idea that *spins out* in various formats and different media.

Some headlines have a supporting line or *subhead.* Think of this as a supporting actor in a movie who plays the lead's best friend. The role of this character is to support the main idea and help explain it further.

Some ads have paragraphs of copy, as in magazine articles, brochures, and online copy. Mini headlines or subheads are used to separate the copy into digestible sections. They're easy to find because they're usually bold or in a contrasting color to highlight them. These separations are considered *blocks of copy.* Blocks range from one to several paragraphs.

Here's a quick overview of the structure of traditional advertising copy. Each part has a specific function.

1. *Eyebrows* – These are lines of text that target a particular audience, like "Arthritis Sufferers," and appear before the headline.

2. *Headlines* – These deliver the main message of the ad. They must be strong enough to stop readers and get them to notice the ad. Headlines in a series of ads should continue stating one big idea with multiple executions. Well-integrated campaigns send a singular impression by presenting variations on one concept. Together, they present one cohesive theme. They also need to have the same format. So, if one headline states a command, they all will. If one headline uses vernacular, they all will. If one headline uses parallel construction (as in the preceding sentences), they all will.

3. *Subheads* – These strengthen the headline and reinforce the stated benefit. The purpose of subheads in lengthy copy is to guide the reader from one key idea to the next. Think of them like directional signs on the highway. Readers can skip ahead to the sections they want to read next.

4. *Body copy* – This is the area where writers can explain specific benefits and features. It helps readers understand why they should buy the product. Effective body copy is fluid. It flows from one point to the next, carrying the reader along. It usually incorporates other writing techniques already discussed, like *weave* (connecting the headline throughout the copy), *ABA* (restating the headline in the closing line), and *alliteration* (using the same first sound in sequential words).

5. *Call to action* – This tells the target what you want them to do: Dial a phone number, hop on a website, visit a store, order online, and so on.

6. *Closing line of copy* – This last line gives readers closure. Do you want to use a *button* (short, catchy phrase) or reinforce the headline through *ABA* format? Remember, you're thanking the reader for getting to the end of your copy. Make it rewarding.

7. *Slogan* – This is a verbal logo. It's the one line that remains constant and doesn't change with each ad or touchpoint. *Slogans* – also called "taglines," "theme lines," or "catchphrases" – encapsulate the brand's message in a sticky phrase. Nike's "Just do it," created in 1988, is still one of the most powerful slogans. It was voted as the number two slogan of the century by *AdAge*.[2] Number one was the De Beers "A diamond is forever." If a slogan is read aloud in a radio or TV spot, the actor's voice should be consistent with the brand's voice. You wouldn't want a comedian to deliver the slogan in jest for a brain surgeon. When appropriate, you may have the slogan incorporated into a jingle, making it a musical slogan.

8. *Sig (signature)* – This is required copy (or "mandatories") that include contact information like the company address, phone, website, and so on.

Remembering the call to action

The final thing your audience needs to know is what you want them to do. Go online. Call an 800 number. Ask their doctor. Go to the store. Redeem a coupon. Comment on a blog. Share a social media post. Create your own product-centric video. Vote for your favorite competitor. Become a Facebook fan. And so on. Although many ads don't include a call to action, they are for brands so well known that consumers don't need any direction. Like Nike, Apple, or Coke.

If you don't tell consumers what to do, chances are they'll do just that: nothing. They need to be encouraged to respond to your message by taking action. Your message has to motivate them to do something. Then, they need to know what they should do.

Now we will discuss several creative areas that explain how to strengthen your writing skills.

Thinking up catchy headlines and subheads

There are many approaches to writing great headlines. Using an unexpected, well-targeted message is always refreshing. Surprising the audience with a shocking, little-known fact is another. You want to get readers' attention so they stop and actually spend three seconds reading your ad. Yes, three seconds. If you think that's a short time, they only spend one second deciding to read it once they look at the *headline*. Amazing, right? Well, now you know how critically important the headline is. It's the main message of the ad and it has to stop readers cold. No matter what they're doing, get them to read on.

To grasp the different ways to create print campaigns, take a look at other books on copywriting for a quick reference. Here's a short list of some of them in alphabetical list by author.

1. Tom B. Altstiel and Jean M. Grow's *Advertising Creative: Strategy, Copy, and Design* (Chapters 9 and 11).

2. Edd Applegate's *Strategic Copywriting* (Chapters 6 and 7).

3. Margo Berman's *Street-Smart Advertising* (Chapter 5).

4. Margo Berman and Robyn Blakeman's *The Brains Behind Great Ad Campaigns* (Chapter 5).

5. Robert W. Bly's *The Copywriter's Handbook* (Chapters 4 and 5).

6. Robert W. Bly's *The Content Marketing Handbook* (Chapter 2).

7. Melanie Deziel's *The Content Fuel Framework* (content examples throughout).

8. Bonnie L. Drewniany and A. Jerome Jewler's *Creative Strategy in Advertising* (Chapter 6).

Realize that the list of strategies already discussed in Chapter 6 can help guide you to a powerful headline. Also, the slogan techniques that follow can be used to generate headlines.

Reviewing different kinds of headlines

Although there are many, here are some of the most common headline approaches.

1. *The results* – This headline highlights the product's benefit. Any time you want to demonstrate products that remove stains, whiten teeth, reduce wrinkles, stimulate weight loss, build muscles, make plants grow, eliminate weeds, and so on, this is a tried-and-true headline. Dramatic changes are often depicted through before-and-after images. The image paired with a candid message can create an "Oh, wow!" moment. Consider the Peloton campaign that shows you how to get that longed-for six-pack.

2. *The comparison* – This allows one brand to challenge another's effectiveness. Instead of just presenting the results of one brand, it's compared side by side to those of a competitor. The point is to show off your brand's advantage in lifting stains, whitening clothes, detangling hair, adding shine to shoes, and so on. Think of it as advertising bragging rights: "My brand can beat up your brand." Think about the Bounty "Quicker-Picker Upper" promise to outperform and outlast its competitors.

3. *The celebrity endorsement* – This approach gives the "microphone" to a celebrity to talk about the product. Celebrities from all industries, from entertainment to sports, instantly raise brand awareness, especially for little-known products. There are also the likability and watchability factors. Ashton Kutcher has wide appeal as the Nikon spokesperson because he seems like someone who feels like a friend. Whoopi Goldberg in Weight Watchers and other campaigns makes you want to watch her. You're curious about what she's going to say. The main downside to using celebrities is the crash-and-burn syndrome. If the star or athlete has a run in with the law, is caught in the center of a controversial issue, or is involved in a personal scandal, that incident can quickly tarnish the brand's image and negatively affect sales.

4. *How to* – This enables you to show consumers how to solve a problem or get a desired result. People can learn "how to have shinier hair," "how to instantly look 10 pounds thinner," or "how to prime and paint in one

coat." Brands like Pantene hair care products, Spanx body-slimming shapewear, and Behr all-in-one paint have used this approach.

5. *The product as the star* – This main message spotlights the product, like the "I'm a PC" campaign. The classic Absolut campaign that used two-word headlines like "Absolut L.A." is another example. One more example is the line, "Have You Elf a Merry Little Christmas," from the popular holiday film *Elf*. Also, its partnership with Pantone Color Institute allowed e.l.f. Cosmetics to introduce the newest, coolest colors to its product line.

6. *The teaser* – This headline tempts the reader with a bit of information. Usually used in a campaign, teasers reveal the advertiser in the last ad in the series only. An example is the campaign that introduced the Florida Lottery with all-type ads that used only one word: "Ha." Each ad added another "Ha." In the end, the vertical strip ad (narrow, vertical panel ad) had many "Ha's" stacked one over the other. The closing line stated that if you play the Florida Lottery you could laugh all the way to the bank. Finally, it revealed the advertiser.

7. *The blind headline* – Here the headline is deliberately vague, sometimes with a surprising "reveal." Once readers find the logo, they get it and are able to grasp the message. *The Economist*, a financial publication, has used blind headlines. One example is this print headline: "Dissection. Good if you're a story. Bad if you're a frog." You don't know who the advertiser is until you see the logo. Then, you, as the reader, put the message together, surmising that you'll read a carefully researched article in *The Economist*.

8. *The stacked headline* – This headline allows writers to use words that are stacked one over the other. Although this is a layout-based headline, it gives writers a way to present related and unrelated words in a numbered or unnumbered list to lead readers to reach the end. For example, the headline could stack this way to draw you into reading the copy[3]:

> Keep
>
> Reading.
>
> You're
>
> Almost there.

There are also visually driven figures of speech headlines like those listed below in numbers 9 through 14.

9. *The metaphor* – Unlike using a simile, the headline shows a comparison without using "like" or "is." One example was the series of one-word ambient ad headlines on three-dimensional objects to advertise the Miami Rescue Mission: (1) "Kitchen" for a dumpster, (2) "Closet" for a shopping cart, and (3) "Bed" for a bus bench. Or the door hanger message created by Knock Knock: "Out to Lunch. But that's a Metaphor."

10. *Personification* – This headline gives human characteristics to an inanimate object, like "time flies." One example was the Tide To Go "Talking Stain" campaign, discussed in Chapter 9 (#3 *emotional blackmail* point of view), where a shirt stain started speaking over the job candidate's replies during his interview. Another one was for Gay Lea spreadable butter, when the product said, "Margarine Is Like So Freaked Out Right Now." A third example was for Workers' Injury Law & Advocacy Group with an image of a weasel in a business suit and the headline "Winning a War Against Weasels."

11. *Hyperbole* – This is an obvious, can't-be-true exaggeration, like "the bag weighed a ton," or this headline for the restaurant 321 East: "How Good Is Our Steak? Last Week a Man Who Was Choking on a Piece of Meat Refused the Heimlich Maneuver." Or this headline for a window cleaner: "Every Window Becomes Invisible to You." This wouldn't be an exaggeration until you saw the visual of a bird with his wing set in a sling and his head wrapped in gauze. The reader had to connect that the bird just crashed into a super clean – or invisible – window.

12. *Irony* – This headline says one thing but means another, like the phrase "laundering money." For example, a lost dog poster read, "Lost: Search & Rescue Dog." Or this headline for an HBO hit TV series, *True Blood*: "All Flavor. No Bite." The visual looked like an alcohol bottle of blood with the label reading "100% Pure True Blood." (The closing line was equally humorous: "HBO reminds vampires to drink responsibly.") Another example is the sign that stated, "Please Vote Against Campaign Signs on City Utility Poles." Or, the "Think-B4USpeak" campaign that tried to teach tolerance and sensitivity to phrases like "That's So Gay" with headlines like these: (1) "That's 'So Jock Who Can Complete a Pass But Not a Sentence,'" and (2) "That's So 'Cheerleader Who Can't Like Say Smart Stuff.'" At first, readers might be amused by the headlines, but then, realized these were stereotypical and offensive messages.

13. *Paradox* – This headline is an absurd, contradictory, or seemingly untrue statement like "Eat More. Weigh Less." Or, as exemplified in the book title, *The Paradox of Choice: Why More Is Less* by Barry Schwartz,

which suggested having more product options may adversely affect consumer-buying behavior. Or this headline: "It's Cheaper to Print on Some Money than Paper," which was superimposed over African bank notes to show how much they had been devalued. Another headline in the same campaign was "Thanks to Mugabe This Money is Wallpaper." The bank notes were spread across a bulletin board and refer to the negative economic effect of the Mugabe regime.

14. *The pun* – This headline uses a play on words, like this headline for Starbucks, "Beware of a Cheaper Cup of Coffee. It Comes with a Price." Or the headline for Mercy (hospital): "All Arteries Connect to Mercy." Or this headline for the film *The Boys in Company C:* "To Keep Their Sanity in an Insane War They Had to Be Crazy." Or, the headline, "Renew Now It's Werth It," in support of keeping baseball pitcher Jayson Werth on the Washington Nationals team.

Here are a few more headline categories presented by Bruce Bendinger in his book *The Copy Workshop Workbook*.

15. *The one-liner* – This catchy, attention-grabbing headline is like the one-line joke. It's fast and immediate, with a little twist. For example, a TV spot for Zazoo condoms with a screaming kid having a temper tantrum in a store was accompanied with two superimposed words: "Use condoms." That line could work as a headline if the campaign went to print.

16. *News* – This technique presents information like a news story. "Wrinkle breakthrough! Fewer lines without surgery." Then, the copy would explain how this new pharmacological product is better than others at reducing wrinkles.

17. *The spiral* – This headline keeps on going, seemingly without end to entice the reader to continue. One line weaves into the next like the children's song *One Potato, Two Potatoes, Three Potatoes, Four*. For instance, a headline for a jewelry store for Christmas could say, "On the First Day of Christmas, Her Boyfriend Gave to Her, a Diamond in a Pear Shape. On the Second Day of Christmas, Her Boyfriend Gave to Her, Two Ruby Earrings, and a Diamond in a Pear Shape."

18. *The story* – This presents a story featuring a consumer, corporate executive, or the brand. If told by the consumer, the stories usually have an emotional appeal and are based on real-life experiences like the customer's weight-loss success, the Mediterranean, Atkins, or other diet plan. For a cosmetic surgery center, a headline could read: "Once

Upon a Time There Was a Little Girl Who Loved Herself, but Hated Her Nose." You'd read on to see what she did about it.

19. *The sermon* – The headline preaches. One example was imprinted on the inside of Vazir Breveries beer bottle caps. Once the bottle was opened the cap was dented in. The message inside simply said: "Don't Drink and Drive."

20. *The outline* – The headline continues down the page using subheads or numbers to continue the message. This allows writers to chunk lengthy copy down to small pieces of easy-to-grasp information. "Ten Reasons to Safeguard Your Credit." Then, the reasons would be numbered one through ten in ten blocks of copy.[4]

One thing that I find invaluable, and I don't really know how a writer can be a writer unless they do this, is to read a lot. Matt Ziselman, Creative Director, Sapient[5]

Making up sticky slogans: The backbone of campaigns

Slogans have an important job. They wrap up the product's message in a tidy package. They remind the audience why they should use that item (or service). They can make a promise to consumers and also establish a relationship with them. Easy-to-remember slogans hang like sticky notes in the consumer's mind. You can probably finish each of these slogans without prompting:

1. "Melts in your mouth, not in your_____"

2. "Better Ingredients Better _____"

3. "The_____of Macy's."

4. "The incredible, edible_____"

5. "Home of the_____"

6. "Once you pop, you can't_____"

7. "America runs on_____"

8. "What would you do for a_____bar?"

9. "Like a good_____, State Farm is there."

10. "Sometimes you feel like a_____. Sometimes you don't."

You get the idea. Whether the slogan is new or old, you can see how these have the unforgettable factor. Did you get them all right? Did you know all the company names? Here are the answers so you can double-check:

1. "Melts in your mouth, not in your *hands*." (M&M'S, 1954)

2. "Better Ingredients. Better *Pizza*." (Papa John's, 1998)

3. "The *magic* of Macy's." (2008)

4. "The incredible, edible *egg*." (American Egg Board, 1977)

5. "Home of the *Whopper*." (Burger King, 1957)

6. "Once you pop, you can't *stop*." (Pringles, 1968)

7. "America runs on *Dunkin'*." (Dunkin' Donuts, 2006)

8. "What would you do for a *Klondike* bar?" (1984)

9. "Like a good *neighbor*, State Farm is there." (1971)

10. "Sometimes you feel like a *nut*. Sometimes you don't." (Peter Paul Almond Joy and Peter Paul Mounds, 1953)

So what makes these particular slogans so sticky? They're catchy and easy to remember. They might be humorous, witty, surprising, or blatantly direct, like "Kotex. Fits. Period." Or "Get to a better State. State Farm Insurance." They can be a line used in a TV spot that suddenly becomes a popular catchphrase like the Budweiser line "Whassup!" or Wendy's "Where's the beef?" They're lines that may repeat a word or phrase like the Meow Mix jingle "Meow. Meow. Meow." Or the Energizer Bunny that "Keeps going and going and going." As simple as they seem, they're both clever and have structure. You'll find they're often based on one of the 16 following techniques. Once you learn these, see if you can identify which techniques were used.

1. *Name* – When you include the company's name in the slogan, you've instantly reinforced name awareness. This is especially true if the slogan is only a few words long. Or, if it's a name that's easy to make fun of or difficult to remember. Let's start with the short slogans like "Toyota. Let's go places." Or "McDonald's. I'm lovin' it." Or "Subway. Eat Fresh." For longer ones, notice how this one supports a challenging name: "With a name like Smucker's, it's got to be good." See how Sensodyne toothpaste clearly states the key benefit: "Lasting protection from sensitive teeth." As almost everyone knows, Aflac simply had an endearing duck quack for the name and that became the slogan. The

slogan and the logo become one: a sLOGOn, coined by Michael New-man.[6] Also, some companies use a secondary or *subslogan*, which some call a *tagline*, for specific campaigns.

2. *Rhyme* – The reason these slogans are so sticky is that we learned nursery rhymes even before we could read. "Jack and Jill went up the hill." "Hickory dickory dock. The mouse ran up the clock." "Old King Cole was a merry old soul." You don't need any more prompting. You know the rest of the rhyme. It's the same with these kinds of slogans. They're easy to recall. "Swiffer gives cleaning a whole new meaning." "Twizzlers. The twist you can't resist." "Must see TV" (NBC). "Feel the heal" (Cortizone-10 for eczema). "Crave the wave" (Ocean Spray). "Flick my Bic" (lighter). "The best part of waking up is Folgers in your cup." "Takes a licking and keeps on ticking" (Timex) was created back in the 1950s by W.B. Doner & Co. and agency predecessors. This type of slogan increases name awareness.

3. *Alliteration* – Repeating the first letter or sound of a word creates alliteration. You've said alliterative phrases many times: Peter Piper picked a peck of pickled peppers. Alliteration slogans are sonorous: "Be certain with Certs," "Intel inside." "Ruffles have ridges." "Whiskas. What cats want." "Fluent in finance" (Barclays Bank). Others have longevity. The famous Campbell's Soup slogan "Mmm mm good!" was created back in 1935 by BBDO. "I'm cuckoo for Cocoa Puffs!" first said by Sonny the Cuckoo bird in 1962, created by Gene Cleaves and illustrated by Bill Tollis, creative head and art director at Dancer/Fitzgerald/Sample.

4. *Play on words* – This is a witty line that has a second meaning: "Chase what matters." Notice, it's only three words long and the first word is the name. This is also an example of a *combination* slogan (technique #16) because it uses the *name* (technique #1), a *play on words* (technique #4), and a command or an *imperative* (technique #11). Other great examples are "All the news that's fit to print" from *The New York Times*. "Don't treat your puppy like a dog" from Ralston Purina dog food. "Discover what One can do" (Purina One dog food). "Works like a dream" (Ambien sleeping aid). "Zero's Subs. We're hot and on a roll." "Takes the 'fur' out of furniture" (Scotch Fur Fighter pet hair remover). "The best tires in the world have Goodyear written all over them." "The best seat in the house" (Jockey underwear). "What moves you" (Scion). "Think outside the bun" (Taco Bell). Morton Salt's slogan, "When it rains, it pours," created in 1912.

5. *Parallel construction* – This was described earlier as a writing technique and it works just as well as a slogan. It's memorable because

it's repetitive. A word, phrase, or part of speech is repeated like these examples. "American by birth. Rebel by choice" (Harley-Davidson). "Kid tested. Mother approved" (Kix cereal). "The few. The proud. The Marines" (U.S. Marine Corps). "Bring out the Hellmann's. Bring out the best." "Sometimes you feel like a nut. Sometimes you don't" (Peter Paul Almond Joy and Mounds). "Be clear. Be confident. Be Proactiv." "Healthful. Flavorful. Beneful." (Beneful dog food).

6. *Statement of use or purpose* – The company gives a promise to the audience. It answers what people can expect when they make a purchase. It's a commitment to the consumer. For example, "Imagination at work" (GE). "We know money" (AIG). "You're in good hands with Allstate." "It's not just for breakfast anymore" (Florida Orange Juice Growers Association). "100% juice for 100% kids" (Juicy Juice). "When banks compete, you win" (Lending Tree). "We do chicken right" (KFC). "We know drama" (TNT). Outback Steakhouse promises your order will be cooked perfectly: "No rules. Just right." "Expect more. Pay less" (Target). "Save money. Live better" (Walmart). "It's the cheesiest" (Kraft Macaroni & Cheese). The problem with the Target and Walmart slogans is that they can be confused. Both chain stores target the same audience with a similar message. You want to create a message that's indisputably your client, not its competitor.

7. *Testimonial* – This type of phrase gives the "microphone" to consumers and lets them praise the product or service. "That was easy" (Staples). "I am stuck on Band-Aid, and Band-Aid's stuck on me." Notice in this one, "Kibbles and Bits! Kibbles and Bits! I'm gonna get me some Kibbles and Bits!" from Kibbles & Bits dog food, the "consumer's voice" is the dog speaking. Another one in the dog's voice is Purina Beggin' Strips tagline, "It's bacon!" A famous celebrity can act like the end user and comment about the brand. People today, however, know that the celebrity is being paid and may make the message less credible.

8. *Simile* – This approach uses "like" or "as" to connect similarities between two items. A metaphor compares without using like or as. "He is a tiger in war." He is not "like" a tiger. He is a ferocious tiger. These are slogans that use similes. "Easy as Dell." "Cats like Felix like Felix" (Felix cat food). "Like a good neighbor, State Farm is there." "Chevy. Like a rock."

9. *Onomatopoeia* – The beauty of this technique is that it engages two senses: sight and hearing. Onomatopoeic words imitate an object or action. Hear the words "Ding-dong" and you're picturing a doorbell. "Click" sounds like the snap of a pen, a computer mouse, or a door

closing. "Click" sounds like the action itself. Listen to the Mazda slogan "Zoom-Zoom" and you think of a car. Alka-Seltzer sounds just like the product in use: "Plop, plop. Fizz, fizz," when dropped into water. Of course, you know how much *"Snap! Crackle! Pop!"* sounds just like Kellogg's® Rice Krispies® when milk is poured over it.

10. *Emotional blackmail* – These slogans conjure up a sense of guilt or fear. They make consumers wonder what would happen if they chose another product. They make people second-guess themselves and doubt their purchasing choices. How sure are you about your deodorant? Probably fine until you were asked to "Raise your hand if you're sure." It makes you wonder. Doesn't it? If "Choosy moms choose Jif" how good a mom are you if you use another brand of peanut butter? Consider: "There's a lot riding on your tires." If you bought another brand, how safe do you feel?

11. *Imperative statement* – One iconic phrase is the Nike slogan, "Just do it." Without preaching, it invites people to continue enjoying whatever sport they choose. Do what you want. But, do it. Some other slogans that use a command or imperative statement are these: "Eat fresh" (Subway). "Play. Laugh. Grow" (Fisher-Price). "Never let 'em see you sweat" (Gillette Dry Idea). "Say it with flowers" (FTD).

12. *Interrogative statement* – A catchy phrase that poses a question is an interrogative slogan. One of the most recognized is "Got milk?" (California Milk Processor Board). Here are a few more: "What's in your wallet?" (Capital One). "Doesn't your dog deserve Alpo?" "Gatorade. Is it in you?" "Have you laughed today?" (The Laughing Cow cheese).

13. *Vernacular* – This type of slogan sounds natural because it imitates consumers' everyday speech or slang. Using common phrases, casual language, and contractions like "gonna," "'em," "wouldn'," "goin'," "yeah," makes people feel comfortable. Some slogans catch on and become part of the American culture, such as "Whassup!" from Budweiser. Others simply tell it like it is, as in KFC's line "It's finger-lickin' good!"

14. *Reason why* – This kind of tagline tells consumers why they should choose this product over another. Reason why slogans encapsulate "because." You purchase this because it offers "Real service, real savings" (Geico). Or, because you want "The world on time" (FedEx). Maybe you enjoy "Hot eats. Cool treats" (Dairy Queen). Or you want to "Drink better water" (VitaminWater). Maybe you need more energy, so you drink Red Bull because it "Gives you wings." When you reach for a chocolate, you expect that "There's a smile in every Hershey's bar."

You know "There's always room for J-E-L-L-O." You ship with FedEx because the underlying message is that you don't need to stress – your package will arrive. Since 1959, when Ogilvy, Benson & Mather created its slogan, Maxwell House has answered "Why buy?" with this promise: because it's "Good to the last drop."

15. *Challenge* – This type of catchphrase dares the audience. It sets up the challenge in the slogan. Everyone on a diet knows you can't eat just one potato chip. That's why the Lay's Baked Potato Chips line is perfect: "Betcha can't eat just one." Here's another line that dares you to say no: "Nobody can say no to the honey nut O's in Honey Nut Cheerios." SlimFast has challenged dieters with this line "Give us a week, we'll take off the weight." The Home Depot invites its audience to take on a home project with "More saving, more doing." Underneath the slogan is the idea that people want to improve their homes. They just don't want to incur steep costs.

16. *Combination* – These theme lines blend several types of slogans together. Notice how "Real people. Real results." from Bowflex uses *parallel construction, statement of purpose*, and *reason why* you would use this fitness equipment. Gerber baby food says, "Start healthy. Stay healthy." It also uses the same techniques as Bowflex: *parallel construction, statement of purpose*, and *reason why*. PlayStation 2 offered this question: "Fun anyone?" It *rhymes* and it's a question (*interrogative*). The "Nothing runs like a Deere" slogan integrates *name, play on words*, and *reason why*. Pringles promises "Once you pop, you can't stop" and utilizes *rhyme, challenge*, and *reason why*. This line, "Don't live a little, live a lotto," incorporates *imperative, parallel construction*, and *reason why*.[7]

The majority of our advertising [for Taco Bell] is all centered around one particular product, one benefit, one main idea that we want to communicate. Teddy Brown, Executive Creative Director at Planet Propaganda[8]

Adding power to your writing

Start today to make the following suggestions a habit. They will help you strengthen your writing immediately. Your copy will sound more conversational. More relatable. And more relevant to your audience. By becoming an active listener, you're fine-tuning your writing. By becoming the consumer, you're focusing on consumer insights. By becoming an interactive consumer, you understand the draw of engagement. By becoming an online and digital shopper, you're experiencing what your audience is considering when they make a purchase. By becoming an avid observer, you're collecting reference material for inspiration.

1. *Become an active listener* – To help your copy sound natural, listen to conversations wherever you are: in restaurants, coffee shops, parks, train stations, gyms, at parties, at meetings, or even in lines at stores. Just listen to how people speak to each other. Notice the short phrases ("Okay, great"), idiomatic expressions ("See what I mean?"), vernacular phrases ("Gotta go"), contractions ("I'm runnin' late"), and connectors ("Yeah, but").

2. *Become the consumer* – Ask yourself what would make you buy that product? Remember to consider how you would feel and think if you were the targeted audience's age. Now, is that message you're writing appropriate for that age group? Is the *tone of voice* the best one to use?

3. *Become an interactive consumer* – What engages you? What piques your attention? What makes you participate with the brand? Is what you're developing exciting enough to capture your imagination?

4. *Become an online and digital shopper* – Okay, you're at the website. Now what? Would a special offer prompt you to take action? Would being able to customize the product excite you? If you're working on a product website that could allow customization for, say, shoes or belts, can you help make that happen?

5. *Become an avid observer* – Pay attention to TV commercials you love. Why do you love them? What visual or verbal techniques could you borrow? Focus on radio commercials. Do the scripts sound contrived or convoluted? If so, why? What makes them sound unnatural? Notice engaging podcasts you enjoy. What pulled you in? Keep a mental note of these observations, so you'll refer to them when you're writing for any medium.

6. *Become a collector* – Save great examples of promotional messages wherever you find them. Use your smartphone to snap a photo. Print out creative work from agency websites. Save powerful social media posts you find. Even keep brochures or fun direct mail pieces you might receive. Yes, there are some great direct mail examples.

Copywriting insights and tips

1. Craig Miller, creative director/copywriter at Craig Miller Creative:

    a. We used to know what it was going to be: TV, radio, and so on, now I have no idea what it's going to be. It's back to the core idea. For all media we think in press releases. We write press releases for the big idea. What's the press going to write about?

    b. Let the idea drive the media, not the media drive the idea. It's purifying. What are you trying to say? What can this campaign do to get attention? Rather than what kind of ad can I do for Domino's? What can I do to make this press worthy?

    c. I do more idea generation in four years than in the 10 years before that.[9]

2. Teddy Brown, executive creative director at Planet Propaganda, discussing the "Why Pay More" campaign:

    a. When you're dealing with humor, it definitely needs to be smart humor. You don't want it to be whacky or goofy or really radical or different just for the sake of being different.

    b. Our briefs from our *point of view*, from any creative's *point of view*, are all trying to drive towards that single most important thing: that main message.

    c. For the most part, there is a habit, or perception, or a belief that we're trying to change or reinforce. Then, we have our main message. And then, we have our consumer take away: "What is it that we want the consumer to like?"

    d. The way we break our briefs down is to get to quite simply: (1) What the consumer currently thinks, (2) what our message is going in, and (3) what will the consumer think as a result of this advertising.[10]

3. Drummond Berman, group creative director/writer at Merkley+Partners.

    a. Be absolutely ruthless because no one other than you can be as ruthless as you could be on your own stuff.

    b. Too many people sit there and write a bunch of lines and the best of those is the one that they'll put forward. It's not about quantity; it's about quality.

    c. Having a clear vision of what it is that you are heading for, and know it when you see it and dismiss it when you don't see it, is really, really important. Just think from the outset about what it is that you're writing because writing is not an accident.

d. The best headlines are based on an idea rather than just moving words around until they sound cool.

e. Absolutely avoid borrowed interest at all costs. And what I mean by that is bringing in other things that have got nothing to do with what you're talking about because you can't think of interesting ways to talk about it. (An example: If you're talking about a breakfast cereal, stay in the world of breakfast cereal. Don't start comparing it to another world. Because you end up just blurring the whole thing.)

f. Make what you've got interesting. Make what you've got make sense. Make what you've got appealing. As a writer, it's important that you really understand that when you have an ability to spin something in a way that makes what you actually have in front of you sound interesting to other people, it's probably one of your best lines.[11]

Making your copy sticky

By creating messages that target the audience with headlines that have stopping power, copy that's relevant to the reader, super-sticky slogans, and media-specific language, you'll develop unforgettable campaigns.

Review the writing tips in each chapter and apply them when you write. Analyze every advertising and content message you read. Dissect each one to see why they work and why they don't. Be sure to collect all kinds of print materials with great copy, so you always have examples you can refer to. The best way to improve your writing is to read great writing. Lastly, and most importantly, become an avid reader who's always looking for inspiration.

Creative writing exercises

Exercise 1: Continuing an existing campaign message

Part 1 Choose a print campaign that you relate to with strong headlines. Analyze why it stopped you. Think about how you can continue the concept of the campaign.

Part 2 Create two more headlines using the same creative approach. For example, if all the existing ads ask a question, your next two headlines must do the same. If the headlines use parallel construction, yours must too. If the campaign uses humor, your ads must also be funny.

Part 3   What other platforms would work: out-of-home, social media, video, or experiential? Which would best spin out this campaign? Would an interactive billboard work? A live event? An in-store display? A direct mail piece? Be open-minded. Consider many options.

Part 4   Write some body copy that integrates a message that fits into the campaign, targets your audience, and relates to or blends with the new ads you just created.

Exercise 2: Write a headline using the techniques below

1. *A blind headline* – The audience shouldn't have a clue what the ad is for until they see the logo.

2. *A news headline* – Develop a message that reflects something in the news or sounds like a news story.

3. *A stacked headline* – Create a headline that would work better if it were set one word above another.

Exercise 3: Creating sticky slogans

Part 1   Using the same brand or product in Exercise 1, now look through the list of slogan techniques in the section "Reviewing different kinds of headlines."

Part 2   Select three techniques and write a slogan using each one. For example, create one using *parallel construction*, another using *testimonial*, and a third using *reason why*. Try to include the *name* in at least one of the slogans.

Part 3   Decide which slogan is stronger. Answer why that one works better.

Exercise 4: Combining headlines and slogans into campaigns that spin out

Part 1   Select a new brand or product. Write a headline based on a consumer benefit. Look for a big idea that can continue in related ads. Choose one headline technique that you can reuse. For example, if you use a question, like "Got Milk?," the next headline would be "Got Cake?"

Part 2   Review the list of slogans mentioned in the chapter. Choose one technique. Create a new slogan that supports the core idea in the same consumer benefit.

Part 3 Create two headlines in a series. They both need to work with the slogan you designed in Part 2. What kind of message would work best: print, out-of-home, table tent (as in restaurants), in-store display sign? Think about the Energizer Bunny campaign. It "Keeps going and going and going." Develop a campaign that will have "legs" and keep running.

Notes

1. Denis Higgins, *The Art of Writing Advertising: Conversations with Masters of the Craft* (Chicago: NTC Business Books, 1965), 24.
2. *AdAge Advertising Century*, "Top 10 Slogans of the Century," 2005, https://adage. com/article/special-report-the-advertising-century/ad-age-advertising-century-top-10-slogans/140156 (accessed February 28, 2024).
3. Margo Berman, *Street-Smart Advertising: How to Win the Battle of the Buzz* (Lanham, MD: Rowman & Littlefield, 2010), 92–93.
4. Bruce Bendinger, *The Copy Workshop Workbook* (Chicago: The Copy Workshop, 2009), 324–365.
5. Matt Ziselman, personal communication, January 30, 2009.
6. Michael Newman, *Creative Leaps: 10 Lessons in Effective Advertising Inspired at Saatchi & Saatchi* (Singapore: John Wiley & Sons, 2003), 232.
7. Berman, *Street-Smart Advertising*, 84–87.
8. Teddy Brown, personal communication, December 14, 2022.
9. Craig Miller, personal communication, April 18, 2022.
10. Teddy Brown, personal communication, December 14, 2022.
11. Drummond Berman, personal communication, April 8, 2009.

11 The Written Word
Print Ads, Posters, Brochures, and More

"The best headlines are based on an idea rather than just moving words around until they sound cool."

Drummond Berman, Group Creative Director/Writer, Merkley+Partners[1]

Writing for print can be more exciting than you realize. Especially with the addition of scent and sound, 3D and holograms, pop-ups, QR codes, and more. In this section, you'll be shown why your message must be just as dynamic today as the special effects. You'll be reminded to always remember the reader. You'll remember to think of your audience not as a statistic, but as real people. You'll realize that great copy appeals to their needs and desires. You'll review the writing techniques in Chapters 9 and 10, apply the strategies in Chapter 6, and learn about *mandatories, eyebrows*, basic copy format, and categories of effective messages.

You'll find out how to construct your copy by a careful consideration of *strategy*, an analysis of *audience*, a clarification of *benefits*, a determination of *tone of voice*, an assessment of *relevance*, a reflection of *concept*, and a presentation of *message*.

You'll also examine examples of exciting print ads, including CAT Footwear, Coravin, Hotel Tango, Paddletek, and ASICS campaigns. In addition, you'll hear from some creative talents who developed them. What's more, you'll delve into the successful use of wit and humor in print ads. Finally, you'll find some helpful writing tips from award-winning copywriters. You'll have a print checklist at the end of the chapter that will help you before you begin the exercises. Now, let's read more about the world of print advertising.

Writing for the printed page

Print advertising, contrary to popular belief, isn't dead. There are still opportunities to develop exciting messages for a wide range of magazines, newspapers, and newsletters, as well as financial and business-to-business (B2B) publications. In fact, with scent and sound chips, pop-up designs, 3D and holographic images, plus other special effects, print ads can practically come to life. Even without any additional creative, executional techniques, print ads on their own can still deliver powerful messages.

Writing for the printed page is different from writing for broadcast, out-of-home, digital, or experiential campaigns. First, it's not a short-lived message because the actual page can be saved and read again, in hard copy. Some ads have a longer shelf life because they are in consumer magazines and business journals that subscribers often save around the house or office to refer to later.

Plus, the printed word delivers a message to the audience in a wide range of vehicles or formats: ads, brochures, postcards, table tents, posters, and flyers. Furthermore, the copy length varies from abridged copy in catalog writing and coupons to longer multiple-page collateral materials, like annual reports and newsletters. Each vehicle demands a special, uniquely suitable approach. Persuasive body copy, regardless of length, will drive home a point as long as the main message, or headline, stopped consumers and made them take a moment to read it.

As with all media, you need to understand the consumers' frame of mind. Sheena Brady, commercial director/creative director, said you must "put yourself in your audience's place." What are they looking for? Do they want to be entertained as in interactive media and TV? Do they want to be surprised as in ambient messages? Do they want to be educated as in newspapers and financial publications? She went on to say:

> *If I'm reading a business journal, I'm probably looking at that medium for information. So you're probably not going to do an ad that's just sheer entertainment value. So I think it really helps to know your medium and tailor that messaging to it. Or even know your medium so you can subvert it. Like if you're a travel company, maybe you tell people they need a vacation because all they do is read boring business journals.*[2]

It's critical to understand your audience's expectations in different media. That will help you target a medium and develop an appropriate message. She added that although you need to tailor the brand attributes, that is, those particular qualities that make a car a car or a shoe a shoe, "the idea of a one-on-one communication with someone, that doesn't change."[3]

Formulating one focused message

Whatever your print vehicle, it's important to focus on one main message. Don't confuse readers with endless benefits and product features. Zoom in on the one take-away you want them to get and stay with it. A conference speaker once demonstrated this point. The presenter had three circular objects in his hand, perhaps soft-foam or ping-pong balls. What the objects were isn't important. What they represented is. He tossed one to an audience member and the person caught it. And he tossed all three at the same time and the person in the audience dropped all three of them. And his point was if you put one message in there, chances are people will remember it. If you put three in, they may not remember any one of them.

The idea is to simplify your message to the audience, so they can absorb it. Stay focused on one singular idea. Even ads without text, or "no-copy ads" with just a visual, make a clear statement. They can still showcase a writer's critical thinking, because the most important talent of a writer is clear communication. Sometimes, a perfect image delivers the intended message.

Writing takes thinking. It's not just about throwing ideas out in a brainstorming session. It's about throwing relevant concepts around. The critical point, when looking for a strong concept with legs, is relevance, not just bold creativity. Drummond Berman, group creative director/writer at Merkley+Partners, clarified that thought this way:

> *Having a clear vision of what it is that you are heading for, and know it when you see it and dismiss it when you don't see it, is really, really important. Just think from the outset about what it is that you're writing because writing is not an accident.*[4]

New writers often get impatient: They want to have a great idea immediately. But, they eventually learn that some headlines take hours of tweaking. Several seasoned copywriters suggested that all writers should be very hard on themselves. They should be demanding and self-critical. Rather than being in love with every idea they have, copywriters should try to become more objective. Let concepts sit for a few days. Then, if they're still excited about them, the ideas are worthy of consideration. Berman said, "Be absolutely ruthless because no one other than you can be as ruthless as you could be on your own stuff."[5]

Remembering the reader

Writers still need to be self-critical even if the number of people reading the ad copy may be smaller than anyone cares to admit. However, the quality of anyone's writing is not contingent upon the size of the audience. Vinny Warren, founder and creative director of The Escape Pod, confessed that he hardly reads all the print copy and he's in the industry. He acknowledged the steep decline of the newspaper audience and the low number of print ad readers. He also explained how readership can impact the copywriter's process. A key point was "presuming interest is a big mistake."[6] Charlie Hopper, principal at Young & Laramore, concurred:

> *There's already so much writing in the world, nobody is actively interested in reading what YOU have to write, especially if it's on behalf of somebody who's trying to sell them something.*[7]

Hopper continued to say, "Everything is [read] in context. That's the key to the writing anyway. I hate long copy. Nobody wants to read."[8]

Warren considered himself one of a small number of people still reading newspapers today. Of those few people, how many actually spend time reading copy at all? If they are reading, what will they absorb and how far into the ad will they read? Warren posed and answered the following question, which gives writers another way to think about how to entice an audience:

> *How do you get people to read what they need to read to get your message? That's the way I always look at it. That means keeping it down to a minimum and making the writing the necessary part of the ad. In other words, the ad isn't complete until you read the copy.*[9]

Keep in mind the audience who bothers to read the copy should be rewarded with clear, concise, persuasive, and engaging copy. You have a living, breathing person who will take the time to read your work. Write with the readers in mind, remembering that, even though you may never meet them, you are still appreciative of their time. Think about that every time you write. Reward readers for reading by bringing copy to closure with techniques discussed in Chapter 9, like:

- *ABA* – reinforcing the headline in the last line of copy.

- *Weave* – continuing the headline idea throughout the body copy.

- *Button* – creating an imaginative closing line, unrelated to the headline.

In addition to writing techniques, you must think about the best way to deliver the message. What's important to your audience? What specific needs do they have? What problem(s) are they trying to solve? How does your product/service/brand help them? Read Checklist 11.1 before you begin to create copy.

CHECKLIST 11.1 Copy checklist

1. Reinforce the *benefits*. Answer, "Why buy?" Show the consumer the reason to make the purchase. Clearly state what the consumer's going to get from the product/brand. For example: Tide To Go gets stains out when you're out and about.

2. Showcase the *product features*. Explain how the product works, like Apple's (iPhone, iPad, etc.) *product-demonstration* messages.

3. Speak in an appropriate *tone of voice*. If you're reaching out to families looking for a fun vacation, look at how Disney vacations always sound like exciting adventures.

4. Choose the most effective *point of view*. Should the *brand* be bragging about its features, design awards, or customer service rewards? Should consumers offer raving *testimonials* about their product/brand experiences? Should people's *conscience* warn them of avoidable problems the brand can prevent? Should the *brand's unique personality* deliver the *brand stand*, for example, as an icon like the Charmin Bears?

5. Look at the audience. How do they live their lives (psychographics)? Does it enhance their lifestyle? What do they *value*? Does the brand share any *core values* with the audience? Which *Decider* (decision-maker) are you targeting? (See Chapter 5.) You'd speak differently to the *User* (end user) than you would to the *Initiator*. To refresh your memory, let's review this list once more.

   a. *Initiator*: suggests buying or trying the product or service

   b. *Influencer*: encourages or dissuades the final shopper

c *Decider*: makes the final purchasing decisions

d *Buyer*: buys the item

e *User*: uses the item or service[10]

6 Consider audience *needs*. What are they looking for? Status? Comfort? Clear skin? Weight loss? Are they *Inner-directed* (make purchases to please themselves, not to dazzle others)? Are they *Outer-directed* (seek to establish status and gain acceptance)? Or are they *Need-driven* (purchase only necessities at this time)?

7 Portray the *brand's personality*. Is it lively like the TGI Fridays restaurant chain? Convenient like an urgent-care center? Sophisticated like a champagne bar?

8 Integrate the *brand's heritage* or *history*. Is there a Colonel as in the KFC story, a Jack Perdue in Perdue Chicken, or an Orville Redenbacher as in Orville Redenbacher's Popcorn? Has it been around for more than 165 years like Macy's (founded in 1858), boasting the largest store in the world?

9 Drive home the message. Make sure it's *relevant* to your audience. Keep it clear, simple, and instantly digestible. If anyone can't read it and "get it," change it.

10 Show what makes the brand *unique*. What separates it from its competitors? Faster service? Newer technology? Better integration between mobile and nonmobile devices?

11 Decide which one of the *50 strategies* you want to use. Start by selecting from the six main categories (see Chapter 6):

a *Consumer-focused* – show benefits.

b *Product-focused* – emphasize product features.

c *Savings as the Star* – focus on price.

d *Emotional Approach* – appeal to consumers' emotions.

e *Storytelling* – present product in a story.

f *Audience Engagement* – encourage consumer participation.

12 Think about the *specific publication(s)* or *location* where the ad or poster will appear. Does anything need to be tweaked for a better fit? For example, the sexy Axe deodorant ads can be even spicier in a magazine like *Maxim*. Would you want to change it for a train station wall or a store window?

13 Check that your overall direction follows the *creative brief*. So, your concept, strategy, message, and tone are all *on-strategy* and in line with the key marketing objective.

There are times when you'll have an attentive, eager reader. For example, when you create annual reports, trade show flyers, newsletters, and manufacturers' literature. You may think these are more informative or promotional than advertising materials. Remember, each printed piece is still communicating a message, whether it's from the company to the consumer or from one business to another (called "B2B" or "business-to-business" marketing) or consumer to consumer (called "C2C" or "customer-to-customer" marketing). With annual reports, you need to think about what investors are looking to learn. In this case, writers should do the following:

- Highlight the company's success and growth.
- Showcase new products.
- Feature awards and recognitions.
- Consider what you would want to hear as an investor.

If you're writing a newsletter, know if it's an internal (to employees) or external (to consumer and/or other businesses) piece.

Discovering basic copy format

All copy needs structure, meaning a format and a *template* or *shell* to follow. This helps you to organize your thinking and prioritize the copy points and *mandatories* (must-have information). The shell is simple. It allows space for the *headline, subhead,* and *body copy* separated by *additional subheads, logo,* and *slogan.* If your ad uses an *eyebrow,* it would be listed before the headline. The *eyebrow,* as discussed earlier in Chapters 10 and 11, is a line of copy that targets a specific audience like this: "Eyeglass Wearers," "Headache Sufferers," or "Cookie Lovers." It singles out that particular individual. Then, it delivers the headline. The signature or "*sig*" normally appears outside the body copy, near the logo. It includes the product, company, service, or store's mandatory information: phone, email, website, location, hours, and so on.

Templates 11.2 and Templates 11.3 are the basic print templates. They can be used for flyers, annual reports, manufacturers' literature, and even web copy.

 TEMPLATES 11.2 Basic print ad copy format

Eyebrow: (if needed)

Headline:

Subhead:

Body copy:

Logo:

Slogan:

Sig:

TEMPLATES 11.3 Basic brochure copy format

Headline:

Subhead: (Identify location, e.g., Inside Left Panel)

Body copy:

Subhead: (Identify location, e.g., Inside Right Panel or Inside Spread if it fits across two pages)

Body copy:

Subhead: (Identify location, e.g., Back Cover)

Body copy:

Logo:

Slogan:

Sig: (Address, phone, hours, website address, etc.)

If you're working at an ad agency, adopt the firm's format immediately. Then, use it for every assignment. Using a consistent copy format has several benefits. It helps do the following:

- Organize your copy.
- Prioritize copy points by sections.
- Facilitate font choices and type placement.
- Focus your writing and readers' attention.

Whether you're writing a small amount of copy for a table tent, sign, small flyer, or print ad, get right to the point. Think in bites of text: tiny messages or packets of information. Edit out all unessential copy. Usually, in advertising messages, less is more. However, there are some products or services that require lengthy copy. Even then, just include the most crucial information. Highlight the *main benefit* and *key message*. The point is, get to the point. But first, get their attention with a *powerful headline*.

Focusing on strategy, audience, benefits, tone of voice, message, and relevance

Before you start brainstorming for a message, implement the strategic thinking in Chapters 5 and 6. This will fine-tune your critical thinking. Next, review the 50 strategies, such as *abundance, continuing story, testimonial,* and *shock.* Consider the various audience categories (VALS), such as *Achievers, Makers, Experiencers,* and *Innovators.* As we've mentioned before, picture your audience as real people, not a list of statistics. Think about how to make your message relevant to this particular *primary,* and possibly, *secondary audience.* Analyze consumer insights. Determine the appropriate *tone of voice.* Should it be emotional: casual, authoritative, flirty, or concerned? Or should it be rational: informative, educational, authoritative, or instructional? Decide which benefit(s) will be featured. Focus on the unique traits that differentiate the product (USP). Choose how you want the audience to think about the brand (positioning in the mind of the consumer). Imagine your message at different *touchpoints.* Be sure you're writing to the correct senses (sight, hearing, scent, touch) for that medium. If you have a *creative brief,* refer to it and let it guide you.

> *If it doesn't speak volumes without you having to explain it to anyone, then it isn't good enough. Drummond Berman, Group Creative Director/Writer, Merkley+Partners*[11]

Ask yourself what kind of *headline* you could use: *results, comparison, how-to, teaser,* and so on. If you need to create a *slogan,* as discussed in Chapter 10, what type would be *sticky* and *relevant*: (1) #1 *name,* (2) #13 *vernacular,* (3) #14 *reason why,* (4) #15 *challenge,* and so on? Question whether you should create a unique word like "Comcastic" for Comcast, or "Hangry" for a Snickers campaign, or "Imagineering" for The Walt Disney Company research and development department. This is an example of a word created, or a *portmanteau,* by joining two words: hungry and angry, or imagination and engineering. However, if the company's customer service has underperformed, the word could be demeaning and tarnish the company's image. Comcastic, unfortunately, has come to mean very poor service or unkept promises.

Whenever you can create something that's unique and easy-to-remember, you've added stickiness to your message. You also have to be able to deliver the brand's promise: satisfy hunger for Snickers or fuel imagination for Disney. The whole point of any advertising campaign is to first get the consumers' attention so the message can persuade them to take action. That's the beauty of the "Just Do It" Nike slogan. The company doesn't tell you what to do, it encourages you to continue what you enjoy doing.

Recognizing categories of effective messages

What makes a headline practically jump off the page and strike up a conversation? How do some of them single you out when you're the consumer? Why do some seem like a personalized, individual message? How do they reach out and tap you on the arm like a good friend about to confide a secret?

Headlines work for different reasons. Their message and *tone of voice* sound credible. They also sound authentic. The humor is unforced. The language reflects the culture. The message is relevant. When creating headlines, check to see if your message resonates with believability. Here's a short list of reasons why headlines work. They've been grouped into different categories for easier reference.

1. *Credible*
   a. Believable
   b. Truthful
   c. Honest
   d. Sincere
   e. Trustworthy

2. *Authentic*
   a. Genuine
   b. True to life (Realistic)

3. *Relevant*
   a. Informative
   b. Comparative
   c. Demonstrative

4. *Natural*
   a. Unforced, natural-sounding humor

b. Vernacular speech

c. Casual

5. *Emotional*

a. Concerned

b. Urgent

c. Serious

d. Sympathetic

e. Empathetic

f. Compassionate

g. Inspiring

h. Motivating

6. *Personal*

a. Friendly

b. Intimate

c. Seductive

d. Secretive

Exploring playful, humorous, empathetic print ads

One campaign that speaks to the audience in an honest and humorous way is CAT Footwear. Created by Young & Laramore, both the ads and out-of-home billboards (Figure 11.1, Figure 11.2, Figure 11.3, Figure 11.4, Figure 11.5, Figure 11.6) talk to the consumer in a lighthearted *tone of voice.*

Each headline reminds consumers how CAT Footwear is created by the same company that builds bulldozers. The connection is that the reliable toughness expected from heavy equipment is what you can expect in its work boots. Writers personified the brand and created the idea that the product line was really a bloodline, as you would have in families. The headline "Our Family Tree > Their Family Tree" (Figure 11.1) shows the lineage as a family-tree depiction. Instantly, you're drawn into the fun of the ad. The play on words is irresistible and forces you to read on.

FIGURE 11.1 This "Our Family Tree" print ad was created by Young & Laramore for CAT Footwear. Image courtesy of Young & Laramore.

The next ad salutes the brand's tough-as-nails reputation and promises to uphold the legend in its footwear. Even the word "icon" bestows honor. (Figure 11.2)

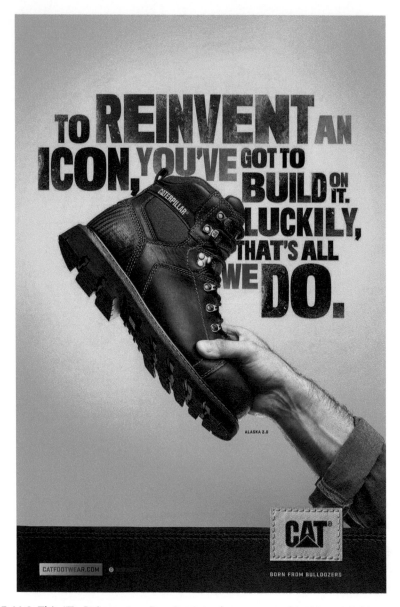

FIGURE 11.2 This "To Reinvent an Icon" print ad was created by Young & Laramore for CAT Footwear. Image courtesy of Young & Laramore.

The copy in the campaign addresses a universal truth: Stuff should last. No copy is necessary because the headlines and subheads (Figure 11.2, Figure 11.3, Figure 11.4) state the consumer benefits and reason to buy this brand: You can count on it performing well for a long time.

You can see that the billboard messages continue the theme. Again, the family history references are reinforced: "Born from bulldozers." and "We both

FIGURE 11.3 This "Built for Anything" print ad was created by Young & Laramore for CAT Footwear. Image courtesy of Young & Laramore.

have the same Grandpa." (Figure 11.5, Figure 11.6). Without question, the entire campaign solidifies the brand in the consumer's mind, as detailed below:

1. "Our Family Tree > Their Family Tree." (Figure 11.1).

2. "To Reinvent an Icon, You've Got to Build On It. Luckily, That's All We Do." (Figure 11.2).

FIGURE 11.4 This "Like a 40 Ton Excavator" print ad was created by Young & Laramore for CAT Footwear. Image courtesy of Young & Laramore.

3. "Built for Anything. You Get to Choose the Anything." (Figure 11.3).

4. "Like a 40 Ton Excavator You Can Wear All Day." (Figure 11.4).

5. "Born from Bulldozers." (Figure 11.5).

6. "We Both Have the Same Grandpa." (Figure 11.6).

FIGURE 11.5 This "Born from Bulldozers" out-of-home message was created by Young & Laramore for CAT Footwear. Image courtesy of Young & Laramore.

FIGURE 11.6 This "We Both Have the Same Grandpa" out-of-home message was created by Young & Laramore for CAT Footwear. Image courtesy of Young & Laramore.

The key to all copy is to tantalize the readers. To draw them in. To hold their attention. In short, you want to keep the reader reading. To understand how to achieve this, Hopper showed how the writer's thought process worked with an interesting comparison:

So, the strategy is how you're going to keep them on the line. It's like dating. It's like wherever it is that you would meet someone – the bar is a cliché – keeping them interested long enough for them to understand that there's something there. You're doing the same thing with the ads. You're trying to keep them from moving on before they get what's good about you.[12]

He went on and explained that the campaign was a true representation of teamwork, blurring and possibly eliminating the lines between writing and designing. They both worked together. Many designers come up with great copy and writers often have exciting visual ideas.

You'll discover that most strong creative teams work as one collaborative idea factory. The titles of copywriter and art director become insignificant. Each one contributes to the strategic thinking and conceptual solutions. When the partnership works, unforgettable and brilliant campaigns are the result.

Studying more ads that empathize with the target

One strikingly effective example of creative work is the Mother London agency response to the 2018 KFC chicken shortage. Yes, they ran out of chicken in the UK. The humorous twist of the brand's iconic letters from "KFC" to "FCK" spoke to the audience. It was on the buckets, and they also appeared in print ads. The underlying idea was "well, FCK, this sucks." The common abbreviated expletive, WTF, wouldn't have been as clear. It cleverly apologized for the inconvenience and made disappointed consumers laugh. After all, a chicken shortage for a brand that primarily serves chicken was so absurdly unexpected, it was funny. The agency played off of that and, by apologizing, it sided with the consumer and showed empathy.

Another campaign that spoke from the consumer's point of view was by Young & Laramore for Coravin, which we discussed in Chapters 2 and 7. The product, the Pivot Wine Preservation System, allows all wine to stay fresh for up to four weeks. People didn't have to decide which bottle to open. They could open more than one. The key phrase "pairs well with" introduces the headlines both as a theme and an eyebrow. Check out the closing line of copy: "So drink a glass of whatever, whenever." It wraps up and reinforces the Coravin benefit. When you read the ads, note how conversational and relatable they are. Look at how each eyebrow prepares the reader for the surprisingly honest next line: the headline.

People are going to critique your work and they're not going to care how much time you spent working on it, or how much sleep you lost worrying about it. Matt Ziselman, Creative Director, Sapient[13]

What this campaign did was solve the wine dilemma and spoke to real people in a real way. The messages were presented in a matter-of-fact language for down-to-earth people. The result was advertising that was *relevant* and *resonated* with authenticity, which made it easy to *remember, respond to,* and *retell.* It encapsulates "The Five Rs" mentioned earlier in Chapter 7.

Let's look at a few print ads now to understand how powerful these to-the-point headlines and closing lines are. The first ad (Figure 11.7) speaks from the partner's point of view. It demonstrates how people sometimes find themselves in boring or condescending conversations at social events.

EYEBROW:	"Pairs Well with"
HEADLINE:	"Listening to Your Boyfriend's Friends Explain the Stock Market to You"
COPY:	"Any bottle lasts up to four weeks. So drink a glass of whatever, whenever."

FIGURE 11.7 This "Listening to Your Boyfriend's Friends Explain the Stock Market to You" print ad was created by Young & Laramore for Coravin. Image courtesy of Young & Laramore.

The second ad (Figure 11.8) underlines how complicated relationships with parents' new partners can be. Look at how the headline not only made that point, but also empathizes with consumers' real issues:

EYEBROW: "Pairs Well with"

HEADLINE: "Meeting Your Dad's New Girlfriend, Crystal"

COPY: "Any bottle lasts up to four weeks. So drink a glass of whatever, whenever."

The headline underscores the inherent awkwardness of meeting anyone, especially your parent's new girlfriend.

FIGURE 11.8 This "Meeting Your Dad's New Girlfriend, Crystal" print ad was created by Young & Laramore for Coravin. Image courtesy of Young & Laramore.

FIGURE 11.9 This "Another Day of School-from-Home, Another Day of Getting Your Ass Kicked by Fifth Grade Math" print ad was created by Young & Laramore for Coravin. Image courtesy of Young & Laramore.

The third ad (Figure 11.9) sympathizes with parents struggling to help their kids with their math homework. It quickly strikes a camaraderie among readers. Many may have silently suffered this humiliation.

EYEBROW:	"Pairs Well with"
HEADLINE:	"Another day of School-from-home, Another Day of Getting Your Ass Kicked by Fifth Grade Math"
COPY:	"Any bottle lasts up to four weeks. So drink a glass of whatever, whenever."

We have already examined other components of this cross-platform campaign in Chapters 2 and 7. You can see its thematic consistency. The brand speaks with one voice: the wine lovers'. It asks, "Why should your wine go bad just because you didn't finish it soon enough?" Now, they don't have to rush or worry about it. The wine-expiration timer has stopped.

Identifying ads with an insider's understanding

One campaign that talks directly to the audience as an athletically driven insider is ASICS. It uses clever play on words that shows it understands how consumers who take their sports endeavors seriously demand more from themselves to reach their athletic goals. Just look at the headlines in these three no-copy ads. The messages were so strong no explanatory copy was needed. The first two ads were for running. The third one was for track sports.

1. "Happiness Is Pushing Your Limits and Then Watching Them Back Down" (Figure 11.10).

2. "Intensity Can Be the Quickest Path to Tranquility" (Figure 11.11).

3. "Funny How Defying Gravity Can Ground You" (Figure 11.12).

FIGURE 11.10 This "Happiness" print ad was created by Vitro for ASICS America Corporation. Image courtesy of Vitro.

FIGURE 11.11 This "Intensity" print ad was created by Vitro for ASICS America Corporation. Image courtesy of Vitro.

FIGURE 11.12 This "Defying Gravity" print ad was created by Vitro for ASICS America Corporation. Image courtesy of Vitro.

The everyday athletes who want to increase their strength and improve their personal performance push themselves in their workouts. They can easily relate to the targeted headlines because each one is speaking their language in a relevant way.

The type is set in a three-dimensional perspective toward a vanishing point. That paired with bold colors energizes the message. When asked whether the visual image preceded the verbal message, KT Thayer, creative director at Vitro, answered:

> *It's hard to say which drove the other, the lines may have come first, but the bold colors and typography definitely influenced the tonality. Once we got the layout to a place we were happy with, we rewrote some of the lines to be shorter, bolder and punchier.*[14]

While developing the strategy for the campaign, Thayer explained, "As a challenger brand, the top priority for ASICS is to build awareness."[15] The objective was to differentiate it from two of its name-brand competitors, Nike and Adidas, giving the consumer a personal choice. He went on to discuss the slogan.

> *"Sound Mind, Sound Body" is more than ASICS' tagline. It is the founding philosophy and the root of the name. Anima Sana In Corpore Sano is a Latin phrase that translates to, "a sound mind, in a sound body." This position drives every decision, innovation, and communication that comes from ASICS.*[16]

The campaign demonstrated that the way to a sound body and sound mind is to be physically fit. The campaign started out showing how running helps consumers achieve mental and physical health. Later, other sports were added, highlighting the same universal benefits. The campaign is based on the *benefit* and *honesty* strategies (#1 and #26 in Chapter 6) and spoke candidly. Thayer shared these thoughts:

> *The 2009 campaign was internally called "Running Truths" as the message had to come from a genuine, honest place that any level of runner could understand and believe. By educating or reminding runners of the full benefits of running, mental and physical, ASICS stood out and carved out an ownable space in running, with plenty of room to grow.*[17]

In the Paddletek campaign, the writers wrote from the perspective of the results-driven athlete. Each headline showed that the brand intimately knew its audience's mindset. We will revisit cross-platform campaigns later in Chapter 14 as a fully integrated idea based on one core message. In one example here, the headline shows the writer's insight into this audience (Figure 11.13). Serious athletes really compete with themselves. They don't only look to set records. They challenge themselves to break the ones they already set.

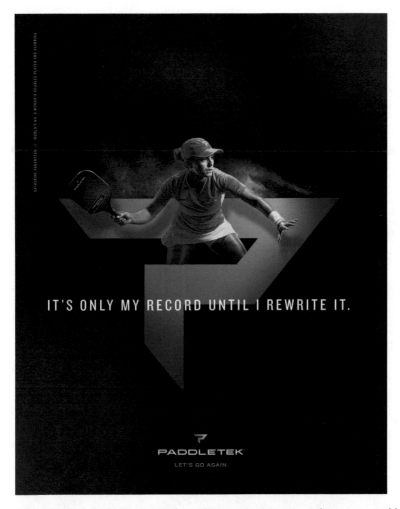

FIGURE 11.13 This "It's Only My Record Until I Rewrite It." print ad was created by Young & Laramore for Paddletek. Image courtesy of Young & Laramore.

The theme continues in the next two Paddletek ads (Figure 11.14, Figure 11.15). You can see the relationship between them with the following headlines:

1. "It's Only My Record Until I Rewrite it." (Figure 11.13)
2. "There Are No Personal Bests. Only Best Yets." (Figure 11.14)

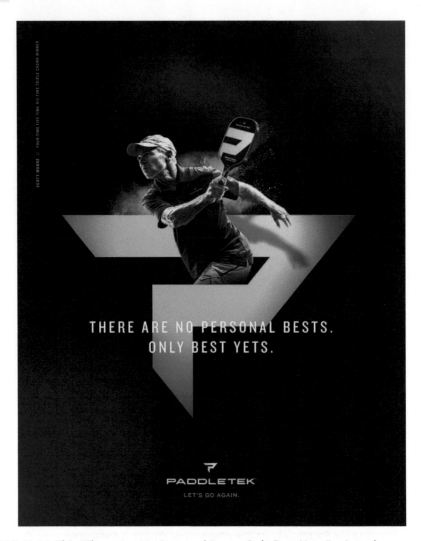

FIGURE 11.14 This "There Are No Personal Bests. Only Best Yets." print ad was created by Young & Laramore for Paddletek. Image courtesy of Young & Laramore.

3. "The Losses Leave You Hungry. The Wins, Even Hungrier." (Figure 11.15)

4. "Yesterday Is Just a Benchmark."

5. "The Come Up Doesn't Come Easy."

6. "Outplay. Outsmart. Outlast. Outdo."

As you can see, targeted communication was delivered through gripping head-lines in the ASICS and Paddletek ads. They reached out to the specific audience

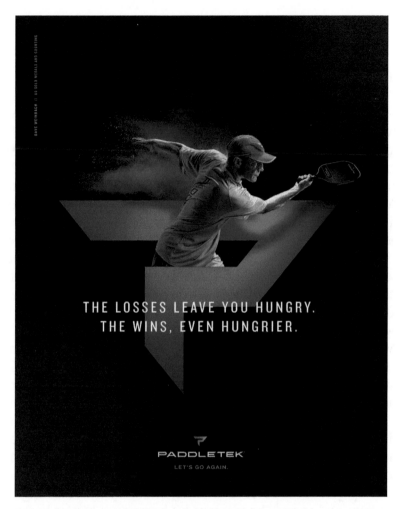

FIGURE 11.15 This "The Losses Leave You Hungry. The Wins, Even Hungrier." print ad was created by Young & Laramore for Paddletek. Image courtesy of Young & Laramore.

and demanded to be heard. The brand's voice demonstrated an unmistakable appreciation for its respective audiences.

Shaping witty headlines that say it all

Sometimes, as we've already seen, the headline carries the entire message. No subhead or copy is required. In the Geek Squad "Wireless Awareness" campaign, created by Crispin Porter + Bogusky, the headlines show a dry wit that engages the audience's imagination. The image is an orange Ethernet cable playfully twisted into the shape of a cause ribbon to add a little more humor. Take a moment to digest each of the headlines.

1. "It's True You Can Get Wireless Just From Talking to a Geek."
2. "If You Have Wireless, You Could Be Giving Wireless to Everyone."
3. "To You It's a Wire. To Us It's a Mission."

Using a play-on-words technique, the first two headlines talk about wireless as if it were a virus that's contagious. They make readers do a double take and then "get" the message. The first one states a simple fact in a clever way. The second one ingeniously warns WiFi users that they inadvertently could be sharing their signal. The third talks about the passion geeks have for their work. Consumers having computer problems want someone passionate, not apathetic. "To You It's a Wire. To Us It's a Mission" separates the computer aficionado from the simple end user. That's who you want working on your system: someone who thrives on solving challenging computer problems.

Notice how these ads address the *audience's objections* and *needs*. Why don't people call for help? Most likely, because they've been disappointed with substandard computer repairs. What do they need? The problem solved right the first time.

One Motel 6 unforgettable print ad is worth discussing here. It spoke honestly to its present and prospective guests. The no-nonsense layout had only a few lines of tiny, white type on an all-black background. It was an *on-strategy* message, both visually and verbally. The *universal truth* here was: Why pay for amenities you don't need? The headline read, "When You're Sleeping, We Look Just Like Those Big Fancy Hotels. Motel 6." The ad stated the obvious, but often overlooked fact: When you're asleep, you don't see the frills of expensive, upscale hotels.

It made a point relevant to many business travelers. They just needed somewhere to sleep because the rest of their day was busy with meetings, conferences, exhibits, and so on. The message hit home even harder because there was nothing on the page to detract from it or distract the reader's attention. Its simplicity reflected the brand's no-frills personality.

Another brand with a distinctive personality is the Aflac Duck. It's funny and lovable. The headline in this ad (Figure 11.16), which was also a poster, integrates the company name: "Get the Aflacts." The subhead follows, creating more urgency: "Why you need Aflac now more than ever." Each subhead that separates the key points spins off the main idea, highlighting the benefits.

Subheads: "Aflac is different from health insurance; it's for daily living."

"Aflac is an extra measure of financial protection."

"Aflac pays you cash benefits to use as you see fit."

"Aflac benefits help with unexpected expenses."

"Aflac belongs to you, not your company."

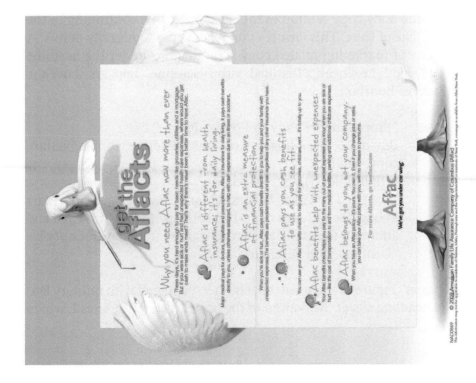

FIGURE 11.16 This print ad was created by the Kaplan Thaler Group for Aflac. Image courtesy of the Kaplan Thaler Group.

The slogan offers another benefit of protection: "We've got you under our wing." Take a close look at the body copy. It's not real copy. It's *Greeked in*. Artists use *Latin* (casually called *Greek*) type (English letters arranged in non-words like "lorem ipsum dolor" to fill space) or copy blocks. It's not designed to be read. It's just to be used for layout purposes. The Aflac Duck has become the main character to present the brand's promise: insurance protection.

When writing any copy, make your message work like a postage stamp, so it sticks to the task until it's delivered. You want one key point to be remembered. So, stick to that core idea throughout the campaign.

Another cohesive and integrated campaign is for Hotel Tango Distillery, a line of alcoholic beverages. It boasts some exceptional headlines that present the brand's promise and explain more in the body copy. Other campaign components will be discussed in detail in Chapter 14. These include web copy (Figure 14.1), digital ads (Figure 14.2), and packaging (Figure 14.3, Figure 14.4). You'll see more packaging copy in Chapter 13 (Figure 13.1, Figure 13.2, Figure 13.3, Figure 13.4, Figure 13.5, Figure 13.6, Figure 13.7).

Below are some copy examples to enjoy. Look at them to understand how powerful these to-the-point print and poster headlines are. The first one, "Propaganda, Ready-to-Propagate" (Figure 11.17), intrigues the viewer to read further. The play on words is unmistakable.

Note how the body copy reinforces the message, while continuing in the same honest *tone of voice*. This ensures that readers don't miss key points. A humorous line of marketing-related copy is set in a box under the headline (Figure 11.17), and the slogan, "Distilled with Discipline," appears above the bottle of Reserve Bourbon.

HEADLINE:	"Propaganda, Ready-to-Propagate."
	Boxed line of ad lingo: "Contains: headline, supplementary copy, 'tagline.'"
SUBHEAD:	"High Proof. Higher Standards."
COPY:	"Founded by Travis Barnes, a Marine who served three tours in Iraq. Hotel Tango crafts fine spirits with the same rigor and attention to detail Sgt. Barnes learned in the line of duty."
SLOGAN:	"Distilled with Discipline"

A second poster (Figure 11.18) again uses humor, peppered with military language. The headline sits at the bottom of the poster. Yet, the subhead, which

FIGURE 11.17 This "Propaganda, Ready-to-Propagate" print ad was created by Young & Laramore for Hotel Tango. Image courtesy of Young & Laramore.

starts at the top, draws the reader in to continue to the last word in the stacked line because of the punctuation. It used a colon, not a period in the subhead.

HEADLINE: "Hotel Tango Recruitment Poster."
SUBHEAD: "Calling ALL:
Brothers, Sisters, Friends, Hackers, *Mensches*, Comrades, and Co-conspirators of Sound Mind, Good Character, and a Penchant for Light Mischief."

FIGURE 11.18 This "Calling All" print ad was created by Young & Laramore for Hotel Tango. Image courtesy of Young & Laramore.

Two arrows drive the viewers' attention down to these two lines of copy:

COPY: "Report: To your favorite local bar, pub, tavern, 'watering hole,' or spirits purveyor.
Secure: One or more Hotel Tango beverage rations."

You can hear the call to join in and lift your glasses in the language. Most importantly, the entire "Distilled with Dignity" campaign has a precision-focused, military voice paired with a sincere, witty, and relatable tone.

FIGURE 11.19 This "Contains 16 Rounds" print ad was created by Young & Laramore for Hotel Tango. Image courtesy of Young & Laramore.

A third poster (Figure 11.19) continues with more tongue-in-cheek humor and armed-forces commentary. You'll see the humorous, advertising-lingo copy set in a box under the headline.

HEADLINE: "Contains 16 (1.5 oz.) Rounds."

BOXED LINE OF AD LINGO: "Supporting message."

SUBHEAD: "Hotel Tango spirits are crafted with the same perfectionist mindset that Travis Barnes, HT founder, gained in his decorated career as a U.S. Marine. Now, he invites you to share with good company one or more rounds of his work: spirits <u>Distilled with Discipline</u>."

BOXED LINE OF AD LINGO: "Visual reference."

Two arrows drive the viewers' attention up to these two lines of copy:

COPY: "Fit to serve.
Made to share."

The fourth poster (Figure 11.20) reminds readers of the founder's distinguished military background, both in the headline and the body copy. You'll again see

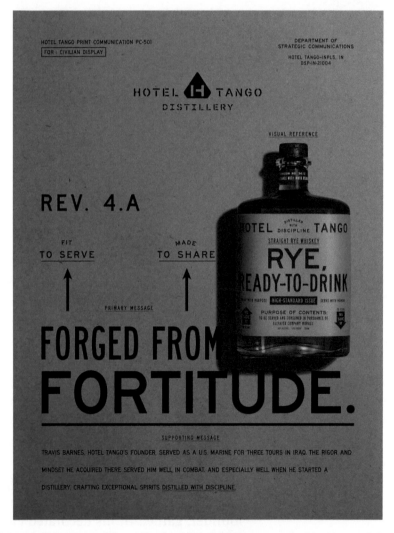

FIGURE 11.20 This "Forged from Fortitude" print ad was created by Young & Laramore for Hotel Tango. Image courtesy of Young & Laramore.

the lighthearted advertising indicators throughout the layout. Notice the use of alliteration in the headline here.

HEADLINE:	"Forged from Fortitude."
UNDERLINED AD LABELS:	"Visual Reference." "Primary Message." "Supporting Message."
SUBHEAD:	"Travis Barnes, Hotel Tango's founder, served as a U.S. Marine for three tours in Iraq. The rigor and mindset he acquired there served him well in combat. And especially well when he started a distillery, crafting exceptional spirits <u>Distilled with Discipline</u>."

Two arrows drive the viewers' attention up to these two lines of copy:

COPY:	"Fit to serve. Made to share."

Take your time to review the copy. Recognize how tightly written it is and how each ad supports the core concept of the campaign. Also be sure to look at the out-of-home examples in Chapter 12 (Figure 12.31, Figure 12.32). Then, see how the concept spins out as an integrated, cross-platform campaign in Chapter 14, mentioned earlier. Review Useful Info 11.4 to better understand similar features in effective campaigns.

USEFUL INFO 11.4 Common qualities in featured campaigns

Notice how each one does the following:

1 Delivers an *on-target* and *on-strategy* concept

2 Shows a deep understanding of the *audience's lifestyle, needs,* and *values*

3 Presents a particularly *relevant* and *relatable message*

4 Shows a *sense of humor*

5 Surprises the reader with an *unexpected concept*

6 Entertains the audience with a *clever turn of phrase*

7 *Thanks the reader* for having "stopped by"

8 *Fulfills* a need, *solves* a problem, *answers* an objection, or *presents* a challenge

Copywriting: A closer look

When you study all these examples, although the campaigns differ, notice they all have several components in common. You can use them as references for future work. Below is a list of helpful writing tips for print. You may want to review them from time to time.

Print writing tips

1. "I find the people that struggle in this business are the ones that can't let go of an idea and move on and come up with something else. If they're not letting go of the idea, what's happening is they're not coming up with new ideas." – Sheena Brady, commercial director/creative director.[18]

2. "If these are tips to young writers or beginner writers, with print, I think more so maybe than even TV – well, I wouldn't say more so, but again – try to be simple-minded. People are turning the pages of a magazine and – in every magazine there are ads for pharmaceuticals, and shampoos, and this and that, and whatever your product is – you want to stop them with something that even with that two seconds they glance at it, they take it away. A lot of times we give print assignments to some of the younger creative teams. Just as I did when I was their age, you're hoping to win this year's Gold Lions at Cannes with every ad you do. So, you break the bank trying to do the greatest print ad of all times. Very often, it becomes a complicated mess. There's nothing wrong if you're trying to sell a Keebler cracker, for instance, which is part of Kellogg's®, with just having a big picture of a cracker and a line that communicates why you should want them. Sometimes I think they think, 'Oh, that's too easy.' But there's a reason it's too easy. Well, because it's so simple. But, that makes for a much better ad quite often, not always.

   But just to be simple visually and copy wise, too. If possible, try tell the story with just a headline and no body copy. You may have to have body copy, but if possible, try to do it without it." – Kevin Moriarty, former vice president and creative director, Leo Burnett.[19]

3. "Writing for print media should typically be more formal, since readers tend to peruse the entire article or spread more thoroughly. One benefit to this is that including sidebars of information, like the resources in these pieces, are more likely to be taken in by the reader." – Deltina Hay, author of *A Survival Guide to Social Media and Web 2.0 Optimization*.[20]

4. "As a writer you have to be able to convey ideas that are sometimes difficult. You have to be able to write about things that are visual. How do you explain that? How do you make people feel something for an idea that they've never seen? Some clients are incredibly visual and can grasp things and some clients aren't. Just like some people are and some people aren't. And so, you have to figure out how to convey your idea in a way that makes it understandable to everybody." – Sara Rose, executive creative director/writer.[21]

5. "Too many people sit there and write a bunch of lines and it doesn't make, you know, the best of those is the one that they'll put forward. It's not about quantity; it's about quality. Simon and I would much rather agonize for three hours on one line than write 20 lines and just pick the best one." – Drummond Berman, group creative director/writer, Merkley+Partners.[22]

6. "Obviously, with print, if they're reading at all, and that's a big if, then keep it short, keep it flowing, and just don't imagine that they're reading it for fun, because they're not." – Vinny Warren, founder and creative director, The Escape Pod.[23]

7. "Have a strategy. You even have a strategy just for getting through your day. You can't just dutifully represent your client. You have to somehow get people engaged in it. That's why we have to think about the strategy. You can't just start talking about Stanley Steemer being this great carpet cleaner. You have to think about what's a way to get people interested in this if they haven't thought about it already. 'Oh, you're walking on crap and tracking it in your house. You don't see it, so you don't really think about it being there. But, it's there.' Boom! You have a Stanley Steemer strategy. Then, everything will fall off of that. That comes from knowing you have to have a way in." – Charlie Hopper, principal, Young & Laramore.[24]

8. Pay attention to everyday conversations at restaurants, on subways, in stores. Listen to what they talk about. Gain insight into what matters to them. Capture the natural speech patterns, casual phrasing, and slang expressions in your writing.

Creative print checklist

So, let's review what makes a terrific print message. Before signing off on your print campaign, answer the questions in Checklist 11.5.

CHECKLIST 11.5 Print campaign checklist of questions

1 About the concept.

  a Is it *relevant* to the audience?

  b Does it speak from the *audience's point of view*?

  c Would it *generate press attention*?

  d Would it *create talk value* or "buzz"?

  e Does it *entertain, inform,* and/or *engage* the reader?

  f Does it *promise a benefit* or *solve a problem*?

  g Does it deliver one instantly *understandable message*?

  h Do all of the related materials project *one cohesive message*?

  i Does it reflect the *brand's personality*?

2 About the body copy (review Chapter 10).

  a Does it *flow*? (Can anyone read it out loud without stumbling?)

  b Does it *weave the main idea* from the first sentence to the last?

  c Does it use short, *concise sentences*?

  d Does it *offer little phrases*? If they work? Like this.

  e Does it use *simple language*, not technical jargon?

  f Does it incorporate *sticky writing techniques* (discussed in Chapter 10) that make your message easy to retain and digest, like the following:

    i *Alliteration* – "The Magic of Macy's" tagline.

    ii *Parallel construction* – "Save money. Live better" (slogan for Walmart).

    iii *Rhyme* – "Hooray for the everyday" (IKEA catalog).

    iv *Simple promise* – "No ordinary airline" (Virgin Atlantic).

    v *Button* – clever closing line, like "Priceless" (MasterCard tagline and closing line that was used in ads and commercials).

    vi *ABA* – last line of copy reiterates the headline, for example, if the headline were "In an Absolut World," the last line could say, "Now you can help create an Absolut world."

    vii *Bullet points* – to emphasize important ideas.

    viii *Connectors* – to join sentences and paragraphs, like on the other hand, because, but, the best part is, etc.

3 About the layout.

  a Can the reader *find* the most *important message*?

  b Does the layout *guide the reader* to the most important points first (referred to as "visual hierarchy")?

  c Does the *visual support the headline*? Do they work as a single conceptual unit?

  d Is the *headline type broken in phrases*, for easier comprehension?

   e   Does the body copy have *objectionable widows* (one word sitting alone at the top of a new copy block) or *orphans* (one word dangling at the end of a paragraph)?

   f   Is the *font* (type style) *appropriate* for the brand and audience? (An example: You wouldn't use a funky or novelty font for a funeral home.)

   g   Is the body *copy set flush left* (aligned on the left side) for a faster read? Centered type is okay for just a few lines. Flush right (last words are aligned on the right side) can work for a visual effect with short copy.

4 About the medium.

   a   Should this be placed in a *media-specific vehicle* (like *Maxim* magazine for a male audience)?

   b   Would you need to *edit down the copy* for a smaller-space ad?

   c   Do you need to *rewrite the headline* and *some of the copy* to target a *different audience*? (For example: Would the concept need to be tweaked for a business publication as opposed to a fitness magazine? Or, is the concept strong enough to work in any publication?)

   d   Is there *another print vehicle* you would suggest?

Creative print ad exercises

Exercise 1: Create a print campaign for Cereality

Cereality is a restaurant chain that primarily serves custom-designed cereals and toppings. Check out www.cereality.com for more details. Be sure to create a campaign for university students. So, use a *tone of voice* and message that would resonate with them.

a. Write two different, but related, *headlines*.

b. Create a *tagline*.

c. Find or create a *visual*.

d. Write at least five sentences or phrases for *body copy*.

e. Remember to make Cereality a "*must-go-to destination*" for a perfect anytime snack or quick meal.

f. Think about *another medium* that would extend the campaign, like out-of-home messages, such as billboards and transit vehicles, or ambient ads, such as lawn signs on college campuses.

Exercise 2: Now, write a print campaign for a possible competitor

This is a direct competitor that offers similar fare. Visit https://www.cereality.com for more information. Repeat all steps (a through f). Try to create a strong campaign to challenge Cereality. You can make up a new cereal café. Remember, each campaign must be distinctive, so as not to confuse the audience. Think about how head-to-head competitors, like Coke and Pepsi or Denny's and IHOP (International House of Pancakes), face off in their campaigns.

Exercise 3: Compare the two campaigns

Be honest. Which one is stronger? Why?

Notes

1. Drummond Berman, personal communication, April 8, 2009.
2. Sheena Brady, personal communication, December 3, 2022.
3. Sheena Brady, personal communication, December 3, 2022.
4. Drummond Berman, personal communication, April 8, 2009.
5. Drummond Berman, personal communication, April 8, 2009.
6. Vinny Warren, personal communication, September 4, 2009.
7. Charlie Hopper, personal communication, November 26, 2021.
8. Charlie Hopper, personal communication, November 26, 2021.
9. Vinny Warren, personal communication, September 4, 2009.
10. Larry Percy, *Strategies for Implementing Integrated Marketing Communications* (Oxford, UK: Butterworth-Heinemann, 2008), 252.
11. Drummond Berman, personal communication, April 8, 2009.
12. Charlie Hopper, personal communication, November 26, 2021.
13. Matt Ziselman, personal communication, January 30, 2009.
14. KT Thayer, personal communication, September 9, 2010.
15. KT Thayer, personal communication, September 9, 2010.
16. KT Thayer, personal communication, September 9, 2010.
17. KT Thayer, personal communication, September 9, 2010.
18. Sheena Brady, personal communication, December 3, 2022.
19. Kevin Moriarty, personal communication, August 24, 2009.
20. Deltina Hay, personal communication, July 19, 2009.
21. Sara Rose, personal communication, November 29, 2022.
22. Drummond Berman, personal communication, April 8, 2009.
23. Vinny Warren, personal communication, September 4, 2009.
24. Charlie Hopper, personal communication, November 26, 2021.

12

The Ambient and Moving Word
Out-of-home and Transit

"Think as a buyer, not a seller. Look for the ultimate benefit."
Drayton Bird, Writer, Speaker, Marketer, and
Author of Commonsense Direct & Digital Marketing[1]

In this chapter, we'll meander through the entertaining world of ambient and transit advertising. You'll see how stimulating and rewarding it is to create innovative, out-of-home messages. You'll be inspired to think up new places to advertise and you'll start to notice "delivery vehicles," like manhole covers, retail store sliding glass doors, and pedestrian crosswalks. You'll scrutinize promotional messages and find out how to categorize them.

You'll realize how important it is to challenge yourself to come up with ingenious copy as well as novel venues. You'll understand how effective it is to surprise and entertain the consumer. You'll find you can be funny and even

Content and Copywriting: The Complete Toolkit for Strategic Marketing,
Second Edition. Margo Berman.
© 2024 Margo Berman. Published 2024 by John Wiley & Sons Ltd.
Companion website: www.wiley.com/go/contentandcopywriting

irreverent, as in the Legal Sea Foods and Feckin Irish Whiskey campaigns. You'll stretch yourself to think visually. So, you can enhance any message. You'll also learn to use traditional out-of-home vehicles in nontraditional ways like the Pet Supplies Plus in-store displays (Figure 12.15, Figure 12.16, Figure 12.17). And, how an ordinary subway message can deliver a far-from-ordinary message, as in the "Packed with Blueberries" 7-Eleven transit sign (Figure 12.6). Or, how a taxi-top sign (Figure 12.26) can create instant double takes, as in the Legal Sea Foods irreverent headline: "This cab gets around more than your sister."

You'll also be inspired to blend technology with signage and create an interactive message that speaks to a very narrow market, such as New York City marathoners and their families. You'll also find an ambient checklist to help you as you're developing your own unique ideas. Now, let's take a closer look at this exciting medium.

Starting from the medium

Today, more than ever, messages are everywhere: on airport luggage carousels, mall escalator sides, sidewalks, shopping cart handles – basically, you name it, and if advertising hasn't appeared there, it will. Writers unfamiliar with these new vehicles of expression will soon find themselves bypassed or replaced by professionals with a wider repertoire of expertise. Here, we will investigate the emerging media opportunities and the kind of imaginative verbal execution they demand.

Once you know where the message will be seen, you can think backward. The first question is always this: Where is the message going to be placed so the targeted consumer will see it? Will it be on any of these out-of-home locations? Or somewhere new?

- Sliding glass doors inside mall stores? (Static cling images of people were on both sides of sliding glass doors in malls across the world from Mumbai, India to Buenos Aires, Argentina. When shoppers approached, the doors parted with the static cling people separating. The message "People Move Away When You Have Body Odor" was for Axe deodorant.)

- Retail store windows in malls and airports? (Static cling image of a woman smashing into a sliding glass door to show how well ICU glass cleaner works.)

- An outdoor field? (With a section "mowed" by a Bic razor leaning against a billboard.)

- Mall escalator steps? (Images of people in roller coaster seats move with the escalator as if they were on the ride at Hopi Hari amusement park in São Paulo, Brazil.)

- Sides of buildings, called "wallscapes"? (A giant, 3D Spiderman crawls along a building side.)

- Bus wheels? (A bus wheel in Japan acts as the lens of a camera, with the rest of the camera drawn on the bus side, around the tire.)

- A Zamboni machine? (With a Gillette Fusion razor in the front of it, the machine was shaving the ice rink at a hockey game.)

- Pedestrian crosswalk stripes? (FedEx Kinko's placed an open, oversized bottle of a liquid white out product on the sidewalk with its brush lying sideways in the crosswalk, as if the lines were just painted.)

- Door hangers? (*The Economist* asking guests "Would you like a wake-up call?" on hotel room doors.)

- Subway overhead handrails? (Barbells are placed along the overhead rails in New York City to remind commuters to work out. They were advertising The Fitness Company.)

- Subway straps? (An image of a Pilot watch on it, the strap suggested, "Try it here. The big Pilot's watch.")

- Power lines? (There was a gigantic wide-tooth comb set into power lines with the Rejoice logo to publicize Asia's number one detangling shampoo by Procter & Gamble.)

- Bendable straws? (This showed a flexible woman bending backward to promote the Y-Plus Yoga Center in Hong Kong.)

- Manhole covers? (A message from Folgers to New Yorkers was placed around a lifelike image of a cup of coffee, painted on top of a manhole cover. The steam floating up looked as if the coffee were piping hot. It read, "Hey, city that never sleeps. Wake up. Folgers.")

- Cocktail umbrellas? (An anti-date drug message created by TBWA\London, "This is how easy it is to spike your drink," was placed in drinks left unattended at London bars.)

Be sure to check out these and other exciting ambient ads online. Look for ads in unusual places. Then, study the copy. Notice how the object or installment stops consumers and how each message draws them in closer.

The above list will give you a few places to start. Each image is well worth your attention and will boost your creative energy.

Also look at Atomic Props & Effects. There, you'll see 3D boards with hard-to-believe images, like "paparazzi" on a billboard photographing a Cadillac and two life-size billboard "workers," one on the scaffold and the other jumping into an impossible-to-resist 3D MINI Cooper at the bottom of the board. There are many other exciting ambient ads, as well. Some are street-lined or bus shelter sculptures. Others are illuminated to replicate the product, as in lit up billboards. Wander around this site. You'll be bombarded with creative ingenuity.

Take a look at outdoor 3D, too, for inflatable designs. You won't forget the 3D monster breaking through the billboard to advertise Monster.com or the giant, one-eyed 3D creature wrapping around the board promoting Halloween shopping at Target.

Be aware that some 3D billboards are expected to be a distraction. But, they may also cause car accidents. The first 3D billboard for Wonderbra at the Waterloo Train Station in London created a media stir. Because Wonderbra claims to be able to make it look as if a woman's bra had increased two cup sizes, the 3D effect only magnified the enhancement. However, without 3D glasses, the image appeared slightly blurry, causing people to stare even more. The idea of using 3D in this way is effective, as you can imagine.

Check out 3D wallscapes and make it a habit to regularly search for innovative ads on Google to keep up with the newest ambient messages. This will give you a steady diet of creative inspiration. Take a quick look at the list in Useful Info 12.1 and use it to refresh your memory.

 USEFUL INFO 12.1 Kinds of ambient media

1 Signage
   a Outdoor
      i *Billboards* (traditional or with movement, 3D, extensions, inflatables, interactivity, etc.)
      ii *Wallscapes* (giant ads on buildings)
   b Indoor (store displays)
      i *POP* – point of purchase
      ii *Shelf talkers* – messages next to products
      iii *Floor talkers* – messages on retail floors
      iv *Window messages*
         1 Stickers (static cling ads)
         2 Flyers (inside store windows)
         3 Posters (free-standing signs in malls)

2 Transit
  a Outdoor (messages on transportation vehicles)
    i Buses
    ii Taxis
    iii Subways
    iv Trains
    v Trolleys
    vi Trucks
  b Indoor (stations)
    i Train
    ii Airport
    iii Subway
        1 Wraps
        2 Kiosks
        3 Signs (inside and out)
  c 3D objects
    i Barbells on subway handrails
    ii Watches on overhead subway hand straps
    iii Art installations

3 Other media
  a Cocktail napkins
  b Elevators
  c Sculptures
  d Free items (with tracking devices) placed in the street for people to take

4 Movies
  a Posters
  b On-screen messages
  c Messages on candy packages, popcorn cartons, etc.

5 Other out-of-home
  a *Arenas* – posters around the stadium, concession stands, etc.
  b *Aerials*
    i Blimps
    ii Hot air balloons
    iii Banner ads on planes
  c *Island displays* – freestanding kiosks inside stores with standalone products like beer or soda in supermarkets

Noticing messages wherever you are

Ambient advertising, that is, messages in unexpected out-of-home locations, is everywhere. Pay attention. Be alert. And, analyze messages wherever you find them. Then, consider what would be the most effective way to use this medium. Think about the following message-influencing questions.

- Is there movement involved affecting how the copy is read? (Sometimes you see this in transit ads on cabs, bus sides, or sliding glass doors.)
- How much space do you have for copy? (Less copy says more on billboards.)
- What could you say to create an impossible-to-ignore message? (Think verbal and visual stopping power.)

Keep in mind that thought-provoking messages can appear in the most mundane places. This is why you need to stretch yourself creatively. Don't dismiss any medium as ordinary. Yes, the medium can be run of the mill, but your message can still be remarkable. Ask: Is the message going to be delivered via one or more of these vehicles?

- Indoors? – Like point-of-purchase signage, window posters, or shelf talkers and videos, which are messages next to products on store shelves.
- Out-of-home? – Like a lawn sign in a park (as PEDIGREE® did to raise awareness for shelter dogs with dog-shaped signs in New York's Central Park and a pleading message saying, "Wish I Was Here."[2])
- On indoor moving objects? – Like shopping cart handles in supermarkets.
- Intrusive? – Like videos inside elevators, pizza box tops, or gas station displays.
- Interactive? – Like quizzes on websites, text messages on billboards, or interactive options in TV spots.
- In print? – Like magazine ads and inserts.
- In broadcast? – Like radio or TV spots.
- On mobile devices? – Like QR codes on smartphones and tablets.
- On transit-related objects? – Like bus wraps, bus sides, bus shelters, train stations, cabs, trolleys, jeeps, boats, or trucks.
- On digital displays? – Like New York Times Square.
- In unusual places? – Like ads in urinals (yes, urinals).

Whenever you're creating ambient messages, think about surprising the audience and reaching them when they aren't expecting it. Once you've stopped them, make sure you reward them with an entertaining, captivating, unexpected, and brilliant statement. If your concept is boring, it will be ignored. If it's *off-target*, it won't be understood. If it's *off-strategy*, it's a waste of time. Focus. Ask more of yourself. Start over if you haven't created a concept and copy that are anything less than terrific.

Looking closely at out-of-home messages

Let's look at a traditional out-of-home vehicle: billboards. These messages should be as brief as possible: seven words or fewer. Sometimes you'll see ordinary, uninspired messages. Other times you'll find extraordinarily creative ones. Read through Tips and Rules 12.2 to improve your ambient-writing skills.

TIPS AND RULES 12.2
Tips for writing ambient copy

1 Less is more. Edit and reedit.
2 Develop traffic-stopping concepts.
3 Catch audience off guard.
4 Create a surprise, verbally and visually.
5 Be irreverent when appropriate.
6 Entertain and engage the viewer.
7 Use interactivity when possible.
8 Allow humor to sell *benefits*.
9 Think visually. How can you enhance the message?
10 Don't stop concepting until you create an idea that *spins out*.

According to Vinny Warren, founder and creative director of The Escape Pod, you'll find more creative billboards in the UK and in Europe than in the US. He said:

> The standards of graphic design are little higher and the medium of outdoor has a better reputation. People put more thought into it than maybe here. If you look around here, I mean I'm looking around here. It's all boring. That's the problem with outdoor.[3]

Of course, not all billboards are unimaginative. Some have extensions (with parts that go above or below the standard rectangular board). Some have moving parts. Some have actual cars, like the MINI Cooper (by Crispin, Porter + Bogusky) on them.[4] And, some even have live people on them like TBWA's Adidas board in Japan.[5] One billboard for Heineken was on a stretchable material and looked as if someone's hand were reaching from behind the fabric to grab a beer. The challenge, as a writer and designer, is to create traffic-stopping billboards, not boring ones.

Every time you're on the highway or on a street with billboards, notice that some catch your attention. What makes you look? The message? The visual? The movement? The extensions that stretch beyond the board? The special effects? If you're able to take a photo at a red light, do it. That way, you can look at the board later and analyze what you liked about it. You'll also have a visual reference when you're working on billboards.

Thinking about surprising the audience

Just think how exciting it is to be stopped right where you are and notice a great message. What can you create that will not only reach the audience you want, but also surprise them? What can you do to hold their attention? How could it be more powerful?

As mentioned in Chapter 4, IKEA used innovative social media as discussed in the article "IKEA Facebook Tag."[6]

The IKEA campaign also displayed creative use of ambient and transit media with these brilliant and unexpected ambient messages:

- Mobile displays of IKEA rooms furnished inside see-through trucks

- Bus stops transformed to look like living room seating

> *The holy grail for me is what I call Culturally Explosive Work™,*
> *work that explodes through pop culture and becomes part of*
> *the cultural lexicon. Craig Miller, Creative Director/Copywriter,*
> *Craig Miller Creative*[7]

You would think that in-store signage is a thankless assignment. You're wrong. The next time you're shopping in a store with whimsical merchandise and see creative messages, snap a picture and send it to yourself. Some in-store messages are very exciting. They stop you and make you think.

Just examine the two in-store displays by DeVito/Verdi for For Eyes (Figure 12.1, Figure 12.2). They're very funny because they make eyeglass wearers think about how their eyewear can project unwanted impressions. It reminds them that the glasses they wear speak about who they are from other

FIGURE 12.1 This "Celibacy Isn't Always a Choice" in-store display was created by DeVito/Verdi for For Eyes. Image courtesy of DeVito/Verdi.

FIGURE 12.2 This "Glasses that Don't Hurt" in-store display was created by DeVito/Verdi for For Eyes. Image courtesy of DeVito/Verdi.

people's viewpoints. It's not about how well they can see out of their glasses. It's about how well others perceive them from what they're wearing. No one wants to look geeky instead of cool.

Understanding your audience's frame of reference

Some campaigns are so authentic in their *tone of voice* they sound as if the consumers wrote them. One that exemplifies this is the 7-Eleven "New York" campaign.

What makes this campaign such a standout? There are several factors. It doesn't look or read like an advertising message. It sounds like a New Yorker speaking frankly to another local. It's bluntly honest. It's persuasive just because of its relatable message and instantly identifiable visuals, such as the 7-Eleven oversized muffins (Figure 12.3, Figure 12.4, Figure 12.5, Figure 12.6) and the to-go coffee cups (Figure 12.7, Figure 12.8, Figure 12.9, Figure 12.10, Figure 12.11, Figure 12.12, Figure 12.13, Figure 12.14).

Created by DeVito/Verdi for 7-Eleven in New York, the messages appeared in the stores, on bus shelters, inside subways, on billboards, and on coffee cups to reinforce the concepts. Notice how the headlines require no body copy. They're immediately grasped, written specifically to the fast-paced, no-nonsense New York commuters.

Look at the following 7-Eleven images and read through all the headlines. See how, together, they create one campaign with the connecting thread of witty writing from the consumer's point of view. Some speak about keeping coffee hot for hours. Others talk about how packed the muffins are with nuts and blueberries. The irreverence in the line "New York is full of nuts. Now so are our muffins."(Figure 12.4) is not offensive because most people probably accept the line as a universal truth. Notice how the two images, the coffee cup and the muffin, spin out to create an integrated, cohesive campaign with multiple concepts. These include: (1) yummy, overstuffed muffins (Figure 12.3); (2) steaming-hot coffee through lunch (Figure 12.7); and (3) the "New York" grind (Figure 12.11).

Notice how whimsical the writing is. The messages play with the audience. You can almost picture them on the subway, smirking in agreement to a head-line that sits above a giant blueberry muffin: "Packed with blueberries like this train is packed with people" (Figure 12.6). Just scan the headlines and subheads below. Then, see them in their respective touchpoints.

1. "Muffins that Can Make Anyone a Morning Person." (Figure 12.3)

2. "New York is Full of Nuts. Now So Are Our Muffins." (Figure 12.4)

3. "If We Can't Have Fresh Air at Least We Can Have Fresh Muffins." (Figure 12.5)

4. "Packed with Blueberries like This Train Is Packed with People." (Figure 12.6)

5. "Enjoy Your Morning Coffee with Lunch." (Figure 12.7)

6. "Hotter than a Cabbie Who Just Got Stiffed on a Tip." (Figure 12.8)

7. "Hotter than Fashion Week and with much Better Taste." (Figure 12.9)

8. "Hotter than The Radiator Your Landlord Won't Fix." (Figure 12.10)

9. "The Perfect Grind for the New York Grind." (Figure 12.11)

10. "Enjoy the Long Commute." (Figure 12.12)

11. "Hot from Battery Park to Central Park." (Figure 12.13)

12. "Hot from Staten Island to Long Island." (Figure 12.14)

FIGURE 12.3 This "Muffins that Can Make" in-store display was created by DeVito/Verdi for 7-Eleven. Image courtesy of DeVito/Verdi.

FIGURE 12.4 This "New York is Full of Nuts" in-store display was created by DeVito/Verdi for 7-Eleven. Image courtesy of DeVito/Verdi.

FIGURE 12.5 This "If We Can't Have Fresh Air" in-store display was created by DeVito/Verdi for 7-Eleven. Image courtesy of DeVito/Verdi.

FIGURE 12.6 This "Packed with Blueberries" transit sign was created by DeVito/Verdi for 7-Eleven. Image courtesy of DeVito/Verdi.

The writing demonstrates a familiarity with the reader. It shows an understanding of consumers going about their daily routines. How much fun were these headlines to discover when grabbing a coffee at 7-Eleven, commuting to work, or riding in a cab? Great copy thanks readers for spending their time and rewards them intellectually with its authenticity and cleverness.

Store displays also speak directly to consumers because they're already shopping. For example, the following in-store display ads easily targeted pet

FIGURE 12.7 This "Enjoy our Morning Coffee with Lunch" in-store display was created by DeVito/Verdi for 7-Eleven. Image courtesy of DeVito/Verdi.

FIGURE 12.8 This "Hotter than a Cabbie" in-store display was created by DeVito/Verdi for 7-Eleven. Image courtesy of DeVito/Verdi.

FIGURE 12.9 This "Hotter than Fashion Week" in-store display was created by DeVito/Verdi for 7-Eleven. Image courtesy of DeVito/Verdi.

FIGURE 12.10 This "Hotter than the Radiator" in-store display was created by DeVito/Verdi for 7-Eleven. Image courtesy of DeVito/Verdi.

FIGURE 12.11 This "The Perfect Grind" OOH (billboard) was created by DeVito/Verdi for 7-Eleven. Image courtesy of DeVito/Verdi.

FIGURE 12.12 This "Enjoy the Long Commute" OOH (billboard) was created by DeVito/Verdi for 7-Eleven. Image courtesy of DeVito/Verdi.

FIGURE 12.13 This "Hot from Battery Park" OOH (bus shelter) was created by DeVito/Verdi for 7-Eleven. Image courtesy of DeVito/Verdi.

FIGURE 12.14 This "Hot from Staten Island" OOH (bus shelter) was created by DeVito/ Verdi for 7-Eleven. Image courtesy of DeVito/Verdi.

"parents" and reminded them why Pet Supplies Plus was a better place to shop. As they passed the adorable end cap displays, they could think about their beloved furry family members. The campaign compared the shopping experience at Pet Supplies Plus to the big-box chains. It challenged the bigger-is-better motto and demonstrated time- and cost-saving benefits, including (1) faster product finds, (2) shorter checkout lines, and (3) lower prices. We already examined the stores' TV spots in Chapter 7 (Figure 7.7, Figure 7.8, Scripts and Examples 7.5, Scripts and Examples 7.6). Here are a few in-store display examples, where you can quickly see how the campaign continued (Figure 12.15, Figure 12.16, Figure 12.17).

You can leave empty-handed But we don't recommend it.

FIGURE 12.15 This "You Can Leave Empty-Handed." in-store display ad was created by Young & Laramore for Pet Supplies Plus. Image courtesy of Young & Laramore.

Writers develop content for different media in various ways. Drummond Berman, group creative director/writer at Merkley+Partners, explained how he approaches out-of-home writing, which he calls "the most disciplined writing that you ever do."

> *Because with out-of-home, you've got somebody speeding past at 50 mph. You've got a very limited amount of space and time. So, you've got to sum up everything you need to say in let's say seven words. We rarely go beyond seven words in a headline. Also, when you're writing it, you're condensing it down into the absolutely shortest form possible, but you can't lose the charm, the wit, the intelligence, or any of that. So, every single word has to work really, really hard.*[8]

FIGURE 12.16 This "Quick! What's Smaller?" in-store display ad was created by Young & Laramore for Pet Supplies Plus. Image courtesy of Young & Laramore.

FIGURE 12.17 This "Oversized is overrated." in-store display ad was created by Young & Laramore for Pet Supplies Plus. Image courtesy of Young & Laramore.

He further explained how the creative process and key components that develop strong out-of-home messages differ from writing print ads.

> So, in out-of-home, you have to work really, really, really hard condensing, trying to find the shortest, snappiest, most memorable way of saying things. But you can't abandon any of the key pillars of the campaign: the tone of voice, the message, the truth, any of that stuff. For me with print, it's just a little easier, I guess.[9]

Berman also described what makes it even more challenging are the similarities between the two media, which he detailed this way:

> It's all the same criteria. You want to stop people in their tracks. You don't want a headline to be banging on and going on forever. It does need to succinctly capture something that is going to resonate with someone and make them want to read on.[10]

Unlike the print medium – where people are sitting down and leafing through the pages, focused on reading – with an out-of-home message, they're not expecting it. So, writers need to interrupt whatever they're doing to get their attention. He said they usually write 15 headlines. Although all would work for print, only four would work for out-of-home.

He continued, explaining how print ads – without having a limited number of words in the headlines – give writers more creative flexibility, while shorter out-of-home messages restrict them.

> I just think the onus on writing a print headline is you have to be creative, you have to be relevant, you have to be truthful, and you have to capture the tonality of the campaign. But you don't have to do it in seven words. You can bring in word play a little more.[11]

That's the test for writers: to create powerful messages wherever they appear, regardless of restrictions. Keep a lookout for brilliant examples, and you'll find them. ASICS is another campaign, created by Vitro that mastered out-of-home messages and showed everyday athletes it understood their *point of view*. In Chapter 11, we discussed ASICS print ads (Figure 11.10, Figure 11.11, Figure 11.12) and in Chapter 4, we examined interactive messages. Now, we'll look at the ASICS out-of-home campaign that involved interactivity. It was created specifically for New York Marathon runners and their supporters. In Figure 12.18, the ASICS ABC SuperSign in Times Square shouted encouragement to all the participants and invited their fans to cheer them on with their

FIGURE 12.18 This "ABC SuperSign" out-of-home sign was created by Vitro for ASICS America Corporation. Image courtesy of Vitro.

X (formerly Twitter) posts. Look at how the language on the boards speaks directly to the runners:

> *Hello Central Park. Goodbye Giving Up.*
> *Hello New York. Goodbye Uncertainty.*
> *Hello New York. Goodbye Limitations.*

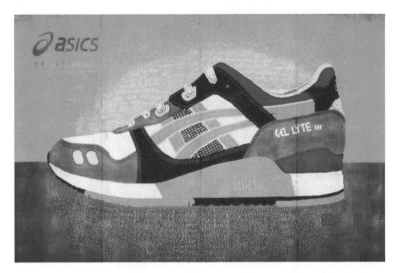

FIGURE 12.19 This "Lite-Brite" art piece was created by Vitro for ASICS America Corporation. Image courtesy of Vitro.

Campaigns that create unexpected communication and catch viewers off guard are more easily remembered. Who would have thought to create a giant Lite-Brite (Figure 12.19) of an ASICS shoe? Vitro did. It's colorful, luminescent, and beautiful, like a work of art. It forced the audience to notice it by its bold creativity. It made an impact in the dozen locations where it was displayed, including the Winter Music Conference in Miami and a launch event at Spotlight Studios in Manhattan.

> *Clichés are dangerous because of that. They just say, "Oh, never mind, there's nothing new here. Move along." Charlie Hopper, Principal, Young & Laramore*[12]

Being irreverent and still effective

Legal Sea Foods' "Fresh Fish" transit ad campaign gained a great deal of press attention when a series of irreverent ads (Figure 12.20, Figure 12.21, Figure 12.22, Figure 12.23, Figure 12.24, Figure 12.25, Figure 12.26) appeared on taxicabs and trolley cars. Developed by the New York ad agency DeVito/ Verdi, some messages on the Green Line trolleys (trams) were considered so offensive, the MBTA (Massachusetts Bay Transportation Authority) banned them. The message particularly disparaging toward train conductors was: "This conductor has a face like a halibut."

FIGURE 12.20 This "Kiss My Bass" out-of-home ad was created by DeVito/Verdi for Legal Sea Foods. Image courtesy of DeVito/Verdi.

FIGURE 12.21 This "Bite Me" taxi-top ad was created by DeVito/Verdi for Legal Sea Foods. Image courtesy of DeVito/Verdi.

FIGURE 12.22 This "Carp" ambient ad was created by DeVito/Verdi for Legal Sea Foods. Image courtesy of DeVito/Verdi.

FIGURE 12.23 This "Halibut" taxi-top ad was created by DeVito/Verdi for Legal Sea Foods. Image courtesy of DeVito/Verdi.

FIGURE 12.24 This "Blowfish" ambient ad was created by DeVito/Verdi for Legal Sea Foods. Image courtesy of DeVito/Verdi.

FIGURE 12.25 This "Movie Sucks" out-of-home ad was created by DeVito/Verdi for Legal Sea Foods. Image courtesy of DeVito/Verdi.

FIGURE 12.26 This "Your Sister" taxi-top ad was created by DeVito/Verdi for Legal Sea Foods. Image courtesy of DeVito/Verdi.

The following list highlights the humor in the Legal Sea Foods irreverent messages. It also shows how a great idea can spin out. Don't be surprised if you find yourself smiling midway through.

1. If that's your girlfriend, I'd throw her back.
2. This cab gets around more than your sister.
3. This cab driver has a face like a halibut.
4. Damn, you smell like carp.
5. Kiss my bass.
6. Bite me.
7. Hey, Chumbug!
8. Is that a worm in your pocket or are you just happy to see me?
9. Your mother's a blowfish!
10. This movie sucks!

Legal Sea Foods CEO, Roger Berkowitz, responded on radio with what started out sounding like a "solemn" apology, but turned out to be an equally impertinent and similarly humorous answer.

We should have never, ever said, "This conductor has a face like a halibut," when the truth is, most conductors don't look anything at all like halibuts. Some look more like groupers or flounders. I've even seen a few who closely resemble catfish. And there's one conductor on the Green Line that looks remarkably like a hammerhead shark. So, we feel badly about this mischaracterization.[13]

The slogan "If it isn't fresh, it isn't Legal!" uses a *play-on-words* slogan technique (#4 in Chapter 10), and *humor* strategy (#25 in Chapter 6). The fact that the brand personality displayed a lack of self-restraint made the campaign even funnier. The line, "This cab gets around more than your sister," which is at first shocking, quickly becomes too funny to take as a serious offense. If you can't laugh once in a while at a mischievous-but-not-malicious remark, you're turning into a somber sour puss. This cheeky campaign also included print and TV.

The Escape Pod created another almost rebellious campaign for its client Feckin Irish Whiskey. You can tell just from the bold name that the brand's personality exhibits a proud sense of defiance.

Turning a once touchy subject into a humorous campaign

Vinny Warren, founder and director of The Escape Pod, talked about the Feckin Irish Whiskey campaign. The three posters (Figure 12.27, Figure 12.28, Figure 12.29), which appeared in many places, including bars and magazine ads, highlight, in a very funny way, Irish terrorism. A topic once considered too volatile to consider using in a campaign. It was used here mostly because of the target audience's familiarity with it. As Warren explained:

I looked at it and my thinking was what if you're a 22-year-old guy from Georgia? What are the two things you might know about Ireland? One of the things that you might know would be the film Snatch, *with the Irish Gypsy background. The other thing that you might know is we have history of terrorism, right?*

That's all finished now, thank God. But, it was one of the things that Ireland was known for. So, I figured let's key into that.[14]

Feckin Irish Whiskey, which ran a national campaign, introduced the brand using the tagline "The Spirit of Irish Rebellion." The language was warm and

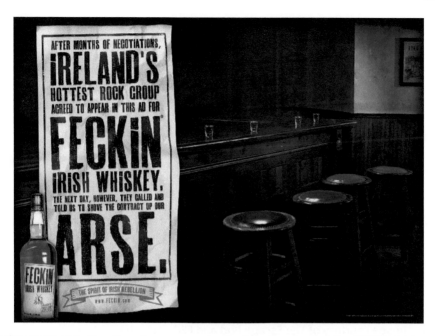

FIGURE 12.27 This "Arse" poster was created by The Escape Pod for FECKIN Irish Whiskey. Image courtesy of The Escape Pod and FECKIN Irish Whiskey.

FIGURE 12.28 This "Piss Off" poster was created by The Escape Pod for FECKIN Irish Whiskey. Image courtesy of The Escape Pod and FECKIN Irish Whiskey.

FIGURE 12.29 This "Abruptly" poster was created by The Escape Pod for FECKIN Irish Whiskey. Image courtesy of The Escape Pod and FECKIN Irish Whiskey.

familiar, as if you were having a drink with a buddy at a bar. Warren described the message, *tone of voice,* and brand positioning this way:

> *If you look at the tone of the ads, we were basically going after the shot whiskey market. So, we were competing with tequila and whatever else people would drink as a shot.*
>
> *That was the idea. It was positioning in that way as opposed to the usual romancing whiskey and all that middle-aged approach. We were just like, "Hey let's just drink it."*[15]

The campaign not only spoke in a bold way, with language like "arse" and "piss off," it also went head-to-head with an unexpected market, not other whiskeys, but with other alcohols used in shots.

Before we move on, look again at the copy in each poster. See how the art director emphasized certain words to draw in the reader. Also pay attention to the slogan and how it makes a direct statement: "The spirit of Irish rebellion."

"After months of negotiations, *Ireland's* hottest rock group agreed to appear in this ad for *Feckin* Irish Whiskey. The next day, however, they called and told us to shove the contract up our *arse.*" (Figure 12.27)

"Ireland's most famous movie star agreed to appear in this ad for *Feckin* Irish Whiskey. But at the very last minute, he cancelled and told us to *piss off.*" (Figure 12.28)

"Ireland's leading soccer player said he'd be happy to appear in this ad for *Feckin* Irish Whiskey. But alas never turned up to be photographed. When we called to ask him why *he just swore* at us and hung up *abruptly*." (Figure 12.29)

There was a fourth poster that continued in the same irreverent *tone of voice*. It demonstrated campaign continuity and read: *Headline*: Go Ahead Drop the F-Bomb. *Subhead*: 1.5 oz. of Feckin Irish Whiskey 16 oz. Beer (Any Kind).

This just shows how you can use potentially offensive language because you know you're speaking to an audience that wouldn't be offended. Realizing that these posters would be read in bars, made the verbiage even more appropriate.

Sometimes the location of the ad could be considered annoying, like TV spots on supposedly commercial-free, audio/video/streaming subscription services or messages in bathrooms. People may be tired of seeing messages everywhere. But now, some unexpected locations have become commonplace, like airline tray tables and quick-service restaurant tray liners. We'll now look at one great example of a tray liner next.

Finding new places to advertise

Just because your audience is already a customer doesn't mean you can't still market to them. In fact, they're the best ones to reach to strengthen the brand-consumer relationship. That's why you'll see creative messages in practical places like the playful Chick-fil-A tray liners (Figure 12.30). Here is a perfect opportunity to invite the target audience to come in for breakfast. They're already fans, so you're not convincing them to try Chick-fil-A, only to return in the morning. Look at how the type is set in the headline and notice the deliberate spelling errors as the cow invites you to come over to eat:

"Therz only one way 2 a great brekfust."

You couldn't expect more from a cow, could you?

When you're creating fun headlines, think about where else the message will appear.

Make sure it's portable. Ask yourself:

- Can your message work in another locale?
- Can you create an idea that *spins out*?
- Can it trigger audience participation?
- What other ideas could you use?

Good Ingredients Prepared Fresh.
It's The Chick-fil-A Way.

Every Chick-fil-A restaurant starts with quality ingredients, preparing all foods fresh daily. First and foremost, we use only 100% whole-breast chicken that's hand-breaded and cooked in peanut oil, which is naturally trans fat and cholesterol free. The cabbage for our Cole Slaw is chopped fresh daily, along with the carrots for our Carrot & Raisin Salad. Our wraps and salads are handcrafted daily with freshly cut vegetables. And it doesn't stop there. Even our delicious Iced Tea is brewed each day with our own special tea blend, and our Chick-fil-A Lemonade is freshly squeezed daily by hand. Freshness: it's key to our famous Chick-fil-A taste, and it always will be.

For complete nutritional details and dietary information, please visit chick-fil-a.com.

	Calories	Total Fat (g)	Saturated Fat (g)	Trans Fat (g)	Carbohydrates (g)	Protein (g)
Entrées						
Chick-fil-A' Chicken Sandwich	430	17	3.5	0	39	31
Chargrilled Chicken Sandwich	260	3	.5	0	33	27
Chargrilled Club Sandwich	380	12	5	0	34	36
Nuggets (8-count)	260	13	2.5	0	10	27
Chick-n-Strips" (3-count)	350	17	3.5	0	17	33
Chicken Salad Sandwich	500	20	3.5	0	53	29
Cool Wrap'						
Chargrilled Chicken Cool Wrap'	410	12	4	0	49	33
Spicy Chicken Cool Wrap'	400	12	4	0	47	35
Chicken Caesar Cool Wrap'	460	15	6	0	46	39
Salads						
Chargrilled Chicken Garden Salad	170	6	3.5	0	10	22
Chick-n-Strips" Salad	450	22	6	0	26	39
Southwest Chargrilled Salad	240	9	4	0	17	25
Chargrilled Chicken & Fruit Salad	220	6	3.5	0	21	22

	Calories	Total Fat (g)	Saturated Fat (g)	Trans Fat (g)	Carbohydrates (g)	Protein (g)
Sides						
Fruit Cup (medium)	70	0	0	0	17	0
Yogurt Parfait (no topping)	180	3	1.5	0	37	6
Waffle Potato Fries" (small)	280	16	3.5	0	31	3
Cole Slaw (small)	360	31	5	0	19	2
Carrot & Raisin Salad (small)	260	12	1.5	0	39	2
Side Salad	70	4.5	3	0	5	5
Hearty Breast of Chicken Soup (small)	150	4	1.5	0	19	9
Desserts						
Icedream' Cone (small)	170	4	2	0	31	5
Fudge Nut Brownie	370	19	6	0	45	5
Cheesecake (slice)	310	23	13	0.5	22	5
Vanilla Milkshake (small)	540	23	13	0	74	13
Chocolate Milkshake (small)	600	23	14	0	88	13
Strawberry Milkshake (small)	610	23	13	0	92	13
Cookies & Cream Milkshake (small)	570	26	14	0	80	14
Lemon Pie (slice)	360	13	6	0	58	6
Breakfast						
Chick-fil-A' Chicken Biscuit	450	20	8	0	48	19
Chicken Breakfast Burrito	420	18	7	0	41	22
Sausage Breakfast Burrito	480	27	11	0	38	21
Chicken, Egg & Cheese on Sunflower Multigrain Bagel	500	20	6	0	49	30
Chick-n-Minis" (3-count)	260	10	2.5	0	29	13
Cinnamon Cluster	400	15	6	0	61	8
Beverages						
Iced Tea -- Sweetened (small)	90	0	0	0	24	0
Freshly Squeezed Lemonade (small)	170	0	0	0	46	0
Freshly Squeezed Diet Lemonade (small)	15	0	0	0	6	0

Chick-fil-A uses 100% refined peanut oil. Nutritional values do not include condiments or dressings. This item is printed on 100% recycled paper that contains at least 26% post-consumer content.

FIGURE 12.30 This "Chikin Maze" tray liner was created by The Richards Group for Chick-fil-A, Inc. All trademarks shown on the tray liner are the property of CFA Properties, Inc. Image courtesy of The Richards Group and Chick-fil-A, Inc.

- Did you consider an alternative message:
  - For a different audience?
  - In another *tone of voice*?
  - With different benefits?

So, to me, the more you read and the more you fill your mind with different types of writing styles, I think that gives you more arrows in your quiver, if you will. Matt Ziselman, Creative Director, Sapient[16]

Driving a key point home with out-of-home ads

As we've seen earlier in Chapter 11 and we'll see later in Chapters 13 and 14, Hotel Tango presented one comprehensive campaign with one core concept: dedication to military precision. This appeared in the print ads (Figure 11.17, Figure 11.18, Figure 11.19, Figure 11.20), billboards (Figure 12.31, Figure 12.32),

FIGURE 12.31 This "Gin, Ready-to-View" out-of-home poster was created by Young & Laramore for Hotel Tango. Image courtesy of Young & Laramore.

FIGURE 12.32 This "Served with Distinction" out-of-home poster was created by Young & Laramore for Hotel Tango. Image courtesy of Young & Laramore.

package design (Figure 13.1, Figure 13.2, Figure 13.3, Figure 13.4, Figure 13.5, Figure 13.6, Figure 13.7, Figure 14.3, Figure 14.4), social media posts, website (Figure 14.1), and digital ads (Figure 14.2). What's most impressive is the consistent and distinctive look and tone. Each vehicle is instantly recognizable as part of the Hotel Tango lighthearted, yet respectful military salute that forms its brand positioning. Review the images and copy to best digest the power of this campaign. In short, it works in all channels, platforms, and formats.

Always look at multiple marketing messages from the same campaigns. Notice whether they're consistent for everyone or modified for each audience. Also, does the brand run multiple concepts simultaneously, while targeting different products or groups? Is it the same content in social media posts as it is for out-of-home, as in the Hotel Tango examples? Be an astute evaluator and apply what works. Keep a running log of your discoveries. They can become excellent sources for inspiration or lessons for what not to do. Read through Checklist 12.3 for some key questions to consider before you create ambient campaigns.

Whatever the medium, think beyond it. See what other ways you can use the message. If it's limited to just one particular platform, can you create a related concept for a different vehicle or channel? Be sure all your communications show a unified idea before settling on the campaign concept. If it's a *big idea*, it's not limited by medium because it's flexible. It's bendable. And it lends itself to adaptation.

CHECKLIST 12.3 Creative ambient checklist

Is it innovative?

Is it unexpected?

Is it relevant (to the brand and audience)?

Is it unusual?

Is it unforgettable?

Is it interactive?

Is it succinct?

Is it in a first-ever medium (or location)?

Is it portable? (Will it work in other venues?)

Is it legible if there is movement (like a subway car, taxi, escalator, or rotating billboard)?

Is it inviting?

Is it a big idea?

Is it press worthy? (Will it generate press attention?)

Creative ambient exercises

Exercise 1: Make a list of ambient messages in places you've never seen before

Exercise 2: Think up two new places for new ambient messages

- What kind of product or service would work in these locations?
- How could you make it more engaging and entertaining?
- Could you use animation? Illumination? Movement? 3D? Interactivity?

Exercise 3: Write stop-'em-in-their-tracks headlines for each of the two ambient messages

- Check that they're appropriate for the brand and they'll target the audience.
- Make sure they work from one concept that can spin out to several, related headline ideas (to prepare for Exercise 5).

Exercise 4: Create a humorous, on-target, on-strategy message for one of the messages

Exercise 5: Spin this message out and create related concepts to use in two other ambient locations

Notes

1. https://draytonbird.com/2015/01/7-money-making-facts-marketers-dont-know/ (accessed November 10, 2022).
2. Margo Berman, *The Brains Behind Great Ad Campaigns: Creative Collaboration Between Copywriters and Art Directors* (Lanham, MD: Rowman & Littlefield, 2009), 200.
3. Vinny Warren, personal communication, December 14, 2022.
4. Margo Berman, *Street-Smart Advertising: How to Win the Battle of the Buzz* (Lanham, MD: Rowman & Littlefield, 2010), 13.
5. Margo Berman, *Street-Smart Advertising: How to Win the Battle of the Buzz* (Lanham, MD: Rowman & Littlefield, 2010), 109.
6. http://viralingoutofcontrol.wordpress.com/page/2/ (accessed February 20, 2011).
7. Craig Miller, personal communication, March 31, 2022.

8. Drummond Berman, personal communication, April 8, 2009.
9. Drummond Berman, personal communication, April 8, 2009.
10. Drummond Berman, personal communication, April 8, 2009.
11. Drummond Berman, personal communication, April 8, 2009.
12. Charlie Hopper, personal communication, November 26, 2021.
13. Roger Berkowitz, personal communication, March 17, 2011.
14. Vinny Warren, personal communication, December 14, 2022.
15. Vinny Warren, personal communication, December 14, 2022.
16. Matt Ziselman, Creative Director at Sapient, personal communication, January 30, 2009.

13

The Abridged Word
Small-space Writing:
Direct Mail, Package
Copy, Coupons,
Freebies, etc.

"Packaging is often the first and only ad the consumer sees."
Carolyn Hadlock, Principal and Executive
Creative Director, Young & Laramore[1]

In the following pages, you'll learn the difference between direct mail and direct response. And why, with direct mail, you need to think about creating the outside message before the inside one. You'll realize that even the most mundane assignments can be creative, like the Hotel Tango packaging. You'll find out why direct mail is still being used and how to make it fun, effective, and strategic. You'll be referred back to Chapter 6, so you can review the 50 types of strategies.

Content and Copywriting: The Complete Toolkit for Strategic Marketing,
Second Edition. Margo Berman.
© 2024 Margo Berman. Published 2024 by John Wiley & Sons Ltd.
Companion website: www.wiley.com/go/contentandcopywriting

You'll also read about writing sales letters. If you're thinking, "Who cares?" You do. You may be writing a letter of introduction to a prospective employer or as a follow up email after an interview. Yes, they're sales letters. And, they need to be persuasive.

You'll be reminded to think about other direct methods of reaching your audience, such as emails, mobile coupons, product-related apps, games, interactive ads, and so on. You'll read about tips for creating successful email marketing campaigns. You'll discover the importance of editing down your writing for small-space messages like coupons, catalogs, signage, and product packaging. Best of all, you'll examine some exciting examples of humorous package copy, including Hotel Tango and Red Brick Beer.

Okay, enough said. Now let's begin our investigation of the delivered word through direct mail, mobile, and small-space messaging.

Exploring direct mail

No matter how many people believe direct mail is an ancient marketing tactic, it still exists. Therefore, well-rounded copywriters need to be equally comfortable in this and in other small-space media vehicles. We'll now examine the writing techniques that create powerful direct marketing communication. So that the received material is read and saved, not ignored and tossed. What's unique about direct mail is that there two parts to consider when writing: (1) the outside and (2) the inside (or reverse side). Writing a compelling message for the outside of the piece instantly captures the recipient's attention. That is true whether it's on the envelope of an inserted piece, on the front side of a self-mailer (marketing materials sent without an envelope), or on a handed-out postcard. For example, if a headline on the envelope reads, "Ummm... there's an ice cream cake inside," you might open it. Inside could be a coupon from Carvel or Dairy Queen.

Here are a few points to remember when creating copy that will be delivered as a *direct mail* piece in the mail. This is often confused with *direct response* mechanisms. Those are messages with a call to action, not necessarily delivered by the post office. They cover a wide range of media: printed pieces like door hangers, magazine sleeves, messages on dry cleaning bags, and coupons; *out-of-home* ads like billboards with 1-800 numbers; digital coupons on websites, texted to mobile devices or sent by email; and so on. Let's get back to direct mail.

Checklist 13.1 is a short, useful list of considerations. The last example (e) is called an "eyebrow" in a print ad. We discussed this in Chapters 10 and 11. As a reminder, it's a line of copy that sits before the headline and targets a specific audience.

Media change; customers don't. Drayton Bird, Writer, Speaker, Marketer and Author of Commonsense Direct & Digital Marketing[2]

Grasping why to use direct mail

Before you write anything that's going to be mailed, you must clearly understand why this particular format was chosen as the medium.

CHECKLIST 13.1 Direct mail handy checklist

1 Consider the outside first.
   a How can you get the recipient to read a self-mailer?
   b What could you say on an envelope or box to entice the addressee to see what's inside?
      i Ask an intriguing question.
      ii Make a seemingly outrageous, yet true statement. ("There's a tractor in this box." Inside is a children's toy.)
      iii Deliver an important and relevant fact.
      iv Offer savings or a coupon.
      v State there's a product sample inside (a small consumer tester, like a tiny bottle of shampoo, a mini bar of soap, or a little box of cookies).
2 Know how this piece will be sent.
   a To an occupant through bulk mail?
   b To a specific, named recipient through standard mail?
   c To a targeted and restricted audience through a priority or rush delivery?
3 Think about how to personalize the message.
   a Feature how the company, product, or service solves problems.
   b Demonstrate why readers need to act now.
   c Propose a limited, time-sensitive offer.
   d Present an immediate or frequent-user discount.
   e Address the consumer as a product user. For example: "Attention Dry-Eye Sufferers" or "Cookie Lovers."

Look at these questions and be sure you can answer them before you start developing the copy:

- What benefits are there in direct mail?
- What's the purpose of the piece?

- What needs to be said first?
- Who's your primary audience?
- What do they need to hear?
- How will this product help them?
- What do you want them to know?

Even if you throw out all the junk mail you receive, you should start looking at the pieces that you at least glanced at. If you receive or discover a great direct mail piece, keep it and start a "clip" or "swipe" file with exciting examples. This way, you'll always have a reference. Also, be sure you're reading award annuals like the *One Show*, going online to see industry award show winners like the Cannes Lions International Festival of Creativity, D&AD, Clio, and the Art Directors Club, or trade publications like *Advertising Age (Ad Age)*, *Adweek*, *Communication Arts*, and more. Some publications have related magazines like *Ad Age's Creativity*.

Drayton Bird, writer, speaker, marketer and author, who ran Ogilvy & Mather Direct in London, has written several advertising and copywriting books. His classic, written more than 25 years ago, *Commonsense Direct & Digital Marketing* is in its fifth edition. There's a quote on the cover by David Ogilvy that reads, "Read it and re-read it. It contains the knowledge of a lifetime." The inside cover added another Ogilvy quote: "Drayton Bird knows more about Direct Marketing than anyone in the world. His book about it is pure gold." In one of his articles, he lists "51 Helpful Direct Mail Ideas." I've selected the following dozen tips and included in parenthesis their original numbers.

1. *(#1) Communicate more than your competitors.*
2. *(#2) Do what a salesman would do.*
3. *(#9) Write from me to you – never from a "team."*
4. *(#14) Online marketing is just accelerated offline marketing.*
5. *(#16) Use "reason why" copy.*
6. *(#21) Always make it easy to respond.*
7. *(#26) Read your copy out loud.*
8. *(#27) Use research for illumination. Not support.*
9. *(#29) Leave well enough alone if tests prove something new won't be better.*
10. *(#32) Search the world and steal the best.*

11. *(#38) Spend 90% of your time thinking about how to single out your prospect.*

12. *(#47) Until you know how to do better, copy.*[3]

From his website (https://draytonbird.com) you can read several helpful articles. Here's an excerpt from "7 Deadly Sins and How to Improve Results."

> *Why do many people call direct mail "junk"? Because most is.*
>   *But sending sloppy junk to people is really a form of personal insult. It says you don't care. Here's where people go wrong – and how you can make your messages work much, much better.*

1. *Not taking it seriously.*

2. *Failure to test.*

3. *Not aiming at the right people.*

4. *Trying to be clever.*

5. *Being too brief.*

6. *Omitting essentials.*

7. *Not having a letter.*[4]

When asked how often a marketer should write to a consumer, Bird said: "The question is not how often do you write, it is what you say when you write." He continued by saying, "The aim is that people should look forward to getting it, not "more bloody sales stuff from them."[5]

Direct mail is not a hit-and-miss medium. Each piece that's sent out can be tested for its effectiveness by tracking the call to action. For example, how many coded (for tracking purposes) people responded? How many calls came in to a designated toll-free number? Or, how many people scanned a QR code to make a purchase? And, so on.

Writing for a direct mail message means being pithy. Get to the point and have a benefit. Before approving the copy ask yourself: "Would I read this or ignore it?" If it's in an envelope, ask, "Would I open it or toss it out?" Be honest. Be painfully truthful with yourself. If it bores you, it will bore the reader. It doesn't matter what the medium. The message is still about being relevant, *on-strategy*, *on-target*, and engaging. So, the audience will respond.

Even if you rarely ever write direct mail, you still need to be versed in the medium. Although his agency doesn't create a great deal of direct mail, Vinny Warren, founder and creative director of The Escape Pod, explained his agency's approach to this vehicle like this:

> *Obviously, it's a cousin of print. Basically, with direct mail what you're doing is hoping that what you're saying is exactly what the person needs to hear. So generally speaking it's like, "Do you need a new boiler?" "Oh, I need a new boiler."*
>
> *So, it's like you have to assume interest, I think. You have to assume interest in general, but in this case, in direct mail, you have to go with the assumption that it is, "Oh, this is exactly what this person needs on some level."[6]*

When you're creating an everyday email or a promotional or informational e-zine (online magazine) message, think about breaking up the copy with bold subheads that move the reader along. Charlie Hopper, principal at Young & Laramore explained, "You can't think of the writing without thinking of how and where and when people will encounter it. The Web has made it very relevant, but it's all in context."[7] He continued:

> *You have to think about what order people are reading it, where they're entering it, where they're exiting, what little stations you give them to get in and out, and that's why the design is very relevant. Because like it or not, your writing is part of a great deluge of words and thoughts and images, not even just in an advertising context, in any context these days. Even if you send an e-mail, don't send a long e-mail. Break it up. Put a little bit up at the top and introduce it with something relevant and deliver your message and get it out.[8]*

The copy has to show the audience why they want the product or service. Think W-I-I-F-Ms. Remember that means "What's in it for me?" If you can't clearly demonstrate the benefit, who cares? No one has time to bother reading irrelevant materials.

Here's a crucial tip: Never underestimate the importance of package design. Yes, that's also an important, sometimes overlooked touchpoint.

> *The campaign starts in aisle with the packaging. Carolyn Hadlock, Principal and Executive Creative Director at Young & Laramore[9]*

Besides marketing materials that you will create for clients, you should also learn how to write strong sales letters, as well. Why? Because you probably will be writing a letter of introduction for a dream job or a global account someday. So, learning how to spark the reader's interest will always serve you well, especially if that person is your prospective employer or client. If your letter is strong enough, it could at least land you an interview or meeting.

Learning a few pointers about writing self-promotion letters

Writing a powerful letter is not a useless skill. And, no, it's not a lost art. It's a vital skill you need to develop. That is, if you want to work at your first-choice agency or company and if you want to write proposal letters that grab the attention of potential clients. Some people have landed interviews and client pitch (presentation) invitations just from the strength of their introduction letters.

Okay, so how do you begin? By becoming the recipient and asking: "What do I need to hear to keep reading?" Creative hiring decision-makers are looking to be entertained, surprised, impressed, and basically swept away by your persuasive copy.

Here are a few basic rules to keep in mind from one of the most respected direct mail marketers, Drayton Bird, whom we've mentioned earlier.

Notice how this list of points in Advice from the Pros 13.2 works equally well whether you're looking to be hired as a job applicant by an employer or as an agency by a client. The most important point is to remember what you can provide, not what you're looking to get, like invaluable experience. Turn the letter around in your mind. Then, feature what you bring to the proverbial table.

ADVICE FROM THE PROS 13.2 Drayton Bird's job-interview writing principles

1 Only approach the right people – the ones you think you can do a good job for; those for whom your "product" – you and your talents – is right.

2 Conduct reconnaissance. Learn as much as you can about the people you want to work for. This will enable you to speak to the right people and address their needs. It also shows you have been keen enough to learn about them. Every time I get a letter from a job applicant, which refers to something my company or I have done, I read with quickened interest. Like everyone else I am interested in people who are interested in me.

3 Following that, talk about the interests of your prospect, not your own (nearly all job application letters I see talk about what the applicant wants rather than "What's in it for me?").

4 Then move on to your special skills, which you must relate to the needs of your potential employer, just as you must relate the needs of your customer to your product or service.

5 Put in some impartial proof that what you say is true. Hardly any letters do. Almost invariably when somebody writes to me for a job, I write back and ask them for comments from previous employers, as well as samples of their work.

6 Include a résumé, which gives every reason why you should be hired.

7 Make it abundantly clear that you're eager to work for the people you're writing to and say why.[10]

For successful sales letters, Bird lists five specific ingredients. These are: (1) Know your product or service. (2) Think about your prospects (potential customers or clients). (3) Create an offer or incentive to take action. (4) Polish your writing technique. (5) Demonstrate your writing talent. Bird pointed out that the first three ingredients, or components, don't include talent, but emphasize content.[11] As long as the content is focused on the product and consumer, and offers an incentive to buy, the letter will still succeed. You might present a trial offer or money-back guarantee (if it's a product). That gives consumers more confidence to make the purchase. First, refer to Advice from the Pros 13.2. Then, consider including the following when writing your own "pitch":

1. Select the agencies or companies you believe are a "fit" for your creative talent.

2. Show that you are highly familiar with the kind of accounts they handle and/or creative work they do.

3. Provide a glimpse into your creativity by writing in an engaging way.

4. Consider using visuals. Yes, in a letter. They're unexpected.

5. State clearly why you're a match.

6. Demonstrate your innovative thinking and unique skills.

7. Sell them on YOU!

Whatever you're creating – whether it's direct mail, email, e-newsletter, or mobile message – you must show readers why they should respond. Paint a benefit-laden self-portrait and present an irresistible offer. Think mutual benefit and reward.

Now, review Checklist 13.3 to polish your email writing skills.

 CHECKLIST 13.3 Some email writing tips

1 Write a targeted, response-driving subject line in emails

Be sure the reader knows what to do: get tickets, renew a subscription, redeem a coupon, download content, etc. If there's a benefit, there may be a reason to read on. Now, make it exciting. Instead of saying, "It's coming," say, "Don't miss it." Replace "New update" with "Get ready to discover." You get the idea.

2 Don't waste the readers' time

If your email message doesn't relate to your readers, they won't read it. Would you? No, of course not. See every message as one that should help your audience. What do they want? What do they need? What do they care about? Start there. If your email or text doesn't target them, change it.

3 Speak directly to them

Don't be self-serving. It's not about your company or services. It's about them. So speak to them using appropriate pronouns. Replace "we" and "our" with "you" and "your." No one cares if your firm won awards. People care that what you offer can help solve their problems. A terrific, but irrelevant product doesn't do anything for that reader.

4 Talk about what matters: benefits

See the letter "i" in "benefits" as the old question: "What's in it for me?" How does this help me, the consumer? Having lower fat content in food is a feature. The benefit is that it helps people eat more healthily and stick to their dietary goals.

5 Get to the point

Who has time to wade through a lot of wordy text? Now, hang on a minute. Drayton Bird, one of the direct mail experts, said just the opposite: Long copy works. It can and it does. But, so does shorter copy, when used correctly. Ask yourself if you have many details that consumers need to understand to make a decision. If they do, cover the topic with details. If not, get in and get out.[12]

Creating messages for mobile email marketing

Messages today reach consumers everywhere they are. Mobile devices have become yet another medium to speak to them. Marketers are using them to stay in touch, as reminder notices for medications, as coupon delivery systems, as product-related apps, as ad vehicles within interactive games (as mentioned in Chapter 4), and more. Rather than being hesitant to develop mobile messages, jump in. You just need to realize, if you have a smartphone or another device, you're already playing in the arena.

When you read a blog, notice how the writer takes you step by step through the process and wraps everything up at the end. Focus every time you're reading. Analyze what made you continue. Then, learn from writers that pull you in.

In addition, study sentence length, organization, tone of voice, and overall writing style. Examine whatever you read. Dissect the prose or copy. Don't be a sleepy reader. Be alert and analytical. Soon, you'll pick up useful techniques just by noticing them. Whether they're journalists, bloggers, novelists, nonfiction writers, or copywriters. If you can't stop until you finish what you're reading, become a student of that writer.

Take a look at the Small-space writing checklist (Checklist 13.4) before you create copy that must fit in a limited space, such as table tents, out-of-home posters, in-store signage, packaging, and so on.

CHECKLIST 13.4 Small-space writing checklist

1 Think Small.
   a Say more in less.
   b Rush to the main idea.
   c Delete all unnecessary copy.
2 Become an Observer.
   a Go shopping for examples.
   b What stopped you in the store:
      i Package design?
      ii Colors on package?
      iii Copy on box?
3 Ask Yourself: What Would Make You Buy?
   With just a few words to say, be critical. Ask, did it:
   a Create curiosity?
   b Answer an objective?
   c Provide a solution?
   d Promise entertainment?
4 Collect Great Examples.
   a Create a swipe or clip file.
   b Save packages, including:
      i Items you purchased
      ii Products with amazing packaging, including:
         1 Perfumes
         2 Alcoholic beverages
         3 Unique teas
      vi Product packaging with exciting copy
         1 Toys
         2 Books
         3 Games
         4 Cereals
         5 Digital devices

Writing copy for product packaging

Brevity is the key to product package copy. Space limitation forces writers to condense their thoughts down to the most minimal expression. Whether they're developing messages for cereal boxes or canned goods, movie DVDs, album covers, or pizza boxes, package writers must say more in less space. Although package design drives the consumers' eye to the product, the message must clarify what it contains to help make the sale. Let's examine the difficulties and solutions to package writing in this small-space overview.

Here's a crucial tip: Never underestimate the importance of package design. Yes, that's also an important, sometimes overlooked touchpoint.

> *This is old, but the package is an ad. Carolyn Hadlock, Principal and Executive Creative Director at Young & Laramore*[12]

In case you think writing copy for packaging is not exciting, think again. The most mundane writing assignments are there to test your creativity. If you were told you needed to write copy for alcohol bottle labels, you might sniff your nose at that. But, before you do, take a look at how the writers at Young & Laramore answered that challenge in Hotel Tango. The writing is clever and honest. It speaks from the founder's life experiences as a combat-wounded, disabled Marine. You feel as if the founder is talking to you.

The slogan, "Distilled with Discipline," tells all. The rest of the copy, including lines such as, "Pour with purpose. Serve with honor." continue the "Corps Competency" theme. Even the campaign on the website, stated: "Made by a Marine = Made the right way." The Young & Laramore creative team shared these ideas on the agency's site:

> *That's the idea at the heart of the Hotel Tango brand. But, without the right messaging, it wasn't coming through. Instead, Hotel Tango's military connection – it's the first combat-disabled, veteran-owned distillery in the country – was seen as a novelty rather than a reason to believe. You might buy a bottle for a relative who served, but you wouldn't buy one for yourself.*
>
> *We addressed that challenge with a complete rebranding that reflects the meticulous approach Travis Barnes, HT's founder, learned in his time as a decorated Marine. It's that mindset that he brings to all nine spirits Hotel Tango crafts – and why we say they're "Distilled with Discipline."*[13]

Read through the on-point, unexpected label copy (Scripts and Examples 13.5). You might never skip reading product packages again.

Examining examples of creative package copy

Just as you should glance at all incoming junk mail, you should also look at every item you buy. Examine every promotional item you receive. And pay attention to the copy, even on your breakfast cereal boxes. If you pay attention, you could discover some entertaining writing at the most unexpected places, such as on the shelves in a liquor store, or specialty shop, or supermarket.

When you find innovative package copy, take a moment and identify the types of techniques and strategies that were used. Notice the use of mandatory copy, generally referred to as "mandatories," gives loyalists a chance to contact the company directly and order more of the products online or in-store.

Let's take a closer look at Hotel Tango packaging. As mentioned above and in Chapter 11, a permanently injured, decorated Marine created the brand with military precision. The headlines and copy reflect this. But, the infusion of humor through marketing language, which was subtly embedded in throughout the campaign, is refreshing. It appears on the bottle labels, outer packaging, posters, and billboards. You might find yourself smiling as you read the copy carefully in the following examples. (See Figure 13.1, Figure 13.2, Figure 13.3, Figure 13.4, Figure 13.5, Figure 13.6, Figure 13.7) We will see more of the cohesive, strategically focused campaign in Chapter 14 (Figure 14.1, Figure 14.2, Figure 14.3, Figure 14.4).

 SCRIPTS AND EXAMPLES 13.5 Package copy for Hotel Tango

1 Distilled with Discipline
2 High-standard issue
3 Pour with purpose. Serve with honor.
4 Fit to serve. Made to share.
5 Purpose of contents: To be served and consumed in pursuance of elevated company morale.

(Copy courtesy of Young & Laramore.)

FIGURE 13.1 This "Reserve Bourbon, Ready-to-Drink" front package design was created by Young & Laramore for Hotel Tango. Image courtesy of Young & Laramore.

FIGURE 13.2 This "Reserve Bourbon, Ready-to-Drink" back package design was created by Young & Laramore for Hotel Tango. Image courtesy of Young & Laramore.

FIGURE 13.3 This "Gin, Ready-to-Drink" bottle-label design was created by Young & Laramore for Hotel Tango. Image courtesy of Young & Laramore.

FIGURE 13.4 This "Gin, Ready-to-Drink" front package design was created by Young & Laramore for Hotel Tango. Image courtesy of Young & Laramore.

FIGURE 13.5 This "Gin, Ready-to-Drink" back package design was created by Young & Laramore for Hotel Tango. Image courtesy of Young & Laramore.

FIGURE 13.6 This "Rum, Ready-to-Drink" front package design was created by Young & Laramore for Hotel Tango. Image courtesy of Young & Laramore.

FIGURE 13.7 This "Rum, Ready-to-Drink" back package design was created by Young & Laramore for Hotel Tango. Image courtesy of Young & Laramore.

The copy was purposeful and amusing, as shown on the labels, packaging, print and digital ads, out-of-home, and online product pages. Notice #8 in the list below. This bourbon label is in red, white, and blue in honor of the veterans. A donation of one dollar would be given to the American Legion in support of programs that help veterans. The directions state, "Drink thankfully."

1. *Reserve Bourbon back of package* (Figure 13.2)

   DESCRIPTION: A well-balanced, dignified, wheated bourbon. Refined sweetness. What Chesty would drink.

   DIRECTIONS: Serve with heightened expectations.

2. *Gin back of package* (Figure 13.5)

   DESCRIPTION: New-wave style. Citrus-forward. Versatile. Pleasing to gin vets and newcomers alike.

   DIRECTIONS: Enjoy with a camaraderie chaser.

3. *Rum back of package* (Figure 13.7)

   DESCRIPTION: Subtle sweetness. Dry on the palate. Soft finish. Elevates any Mai Tai.

   DIRECTIONS: Never to be used in the same sentence as "chug."

4. *Bourbon back of package* (Figure 14.4)

   DESCRIPTION: Young and approachable, cocktail whiskey. Corn-sweetness, balanced by rye. Best in a cocktail.

   DIRECTIONS: Serve with heightened expectations.

5. *Rye (web)*

   DESCRIPTION: Spicy finish. Subtle sweetness. Deceptively smooth. Sazerac-ready.

   DIRECTIONS: Water down at your own risk.

6. *Cherry Liqueur (web)*

   DESCRIPTION: Tart, Montmorency Cherry Juice. Balanced. Vibrant sweetness. Gives your mule a real kick.

   Directions: Not to be confused with anything "cordial."

7. *Lemoncello Liqueur (web)*

   DESCRIPTION: Citrus-forward, new world Lemoncello. Higher proof. Hand-peeled. Lemon drop-able. Best consumed within 60 days of opening. Shake well. Serve chilled.

   DIRECTIONS: Sip. Pucker. Repeat.

8. *American Straight Bourbon Whiskey (web): "Red, White & Bourbon"*

   DESCRIPTION: For every bottle of Hotel Tango "Red, White & Bourbon" sold, $1 will be donated to the American Legion to support veteran programs.

   DIRECTIONS: Drink thankfully.

It's important to notice how the online product pages of Hotel Tango Distillery also introduced additional clever copy, including "Drink responsibly. Behave less so." That's a fun use of the *imperative* or *command* technique (#11), as discussed in Chapter 10.

Don't just look at imaginative package copy, emulate it. The best way to improve your small-space writing is to discover and review imaginative writing. Then, use the copy as inspiration for your assignments and future or current clients.

Learning some tips for small-space writing from Charlie Hopper

Charlie Hopper, principal at Young & Laramore, explained that writers need only to write enough lines to get the point across. Regardless of the advertising vehicle, small-space messages must punctuate the points. Eliminate everything that's superfluous and focus on what you want the reader to know. Here are his tips for writing with space restrictions.

Charlie Hopper's tips for small-space writing

1. In every case – and every single medium from banner-being-flown-off-the-back-of-an-airplane-at-the-seashore to a blog entry – the same basic rule always applies: only say what you have to say, and get out. Don't assume people are looking to fill their time by reading your wonderful writing. Say it, and get away.

2. In this age, you have to be interesting or just forget it. Even in a small space, you have to say something worth thinking about, worth spending time with. Because whether you have a Super Bowl ad or a small space, and somehow you induce the reader to spend a moment looking at your copy, they'll instantly forget it and it will be the same net result as if they didn't read it. Be relevant, and surprising, no matter how much or how little space you have. Say it, be charming (but don't fool around using a lot of space being charming) and get away.

3. Skip the intro. Don't tell them that you're going to be interesting in a moment.

4. Short sentences help. It makes your writing a lot more muscular, and it lures in the reader. They subconsciously note that the sentences are brief. They figure, they can get in and get out. Then they're stuck. Eventually, for rhythm, you might introduce a longer sentence just so you don't sound punchy. But then, be brief again.

5. Go back and edit. In that second sentence in the previous paragraph, I'd originally written, "It makes your writing a lot more muscular..." By removing "a lot" I didn't lose much, and I have two words I can spend later on something else.[14]

Other product package copy only used a branded name, a slogan, or a headline. For example, when The Escape Pod developed an OfficeMax brand of "Back-To-School" items, it named the line "Schoolio Von Hoolio." It was fun, catchy, and it *rhymed* (#2 writing technique we discussed in Chapter 10). It also had no copy and what agency president and founder Vinny Warren called "crazy design." It was easy for kids to ask their parents for it and it was a clever way to introduce a new product line. Vinny Warren explained the packaging like this:

> *It was more of a brand idea that the packaging was integral to. The idea was packaging in a way. It's a "Back-To-School" brand designed to compete. It's an OfficeMax brand. It was designed to compete with Crayola. Their thinking was crayons are crayons. Most of this stuff is generic. So, basic packaging is the thing that can make the difference.*
>
> *And so our "Schoolio Von Hoolio," if you were a kid at age 10, "Schoolio Von Hoolio" is going to appeal to you more than Crayola, I'm guessing. Because it's more whimsical.*
>
> *The "Hoolio" is about all the "Back-To-School" stuff. Folders, you name it. It became their internal brand.*[15]

When you're developing copy for packages, you may only need to focus on creating a sticky brand name. Sometimes the package design says everything. For example, when a plastic yellow lid was placed on top of a Heineken beer, it resembled a tennis ball container. The design said it all. It was a clear visual statement that instantly connected Heineken to a tennis tournament as a US Open sponsorship. Heineken has continued this relationship for more than 19 years, creating promotional items to increase consumer brand recall.[16]

One more package design and copy worthy of your full attention is Red Brick Beer, created by 22squared. Developed by Red Brick Brewery, this was a regional beer. The challenge was to reach 120 million Southern beer lovers. How? By speaking "Southernese." And, by integrating iconic Southern phrases and recognizable visuals. The unifying and catchy campaign slogan was "Beer from around here." It had a friendly, familiar, and neighborly tone. It also implied a *universal truth*: "The rest of the world is crazy."

With a tiny media budget, 22squared utilized the packaging itself to sell the product (Figure 13.8, Figure 13.9, Figure 13.10, Figure 13.11). The copy made interesting statements and humorous comments on each of the six-packs, such as:

1. *Pale Ale* – Like a classic California pale ale, but from America. Best served cold. Straight from the bottle. Or a glass. Or a mason jar.

2. *Blonde* – This Blonde has a good crisp body. Stop your snickerin. Best served cold. On the porch. In the early evening. With a dog.

3. *Brown* – A nice, smooth ale. Says "Yes sir" and "Yes ma'am." Best served cold. Best served below the latitude of 39° 43° 20° N.

4. *Porter* – As thick and stout as a BBQ line cook. Best served cool. On a cold day. But not "Boston" cold. That weather should be illegal.

FIGURE 13.8 This "Beer from around Here" Pale Ale package design was created by 22squared for Red Brick Beer. Image courtesy of 22squared.

FIGURE 13.9 This "Beer from around Here" Brown package design was created by 22squared for Red Brick Beer. Image courtesy of 22squared.

FIGURE 13.10 This "Beer from around Here" bottle package design was created by 22squared for Red Brick Beer. Image courtesy of 22squared.

FIGURE 13.11 This "Beer from around Here" Southern Sampler package design was created by 22squared for Red Brick Beer. Image courtesy of 22squared.

There are also funny quotes on each six-pack from "Bob," as if consumers knew him.

Here are a few examples (Figure 13.12, Figure 13.13). "Bob at Red Brick says:" ...

1. "My friend started drinking Northern brews and soon he was saying the word pop."

2. "When you buy New England beer you're just giving more money to the Queen."

3. "The problem with beer from Milwaukee is that the label's all in Milwaukeean."

4. "We call it Helluva Bock. But you can call it Heckuva Bock if you're drinking it in church."

Curt Mueller, creative director and writer for the Red Brick campaign explained how he and the designer worked together, exchanging ideas back and forth:

> During this project, I sat directly next to the designer and we constantly traded copy and designs back and forth. We inspired each other, and we were brutally honest with each other. As a writer on packaging design projects, you have to leave your ego at the door. Your words are only important in so far as they complement the overall design and tone.[17]

He described the brand's uniquely Southern personality and whimsical *tone of voice* in this way:

> The South has always seen itself as its own country. We leveraged this attitude and created a new enemy to fight against: the non-Southern import. Our packaging reflected Southern sensibilities and the idea that all beer from outside the South is an import. We added Southern visual references and a lot of Southern humor to make it go down easy.[18]

Once you look at the campaign carefully, you're able to see how strategically driven the message was. Mueller reduced the creative brief down to one concise sentence:

> Immediately increase sales of Red Brick beer by appealing to Southern craft beer drinkers.[19]

FIGURE 13.12 This "Beer from around Here" "Bob Says" side of Pale Ale package design was created by 22squared for Red Brick Beer. Image courtesy of 22squared.

FIGURE 13.13 This "Beer from around Here" "Bob Says" side of Brown package design was created by 22squared for Red Brick Beer. Image courtesy of 22squared.

He shared the strategic thinking behind the copy in four points:

1. *Their marketing needed a single voice.*

2. *Their budget didn't allow for a significant marketing push.*

3. *We would have to take advantage of their free media: their packaging. The packaging would have to tell the story of Red Brick and be their "advertising."*

4. *99% of craft beer brands speak like someone you'd hate to have a beer with. We wanted to talk like an old friend – a self-deprecating, half-drunk, Full-Southern friend.*[20]

What is interesting to note is when asked if the copy changed from market to market. Mueller commented, "No, being proudly xenophobic is part of Red Brick's charm."[21]

He went on to describe how the slogan was the catalyst behind the concept, message product names, and package design, creating an instantly recognizable visual impression.

> *Red Brick is a craft beer made by Atlanta Brewing Company in Atlanta, GA. We redesigned not just their packaging, but their entire visual identity, using the tagline "Beer From Around Here" and the concept that all beer from outside the Southern states is effectively an import. We simplified the names of their products, added writing with Southern personality, and incorporated visual cues from Southern industrial products. With a limited ad budget, we made the packaging the advertising, and managed to turn a brand with no recognizable identity into a brand with not just an identity, but a rich cultural story.*[22]

What were the objectives and results of this campaign? Red Brick wanted to increase sales by 100%. Sales far exceeded that goal within a year. There's no question that this humorous package copy's success was nothing to laugh at.

Take a moment to review the Basic writing tips listed here (Advice from the Pros 13.6). Think of them when you're creating copy.

What you should notice is how product-centric campaigns, like those mentioned above, can create buzz. They created attention because the ideas

ADVICE FROM THE PROS 13.6 Basic writing tips from Curt Mueller

1 Inhale writing that isn't advertising, from Tolstoy to Twilight.

2 Don't have a style. You're a copywriter, not a novelist. Be adaptable.

3 Don't work as hard as senior writers and creative directors, work harder. You're not yet adept at recognizing when you're "there." Keep going long past when you think it's time to quit.

4 Start by writing exactly what you want to say, as simply as possible. Write it at the top of the page and refer to it often.

5 At times you'll feel like a genius; at times you'll feel like an illiterate hack. Neither is true.[23]

were unique and unexpected. Challenge yourself to use interesting media (like smell marketing) in an innovative way for future clients.

Copy for all small-space vehicles requires a special kind of thinking. Writers know the space is limited, so they must begin by deleting whatever is not crucial to the message and distill the copy down to its bare bones of necessary facts.

Creating coupon copy, digital discounts, and freebies

Other examples of restricted-space messaging are coupons, from traditional print to digital, including online, email, mobile, such as QR codes (as in coupons for print ads, digital deals, during TV program pauses, or commercials), and more. When people look for coupons, they want two things: savings and a great or free offer. When Teddy Brown, senior vice president, executive creative director at Planet Propaganda, was asked to talk about Taco Bell coupons, he said:

> They'll do coupons to stimulate traffic. For instance, right now there's a Black Jack Taco spot on the air and they are running a free taco night giveaway. But usually it's this notion of free that stimulates traffic pretty decently. So it's a "Free Taco After Dark," from 6 p.m. to midnight on Halloween.
>
> They'll do things like that. They'll do tie-ins with major league baseball like America gets a free taco if someone steals the base.[24]

He was talking about the "Steal a Base, Steal a Taco" campaign. During the World Series, whenever a baseball player from either team stole a base, Taco Bell gave away a free "Beef Crunchy Taco" to anyone who wanted one.[25] Although the type of free taco changes. The promotion has continued since 2007, with a few short breaks in between years.

Coupons can generate new and repeat business, traffic, interest in an everyday special, or introductory item, and can increase sales on slow days. If your coupon has a strong offer and also uses unexpected, creative copy, it will stand out from the competitors.

Vinny Warren, founder and creative director of The Escape Pod, also commented about coupon writing. What was interesting was that the audience, in this case, really wanted to see the message, unlike other advertisements or promotions. Someone clipping coupons is looking to save. Here's what he said:

> *Basically, you have to presume interest.*
>   *Yes, you've got to go, "Oh, you're interested in ten cents off the frozen peas." It is what it is. Mostly, you can finesse the execution of them. Ultimately again, people aren't reading them for fun. They're like, "How much do I get off of this?"*[26]

Now, let's focus on another type of small-space ad: online banners.

Examining online banner ad copy

Small print ads were one challenge. They didn't have very much physical space to make an impression. So, they had to be very creative to work. Online banner ads appear on sites people are already visiting. They're right in front of consumers; yet they need to offer something valuable or they'll be ignored. Creating an impact in a tiny space is still a challenge. The difference is that digital banners can be interactive and ask viewers to click on something, play a game, answer a question, take a quiz, and so on. They can start a brief dialogue with the consumer.

Interactive banner ads encourage engagement. Site visitors don't just view the page, they can get involved with it and thereby increase click-through rates. The following three interactive banner ad campaigns gained traction. (1) Rock Content allowed music fans to stay up-to-date with news and trends by subscribing to the newsletter. (2) McDonald's created a game-like interaction around one of its products, Filet-O-Fish, in cities where it was most popular. The element of play encouraged visitors to engage with the Filet-O-Fish banner ad. By circumventing challenging obstacles, players could receive the menu item as a reward. (3) Wheat Thins invited guests to stuff a virtual serving bowl with as many Wheat Thins as they could. Players had to catch the chips that spilled over by strategically positioning a moving bowl under them as they fell.[27]

Take time to visit digital agencies' websites where you'll see examples of their work, and possibly, some banner ads. The Ovation Guitars sweepstakes let participants win one of 12 celebrity guitars or a $5,000 custom Ovation guitar. Contestants created and posted video guitar lessons. Consumers voted for their favorite lesson and Joe Tunan was the winner. One banner ad (Figure 13.14) linked to the Ovation Guitars website. Both banner ads had a call to action: (1) "Check it out" and (2) "Enter to win."

Notice in the first ad how the copy uses vernacular or everyday language (Scripts and Examples 13.7) as discussed in Chapter 6 (*pop culture* strategy #50). "Blah. Meh. Ugh. Yawn." Then, it wakes up the audience with "Hello" and invites them to "go against the grain," using a *play on words* (slogan technique #4), as explained in Chapter 10.

FIGURE 13.14 This "Blah–Meh–Ugh–Yawn" animated online banner ad was created by Digital Surgeons for Ovation Guitars. Image courtesy of Digital Surgeons.

SCRIPTS AND EXAMPLES 13.7 Ovation Guitars copy

1 Banner ad #1 (Figure 13.14)
   Blah. Meh. Ugh. Yawn.
   Hello. Go against the grain.
   Unique tone. Better projection. Unmatched Playability.
   The all new
   OvationGuitars.com.
   Check it out.
2 Banner ad #2
   Ovation's Video Lesson Contest
   Guitar Giveaway.
   Win one of 12 celebrity guitars
   or a
   $5,000 custom Adams
   Enter to Win!

(Copy courtesy of Digital Surgeons.)

When you think about online banner writing, think about out-of-home billboards. Writers strive to keep the message to seven words or less because people are driving more than 55 miles per hour down the highway. Well, online consumers are usually going even faster, surfing from one website to another. So, you need to stop them and engage them. Or, they're gone. Remember, if you can present a good deal or a great prize for a sweepstakes, your message will be relevant to a particular target. As with all advertising, be sure you're clear on who those people are. What their needs or problems are as discussed in Chapters 1 and 5.

Small-space writing also includes online and printed catalog copy. This form of copywriting is some of the briefest around. You have to include all the main points because these shoppers are looking for information. And, they want it fast.

Understanding catalog copywriting

Today, catalog companies, may also have retail and e-stores. Some, like Harry & David, 1-800-Flowers, Walter Drake, and Hammacher Schlemmer (America's longest running printed catalog, which started out in 1848 as a

Manhattan hardware store with unusual items) exist via digital catalogs and e-stores, alone.

If you end up writing catalog copy for some clients, hop online so you can study them. Also, start collecting printed examples and bookmarking digital catalogs wherever you find them. Pay attention to the brevity of each item description. To get an idea how crisp this writing is, describe yourself in a sentence of seven words or less. Make sure this one sentence could actually depict your talent to an employer or client. Not so easy, right?

Refer to this handy checklist (Advice from the Pros 13.8) when you're developing marketing messages. You'll find it a valuable reference.

 ADVICE FROM THE PROS 13.8 A very useful marketing checklist for you by Drayton Bird

This list is based on my 56 years' experience of what makes for profitable marketing.

You may find using it a bit of bore. But if you want to sell it's a lot better than stuff that flops.

You'll see that some – perhaps many – of your messages miss one or more of the points below. Mine often do before I've double-checked.

1   Does your opening quickly offer or clearly imply a strong benefit?

2   Is everything instantly clear? If it's funny, clever or obscure – beware.

3   Have you told the whole story? Unless you give every sensible reason to buy, answer obvious questions and overcome all reasonable objections, you'll lose sales.

4   Is what you sell fully and clearly described?

5   Is the tone right? Don't be funny about serious things (e.g., charity, business or money).

6   Do you demonstrate the benefit – give examples, quantify it, compare it to alternatives? People want to know how and why you are better.

7   Do you prove your claim is true? Testimonials? Independent research?

8   Do you ask firmly enough for a reply, telling people precisely what to do? Repeat your arguments at that point.

9   Is the coupon, order form or request to reply big enough, clear, simple and easy to use?

10 Does your copy, when read aloud, sound like someone talking? Good!

11 Have you shown it to someone uninvolved, preferably a likely prospect? Ask if they understand it – and if they would buy.

By the way, these principles are similar, but not identical, for advertising not designed to sell immediately, which usually (but not always) has less copy. And usually (but not always) would be a damn sight better if it did try to sell immediately.[28]

When writing for catalogs, be sure to read through Checklist 13.9.

CHECKLIST 13.9 Catalog copywriting checklist

1 Put key features first.
2 Write crisp, concise copy.
3 Sell the USP (unique selling point or proposition).
4 Be persuasive.
5 Be truthful. Do not exaggerate.
6 Capture the reader's interest.
7 Say more in fewer words.
8 Reread copy and edit superfluous words.

Creative abridged writing exercises

Exercise 1: Write an introduction letter for a prospective employer

Part 1 To start, just write three strong paragraphs.

Part 2 Now read it out loud. Ask: Would you call in this applicant for an interview?

1. Is the copy:
   a. Catchy?
   b. Personable?
   c. Informative?
   d. Engaging?
   e. Creative?
   f. A reflection of your talent?
   g. Persuasive?

2. Does the letter show:
   a. Your understanding of the company?
   b. What you have to offer?
   c. How you could help this firm grow?
   d. Why you're an ideal fit?
   e. W-I-I-F-M (What's in it for "me," meaning the employer.)

Part 3 Fine-tune the letter to make you sound like the right candidate for the job.

Make it tempting. Add one more paragraph to encourage the employer to call you for an interview.

Exercise 2: Write an interactive banner ad

1. How can you animate it?

2. What can you ask the audience to do? (Enter a contest, write a comment, or create a video showing them using the product or service and having them post it on social media.)

Exercise 3: Find two examples of great digital ads. You can quickly search for them online.

Why were they effective? How could you continue the campaign? Would interactivity work? Could you integrate an experiential component with a live activation, augmented or virtual reality aspect, gamification, or a combination of social media and live events, such as the Wheat Thins "The Crunch Is Calling" X (formerly Twitter) campaign, as discussed in Chapter 4?

Notes

1. Carolyn Hadlock, personal communication, March 16, 2022.
2. Drayton Bird, personal communication, November 23, 2022.
3. https://draytonbird.com/articles/ (accessed November 1, 2022).
4. https://draytonbird.com/welcome-to-our-free-marketing-library/7-deadly-sins-and-how-to-improve-results/ (accessed November 1, 2022).
5. Drayton Bird, personal communication, November 23, 2022.
6. Vinny Warren, personal communication, December 14, 2022.
7. Charlie Hopper, personal communication, November 15, 2021.
8. Charlie Hopper, personal communication, November 15, 2021.
9. Carolyn Hadlock, personal correspondence, March 16, 2022.
10. Drayton Bird, *How to Write Sales Letters That Sell: Learn the Secrets of Successful Direct Mail* (London: Kogan Page, 2004), 21.
11. Bird, *How to Write*, 17–18.
12. Carolyn Hadlock, personal correspondence, March 16, 2022.
13. https://yandl.com/brands/hotel-tango/distilled-with-discipline (accessed July 25, 2022).
14. Charlie Hopper, personal communication, November 26, 2021.
15. Vinny Warren, personal communication, December 14, 2022.

16. Sandi Karchmer, "Heineken a Winner in the U.S. Open," *Marketing Through the Clutter*, posted October 1, 2007, https://sandisolow.blogspot.com/2007/10/heineken-winner-at-us-open.html (accessed February 29, 2011).
17. Curt Mueller, personal communication, November 21, 2022.
18. Curt Mueller, personal communication, November 21, 2022.
19. Curt Mueller, personal communication, November 21, 2022.
20. Curt Mueller, personal communication, November 21, 2022.
21. Curt Mueller, personal communication, November 21, 2022.
22. Curt Mueller, personal communication, November 21, 2022.
23. Curt Mueller, personal communication, November 21, 2022.
24. Teddy Brown, personal communication, December 14, 2022.
25. https://www.today.com/food/restaurants/taco-bell-steal-a-base-steal-a-taco-promo-world-series-2023-rcna119102 (accessed February 27, 2024).
26. Vinny Warren, personal communication, December 14, 2022.
27. https://rockcontent.com/blog/interactive-banners/ (accessed March 2, 2023).
28. https://draytonbird.com/articles/useful-marketing-checklist/ (accessed November 16, 2022).

14 The Cross-platform Word

Integrated Campaigns: Traditional, Social Media, and Interactive

> *"Saturate yourself with great advertising from around the world. The best work is coming from all over."*
>
> Tom Amico, Creative Director/Writer, Tom & Eric 911[1]

It's important to analyze as many references as possible in myriad platforms, channels, and formats. Compile examples that will help you become mentally flexible and consider various ways of executing cross-platform campaigns.

Content and Copywriting: The Complete Toolkit for Strategic Marketing, Second Edition. Margo Berman.
© 2024 Margo Berman. Published 2024 by John Wiley & Sons Ltd.
Companion website: www.wiley.com/go/contentandcopywriting

By doing this, you'll see how strategic thinking about the idea's execution and distribution will guide the creative process.

Most of all, you'll discover that creating communication that addresses people's needs and desires (as discussed in Chapter 1 and Chapter 5), while solving problems, will always be relevant. And, how interacting with consumers in an exciting way will create dialogues, build relationships, and strengthen brand loyalty. By paying attention to campaigns that spark your attention, engage your imagination, and stimulate your response, you'll see what kinds of ideas work and use them as reference points. Powerful campaigns, not only succeed in many different social media channels and other platforms, but also stick around for a while. This is because their messages are unique, unexpected, and engaging. We'll begin our exploration of cross-platform advertising by looking at a campaign with big ideas.

Developing ideas that spin out

A *big idea*, as you've probably heard many times before, is one that has legs, has a long "shelf life," and can work in all formats. With so many new communication vehicles emerging, writers must be thinking about conceptual flexibility. They must strive to develop ideas that can be chameleons and blend easily into diverse media environments. If you're creating a digital ad, you may want to think about where else the message could be used. Hotel Tango is one such example. As mentioned earlier, the copy and concept on packaging extended to print ads (Figure 11.17, Figure 11.18, Figure 11.19, Figure 11.20), billboards (Figure 12.31, Figure 12.32), website descriptions (Figure 14.1), digital ads (Figure 14.2), social media posts, and videos.

As you can see in the copy below, regardless of medium, this is a campaign with a consistent message. One that easily *spins out*. The message here addresses a *universal truth*: the military means commitment and discipline. The connection, as discussed in earlier Chapters 11, 12, and 13, is to the decorated Marine who founded the Hotel Tango Distillery brand. Notice, how confident the *tone of voice* is. To refresh your memory, one headline stated, "Forged from Fortitude." The slogan supported the campaign and promoted the brand promise: "Distilled with Discipline."

The website navigation pages, out-of-home billboards, digital ads, bottle labels, and packaging carried the same visual look and message (Figure 14.1, Figure 14.2, Figure 14.3, Figure 14.4).

FIGURE 14.1 This homepage navigation was created by Young & Laramore for Hotel Tango. Image courtesy of Young & Laramore.

FIGURE 14.2 These "Banner, Ready-to-Click" digital ads were created by Young & Laramore for Hotel Tango. Image courtesy of Young & Laramore.

FIGURE 14.3 This "Bourbon, Ready-to-Drink" front package design was created by Young & Laramore for Hotel Tango. Image courtesy of Young & Laramore.

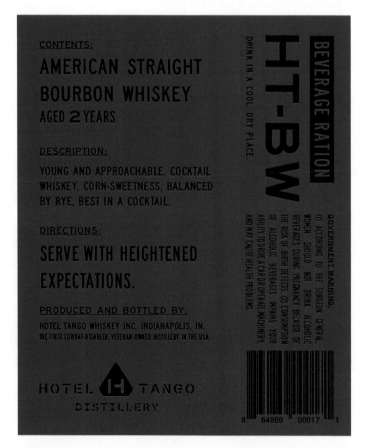

FIGURE 14.4 This "Bourbon, Ready-to-Drink" back package design was created by Young & Laramore for Hotel Tango. Image courtesy of Young & Laramore.

Writers must consider which channel or platform will be used and look for a way to create a message that will be equally effective in each, as well as have a definitive plan to weave them together. Realizing that what works in TV may not be relevant or applicable in social media videos may force writers to reexamine their initial creative direction and refocus their message.

Creative teams are always looking for a *big idea*. One that transcends media and cultural barriers. Ideas that *spin out* and have legs. Ideas that are flexible and nimble. Like catchy slogans (Nike's "Just Do It"), seemingly endless campaigns (De Beer's "A Diamond Is Forever"), and long-running characters or icons (Planter's "Mr. Peanut"). See *Ad Age*'s list of "Top 10 Advertising Icons of the (20th) Century." The top five were The Marlboro Man, Ronald McDonald, The Jolly Green Giant, Betty Crocker (retired), and The Energizer Bunny. The rest of the list were The Pillsbury Doughboy, Aunt Jemima (also retired), The Michelin Man, Kellogg's® Tony the Tiger®, and Elsie (the cow).[2] You've probably also seen other popular icons, including the Nabisco Keebler Elves; Rice Krispies' Snap, Crackle, and Pop; and the Michelin Tire Man, one of the oldest ones, dating back to the 1894 Lyon Exhibition.

Thinking about how small-space writing differs from other media

Each medium has its challenges. And, as we've seen in writing for direct mail and small-space messages like coupons and packaging (Chapter 13), the trick is to say something memorable in as few words as possible. Charlie Hopper, principal at Young & Laramore, adds this bit of insight:

> *Well, I think it's an example of always being sure you understand who is going to see your work, where they're going to see it, and how. It's definitely different than a temporal medium, like radio or TV, which has to tease you into staying interested from moment to moment – and in this case, it's different than a billboard or web banner or coupon tucked into a "ValPak" with a bunch of other coupons, that has to grab you quickly with a focused message and then assume you've moved past.*
>
> *Here, you know the person is going to hold the door hanger – or, if it's stitched into a magazine, the ad – in their hand. So, if you're clever enough into charming them into spending a moment satisfying their curiosity (if you've managed to arouse their curiosity), you have the chance to say a little more than in some other media.[3]*

Regardless of the channel or platform, it's always crucial to understand where the consumer will encounter it. Specifically, at which touchpoints? This helps writers comprehend the readers' mindset. Are they surfing online? Texting on their phones? Driving past a billboard on the highway? Watching TV? Reading a magazine? Listening to a podcast? Following a blogger? Chatting on a social network? Participating in a contest? Creating consumer content? And, so on. Knowing where they are can help writers talk to them in a more personal way.

For instance, if you catch people in the middle of their everyday activities, like walking across a park, riding a mall escalator, or hailing a cab, you're using ambient or transit messages to reach them. You've already interrupted their day and, if the ad is strong enough, caught their attention. Just to see how one promotional message can convert to another type of marketing, let's take a glance at other ambient ads that started out as something else.

Creating messages that move from one platform into another

Understanding what the core essence of the brand says often starts with a general, architectural overview, such as the example (Figure 14.5) for Natürlich yogurt by Tom & Eric 911. It shows the thinking that goes on long before the messaging, which resembles the insights in a creative brief. Some key points that the brand wanted to determine were:

- Brand mission
- Brand voice and values
- Key selling proposition
- Consumer benefits
- Brand iconography, look, allure

After each of these are answered, the chart is completed as shown in Figure 14.6. There were many other details that were distilled down to those bullet points. For example, here are the questions asked and answered in the brand manifesto.

> **What if the yogurt we enjoy** …
>
> … **tasted better?** Using only the better milk that comes from grass-fed Jersey cows from the fields of central Pennsylvania.

In Summary: Brand Architecture

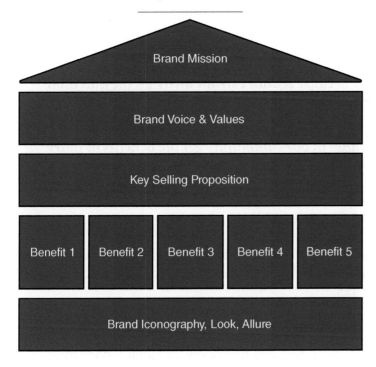

Brand Mission

Brand Voice & Values

Key Selling Proposition

| Benefit 1 | Benefit 2 | Benefit 3 | Benefit 4 | Benefit 5 |

Brand Iconography, Look, Allure

FIGURE 14.5 This "Brand Architecture Overview" presentation image was designed by Tom & Eric 911 for Natürlich. Image courtesy of Tom & Eric 911.

Natürlich: Brand Architecture

Our Mission

Natürlich is a brand committed to raising the potential of what better (vs. bigger) dairy can provide to a healthy, more vibrant society.

Values: "Better Dairy Pledge"

- We believe all should strive to make things better (striving)
- We believe better is a journey, not a destination (progressive, active)
- We believe we must live the change we want to see (principled)
- We believe in staying positive along the way (optimistic)

Unique Selling Proposition

"It starts with better milk yogurt. And everything better that comes with it."

| Organic, Grass-fed Jersey cow milk | Unstrained, non-homogenized milk so cream & whey naturally rise to the top | 100% natural ingredients & flavor powders | Made by a chef to work better in recipes | Better dairy: Buy-forward food waste recovery program / fair trade practices |

FIGURE 14.6 This "Brand Architecture in Detail" presentation image was designed by Tom & Eric 911 for Natürlich. Image courtesy of Tom & Eric 911.

*... **was made better**? Without the unnecessary step of homogenization that is only used to standardize cheap milk.*

*... **worked better in recipes**? Blending naturally with other ingredients because it hasn't been manipulated through homogenization.*

*... **was healthier because it didn't strain away all the nutrition found in the whey**? And let it rise to the top of the yogurt, along with the cream.*

*... **also helped those in our community get the benefits of dairy on a daily basis**? Pound-for-pound for every cup purchased.*

*... **is now available at your local Whole Foods**? Well, it is.*

Introducing Natürlich. Better Milk Yogurt. A better way forward.[4]

Other important questions were answered, including: (1) Who is the audience? and (2) What distinguishes it from other brands? First, Natürlich specified three targeted audiences:

1. *Consumers* – Affluent, educated women under the age of 35
2. *Trade* – Potential retail partners in grocery and food service trade
3. *Chefs* – In-launch markets to build initial social community

Then, it defined the *unique selling proposition* (USP) with the following points. It answered why Natürlich was different from other yogurts this way: Because it's made:

- In the traditional way of making yogurt, non-homogenized, with the cream on top.
- From the finest Jersey cow milk, which comes from small local dairies, making the yogurt richer and creamier.
- From an ancient Mediterranean recipe.
- By a chef to work better in recipes.

And it's:

- Unstrained, so keeps all of the nutrients found in the whey.[5]

You can review more of the strategic thinking in the completed brand architecture chart (Figure 14.6). Pay attention to the USP, "It starts with better milk yogurt. And everything better comes with it." Notice how the focus is on the milk. The brand specifically attributed the core difference to the cow milk itself. The yogurt came from Jersey cows, not Holstein cows. Then, the copy explained that the milk is creamier to emphasize the differentiation point between Natürlich and other yogurts. It continued detailing the production process. The milk was not homogenized to allow the cream to rise to the top. The whey was retained, not removed, to preserve the nutrients. These details helped yogurt lovers fully understand the brand's features and how they translated into consumer benefits.

Notice how the ad started with a friendly "hi." Then, the copy stated what differentiated this yogurt in clear, simple-to-grasp copy. In the first ad (Figure 14.7), look how the copy explained why the milk was creamier. It emphasized the differentiation points between Natürlich and other yogurts. These details helped yogurt lovers fully understand the brand's features and these key benefits: (1) more protein and (2) better blending when used in recipes.

HEADLINE:	"We're Natürlich. The better milk yogurt."
COPY:	"Hi. We're Natürlich, the better milk yogurt that's also better for recipes. Our founder, a professionally trained chef from Turkey, came to this country to replicate the taste and texture

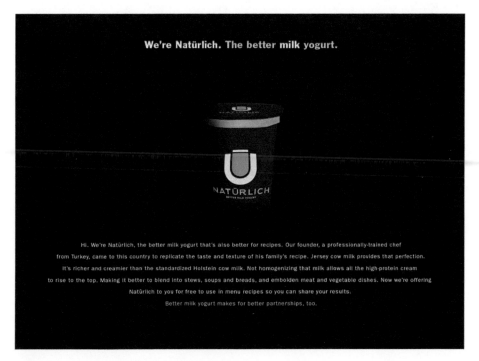

FIGURE 14.7 This "Better Milk Yogurt" print ad was created by Tom & Eric 911 for Natürlich. Image courtesy of Tom & Eric.

of his family's recipe. Jersey cow milk provides that perfection. It's richer and creamier than the standardized Holstein cow milk. Not homogenizing that milk allows all the high-protein cream to rise to the top. Making it better to blend into stews, soups and breads, and embolden meat and vegetable dishes. Now we're offering Natürlich to you for free to use in menu recipes so you can share your results.
Better milk yogurt makes better partnerships, too."

In the second ad (Figure 14.8), see how the copy again showcased why the milk was creamier. It reiterated the distinctive differences and production process mentioned earlier. The clear explanation highlighted the line of the products' features and buyers' benefits. In addition, the ad also spoke to the

FIGURE 14.8 This "Cow" print ad was created by Tom & Eric 911 for Natürlich. Image courtesy of Tom & Eric.

brand's commitment to social responsibility to different communities, from independent farmers to local business owners. It promised a sought-after quality: honesty through transparency.

SLOGAN ACTS
AS HEADLINE: "We're Natürlich. The Better Milk Yogurt."
(It sits at the bottom of the ad)

COPY: "Are there a lot of good yogurts out there?
Maybe. We're the one that set out to be better. Better milk is why. We use only grass-fed Jersey cows that produce richer, creamier milk. Then we don't homogenize it so the cream naturally rises to the top. Finally, we don't strain the whey so we retain more nutrients. It could be the best yogurt you've ever had. But for us, we're happy to work at just being better. For our communities, including independent farm owners. And for business, with better practices and complete transparency. It starts with better milk yogurt.
And everything better that comes out of it."

In the next ad, "Splash" (Figure 14.9), the headline posed a question. Sometimes, if the answer to a question can be dismissed by a quick yes or no, writers avoid using it in headlines. However, here, the subhead immediately negated the readers' reply with a "reason why" answer. Be sure not to miss the closing line. It wasn't just a standard call to action. It was an invitation to actually contact someone directly at the company. Her phone number and email were listed. You have to admit, that was a bold action. It instantly validated the brand's pledge to uphold corporate accessibility, accountability, and transparency.

HEADLINE: "Does the world need another yogurt?"
SUBHEAD: "If it's made with better milk, then yes."
COPY: "We're unleashing better milk yogurt to a generation who missed out on what dairy was like before standardization and homogenization made milk look and taste the same. Our "better milk" comes from grass-fed Jersey cows and is A2

certified and Non-GMO Project verified. Original, Strawberry, Maple and Honey flavors.
Call Donna Serio at 908-209-8238 or dserio@naturlich.com to find out more."

SLOGAN: "Natürlich. Better Milk Yogurt."

FIGURE 14.9 This "Splash" print ad was created by Tom & Eric 911 for Natürlich. Image courtesy of Tom & Eric.

The Natürlich campaign used the *product as hero* strategy (#13), as mentioned in Chapter 6, and satisfied health-conscious consumers' craving for natural yogurt equally well in all media. That's the key to a strong cross-platform campaign: present a message that's flexible enough to perform well wherever it appears. Here, even though some of the images looked unrelated, the core concept and USP were echoed throughout the campaign.

Planning cross-platform campaigns from the beginning

Don't just think about a concept. Think about a fleet of delivery vehicles. Right from the beginning, allow yourself to consider other idea modes of transportation. Stretch your strategic thinking. Challenge yourself. Ask if any of these message delivery systems would work:

- Ambient
- Transit
- Out-of-home messages
- Print
- Broadcast
- Digital
- Online
- Interactive
- Packaging
- Indoor signage
- Social media
- Coupons
- Immersive
- Mixed Reality (MR)
- Emerging media

Successful integrated campaigns, such as the Hotel Tango examples, mentioned earlier (Figure 14.1, Figure 14.2, Figure 14.3, Figure 14.4), and in Chapters 11, 12, and 13, demonstrate how one consistent message moves fluidly from one platform to another. It went from clever print ads (Figure 11.17, Figure 11.18, Figure 11.19, Figure 11.20) and out-of-home posters (Figure 12.31, Figure 12.32) to witty bottle-label and package-design copy (Figure 13.1,

Figure 13.2, Figure 13.4, Figure 13.5, Figure 13.6, Figure 13.7, Figure 14.3, Figure 14.4), as well as online content (Figure 14.1) and digital ads (Figure 14.2).

The brand saluted the seriousness of military precision, discipline, and commitment to purpose. Yet, it did that with unexpected, easy humor. The out-of-home posters offered whimsical, marketing lines that stated the obvious, such as: (1) "Billboard," identifying what it is and (2) "This Side Up to Install" with a vertical arrow (Figure 12.31).

The ads in Chapter 11 followed suit with their own clever labels. For example, the "Propaganda, Ready-to-Propagate" ad (Figure 11.17) entertained readers with this marketing descriptor: "Contains: Headline, Supplementary Copy, 'Tagline.'" They displayed agency-directed pointers, with terminology, such as: "For Civilian Display" and "Department of Strategic Communication," as listed below. Each ad restated the line "Distilled with Discipline" as a persuasive message to discerning drinkers that the product shown is of the highest quality.

The body copy in the "Forged from Fortitude" ad (Figure 11.20) offered other labels to identify parts of the ad. These included:

1. *Visual reference* over the product shot of the bottle

2. *Supporting message* above the body copy

3. *Rev. 4.A* (sharing the ad's revision number) above the headline

The packaging included comical up and down arrows, next to copy. Look how the symbols were similar to what you'd usually see on delivery boxes:

- *Up arrow:* This side (up) to store

- *Down arrow:* This side (down) to pour

Also comical was the following copy, as discussed above, which is usually reserved for in-house reference:

1. *File name and job number:* Hotel Tango Print Communication PC-501

2. *Agency department:* Department of Strategic Communication

3. *Medium:* For Civilian Display

Every message included wit. For example, in social media posts, the content read "Click here for gin," or "Banner, ready-to-click," as if you could pour a drink right there.

The digital ads (Figure 14.2) continued to feature ad agency language, such as: "Desired Action Click Here," "Hotel Tango Digital Ad," "Primary Message," which sat near the headlines, and "Visual Reference," which again accompanied the product beauty shot. Of course, none of these were necessary. Yet, they showed how the brand didn't take its advertising as seriously as it did its product quality.

The package copy was an exciting reference for writers because it demonstrated how the concept was integrated throughout the campaign: with packaging, ads, out-of-home, and digital content.

Below are more examples of clever, brand-core-related lines, which were reinforced by appearing on the outside of the boxes: (1) "Pour with purpose," (2) "Serve with honor," (3) Drink in a cool dry place," and (4) "Purpose of contents: to be served and consumed in pursuance of elevated company morale." Although we looked at this under packaging copy in Chapter 13, notice how some of the product copy is different on the website, as shown in examples #1 and #2, here.

1. *Bourbon* (Figure 14.4)

   Package copy (back side):

   - DESCRIPTION: Young and approachable, cocktail whiskey, corn-sweetness, balanced by rye, best in a cocktail.

   - DIRECTIONS: Serve with heightened expectations.

   Web copy:

   - DESCRIPTION: Aromas of caramel, balanced by rye. Best in a cocktail (e.g., Old Fashioned)

   - DIRECTIONS: Drink responsibly. Behave less so.

2. *Reserve Bourbon* (Figure 13.2)

   Package copy (back side):

   - DESCRIPTION: A well-balanced, dignified, wheated bourbon, refined sweetness. What Chesty would drink.

   - DIRECTIONS: Serve with heightened expectations.

   Web copy:

   - DESCRIPTION: Third in the rotating Reserve Bourbon series, aromas of cherry, vanilla, and burnt sugar, soft oak finish. What Chesty would drink.

   - DIRECTIONS: Serve with heightened expectations.

The directions in each of the examples embody the understated humor that runs throughout the campaign. For example, "Serve with heightened expectations," "Enjoy with a camaraderie chaser," and "Water down at your own risk." The Rum package directions discussed earlier (Figure 13.7) stated, "Never to be used in the same sentence as 'Chug.'" This wittily reminds consumers that they're drinking a fine alcohol and shouldn't chug it as if they were drinking beer. Of course, these are tongue-in-cheek remarks, not designed to sound preachy. The subtle humor draws the reader in to take a second look.

In discussing packaging, Carolyn Hadlock, principal/executive creative director, stated the following two key points. Although we mentioned the second one before, it's worth repeating.

1. *Packaging is often the first and only ad the consumer sees.*
2. *The campaign starts in aisle with the packaging.*[6]

When you consider how important these two statements are, you'll realize the power of product packaging. It's more than copy on a box. It's a direct-to-consumer message.

Notice that the slogan was always underlined in all promotional material. Carefully review each example and pay close attention to the writing. It's a masterclass of "tight" copy, meaning it contains carefully chosen words that deliver and reinforce the core concept.

For example, the bottle labels (Figure 13.3) restated "high, standard issue," "fit to serve," and "ready-to-drink." Then, the billboards (Figure 12.31, Figure 12.32) playfully answered with "ready-to-view," showing a clear-to-see relationship between the platforms and channels.

The beauty of the campaign was the consistency in the design layouts, visuals, copy, and tone of voice. There's no question which brand it was and what the brand was trying to say. Creating instantly identifiable campaigns is crucial for brand recall. That is precisely what Hotel Tango accomplished.

She also explained the campaign components in the following statement:

> *We created print. We created outdoor. We created in-store. We made the website. We did every touchpoint for the brand. Each piece is written for its particular media form, but it all comes from the same place – MRE (military ready-to-eat) lexicon.*[7]

Checking that you're writing for the eye, ear, and imagination

In addition to packaging, out-of-home, and digital ads, consider what else you can do to specifically target a particular audience. After you've considered various media, now ponder how you can use a specific medium to leverage its communication adaptability. For example, look at this short list. Could you add to it?

- Use *eyebrows* in print and digital ads.

- Create *opt-in* mobile messages.

- Develop an online reward point system for repeat customers.

- Provide subscriber offers, *shelf talker* coupons (automated coupon distributers on store shelves), digital discounts, and *QR codes*.

- Establish a Facebook fan page.

- Create social media ads.

- Design an interactive vehicle: online product size matching (like Levi's jean "Curve ID" online shape quiz), e-catalog, mall kiosks (booth or free-standing terminal), in-store imaging (like showing clothes on you without trying them on).

- Invite *consumer-created* or *user-generated content* (like TV commercials or logos).

- Produce immersive experiences.

Remember, with interactive campaigns, you can ask their opinion. Engage their curiosity. Create intrigue. You want to connect consumers' creativity to the brand in a new and compelling way.

Also think about how you could reach a broader audience. What could you integrate into your campaign to broaden your market? Consider future media. What new *touchpoints* could you create? Here are examples, some which we already discussed, that were breakthrough ideas when they were first introduced:

- Manhole covers in New York City – The realistic image of a cup of Folger's coffee looked as if it were steaming by the air being released under the manhole.

- Bus tires – The tire looked like the lens of a Canon camera.

- Subway platform pillars – The pillars were painted to look like brown markers to remind commuters of the UPS "Whiteboard" campaign.

Reminding consumers of the benefits in all media

Always examine how a campaign modulates from one communication format to another. When you see it on one channel or platform, notice it on another. Below, we'll examine campaigns that fluently move across platforms to create integrated campaigns. If people are engaged and entertained in a dialogue that addresses their needs, they're more likely to support the brand, especially if the benefit is reinforced at all *touchpoints*. Now, let's take another look at the Trane campaign. We examined the radio scripts in Chapter 8 from the "We Run Together" (Script 1, Script 2) and "Tested to the Extreme" campaigns (Script 3, Script 4).

The radio spots showed that the brand fully understood consumers' thinking. People don't want to worry about whether or not their heating or cooling units work. They expect them to. The campaign promised that at the Trane testing facility, every heating and cooling system was being put through grueling, relentless trials. So, when consumers were going about their daily pursuits, the products were going through punishing challenges to ensure their reliability. The slogan promised the consumer freedom of mind with this commitment: "We test. So it runs."

The headline, "We Run Together," copy, and slogan were the same in all three ads (Figure 14.10, Figure 14.11, Figure 14.12). Only the visuals were

FIGURE 14.10 This "We Run Together in Rain" print ad was created by Young & Laramore for Trane. Image courtesy of Young & Laramore.

FIGURE 14.11 This "We Run Together in Heat" print ad was created by Young & Laramore for Trane. Image courtesy of Young & Laramore.

FIGURE 14.12 This "We Run Together in Snow" print ad was created by Young & Laramore for Trane. Image courtesy of Young & Laramore.

different. The idea was that Trane would run regardless of the weather or whatever consumers were doing. So, the underlying message was we would run together in rain, heat, and snow. The visuals showed people taking their pet out in the rain, sweating during a workout in the heat, and scraping ice off the car windshield. You could run your errands because when you got home, your heating and cooling unit would be running.

> HEADLINE: We Run Together.
> COPY: Every Trane air conditioner, furnace, and heat pump is engineered, built, and tested to run, run and run – just like you.
> SLOGAN: *It's Hard to Stop a Trane.*

These side-by-side, one-word billboards (Figure 14.13, Figure 14.14) reinforced the rigorous testing that every product endured. The pair of short headlines simply labeled the tests: "Slam" and "Shake," "Dry" and "Wet." The copy simply said, "Tested for every extreme." The standalone out-of-home ad (Figure 14.15) reminded passersby of the brand promise: "We test. So it runs." Every message was succinct and powerful. Truly, here less was more.

FIGURE 14.13 These out-of-home "Slam" and "Shake" billboards were created by Young & Laramore for Trane. Image courtesy of Young & Laramore.

FIGURE 14.14 These out-of-home "Dry" and "Wet" billboards were created by Young & Laramore for Trane. Image courtesy of Young & Laramore.

FIGURE 14.15 This out-of-home "We Test. So It Runs." billboard was created by Young & Laramore for Trane. Image courtesy of Young & Laramore.

PAIR OF HEADLINES:	Slam. Shake.
COPY:	Tested for every extreme.
SLOGAN:	*It's Hard to Stop a Trane.*

PAIR OF HEADLINES:	Dry. Wet.
COPY:	Tested for every extreme.
SLOGAN:	*It's Hard to Stop a Trane.*

HEADLINE:	We Test. So It Runs.
TEXT IN BOX:	Test 10072
COPY:	Acoustic sound chamber.
PRODUCT:	XV20i
	4dB below average
SLOGAN:	*It's Hard to Stop a Trane.*

The unmistakable singularity of message instills confidence. Every campaign, whether it was "We Run Together" or "Relentless Testing," strengthened brand trust and consumer loyalty. The overarching deliverable was reliability under all conditions.

Promoting environmental consciousness and social responsibility

Some topics are important to discuss, but often considered distasteful to mention. So, how can a campaign talk about animal waste in a descriptive, yet tasteful way? This was the challenge Tom Amico, creative director/writer of Tom & Eric 911, faced. How should he discuss the benefits of treating and managing animal manure to reduce or prevent soil pollution and air emissions? With proper treatment, the waste can be safely reintroduced into the soil as a valuable fertilizer. The goal was to point out the importance of reusing or upcycling "wet" waste, especially for municipal wastewater and agricultural waste.

This was his explanation of the Upcycle campaign:

> *We named this start-up company, designed the logo and website (upcycletech.com) and launched the brand across all platforms, while transforming an old-school sector of waste management into Bio-Asset Recovery Systems.*
>
> *We wanted to create a movement. Why not turn it into something useful? We wanted to get the word 'waste' out of there and make it forward and positive.*[8]

In one Upcycle ad (Figure 14.16), the headline brought up the subject of "wet waste" with this headline "Don't Take the Wet Waste Revolution Lying Down." The use of a cute, baby pig made the campaign charming.

A similar approach was used for the Charmin Bears "Enjoy the Go" campaign. Instead of shying away from the topic, this campaign honestly said, "We all go. Why not enjoy the go with Charmin?" The ads explained the softness and effectiveness of this toilet tissue. By using adorable characters in the Charmin Bear family, they appealed to kids and adults, as well.

FIGURE 14.16 This "Don't Take the Wet Waste" print ad was created by Tom & Eric 911 for Upcycle. Image courtesy of Tom & Eric.

Look at how this *imperative*, or *command-style* Upcycle headline (#11 in Chapter 10) invited the reader to find out more about Upcycle (Figure 14.16).

HEADLINE: "Don't Take the Wet Waste Revolution Lying Down."
COPY: "The mission of Upcycle is simple and game-changing. To repurpose wet waste as renewable, profitable resources. An unheard of 95% potential asset yield of water, energy and minerals. In minutes, not months. Upcycle 15 tons of wet waste a day with low-carbon emissions. Ecological. Economical. Transformational.

Welcome to The Age of Bio-Asset Recovery. Let's get started at Upcycletech.com. Or call 1-844-WASTE-NOT."

The copy pointed out that upcycling animal waste is not just good for the environment, it's also good for the bottom line. The website showed slides with the same headline and visual, but with new copy and a call-to-action, click-through button.

SAME HEADLINE: "Don't Take the Wet Waste Revolution Lying Down."
NEW COPY: "Now, any kind of wet waste can add to your net worth. Upcycled in minutes, not months. With an unheard of 95% potential yield in recovered assets. Water. Energy. Minerals. 'Waste management' is no longer unmanageable. It's economical, even profitable."
BOLD: "Introducing The ReGenerator™."
CLICK BUTTON: "Tell Me More."

The agency's and brand's website also showed another easy-to-grasp message with just a clear glass of water as the visual. Here's the rest of the content:

HEADLINE: "Waste Redefined."
COPY: "Why waste your waste? Now, any kind of wet waste can be upcycled into assets with economic value. Fifteen tons a day, or more. In minutes, not months. Just plug in and go. Ecological. Economical. Transformational."
BOLD: "Introducing The ReGenerator™."
CLICK BUTTON: "Tell Me More."

Another slide presented a chart depicting the process with this to-the-point headline: "Wet Waste in. Bio-Asset Recovery Out." A fourth slide presented a list of short, bite-size facts, making a hard-to-discuss topic interesting and informative.

HEADLINE: "Welcome to the Wet Waste Revolution."
COPY: "We're Upcycle Technologies.
We're giving waste a good name.
We're snuffing out swollen lagoons.
We're drying up toxic wastewater.
We're not **hauling** waste away.
We're **overhauling** an industry.
We're turning **pollutants** into **power**. **Manure** into **minerals**.
Waste into **water**. And steam. Real economic assets.
An unheard of 95% yield potential.
Our patented process takes **minutes**, not **months**.
Introducing The ReGenerator™."
And the end of waste management as we know it.
The Age of Bio-Asset Recovery has begun.
So why waste time? Come join us.

Just fill out the Contact Us form if you would like additional information about Upcycle Technologies.
Or call 1-844-WASTE-NOT."
(Copy courtesy of Tom & Eric 911)

Study the use of all the writing devices listed below and set in bold type above. These and other techniques were described in Chapter 9:

1. *Parallel construction*: We're giving, we're snuffing, we're drying, we're not hauling, we're overhauling, and we're turning.

2. *Alliteration:* (a) Pollutants into power. (b) Manure into minerals. (c) Waste into water. (d) Patented process. (e) Minutes, not months. (f) Why waste time?

3. *ABA construction*: The headline is repeated or rephrased in the closing line: "So why waste time?"

4. *Weave*: The concept of waste is woven throughout the copy.

5. *Call to action*: "Come join us." "Just fill out the Contact form."

You can see how many techniques writers incorporated into this copy block. The "tight" or succinct writing makes the slide content easy to follow and finish.

Let's return to the ads. How could you not read on when an adorable piggy is looking directly into the camera and asking: "Why Let My Waste Go to Waste?" In the next ad (Figure 14.17), the piggy asks a simple question, using an *interrogative* headline. Then explains how this waste upcycling system,

FIGURE 14.17 This "Why Let My Waste" print ad was created by Tom & Eric 911 for Upcycle. Image courtesy of Tom & Eric.

The ReGenerator™, works. It also informs consumers that pigs produce 20 times more daily waste than people. That is a surprising-to-most fact. The ad is deceptively educational. It draws readers in with the endearing piggy image.

Headline: "Why Let My Waste Go to Waste?"

Copy: "Waste management is no longer manageable. I know. I produce 20 times more waste than a human in a single day. But now, any kind of wet waste can add up to your net worth. Water. Energy. Minerals. An unheard of 95% potential yield. Introducing The ReGenerator™. Its patented process takes minutes, not months. What's more, The ReGenerator™ pays for itself in as little as three years.

       Economical. Ecological. Transformational.

Welcome to the Age of Bio-Asset Recovery. Let's get started at Upcycletech.com Or call 1-844-WASTE-NOT."

One of the out-of-home messages (Figure 14.18) showed a three-dimensional chicken as an *extender* (a visual that goes higher than the top of the billboard) and used the same message, "Don't Let My Waste Go to Waste." The call-to-action line stated a clever, and an easy-to-retain phone number, especially for highway drivers: 1-844-WASTE-NOT.

FIGURE 14.18 This "Don't Let My Waste" billboard was created by Tom & Eric 911 for Upcycle. Image courtesy of Tom & Eric.

The next two out-of-home ads (Figure 14.19, Figure 14.20) showed a day-and-night version of an almost identical ad. What's interesting to notice is in

FIGURE 14.19 This "Wasted Redefined" day billboard was created by Tom & Eric 911 for Upcycle. Image courtesy of Tom & Eric.

FIGURE 14.20 This "Wasted Redefined" night billboard was created by Tom & Eric 911 for Upcycle. Image courtesy of Tom & Eric.

the day version, the same phone number was used as discussed above. Yet, in the night outdoor sign, the call-to-action line changed and sent viewers to a website, instead of a toll-free number.

The purpose of the campaign was to announce the release of a new energy conservation technology. It turned carbon-based waste into clean, safe, and sustainable energy. The applications included converting city wastewater and agricultural/food processing waste into profitable power.

The cross-platform ads demonstrated how waste upcycling could serve a purpose while helping to protect the environment. The brand used three specific strategies, as discussed in Chapter 6, including:

1. *Product as hero* (#13)

2. *Green* (#43)

3. *Cause-related* (#49)

With environmental issues being central to many people's concerns, consumers, farmers, and business owners are choosing vendors that align with their core beliefs. Socially responsible companies are implementing new policies to address these types of issues to be relevant to a wider audience. Marketers today know that people want to know about companies' responsible actions, not just promises. So, the marketing needs to be informative, engaging, and entertaining. When a brand's communication addresses target audiences' values, as well as their needs, it's more likely to be embraced, especially if the benefit is reinforced at all touchpoints.

Now we'll look back at the ASICS campaign already discussed in Chapters 4, 11 and 12.

Including target-specific ambient and interactive advertising

When asked about the strategic thinking behind the ASICS "New York City Marathon" campaign, KT Thayer, former creative director at Vitro, explained that the objective was to build awareness. The creative team realized this was a "challenger brand" and was competing head-to-head with the category mega-stars, including Nike and Adidas. The idea was to showcase the unique qualities of ASICS and to offer consumers another option.

Thayer went on to explain how "Sound Mind, Sound Body" was more than just the ASICS slogan. As he said in Chapter 11:

> It is the founding philosophy and the root of the name. Anima Sana In Corpore Sano is a Latin phrase that translates to, "a sound mind, in a sound body." This position drives every decision, innovation, and communication that comes from ASICS.[9]

Fitness is one way of creating a "Sound Mind" resting in a "Sound Body." Consumers could choose any activity. Running might be one solution. The campaign wanted to present another reason to run besides the physical benefits. It also emphasized the mental and emotional benefits. This distinguished ASICS from its competitors and enabled it to create and continue to grow its own identifiable message in the market. It informed and reminded consumers of the benefits of every sport, specifically running.

> The campaign was internally called "Running Truths," as the message had to come from a genuine, honest place that any level of runner could understand and believe.[10]

One interesting question with this campaign was whether the language or the images came first. Thayer explained that although some of the headlines may have been created first, the graphics impacted the message. Once the art director designed the layout, chose the font, set the type, and added bright colors, the copy was rewritten to be "shorter, bolder, and punchier."[11] In case you can't recall the campaign, take a moment to review it in Chapters 4, 11 and 12. For a quick reference and to refresh your memory, look at Figure 11.10,

Figure 11.11, Figure 11.12, Figure 12.18, Figure 12.19. Can you see how the typography gave the ads a three-dimensional perspective and a sense of movement?

When asked to give new copywriters a few helpful tips, Thayer offered the following advice.

> *Try to learn discipline. Don't be satisfied too quickly. It's tough when you write something you like but it doesn't fit for one reason or another (it's too long, sounds like another brand, it's not on strategy, etc.), but more times than not if you keep at it, you get to a better place than where you started.*[12]

As other writers have suggested, be tough on yourself. Don't settle with your first idea. Think about it. Ask if that's the best you can do? Remember to challenge yourself. Always stretch yourself creatively. Try to demand more from yourself. You may not only surprise, but even amaze, yourself!

Take a moment to revisit the Legal Sea Foods campaign also found in Chapter 12 and read the irreverent headlines (Figures 12.20, Figure 12.21, Figure 12.22, Figure 12.23, Figure 12.24, Figure 12.25, Figure 12.26).

Being irreverent can create unforgettable messages

If you're wondering how the creative team came up with the sassy, high-impact "Fresh Fish" campaign for Legal Sea Foods, Paul McCormick, director of new business at DeVito/Verdi, answered the question. He explained that Legal Sea Foods prides itself on being able to prove ultimate freshness by its "ability to track every meal from pier to plate."[13] The Boston-based company conducts on-dock testing of all fish and buys only top-of-catch and freshly caught fish and shellfish from day boats.

The question was how to relay that freshest-fish-anywhere message in a penetrable message. The result was a remarkably cheeky, yet undeniably clever, *play-on-words* slogan (#4, as described in Chapter 10): "If it isn't fresh, it isn't Legal." The entire campaign drives home the benefit to the consumer in an intrusive, yet fun manner in just three strong, simple words: "Really Fresh Fish."

The agency created a cost-effective, cross-platform campaign with various *touchpoints* and a consistently whimsical *tone of voice*. The carefully integrated use of media included:

- 15- and 30-second TV spots
- Local radio

- Viral videos

- Out-of-home messages

- Cinema advertising

- Guerilla street signs (like *floor talkers*, giant sticky notes, and creative street signs)

- Newspaper

- *Wild postings* (repeated, often edgy posters placed in nontraditional locations like construction sites, building sides, alleys, windows, bus shelter sides)

- Ongoing public relations

This campaign ran exclusively in Boston and was tailored for the cabs and MTBA ("T") Green Line trolleys (trams). To make the campaign particularly relevant to the medium, the creatives knew where the ads would run.[14] This is why the marriage between the messages and the media are so perfectly matched. You can quickly see that from the already discussed examples below:

- "This movie sucks!"

- "This cab gets around more than your sister." (Later adapted for the "T.")

- "This cab driver has a face like a halibut." (Later also adopted as "conductor" on the "T.")

With campaigns like Legal Sea Foods, it's no surprise that DeVito/Verdi has been voted "The Best Ad Agency in the US" six times by the American Association of Advertising Agencies.

Agencies of all sizes can generate national attention. And campaigns that start out as a spark of an idea can go global. Just think back to the Wendy's "Where's the Beef" and Budweiser "Whassup!" campaigns.

Creating writing that sounds natural

All writing should speak in a sincere and truthful *tone of voice*. It's especially effective when the campaign incorporates an *honesty* strategy (#26), as discussed in Chapter 6. Let's examine the conceptual approach and writing process to achieve this from a creative team. Drummond Berman, group creative director/writer at Merkley+Partners, explained that he and his creative partner, Simon Nickson, group creative director/art director, look to create concepts that project "absolute realism."[15] He explained how they come up with and, then, develop their ideas:

> *Our planners go out and they, as we said, they do these ethnographies. They go to people's houses. They talk to them. They find common patterns between the things people believe and what they don't believe and all of that. Then they share that with us. We use that to create the advertising. Then we sit with our client and we pick the best stuff, and then we put it straight out in market. We don't show it to anyone. We don't ask anyone's permission. We just run it.[16]*

He shared how they work with the research to create an authentic voice that sounds genuine. He continued to talk about the creative process saying:

> *We try to just capture the way people truly feel. Very often, somebody will say something in one of the ethnographies that is put in their way rather than just the kind of stereotypical way, and we'll use that word-for-word. Or we'll always try to write something so that it sounds like a real person talking the way they really speak by using those kinds of idiosyncratic words that only they use. So, if you look at all the spots, there's always something in there that makes it not just a person speaking, but that person speaking.[17]*

Nickson explained that TV scripts tended to be "incredibly real," which is slightly different than print and out-of-home messages, which interpret people's feelings in a witty way, rather than "just writing exactly the way people speak."[18] Whereas with TV, Nickson said:

> *We write scripts that are based on one person and not one person that's talking for 100,000 people, but* **one person** *who is talking* **for himself** *about* **his situation** *and how he feels about it in* **his language** *that then obviously resonates with other people.[19]*

He likened the scripts to natural conversations you might have at a dinner party with someone who's expressing how you feel, but in his or her own manner of speech, using different expressions, clichés, or choice of language. But yet, you're being drawn into the conversation because it resonates with you, and you agree with what they're saying.

The communication feels more like a dialogue rather than an advertising message. Although it's contemporary, Nickson said, "there's also something slightly retro about it as well, slightly comforting. Like you feel like you've seen it before, or you've been around it before, or whatever."[20]

To create one cohesive message, Drummond said a team of people work on the account, who handle reports, design exhibitions, create marketing pieces, and develop other components that keep this well-integrated campaign "really unified and consistent."[21]

Drummond also added a tip on writing for print, explaining that there are multiple elements to consider, and writers need to think about the "hierarchy of messaging."[22] In other words, writers need to decide what part of the message should be emphasized as a headline. What should be a subhead. And what needs to be stated in the body copy. He explained:

> *Very often you have copy with a subhead that sort of summarizes what this ad is about in a very simple, non-creative, more informational way. So, you* **don't** *have to have everything in the headline. You* **do** *have to have everything in the ad. So, you constantly need to be thinking about what that hierarchy of the ads is going to be and what you're going to say to pay that off in order for it to quickly make total sense to people.*[23]

Learning Charlie Hopper's media-focused writing tips

As mentioned in Chapter 6 in Advice from the Pros 6.1, Hopper stated that creative teams begin thinking about where people will see the work. Creatives look to catch consumers off guard, interrupt their lives, and create a personal communication. Each message is perfectly tailored to that specific medium. Hopper explained the creative process this way.

Today, there are more imaginative touchpoints to reach the consumer, as we've discussed throughout this work. In addition to the innovative outdoor signs of years ago, now there are interactive TV spots, podcasts, mixed reality, art installations, transit, ambient, and other unexpected places. Hopper explained that the most important strategy is to keep the consumer interested long enough for them to see there's a reason to stay engaged. He compared it to dating, and said:

> *You're doing the same thing with the ads. You're trying to keep them from moving on before they get what's good about you.*[24]

Hopper added his best writing tips (Advice from the Pros 14.1). Use them to improve your content writing and copywriting.

ADVICE FROM THE PROS 14.1 Hopper's top writing tips

1. *Just stay away from the puns.* What the pun will do is distract you. The pun wins. But the pun is always off topic. The pun is never making any new ideas. The pun is never really convincing anybody about anything new. Even feeling as I do, I can't get rid of them entirely, like cockroaches or crabgrass.

2. *Write less.* You can always write less. You can always shock yourself at how concise you can get. You can take out all kinds of unnecessary clauses and qualifying words that don't get you anywhere. You can almost 100% of the time cut off the first paragraph, no matter what you're writing. Just cut off the first paragraph. That always works.

3. *Don't let grammar freak you out.* Concentrate on expressing an original thought. A lot of great thinkers would not be able to summon an example of a subordinate clause or tell you what the subjunctive mood is.

4. *Learn grammar.* It frees you. Picasso could draw an accurate, controlled and identifiable picture of a woman, that's why it was okay for him not to. If you can develop a certain comfort with grammar, it gives you confidence to mess around with it a little.

5. *Don't let bad grammar get you expelled before you make your point.* People are unaware of good grammar and really aware of bad grammar. It's like manners. And if you have good manners, you have a chance of making your point. If you do the English grammar equivalent of scratching your armpits while you talk, you may be rejected without a fair hearing.

6. *Pretend your reader has an excited dog on a leash, or impatient child repeatedly saying her name.* That way, you'll make sure you're concise, and you won't make people figure stuff out and guess what you're trying to say. And you won't be as interested in making them say, "Gosh, that person was quite clever."

7. *Don't ask a question that is easily answered "no."* Like "Are you tired of never having enough ice cubes?" or "Isn't it time you considered making a will?" It's for two reasons: people are impatient and if you ask them hypothetical questions as a way of supposedly trapping them into following you, it's just annoying and they think they have you sized up and think to themselves "forget it." And about three-quarters of the time when you do ask a question like that, it's a trite, tired question-device that automatically signals, "No need to read this. It's full of old ideas you've seen before."

8. *Be the first to say something.* Don't just mush around things other people have said. It's ambitious to think you'll be first. But it's the difference between being a writer and being a supplier of verbiage.

9. *Provide variety.* Switch it up. Be almost mechanically aware of varying the lengths of your sentences. Don't write the same length of sentence over and over and over. It's just a simple, mechanical thing to try.[25]

Looking at more cross-platform campaigns

Let's examine a few more cross-platform campaigns. The campaign for Mount Sinai Medical Center, created by DeVito/Verdi (Figure 14.21, Figure 14.22, Figure 14.23, Figure 14.24), shows how writers can create a series of unexpected, thought-provoking headlines. Again, the benefits of going to Mount

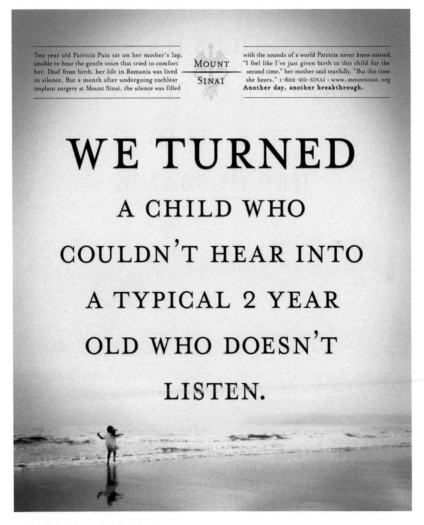

FIGURE 14.21 This "Two-Year-Old" print ad was created by DeVito/Verdi for Mount Sinai. Image courtesy of DeVito/Verdi.

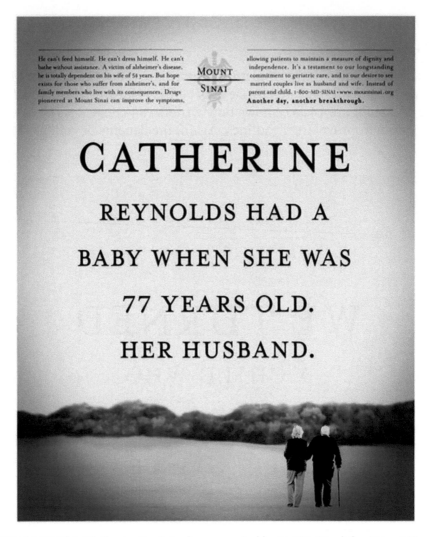

He can't feed himself. He can't dress himself. He can't bathe without assistance. A victim of alzheimer's disease, he is totally dependent on his wife of 54 years. But hope exists for those who suffer from alzheimer's, and for family members who live with its consequences. Drugs pioneered at Mount Sinai can improve the symptoms,

MOUNT SINAI

allowing patients to maintain a measure of dignity and independence. It's a testament to our longstanding commitment to geriatric care, and to our desire to see married couples live as husband and wife. Instead of parent and child. 1-800-MD-SINAI • www.mountsinai.org
Another day, another breakthrough.

CATHERINE

REYNOLDS HAD A

BABY WHEN SHE WAS

77 YEARS OLD.

HER HUSBAND.

FIGURE 14.22 This "Catherine" print ad was created by DeVito/Verdi for Mount Sinai. Image courtesy of DeVito/Verdi.

Sinai are summarized in the *combination* (#16) slogan "Another day. Another breakthrough." (This line combines these three types of slogans: [1] #5 *parallel construction*, [2] #6 *statement of use or purpose*, and [3] #14 *reason why*, as discussed in Chapter 10.) Notice also how it closes the copy in every ad. Rather than sitting in its normal position, it's close to the logo.

Let's look at the ads one at a time. Then, we'll read the radio script. Each ad has a *call to action*, and the *mandatory* information, called the "signature lines" (or "sig"), which include the phone number and website. Pay special attention to how the copy jumps into the story, without an introduction.

A car accident left Ruby Gaynor with a serious brain injury. And a severely impaired future. But doctors at Mount Sinai Rehabilitation Center weren't impaired by the constraints of ordinary care. Through intensive therapy, she relearned the basic skills that she once took for granted, and fine-tuned the advanced skills that could take her through college. Which turned a tragedy into a triumph. And tears into, well, more tears. 1-800-MD SINAI. For a list of our doctors log onto www.mountsinai.org **Another day, another breakthrough.**

MOUNT SINAI

RUBY

GAYNOR'S PARENTS CRIED

WHEN SHE SUFFERED BRAIN DAMAGE.

THEY CRIED EVEN MORE

WHEN SHE GRADUATED COLUMBIA.

FIGURE 14.23 This "Ruby" print ad was created by DeVito/Verdi for Mount Sinai. Image courtesy of DeVito/Verdi.

This way the reader is drawn in, and not turned off, before absorbing the information.

"Two-Year-Old" (Figure 14.21)

HEADLINE: We Turned a Child Who Couldn't Hear into a Typical 2 Year Old Who Doesn't Listen.

COPY: Two-year-old Patricia Puia sat on her mother's lap, unable to hear the gentle voice that tried to comfort her. Deaf from

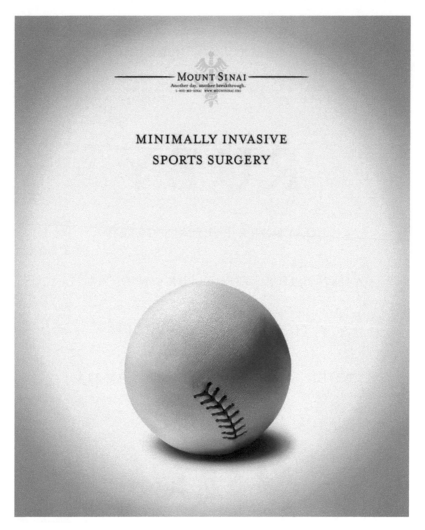

FIGURE 14.24 This "Baseball" print ad was created by DeVito/Verdi for Mount Sinai. Image courtesy of DeVito/Verdi.

birth, her life in Romania was lived in silence. But a month after undergoing cochlear implant surgery at Mount Sinai, the silence was filled with sounds of a world Patricia never knew existed. "I feel like I've just given birth to this child for the second time," her mother said tearfully. "But this time she hears." 1-800-MD SINAI. www.mountsinai.org.

Look at how the headline catches the reader off-guard. It talks about a deaf toddler who, through surgery at Mount Sinai, eventually, turns a deaf ear. Just like all little kids her age. At first, you feel sympathy. Then, you feel joy. What a wonderful way to tell the story, in just a few words.

"Catherine" (Figure 14.22)

HEADLINE: Catherine Reynolds Had a Baby When She Was 77 Years Old.
SUBHEAD: Her Husband.
COPY: He can't feed himself. He can't dress himself. He can't bathe without assistance. A victim of Alzheimer's disease, he is totally dependent on his wife of 54 years. But hope exists for those who suffer from Alzheimer's, and for family members who live with its consequences. Drugs pioneered at Mount Sinai can improve the symptoms, allowing patients to maintain a measure of dignity and independence. It's a testament to our longstanding commitment to geriatric care, and to our desire to see married couples live as husband and wife. Instead of parent and child. 1-800-MD-SINAI. www.mountsinai.org.

Here the headline makes you stop and ask, "How is that possible?" Then, the subhead explains the answer. You go from confusion to comprehension in just two words: "Her husband." Again, the woman's life experience is summed up in a headline and subhead.

"Ruby" (Figure 14.23)

HEADLINE: Ruby Gaynor's Parents Cried When She Suffered Brain Damage.
SUBHEAD: They Cried Even More When She Graduated Columbia.
COPY: A car accident left Ruby Gaynor with a serious brain injury. And a severely impaired future. But doctors at Mount Sinai Rehabilitation Center weren't impaired by the constraints of ordinary care. Through intensive therapy, she relearned the basic skills she once took for granted, and fine-tuned the advanced skills that could take her through college. Which turned a tragedy into a triumph. And tears into, well, more tears. 1-800-MD-SINAI. For a list of our doctors log onto www.mountsinai.org.

This headline connects to everyone. Who wouldn't feel terrible about anyone's daughter with brain damage? Then, the subhead rewards the reader with instant relief. How wonderful that Ruby recovered. It doesn't matter whether you know her or not. You're happy for her parents. Why? Because this headline immediately conjures up empathy and compassion.

"Baseball" (Figure 14.24)

HEADLINE: Minimally Invasive Sports Surgery.

COPY: None. (There was no need to explain it because the headline and visual said it all.) When the headline and the visual deliver the entire message as a unit, copy is sometimes not needed. That's the case in this "Baseball" ad. The image cleverly shows a short surgical incision as if the baseball were repaired.

Now, let's look at how the Mount Sinai radio script (Scripts and Examples 14.2) parallels the print ad copy for the two-year-old Patricia Puia's story. The spot restates how her hearing was restored through surgery at the hospital. See how the script uses *parallel construction* (#9 writing techniques in Chapter 9) with the second announcer repeating and then modifying the first announcer's lines.

 SCRIPTS AND EXAMPLES 14.2 Mount Sinai, :60 radio script: "Two-Year-Old"

MAN 1:	Two-year-old Patricia Puia was born deaf in Romania.
MAN 2:	Two-year-old Patricia Puia was born deaf in Romania.
MAN 1:	Her life was lived in silence.
MAN 2:	Her life was lived in silence.
MAN 1:	She had never heard a lullaby or the voice of another human being.
MAN 2:	She had never heard a lullaby or the voice of another human being.
MAN 1:	Her parents were told nothing could be done.
MAN 2:	Her parents were told that Mount Sinai in New York could restore Patricia's hearing.
MAN 1:	Patricia's parents were filled with despair.
MAN 2:	Patricia underwent cochlear implant surgery.
MAN 1:	Patricia withdrew into a shell.
MAN 2:	Patricia was able to hear for the very first time.
MAN 1:	Life has been difficult for Patricia and her parents.
MAN 2:	Life for Patricia is that of a typical two-year-old. She can hear, but she doesn't listen.

> WOMAN: Which hospital you choose can make all the difference in the world. Mount Sinai. Another day. Another breakthrough. For more information call 1-800-MD-SINAI.
>
> *(This "Two-Year-Old" :60 radio spot was created by DeVito/Verdi for Mount Sinai. Script courtesy of DeVito/Verdi.)*

The same echo technique is used in the "Father" script (Scripts and Examples 14.3). The small differences from one line to the next highlight how the new medication developed by Mount Sinai doctors changed this man's life and that of his children. For example, look how the bolded copy emphasized the quality-of-life improvement.

MAN 1: He could **barely speak**.
MAN 2: He began **speaking in full paragraphs.**
MAN 1: His family found they could **no longer** communicate with him.
MAN 2: His family found they could **now** communicate with him.
MAN 1: His children felt as if they had **lost their father.**
MAN 2: His children were thrilled to **have their father back.**

 SCRIPTS AND EXAMPLES 14.3 Mount Sinai, :60 radio script: "Father"

MAN 1: Sixty-four-year-old Norman Lewis suffered from Alzheimer's Disease.

MAN 2: Sixty-four-year-old Norman Lewis suffered from Alzheimer's Disease.

MAN 1: His children suffered with him.

MAN 2: His children suffered with him.

MAN 1: His condition grew progressively worse.

MAN 2: His condition grew progressively worse.

MAN 1: His speech in particular had badly deteriorated.

MAN 2: His speech in particular had badly deteriorated.

MAN 1: No treatment was available.

MAN 2: He was treated with a new drug developed by a team of doctors at Mount Sinai.

MAN 1: He could barely speak.

MAN 2:	He began speaking in full paragraphs.
MAN 1:	His family found they could no longer communicate with him.
MAN 2:	His family found they could now communicate with him.
MAN 1:	His children felt as if they had lost their father.
MAN 2:	His children were thrilled to have their father back.
WOMAN:	Which hospital you choose can make all the difference in the world. Mount Sinai. Another day. Another breakthrough. For more information call 1-800-MD-SINAI.

(This "Father" :60 radio spot was created by DeVito/Verdi for Mount Sinai. Script courtesy of DeVito/Verdi.)

Next, we'll discuss single medium campaigns. Those are the ones that run only in one medium.

Celebrating single medium campaigns

Some messages are so powerful, they only need to appear in one medium. The Apple "1984" TV spot, created by TBWA\Chiat\Day, that ran in the Super Bowl of that year, made such an impact, it was replayed and discussed in the news. Today, it would have been shared online and viewed by thousands, if not millions of people, practically overnight.

Another message, created in 1999 by DeVito/Verdi for the American Civil Liberties Union (ACLU),[26] ran only as a print ad. It drove home the problem of racial profiling with the image of Dr. Martin Luther King on the left and murderer Charles Manson on the right (Figure 14.25). Just look at how the headline clearly made the point:

HEADLINE:	The Man on the Left is 75 Times More Likely to Be Stopped by the Police While Driving Than the Man on the Right.
COPY:	It happens every day on America's highways. Police stop drivers based on their skin color rather than for the way they are driving. For example, in Florida 80% of those stopped and searched were black and Hispanic, while they constituted only 5% of all drivers. These humiliating and illegal searches are violations of the Constitution and must be fought. Help us defend your rights. Support the ACLU. To learn more and to send your Members of Congress a free fax go to www.aclu.org/racialprofiling.

FIGURE 14.25 This "Dr. King" print ad was created by DeVito/Verdi for American Civil Liberties Union. Image courtesy of DeVito/Verdi.

The copy explained that black and Hispanic drivers were pulled over by the police even though they represented only 5% of all drivers (at that time). People profiled sarcastically coined the phrase "DWB" (driving while black) as a humorous reference or parody to the then-used phrase "DWI" (driving while intoxicated), now commonly called "DUI" (driving under the influence). The ad was designed to create pressure for those "persuaders" in political power to create change.

Another controversial campaign, also created by DeVito/Verdi, shortly after opening its agency in 1991, was for Daffy's. The first headline read: "Shirt. Bullshirt." (Figure 14.26). It showed a shirt with a $20 price tag on the left and one with a $68 price tag on the right.

FIGURE 14.26 This "Bullshirt" print ad was created by DeVito/Verdi for Daffy's. Image courtesy of DeVito/Verdi.

The copy simply stated:

> *Men's women's and children's fashion & designer clothes 40–75% off, every day.*

It finished with a list of addresses. Plus, the logo. That's it. The headline said it all.

The next headline, "If you're paying over $100 for a dress shirt, may we suggest a jacket to go with it?" (Figure 14.27), implied that you had to be crazy to spend $100 on a fancy shirt. Unfortunately, showing a straitjacket in the ad ruffled feathers for mental-health advocacy groups, who found the image offensive.

Under the logo was an easy-to-recall slogan that used several techniques: (1) *#2 rhyme*, (2) *#4 play-on-words*, (3) *#6 statement of promise* (as discussed in Chapter 10). It cleverly restated the point:

Clothes that will make you, not break you.

Again, the copy just said:

With men's, women's and children's fashion & designer clothes 40–75% off, every day, you'd be crazy to shop anywhere else Elizabeth, East Hanover, Paramus, Wayne and New York City.

FIGURE 14.27 This "Jacket" print ad was created by DeVito/Verdi for Daffy's. Image courtesy of DeVito/Verdi.

Even though the ad uses a humorous *tone of voice*, it was still considered offensive to one group sensitive to mental-health issues, as mentioned above. However, by saying you'd have to be crazy to overpay for something is a common expression that resonates with everyday shoppers, especially in a challenging economic climate.

Humor, of course, is subjective. However, clever copy that can work in multiple platforms, amuse the audience, and feature benefits can be very persuasive. The humorous tone makes the audience feel comfortable, as if they know the brand and the brand knows them. They're sharing a little joke between them, and the consumer feels as if the brand "gets" or understands them. The *benefits* remind shoppers their needs are recognized. The multiple *touchpoints* show consumers can be reached in their everyday activities because their lifestyles are considered. In short, reaching the consumer in a disarmingly simple, yet creative way bears fruit.

Thinking globally

One last area we should consider is: the international messages. Reaching audiences through multiple *touchpoints* is equally applicable to multicultural and multilingual campaigns. Those messages also need to make consumers feel as if they're having a private, one-on-one conversation with the brand. Whether you create the dialogue in one language or more, the key is to know when and where to use which language. Some agencies write differently for different markets. Others want to create a universal message that's applicable to all audiences. Let's look at how McDonald Marketing, an agency specializing in targeting Hispanic audiences, creates messages for specific consumer groups.

> *So, when we're doing national marketing messages that need to go everywhere, we use neutral Spanish. It's dialect-free and it's what we would call Tom Brokaw Spanish.* Kelly McDonald, President of McDonald Marketing[27]

Writing for Hispanic markets

Kelly McDonald, the president of McDonald Marketing, shared how her agency specifically addresses one of four particular Hispanic mindsets "to identify our client's high-potential target or targets."[28] She developed an "Acculturation Stratification Model" to define each group. She explained the difference between assimilation and acculturation because many people confuse the two words and use them interchangeably. McDonald clarified them this way:

1. *Assimilation means that I forfeit my culture and I adopt yours.*

2. *Acculturation means, "I forfeit nothing." There are certain things that I really like about your culture and I want those. But, there are certain things that I really like about my primary culture and I want to keep those, too.*

   So, an overly simplistic way to look at it is, assimilation is about "either or." It's about I'm either in my culture or I'm in yours and adapted to yours. And acculturation is not about "either or" it's about "and."[29]

She gave this example of acculturation by talking about a little eight-year-old American girl of Mexican descent. "On Christmas, she's eating tamales *and* waiting for Santa. Then, a week later, she's celebrating Three Kings Day. She differs from the recently arrived Spanish-dominant Latinos, who are going to be immersed in their primary culture. They tend to live among other Spanish-speaking people, work among other Spanish-speaking people, live in Little Mexico, their Little Mexico part of town."[30]

McDonald then breaks the Hispanic market into four subgroups or levels of acculturation:

1. *Cultural loyalist* – They could have just arrived or could have lived in America for 20 years, yet still think they're going back "home." They still see themselves as visitors, not residents. They're the least acculturated.

2. *Cultural embracer* – Like the cultural loyalists, they were born outside the country, but have adopted the United States as their permanent home.

3. *Cross culture* – They're Latinos who are first-generation Americans. They were born here, but their parents weren't. So, they've been raised biculturally. They have a different mindset.

4. *Cultural integrator* – They're US born Latinos who are second, third, fourth (and so on) generation. They prefer to speak English, but are proud of their Hispanic heritage. They might ask their parents to call them Joey, not José so they'll fit in. Today, the same kids are saying, "No, it's okay to call me José." Because now being Latino creates a professional advantage.[31]

She explained how this helps when you're marketing to each group. For example, if your client is a bank, the way you would approach a newly arrived *cultural loyalist* would be different from a *cultural integrator* or *cross culture*. You might target a *cultural loyalist* with information about a checking or savings account and money wiring. However, you wouldn't mention money wiring to any other of the Hispanic subgroups because they wouldn't be sending money home to anyone. Most of their family members are in the U.S. Likewise, you wouldn't try to sell a mortgage to recent arrivals because they wouldn't have the required credit history.

For bilingual targeting, McDonald said it's not right for every market. For instance, if the same bank were targeting cultural embracers, it might use Spanish. The reason is this. Although *cultural embracers* are quickly becoming bilingual, they might still prefer to receive information in Spanish, because it's their first language and therefore easier to comprehend.

McDonald also mentioned if the client, such as a telecommunications company, were targeting youth, its natural primary audience, it would use Spanglish (a mix of English and Spanish), rather than with a bilingual campaign. And, when they create bilingual campaigns, they don't "translate" the message, they "*transcreate*" it. That means they develop a similar, culturally relevant message, that isn't necessarily a word-for-word translation.

Finally, when targeting the *cultural integrator*, she would use English, the group's dominant language, peppered with culturally relevant references in the message. She explained, like African–American marketing, it's not a linguistic, but a cultural difference, which would be addressed with African–American humor, situations, family scenes, and so on.

Research delivers insights into each demographic group. For instance, if a charitable organization wanted people to donate their vehicles, that kind of message wouldn't be something Hispanics would necessarily respond to. They would tend to give their cars to family members. She became enthusiastic when she discussed the importance of research in the strategic development process:

> *We love research. We believe nothing speaks like the consumer. So, wherever possible, we actually augment our own experience and insights with concrete research.*[32]

She shared some interesting research results after her agency conducted 200 person-on-the-street interviews in six different cities. When they questioned people, they asked:

1. Do you have insurance?

2. Do you have a license, and do you have insurance?

What they found out was surprising. Although many people didn't have a license, every one of them had insurance. When they asked consumers why they would have insurance without having a license, people answered, "Because it's the law."[33]

Another interesting insight she learned was to separate men and women in Hispanic focus groups because men will be more forthright without women in the room. On the other hand, women will be more vocal without men around them. How did she use this information? When her agency wanted to talk to the do-it-yourself painter for Sherwin-Williams, one of her clients, they spoke to the men and women separately. No macho man will admit he doesn't know how to paint something in front of a woman.

When they asked men, "Do you feel like you need to go to the paint store to get expert advice, and the proper guidance you need for the tools and the prep work?" they gathered more honest answers when there were no women in the room. Hearing from each group separately helped guide the advertising. McDonald said:

> *It absolutely drives the messaging because what it does is identifies barriers to entry that we can then overcome with messaging or identifies what their desires are that we didn't know.*[34]

One final question was telling. It was free-form: "If you had the president of Sherwin-Williams here in front of you today, what would you tell him or her?" They were able to say anything at all, like, "Oh, I like your products." Or "I wish there was a store near my house." But, here's what was said over and over: "It would be really nice if you had coupons."[35]

Just learning that this audience wanted coupons drove the creative teams to develop them because they knew they would be appreciated and redeemed. In a direct mail piece, Sherwin-Williams offered a coupon with $10 off a $50 purchase.

Perhaps assuming that everyone enjoys a discount and applying that as a *universal truth* would have worked. However, once the research confirmed that this audience wanted to save money, it became the core message that was definitely on-target.

When considering a cross-platform campaign, think about whether or not it will need to speak to an international audience, to target a specific ethnic group, or to be *transcreated* into another language. Be mindful of cultural differences and make sure your messaging is sensitive to words that could be incorrectly translated. Every audience deserves to be respected and honored. Cultural errors can inadvertently become controversial and/or offensive.

Think big picture. Can this campaign speak to a wide audience and still deliver a universal truth? If so, you might use only one core message that is universally understood as the Volkswagen "Das Auto" slogan. The word "car" or "auto" is quickly grasped worldwide.

Most importantly, say what you want to say as clearly as possible. No one has time to figure out a complex message. Here's what Charlie Hopper said:

> *You've got to hate big words where small words will do. The ones that come to mind immediately are "utilize" instead of "use." "Verbiage" instead of "words" or "copy." But, there are millions of other examples. You've got to hate clichés.* *Charlie Hopper, Principal, Young & Laramore*[36]

Refer to Checklist 14.4 when you develop cross-platform campaigns with multiple touchpoints. It will help you design persuasive, on-target, and on-strategy marketing.

As you create campaigns, whether they're local or global, create the brand's voice and story. Know your audience. Develop useful content. Offer solutions. Share it across platforms. Generate a following. Earn advocacy. Be respectful and responsive to your audience. Be engaging and experiential. Be bold.

Finally, remember this: Sticking to the status quo is like using a compass and the North Star to fly to the moon. It's just not going to cut it.

 CHECKLIST 14.4 Cross-platform writing tips checklist

1 Think simple. Look for a message that's instantly understood.

2 Focus on flexibility. Ask how the message would lend itself to other channels and platforms.

3 Include interactivity. Make it a point to engage the audience. Remember what ASICS did to target New York Marathoners, as we mentioned earlier in Chapters 4, 11, and 12.

4 Consider specific interest groups. If you're addressing hockey or ice-skating fans, forget age and think about what unifies them. Then, speak to those common interests.

5 Remember to include *universal truths*.

6 Be irreverent when appropriate. Review the Legal Sea Foods and FECKIN Irish Whiskey campaigns in Chapter 12.

7 Decide if humor would work as it does in the 7-Eleven campaign in Chapter 12 and Red Brick Beer packaging in Chapter 13.

8 Be sensitive to different audiences, so your message will be embraced, not rejected.

9 Promote the brand through traditional, digital, immersive, social, and mobile media.

10 Create an open dialogue. Just realize, today's audience can answer back.

Cross-platform messaging exercises

Exercise 1: Thinking about writing for diverse audiences

Part 1 Go online and find a campaign that targets a specific ethnic or lifestyle group. For instance, cruise lines that allow specific groups to customize a cruise just for them, like art aficionados, music devotees, fitness buffs, gardening enthusiasts, wine connoisseurs, gourmands, writers, fundraisers for charitable organizations, industry associates, wedding parties, same-sex couples, singles, retirees, seniors, and so on.

Part 2 Create a new campaign for the same audience. Develop a slogan and two headlines that could work in any media, including social media posts.

Part 3 Choose your media. Consider using:

- Interactive components, like:
    - Contests (for example: best new cruise activities or excursions)
    - Blogs with people sharing their stories
    - Social networking channels where consumers can exchange ideas
- Mobile announcements
- Online coupons
- Immersive experiences
- Digital discounts
- TV or radio
- Print ads, flyers, brochures
- E-zines (online magazines) or e-newsletters
- Ambient signs
- Direct mail
- Transit messages

Exercise 2: Create another campaign for a different group

Part 1 How would you target this group? You could consider:

- *Eyebrows* (lines that appear before the headline to speak to a specific group, like: "Attention Pet lovers!" as discussed in Chapters 10 and 11).

- Language *relevant* to a specific group, like "Expert Yoga instructors."

- *Benefits* that speak to an interested group, like "Strengthen your core muscles," for Pilates' students.

Part 2 What other types of media would you use? Before deciding, ask yourself why you would choose those particular vehicles? Are there any other ones you should consider, such as: social media posts or videos, out-of-home, YouTube videos, immersive campaigns, or TV spots?

Exercise 3: Thinking past different groups

Part 1 If you know which audiences you're targeting, you may be able to see if there are any common values or interests. Think about events or activities that unify people across the world like soccer, fitness, literature, art, music, and so on.

Consider how you could create a campaign that would be equally effective in two languages and speak directly to each market.

Part 2 Create a single, simple message that can be repurposed. Start with a *universal* or *global truth* that could work as the slogan for both audiences.

Part 3 Modify the message to act as a series of headlines in the campaign.

Part 4 Consider an international audience. How would you adapt this message?

Part 5 Start by creating a strictly transit-oriented campaign. Can you make it interactive with a QR code or an invitation for commuters to post about the product for a reward? Consider using:

- Taxi cabs
  - Outside (top or side of cabs)
  - Inside
- Bus
  - Sides
  - Benches
  - Shelters
- Subways
  - Interiors

- ▪ Exteriors
- ▪ Platforms
- ▪ Trolleys (trams)
- ▪ Trains
  - ▪ Cars/Carriages
  - ▪ Stations
- ▪ Airplanes
  - ▪ In-flight magazines
  - ▪ Tray tables
  - ▪ Outside of plane (body and tail wings)

Exercise 4: Adding interactivity

Part 1 What types of engagement could you use? Would augmented or virtual reality work? Could a live activation event promote the brand? Would a branded app entice a response? Remember to review the types of common interests your audience(s) have, including foreign films, musical genres, diet and fitness, gymnastics, salsa dancing, cooking, and so on.

Part 2 Choose the type of interaction. Remember to connect the (1) brand, (2) audience, and (3) strategy. Just developing an idea isn't enough. It has to work on all three levels.

Part 3 Write a social media post or video to promote the interaction.

Notes

1. Tom Amico, personal communication, April 20, 2022.
2. https://adage.com/article/special-report-the-advertising-century/ad-age-advertising-century-top-10-icons/140157 (accessed January 30, 2022).
3. Charlie Hopper, personal communication, November 26, 2021.
4. Tom Amico, personal communication, April 20, 2022.
5. Tom Amico, personal communication, April 20, 2022.
6. Carolyn Hadlock, personal communication, March 16, 2022.
7. Carolyn Hadlock, personal communication, March 16, 2022.
8. Tom Amico, personal communication, April 20, 2022.
9. KT Thayer, personal communication, September 9, 2010.
10. KT Thayer, personal communication, September 9, 2010.
11. KT Thayer, personal communication, September 9, 2010.

12. KT Thayer, personal communication, September 9, 2010.
13. Paul McCormick, personal communication, November 8, 2022.
14. Paul McCormick, personal communication, November 8, 2022.
15. Drummond Berman, personal communication, April 8, 2009.
16. Drummond Berman, personal communication, April 8, 2009.
17. Drummond Berman, personal communication, April 8, 2009.
18. Simon Nickson, personal communication, April 8, 2009.
19. Simon Nickson, personal communication, April 8, 2009.
20. Simon Nickson, personal communication, April 8, 2009.
21. Drummond Berman, personal communication, April 8, 2009.
22. Drummond Berman, personal communication, April 8, 2009.
23. Drummond Berman, personal communication, April 8, 2009.
24. Charlie Hopper, personal communication, November 26, 2021.
25. Charlie Hopper, personal communication, November 26, 2021.
26. https://www.devitoverdi.com/work/aclu/ (November 8, 2022).
27. Kelly McDonald, personal communication, May 12, 2009.
28. Kelly McDonald, personal communication, May 12, 2009.
29. Kelly McDonald, personal communication, May 12, 2009.
30. Kelly McDonald, personal communication, May 12, 2009.
31. Kelly McDonald, personal communication, May 12, 2009.
32. Kelly McDonald, personal communication, May 12, 2009.
33. Kelly McDonald, personal communication, May 12, 2009.
34. Kelly McDonald, personal communication, May 12, 2009.
35. Kelly McDonald, personal communication, May 12, 2009.
36. Charlie Hopper, personal communication, November 26, 2021.

Resources

A Short, Handy List of Resource Links

U se this as a reference guide. Of course, this is only a brief overview of some of the information available. Regularly search for updated content. Then, edit or add to this list as a personalized reference for yourself.

Best times for social media posts

Influencer Marketing Hub – https://influencermarketinghub.com/social-media-post-reach-engagement/

Sprout Social – https://sproutsocial.com/insights/best-times-to-post-on-social-media/

Status Brew – https://statusbrew.com/insights/best-times-to-post-on-social-media

Business strategies (growth hacks: affordable, business growth strategies)

Growth Hacks – https://coschedule.com/blog/growth-hacks

WordStream – https://www.wordstream.com/blog/ws/2015/06/02/growth-hacking

Content marketing

HubSpot – https://blog.hubspot.com/marketing/content-marketing

Content and Copywriting: The Complete Toolkit for Strategic Marketing,
Second Edition. Margo Berman.
© 2024 Margo Berman. Published 2024 by John Wiley & Sons Ltd.
Companion website: www.wiley.com/go/contentandcopywriting

Content scheduling

Canva – https://www.canva.com/for-teams/content-planning-scheduling/

CoSchedule – https://coschedule.com

Digital Marketing Institute – https://digitalmarketinginstitute.com/resources/lessons/content-marketing_content-scheduling_2yyu

Hootsuite – https://www.hootsuite.com/

Influencer Marketing Hub – https://influencermarketinghub.com/social-media-posting-scheduling-tools/

Sprout Social list of tools – https://sproutsocial.com/insights/social-media-scheduling-tools/

Conversion improvement – landing page tools

WordStream – https://www.wordstream.com/blog/ws/2015/06/24/landing-page-tools

Customer testimonial page examples

HubSpot – https://blog.hubspot.com/service/testimonial-page-examples

MarketSplash – https://marketsplash.com/customer-testimonial-examples/

WordStream – https://www.wordstream.com/blog/ws/2017/07/19/customer-testimonial-examples

Definitions and terms

Hootsuite – https://blog.hootsuite.com/social-media-definitions/

HubSpot – https://blog.hubspot.com/marketing/social-media-terms

One2Create – https://www.one2create.co.uk/?s=terminology

Outbrain – https://www.outbrain.com/blog/digital-advertising-glossary/

SimpliLearn – https://www.simplilearn.com/social-media-marketing-terms-article

Sprout Social – social media definitions – https://sproutsocial.com/glossary/

Editorial calendar

Asana – https://asana.com/templates/editorial-calendar

CoSchedule – https://coschedule.com/blog/content-marketing-editorial-calendar-template

Hootsuite – https://blog.hootsuite.com/how-to-create-a-social-media-content-calendar/

HubSpot – https://offers.hubspot.com/editorial-calendar-templates?utm_campaign=kickback-email&utm_medium=email&utm_content=186820869&utm_source=hs_automation

SmartBlogger – https://smartblogger.com/editorial-calendar/

Funnel examples

Launch marketing/sales funnels

Copyhackers – https://copyhackers.com/how-to-plan-your-launch-funnel/

Social media marketing funnel – Drives social media followers to website

Sprout Social – https://sproutsocial.com/insights/social-media-marketing-funnel/

Guides and other resources

Sprout Social – https://sproutsocial.com/insights/resources/

Marketing analytics

Adobe Analytics – https://business.adobe.com/blog/basics/marketing-analytics

BuzzSumo – https://appsumo.com/products/buzzsumo/

Coursera – https://www.coursera.org/articles/marketing-analytics

Marketing Evolution – https://www.marketingevolution.com/marketing-essentials/marketing-analytics

Quid – https://www.quid.com/knowledge-hub/resource-library/blog/what-is-social-listening-why-is-it-important/

SAS – https://www.sas.com/en_us/insights/marketing/marketing-analytics.html

WordStream – https://www.wordstream.com/blog/ws/2021/10/19/ppc-metrics

Marketing trends (sites, blogs, and articles)

Canva – https://www.canva.com/learn/marketing-trends-guide/

Entrepreneur – https://www.entrepreneur.com/growing-a-business/7-marketing-trends-that-will-define-success-in-2022/394483

Envato – https://www.envato.com/blog/marketing-trends/

Forbes – https://www.forbes.com/sites/henrydevries/2023/01/30/10-marketing-trends-and-predictions-for-2023/?sh=6c76cb5b7f26

HubSpot – https://blog.hubspot.com/marketing/marketing-trends

LinkedIn – https://www.linkedin.com/pulse/top-5-2023-marketing-trends-bold-agency-llc

Social media analytics

Hootsuite – https://blog.hootsuite.com/what-is-social-media-analytics/

HubSpot – https://blog.hubspot.com/marketing/social-media-analytics

IBM – https://www.ibm.com/topics/social-media-analytics

LinkedIn – https://www.linkedin.com/pulse/how-understand-your-social-media-analytics-naturally-social

Qualtrics – https://www.qualtrics.com/experience-management/research/social-media-analytics/

Quid – https://www.quid.com/knowledge-hub/resource-library/blog/what-is-social-listening-why-is-it-important/

SocialPilot – https://www.socialpilot.co/social-media-analytics-tools

SpiceWorks – https://www.spiceworks.com/marketing/advertising/articles/what-is-social-media-analytics/

Templates (design, social media, video, coding, etc.)

Canva – https://www.canva.com

Convince&Convert – https://www.convinceandconvert.com/social-media-strategy/successful-social-media-writing/

Envato Elements – https://elements.envato.com/

Hootsuite – free social media templates – https://blog.hootsuite.com/social-media-templates/

Hubspot – various free templates for design, social media, coding, etc. – https://www.hubspot.com/resources/template

Marketing plan template generator – https://blog.hubspot.com/marketing/marketing-plan-template-generator

Marketing plan template link – https://blog.hubspot.com

Tutorials (just a short list of examples)

Design trends and tutorials

https://www.youtube.com/watch?v=pnymSjlWmCE

https://designschool.canva.com/

https://Yesimadesigner.com/courses

https://bringyourownlaptop.com/files

How to make video ads

https://animoto.com/make/video-ads

https://www.envato.com

Video templates and overlays – https://www.youtube.com/watch?v=3yQmBLeOc7A

About interactive videos – https://www.youtube.com/watch?v=6cpIHzkHpKw

Marketing

https://blog.hubspot.com/marketing/social-media-marketing-courses

Marketing word list – https://www.wordstream.com/blog/ws/2021/01/13/best-words-and-phrases-for-marketing

Social media trends

https://www.youtube.com/watch?v=3yQmBLeOc7A

Intro to social media – https://academy.hubspot.com/

User experience design course with Adobe XD course

https://www.youtube.com/watch?v=68w2VwalD5w

Writing

Content Marketing Institute – https://contentmarketinginstitute.com

Convince&Convert – https://www.convinceandconvert.com

Copyhackers – https://copyhackers.com/copywriting-tutorial/

Digital Marketers World – https://digitalmarketersworld.com

Hemingway App – https://hemingwayapp.com (measures the grade level. Go to WRITE to begin.)

Proofed – https://proofed.com/writing-tips/how-to-determine-a-piece-of-writings-tone/ (analyzes the way the content is expressed, such as in a positive, negative, or neutral tone.)

Wordstream – https://www.wordstream.com/blog/ws/2020/11/23/content-marketing-trends

Terminology

U se this glossary of terms as a fast reference for unfamiliar words or as a refresher for those you already know.

Check the Notes at the end for some helpful sources.

A/B testing – Test content with two or more versions to see which one performed better. It can also be used to specifically compare two different audiences' reactions.

Acronyms – One source for social media and slang acronyms: https://sproutsocial.com/insights/social-media-acronyms/.

Action – Part of a contact's behavior when interacting with your business, e.g., they clicked a link, visited a page, registered for a seminar, etc.

Ad blocker – Software that blocks digital advertising messages and pop-up ads. More than 11% of consumers are blocking ads.[1]

Ad fatigue – What consumers experience with an overload of online ads, especially when they see the same advertisement again and again.

Ad format – Different types of ads designed for their respective placement (platforms where they will appear):

- Photo and video ads
- Shopping ads
- Lead ads
- Message ads
- And more....

Content and Copywriting: The Complete Toolkit for Strategic Marketing,
Second Edition. Margo Berman.
© 2024 Margo Berman. Published 2024 by John Wiley & Sons Ltd.
Companion website: www.wiley.com/go/contentandcopywriting

Affiliate marketing – Affiliates are paid only when their links lead directly to a sale, as seen with Amazon links. However, sponsors are rewarded for their participation.[2] This is the step-by-step payment process:

1. Creator shares a link to the purchase of a particular product or service.
2. A viewer uses that link and makes said purchase.
3. The creator gets a percentage of that sale.

AI – Artificial Intelligence. Many uses to develop visual and verbal content, such as logo designs, written content, and captions for social media posts across platforms.

AI-powered copy – Computer-generated content services, such as OpenAI, ChatGPT, and Contentyze, which use AI to examine data, summarize it, and write content, including blogs.

Analytics – Measurement tools for the analysis of data to find patterns and draw insights into business performance (ROI or return on investment), marketing effectiveness (websites, videos, social media, etc.), consumer behaviors, and other relevant research areas.

API – Application Programming Interface. A way for two or more computer programs to communicate with each other.

AR – Augmented reality. AR adds or overlays images/text over what you see. AR can put answers right where your questions are by overlaying helpful visual content and information on your real world.[3]

AR ecosystem – Augmented reality environments.

Art installation – Oversized, eye-catching display to showcase a brand's products and appeal to varied communities.

Attribute – A quality or feature *about* a contact, e.g., their budget, contact location.

Audience engagement – Consumers interact with marketing prompts.

Banner ad – An online display ad, often on a web page, which can be interactive.

Behavior-based segmentation – Based on patterns of behavior, marketers can better predict how a consumer will react to a product, service, or brand information.

Blipvert – Commercials that run three seconds or less.

Bot (and integration) – A software program that can execute commands, reply to messages, or perform routine tasks, such as online searches, either automatically or with minimal human intervention (often used in combination). Here are a few examples: a social media bot reposting certain posts; a customer service chatbot to answer product questions; or a chatbot where consumers can get help with their accounts, travel plans, online orders, dinner reservations, and so on.

Bounce rate – Measures how often people go to your site and don't go to any other pages.

Brand purpose – The social consciousness and core value of the brand. What does it represent and how does it benefit causes, such as environmental and social justice issues? Consumers choose brands whose "mission" supports what's important to them.

Brand voice – How a brand usually talks or sounds. (See also Reverse engineering).

Business impact – Business leadership that shows it cares about business competitive advantages, customer satisfaction.

Calendaring – The scheduling of content and ad campaign release dates.

CGI – Computer-Generated Imagery. Digitally designed visuals (created by computers).

Click trigger – Encourages consumers to make a purchase by soothing their objections.

CLV – Customer Lifetime Value. Tracks total income from one customer.

CMS – Content Management System. Software to help arrange, generate, edit, and share (publish) content, such as WordPress.

Conditional content – A way to address a specific audience with customized tags to target (1) audience interest, (2) geographic location, (3) specific sales-team members, and (4) others.

Content community – Group of people who can create and share their work, especially useful for marketing teams.

Content grouping – Placing similar content into groups for easy reference.

Conversion – What is the ad's conversion rate compared to same-audience competitors (as seen in Facebook).

Conversion rate – Measures how many leads became customers. The rate is based on this formula: The number of people who took an action divided by the total number of people who saw the message, but didn't.

CRM – Customer Relationship Management. Tools that enable companies to monitor their relationships, interactions, and customer marketing.

CRM platform – A tool to manage and record customer-interaction information.

Cross-post – Repurpose content over multiple channels. It's efficient. But, can have drawbacks. Followers don't like to reread the same message.

CTA – Call to Action. Words or buttons that prompt consumers to do something: order, register, opt-in, etc.

CTR – Click-through Rate. Measures the percentage of viewers who clicked on a link, ad, or call-to-action button while they were searching The CTR formula is: # of clicks ÷ # of impressions × 100.

- Divide # of clicks on a link (or CTA) by total # of impressions (number of times someone saw the ad/content).
- Multiply the result by 100 to create the percentage.

Custom audience – A list of people your company would like to target with your ads, whose e-mail addresses you already have.

Custom field, list, or tag – Store data that is unique to each contact.

Customer acquisition cost – What marketers spend to gain a customer.

Customer data platform – Connects information from various sources, normalizes the data, and sends it down for activation.

Customer journey (funnel) – Ushers the shopper from product awareness, interest generation, and increased desire to a final purchase.

D2C – Direct to Consumer. To interact with consumers where they are, capture feedback and apply it to product design and customer service improvements, and customize consumer engagement.

Digital advertising – Targets online consumers through channels and platforms with data-driven research to escort them through the buyer's journey: from (1) awareness, (2) consideration, and (3) decision to (4) the actual purchase.

Digital maturity – Demonstrates a firm's ability to rapidly adjust marketing strategies as technology changes, sometimes called "hyper-personalization."

Digital tracking – Monitors all online and mobile activities across digital channels and platforms with the use of various tools, including geolocation and device IDs. For example, this can include day-to-day activities, such as banking and shopping, to gain insight into consumer behavior.

DM – Direct Message. Not visible to the public, e.g., Facebook Messenger.

Dwell time – How long visitors stay on a site.

Engagement analytics – How much engagement content created compared to competitors with the same target audience.

Diagnosis example: Low score = doesn't drive enough interactions. Measures these and other activities: number of pages visited per session, bounce rate (stopped by and left), how long visitors stayed (session duration), number of unique (not repeat) visitors and first-time and past visitors, etc.

Ephemeral video – Disappears in 24 hours (by invitation only).

FB – Facebook.

Free trial – Offer has an expiration date, then users can upgrade to full functionality. 30% of trial users choose to upgrade (mostly B2B).

Freemium – No time limit, users have access to basic features, only 1–10% of users upgrade to paid or premium subscriptions.[4]

Geosocial – GPS info connects people to local businesses and events.

Hero banner – Compelling message at the top of the home page.

IG – Instagram.

Impressions – Number of times someone saw the ad or read the content.

1. Types of impressions:
   - *Served impressions* – Measures (1) when the website posts the ad and (2) when visitors left before seeing the content.
   - *Viewed impressions* – Tracks whenever visitors appeared to view or scrolled down to see the message.
2. A few impression measurement tools:
   - *Total impressions* – Represents how many times the content appeared.
   - *Impression share* – Indicates percentage of impressions that the ad or content receives divided by how many it could have received. Marketers can see how many users are actually viewing their content.
   - *Search impression rate* – Lists the content's search engine page results.

In-app tour copy – How to get users to start engaging with an app when they sign up.

Inbound marketing – Content audience wants to receive (versus outbound – content that invades audience's lives, not necessarily wanted).

Influencers – People who (1) prompt followers to take action because of their perceived expertise or social media clout, and/or (2) promote brands or products through comments, reviews, or recommendations.

Infographic content marketing – Depicts content, information, and data in a simple-to-grasp, graphic format.

Integrated campaign – Using multiple channels and platforms to share content and post ads, for example:

- Digital ads and social media.
- Email with social media marketing:
  - Constant Contact + Instagram, Pinterest, X (formerly Twitter), YouTube, and LinkedIn.
  - Snapchat, TikTok.
- Social media and traditional media with coordinated scheduling.

Interactive TV – Commercial allows the viewer to interact by using buttons on TV remotes, tablets, mobile phones, or other devices.

Interactive video tools – Camtasia, Adobe Premiere Pro, tutorials (as examples).

Interruptive marketing – Disturbs consumers during their everyday activities. People often want to avoid these types of disruptions.

IRL – In Real Life. In the real world as opposed in a digital environment (or "virtual world").

Keywords – Common link between what brands offer and what consumers search for. Used to (1) summarize web page, social media post, video content, etc., (2) target audiences by topic or interest, (3) help surfers quickly find what they want, and (4) guide marketers in choosing relevant "focus" words. Correct keywords drive relevant content to targeted consumers.

Launch copywriter – Writer who focuses on rebranding or product-introduction copy.

Launch funnel – Designed to attract consumers to a new brand, create interest, guide the decisions process, and ultimately result in sales.

Lead generation list – Represents a broad spectrum of contacts who have one main, common interest.

LI – LinkedIn.

Lookalike audience – A group of people who are similar to an existing audience.

Meta tag – Small piece of code that provides details about your page to search engines.

Micro audience – Targets a niche group of people with similar demographics, interests, behavior, and/or geographics.

Mobile marketing – Promoting brand/product via mobile devices.

Mobile websites – Sites specifically designed for hand-held devices.

MR – Mixed reality. MR can blend physical and virtual worlds by integrating overlays and real-world objects into digital environments, creating unique interactions.

MT – Modified tweet, e.g., edited down to fit.

Native advertising – Looks like editorial info designed to encourage audience response with relevant headlines, images, content, description text, and more.

Native content – Blends into the format of where it appears.

Netnography – Analysis of online consumer behavior, using ethnographic-research techniques, to gain applicable marketing insights.

Newsjacking/Trendjacking – Borrowing current, popular topics in the news and on social media, then featuring them in your content.

Organic CTR – Organic Click-through Rate. The number of times visitors click on your page when it appears in an unpaid (organic) search.

Organic search – People find the site on their own, not through a paid search or sponsored content.

Outbound marketing – Content, such as advertising, that invades audience's lives. Not necessarily wanted.

Paid ads – Companies pay to digitally display their ads on web banners; social media posts; landing pages; sponsored content; and influencer, video, and other digital platforms. These include Google, Facebook, Instagram, LinkedIn, and YouTube.

Personalized ads – Used to be called eyebrows. A phrase that preceded the headline in ads and targeted a specific audience: "Hey, HR Managers…"

PM – Private Message. Not visible to the public.

Pinners – Pinterest users.

Podcast – Episodic audio/video program.

Pogo-sticking – Consumers who use a key phrase to search, click on the link, return to the search, click on another link and so on. They don't stay and read past the link because they didn't find the information they needed.

PPC – Pay-per-click. Advertiser pays when people who see an ad click through to websites or landing pages.

- *PPC ads* – Appear in sidebars on search engines, native ads, apps, social media ads.
- *PPC advertising* – Advertisers pay for each ad that's clicked.

Programmatic advertising – Automated software that enables advertisers and publishers to participate in real-time bidding (RTB) to buy and sell online ads.

PWA – Progressive Web App. Uses one commonly shared coding system for every platform to provide easy accessibility.

Quality – How your ad measures up compared to competitors for the same audience (FB).

Diagnosis: Low quality means (1) infrequency and (2) high delivery cost.

RankBrain – Part of Google's search algorithm for more accurate search results to analyze how people:

- Search with keywords.
- Interact with the results (UX = user experience).

Ratings and reviews – Consumers post their opinions of brands/products on Amazon, Google, medical sites, Yelp, and so on.

Repost – Repost content you enjoy or find useful to your friends, colleagues, family, and followers, which can result in a wider audience.

Reverse engineering – Used by copywriters/content writers to mimic or match a brand's manner of expression, including:

- *Voice* (brand personality) – How a brand usually talks or sounds.
- *Tone* – Sentence length, language, and style that change with context.

For example:

- How many sentences? How long are they?
- How do they use punctuation? (Sentence length and punctuation use: the more commas, the longer the sentence).
- What's the grade level?
- Do they use italics, bold, underlining, colors, emojis, curse words?
- What keywords are used? Look for a phrase or famous person that represents the writing.
- Look at context. What's the reference: personal or political?

ROI – Return on Investment. Measures sales profits in relation to the total marketing costs (a quick way to look at it is sales minus total cost.)

RSA – Responsive Search Ads. Shows users' past search history, including keywords, clicks, and what device they were using.

RTB – Real-time Bidding. Allows advertisers and publishers to engage in automated auctions. (You may have participated in similar auctions on eBay, for example.)

SaaS – Software as a Service. Allows consumers to use cloud-based, updated apps online.

- *BDR* – Business development representative.
- *SDR* – Sales development representative.

SaaS marketing – The way SaaS companies promote their services, such as subscription-based products.

Search advertising – Ads on sidebars within search engine results pages (SERPs), also called "SEM" (search engine marketing).

Self-aware marketing – Brands point out their mistakes for authenticity.

Sequence of copy – How the content is organized, meaning in what order the information appears.

SERP – Search Engine Results Page. The web pages that appear after an online search.

SMB – Server Message Block. The protocol, or way a client or server communicates, which controls file access, and directories, as well as printers, routers, etc.

Social bookmarking – Used to mark, save, and share information.

Social commerce – Offers links to e-commerce, such as via social media platforms, QR codes, websites, etc., for example:

- *Instagram Skinskool* – cosmetic shop.
- *Levl's digital shop* – in app or on desktop + link to e-commerce site for purchase.
- *Pinterest* – with catalog functionality.

Social knowledge – Where people search for shared info, like Wikipedia.

Social listening – Analyzes what's being said on reviews, comments, and posts to better gauge customer sentiment to gain insights.

Social media advertising – Google, X (formerly Twitter), Instagram, Pinterest, Snapchat, Tumblr, YouTube.

Social media engagement – When people interact on social media channels, such as LinkedIn, Facebook, Instagram, etc.

Social media intelligence – Similar to social media analytics, it includes the tools and systems used to track social media activity, from discussions to current topics/trends.

Social media marketing funnel – Drives social media followers to a website.

Social media templates – Predesigned layouts to be modified or reused (with permission).

Social monitoring – Concentrates on opportunities to engage with customers, especially if they've posted complaints, such as airport delays and poor airline response times.

SoLoMo – Social, Local and Mobile marketing.

Soundless optimization – Improve attention by adding written content, such as titles, subtitles, captions, and animated text, because most people watch videos with the sound turned off.

Specific target audiences and new audiences – Address the message to (1) a particular group of people or reach out to (2) a different, newly designated group of consumers.

Sponsored blog post – With sponsored posts, writers are set up to get immediate payment for their work. This differs from "Affiliate marketing" where writers get paid on a per-click or reach basis. The decision on how to compensate the influencer should come down to campaign goals:

- *Sponsored posts* are effective at generating brand awareness.
- *Affiliate marketing* is a viable option when a brand wants lead generation and increased sales. It can often result in a less expensive return on investment.

Sponsored display ads – Target a selected audience as they're shopping or surfing and often mask themselves because they blend into the surrounding content.

Strategic content plan – Created to solve a particular marketing problem. This differs from a useful content plan, which offers helpful advice to the reader, but doesn't include a sales pitch.

Tag Category (in databases) – Name of tags, such as:

- *Action tag* – To signify behavior that changes the contact's status. This tag can be used to describe any kind of contact behavior.
- *Engagement tag* – To track how engaged or disinterested a contact may be. The tag will update based on the contact's actions and engagements.
- *Product tag* – To indicate what product a contact purchased.

- *Source tag* – To track where your leads came from, for example: a live event, webinar, blog article social media post, etc.
- *Trigger tag* – To initiate processes by triggering an action.

Tags (in databases) – Organize the contacts in your database.

Targeted (digital) advertising – Helps you reach an audience segment online, via these and other methods:

- *Behavioral targeting* – Finding consumers by their searching and shopping habits.
- *Contextual targeting* – Offering relevant content based on consumers' interests.
- *Geographic targeting* – Reaching people where they are located.

Template – Layout to use as a verbal and visual reference for logos, social media posts, scripts, storyboards, and so on.

Temporal framing – Write or "frame" content to guide the consumer to take the desired action and say "yes".

Thought leadership – Ideas expressed in a way that shows topic expertise.

UAT – User Acceptance Testing. Also known as "beta" or "end-user testing" and defined as testing of the software by the user or client to determine whether it can be accepted or not. This is the final testing performed once the functional, system, and regression testing are completed.

UI – User Interface. Describes how the consumer interacts with the software: how seamlessly the buttons, icons, or other interfaces function with only digital products or services. To be successful, designers use icons, functions, and language that are familiar to the user, such as the magnifier icon and common cut-and-paste commands.

URL – Uniform Resource Locator. The web address used for website or page identification.

UV – Unique Views. The number of individual viewers for a page, video, or image.

UX – User eXperience. Includes every interaction consumers experience during their product/service journey. Focuses on understanding and resolving any problems users might face with the software. The goal is to simplify consumer interaction with any product by applying best practices to facilitate users' actions in a website or app.

UX/UI – User eXperience, User Interface.

Views – Number of times consumers engaged with the post or content, as opposed to impressions, which tells the number of times people only saw the ad or content.

- *Total views* – How many times one video received views.
- *View rate* – How many visitors saw the video after it appeared as an impression.
- *Average watch time* – How long viewers looked at the video.
- *Average cost per view* – How much it cost to create the video for a single view (based on the total number of views).[5]

Viral marketing – Popularized content by unpaid, naturally occurring shares, such as word-of-mouth.

VR – Virtual reality. VR transports you somewhere else, as if you traveled there. VR can bring you anywhere and help you learn about different places, products, exhibits, and ideas by experiencing them as if you were really there.

VSO – Voice Search Optimization. Identification and use of commonly used keywords in spoken or voice-activated searches.

Web-hosted ads – Appear on websites to drive traffic to another site.

Website card – Small, flexible designs with company information, icons, clickable call-to-action buttons, and linkable images to drive website traffic from social media channels, especially X (formerly Twitter).

Wikis – Websites that allow users to add, delete, or revise content.

X – X (formerly Twitter).

XR – Extended Reality. Used as a catch-all abbreviation that refers to Augmented Reality (AR), Virtual Reality (VR), and Mixed Reality (MR).

YT – YouTube.

Notes

1. https://www.outbrain.com/blog/digital-advertising-glossary/ (accessed February 20, 2021).
2. https://blog.gamesight.io/affiliates-vs-sponsorship-which-how-and-why/ (accessed May 6, 2022).
3. https://www.wordstream.com/blog/ws/2020/11/23/content-marketing-trends (accessed May 16, 2021).
4. https://www.reliabills.com/blog/freemium-tools-for-small-business/ (accessed Jan. 7, 2022).
5. https://www.indeed.com/career-advice/career-development/impressions-vs-views (accessed Feb. 26, 2022).

Suggested Reading

Applegate, Edd. 2015. *Strategic Advertising: How to Create Effective Advertising*, 2nd ed. Lanham, MD: Rowman & Littlefield.

Astiel, Tom, Grow, Jean M., and Jennings, Marcel. 2019. *Advertising Creative: Strategy, Copy and Design*, 5th ed. Thousand Oaks, CA: Sage Publications, Inc.

Berger, Arthur Asa. 2021. *Ads, Fads and Consumer Culture: Advertising's Impact on American Character and Society*, 6th ed. Lanham, MD: Rowman & Littlefield.

Berman, Margo. 2010. *Street-Smart Advertising: How to Win the Battle of the Buzz*. Lanham, MD: Rowman & Littlefield.

Berman, Margo. 2012. *The Copywriter's Toolkit: The Complete Guide to Strategic Advertising Copy*. Chichester, UK: John Wiley & Sons.

Berman, Margo. 2017. *The Blueprint for Strategic Advertising: How Critical Thinking Builds Successful Campaigns*. New York, NY: Routledge.

Berman, Margo and Blakeman, Robyn. 2009. *The Brains Behind Great Ad Campaigns: Creative Collaboration Between Copywriters and Art Directors*. Lanham, MD: Rowman & Littlefield.

Bird, Drayton. 2004. *How to Write Sales Letters That Sell: Learn the Secrets of Successful Direct Mail*. London: Kogan Page.

Blakeman, Robyn. 2011. *Strategic Uses of Alternative Media: Just the Essentials*. Armonk, NY: M.E. Sharpe.

Bly, Robert W. 2020. *The Content Marketing Handbook: How to Double the Results of Your Marketing Campaigns*. Irvine, CA: Entrepreneur Press.

Bly, Robert W. 2020. *The Copywriter's Handbook: A Step-by-Step Guide to Writing Copy That Sells*, 4th ed. New York, NY: St. Martin's Griffin.

Deziel, Melanie. 2020. *The Content Fuel Framework: How to Generate Unlimited Story Ideas*. Canada: Storyfuel Press.

Drewiany, Bonnie L. and Jewler, Jerome A. 2014. *Creative Strategy in Advertising*, 11th ed. Boston, MA: Wadsworth.

Gladwell, Malcolm. 2002. *The Tipping Point: How Little Things Can Make a Big Difference*. Boston, MA: Back Bay Publishing.

Gladwell, Malcolm. 2007. *Blink: The Power of Thinking Without Thinking*. New York, NY: Little, Brown and Company.

Gladwell, Malcolm. 2011. *Outliers: The Story of Success*. New York, NY: Back Bay Publishing.

Griffin, Glenn W. and Morrison, Deborah. 2010. *The Creative Process Illustrated: How Advertising's Big Ideas Are Born*. Cincinnati, OH: HOW Books.

Johnson, Spencer and Blanchard, Kenneth. 2002. *Who Moved My Cheese? An Amazing Way to Deal With Change in Your Work and in Your Life*. New York, NY: G.P. Putnam.

Marsh, Charles, Guth, David W. and Short, Bonnie Poovey. 2021. *Strategic Writing: Multimedia for Public Relations, Advertising and More*, 5th ed. New York, NY: Routledge.

Ogilvy, David. 1981. *Confessions of an Advertising Man*. New York, NY: Atheneum.

Ogilvy, David. 1985. *Ogilvy on Advertising*. New York, NY: Random House.

Ogilvy, David. 2004. *Confessions of an Advertising Man*. London: Southbank Publishing.

Popcorn, Faith. 1992. *The Popcorn Report: Faith Popcorn on the Future of Your Company, Your World, Your Life*. New York, NY: Doubleday.

Postman, Joel. 2009. *SocialCorp: Social Media Goes Corporate*. Berkeley, CA: New Riders.

Quesenberry, Keith A. 2020. *Social Media Strategy: Marketing, Advertising, and Public Relations in the Consumer Revolution*, 3rd ed. Lanham, MD: Rowman & Littlefield.

Sheehan, Kim Bartel and Robertson, Charlie. 2019. *Hitting the Sweet Spot Again*. Irvine, CA: Melvin & Leigh, Publishers.

Sullivan, Luke. 2022. *Hey Whipple, Squeeze This: A Guide to Creating Great Ads*, 6th ed. New York, NY: John Wiley & Sons.

Underhill, Paco. 2009. *Why We Buy: The Science of Shopping*. New York, NY: Simon & Schuster.

Index

Content and Copywriting: The Complete Toolkit for Strategic Marketing,
Second Edition. Margo Berman.
© 2024 Margo Berman. Published 2024 by John Wiley & Sons Ltd.
Companion website: www.wiley.com/go/contentandcopywriting